Tyndale New Testament Commentaries

Volume 15

Hebrews

To Peter O'Brien,
scholar, pastor and friend

Tyndale New Testament Commentaries

Volume 15

Series Editor: Eckhard J. Schnabel
Consulting Editor: Nicholas Perrin

Hebrews
An Introduction and Commentary

David G. Peterson

Academic
An imprint of InterVarsity Press
Downers Grove, Illinois

Inter-Varsity Press, England
36 Causton Street, London SW1P 4ST, England
Website: www.ivpbooks.com
Email: ivp@ivpbooks.com

InterVarsity Press, USA
P.O. Box 1400, Downers Grove, IL 60515, USA
Website: www.ivpress.com
Email: email@ivpress.com

Inter-Varsity Press, England, publishes Christian books that are true to the Bible and that
communicate the gospel, develop discipleship and strengthen the church for its mission in the world.

IVP originated within the Inter-Varsity Fellowship, now the Universities and Colleges Christian
Fellowship, a student movement connecting Christian Unions in universities and colleges throughout
Great Britain, and a member movement of the International Fellowship of Evangelical Students.
That historic association is maintained, and all senior IVP staff and committee members subscribe
to the UCCF Basis of Faith. Website: www.uccf.org.uk.

InterVarsity Press®, USA, is the book-publishing division of InterVarsity Christian Fellowship/
USA® and a member movement of the International Fellowship of Evangelical Students. Website:
www.intervarsity.org.

Unless otherwise indicated, Scripture quotations are from NIV 2011 (Anglicized). For Bible
acknowledgments, see p. xiii.

First published 2020

Set in Garamond 11/13pt
Typeset in Great Britain by CRB Associates, Potterhanworth, Lincolnshire
Printed and bound in Great Britain by Ashford Colour Press Ltd, Gosport, Hampshire

Produced on paper from sustainable forests.

UK ISBN: 978–1–78359–962–2 (print)
UK ISBN: 978–1–78359–963–9 (digital)

US ISBN: 978–0–8308–4299–5 (print)
US ISBN: 978–0–8308–5072–3 (digital)

British Library Cataloguing-in-Publication Data
A catalogue record for this book is available from the British Library.

Library of Congress Cataloging-in-Publication Data
A catalog record for this book is available from the Library of Congress.

CONTENTS

General preface   vii
Author's preface   ix
Abbreviations   xi
Select bibliography   xv

Introduction   1

1. Character and style   1
2. Structure and argument   5
3. Occasion and purpose   15
4. Destination and date of composition   19
5. Authorship and authority   23
6. Theology   27

Analysis   57

Commentary   61

GENERAL PREFACE

The Tyndale Commentaries have been a flagship series for evangelical readers of the Bible for over sixty years. Both the original New Testament volumes (1956–1974) as well as the new commentaries (1983–2003) rightly established themselves as a point of first reference for those who wanted more than is usually offered in a one-volume Bible commentary, without requiring the technical skills in Greek and in Jewish and Graeco-Roman studies of the more detailed series, with the advantage of being shorter than the volumes of intermediate commentary series. The appearance of new popular commentary series demonstrates that there is a continuing demand for commentaries that appeal to Bible study leaders in churches and at universities. The publisher, editors and authors of the Tyndale Commentaries believe that the series continues to meet an important need in the Christian community, not least in what we call today the Global South, with its immense growth of churches and the corresponding need for a thorough understanding of the Bible by Christian believers.

In the light of new knowledge, new critical questions, new revisions of Bible translations, and the need to provide specific guidance on the literary context and the theological emphases of the individual passage, it was time to publish new commentaries in the series. Three authors will revise their commentary that appeared in the second series. The original aim remains. The new commentaries are neither too short nor unduly long. They are exegetical and thus root the interpretation of the text in its historical context. They do not aim to solve all critical questions, but they are written with an awareness of major scholarly debates which may be treated in the Introduction, in Additional notes or in the commentary itself. While not specifically homiletic in aim, they want to help readers to understand the passage under consideration in such a way that they begin to see points of relevance and application, even though the commentary does not explicitly offer these. The authors base their exegesis on the Greek text, but they write for readers who do not know Greek; Hebrew and Greek terms that are discussed are transliterated. The English translation used for the first series was the Authorized (King James) Version, while the volumes of the second series mostly used the Revised Standard Version; the volumes of the third series use either the New International Version (2011) or the New Revised Standard Version as primary versions, unless otherwise indicated by the author.

An immense debt of gratitude for the first and second series of the Tyndale Commentaries was owed to R. V. G. Tasker and L. Morris, who each wrote four of the commentaries themselves. The recruitment of new authors for the third series proved to be effortless, as colleagues responded enthusiastically to be involved in this project, a testimony both to the larger number of New Testament scholars capable and willing to write commentaries, to the wider ethnic identity of contributors, and to the role that the Tyndale Commentaries have played in the church worldwide. It continues to be the hope of all those concerned with this series that God will graciously use the new commentaries to help readers understand as fully and clearly as possible the meaning of the New Testament.

Eckhard J. Schnabel, Series Editor
Nicholas Perrin, Consulting Editor

AUTHOR'S PREFACE

Recollecting the impact that earlier versions of the Tyndale Commentaries have had on my development as a Christian and my ability to expound biblical texts, I feel privileged to contribute to this third series. I am especially pleased to write again on Hebrews, which has occupied my close attention for more than fifty years. Throughout that period, I have benefited from the insights of many other scholars, particularly my colleague and friend Peter O'Brien. His academic expertise and godly character have been an encouragement to me ever since my undergraduate days. I also had the great honour of doing doctoral research on Hebrews under the supervision of Professor F. F. Bruce.

Although Hebrews may seem daunting at first, once the interplay between doctrinal exposition and exhortation is understood, the application becomes clearer. The author's central concern was for those he addressed to 'move beyond the elementary teachings about Christ and be taken forward to maturity' (6:1). My prayer is that the readers of this commentary will be greatly assisted in achieving that goal. The new format of the series, with an outline of the theology of the book in the Introduction and theological reflections at the end of each section of the argument, should help to expose the contemporary relevance of this 'word of exhortation' (13:22).

I am thankful to another friend and colleague, Tim Escott, who has carefully read through my work as it progressed and given me valuable feedback. I am also grateful that Professor Eckhard

Schnabel has been able to make helpful suggestions in the final stages of revision. I also thank my wife Lesley for her loving support and for being an eager conversation partner in the project.

David Peterson

ABBREVIATIONS

General

BDAG	*A Greek–English Lexicon of the New Testament and Other Early Christian Literature*, ed. W. Bauer, F. W. Danker, W. F. Arndt and F. W. Gingrich, 3rd edn (Chicago: University of Chicago Press, 2000)
Bib	*Biblica*
BJRL	*Bulletin of the John Rylands Library*
BTCP	Biblical Theology for Christian Proclamation
CBQ	*Catholic Biblical Quarterly*
CBR	*Currents in Biblical Research*
EBTC	Evangelical Biblical Theology Commentary
ET	English translation
Louw and Nida	*Greek–English Lexicon of the New Testament: Based on Semantic Domains*, ed. J. P. Louw and E. A. Nida, 2nd edn (New York: United Bible Societies, 1989)
LXX	Septuagint (Greek) Text of the Old Testament
mg.	marginal reading
MT	Masoretic (Hebrew) Text of the Old Testament
NICNT	New International Commentary on the New Testament
NICOT	New International Commentary on the Old Testament

NIDOTTE	*New International Dictionary of Old Testament Theology and Exegesis*, 5 vols., ed. W. A. VanGemeren (Carlisle: Paternoster, 1997)
NovTSup	Supplements to Novum Testamentum
NSBT	New Studies in Biblical Theology
NT	New Testament
OT	Old Testament
par.	and parallels
PNTC	Pillar New Testament Commentary
SBLDS	Society for Biblical Literature Dissertation Series
SBLMS	Society for Biblical Literature Monograph Series
SNTSMS	Society for New Testament Studies Monograph Series
TDNT	*Theological Dictionary of the New Testament*, 10 vols., ed. G. Kittel and G. Friedrich (Grand Rapids: Eerdmans, 1964–1976)
TrinJ	*Trinity Journal*
TynBul	*Tyndale Bulletin*
WTJ	*Westminster Theological Journal*
WUNT	Wissenschaftliche Untersuchungen zum Neuen Testament

Ancient texts

b. Sabb.	*Shabbat* (Babylonian Talmud)
1 En.	*1 Enoch (Ethiopic Apocalypse)*
2 En.	*2 Enoch (Slavonic Apocalypse)*
4 Ez.	*4 Ezra* (= 2 Esdras 3 – 14)
Josephus, *Ant.*	Josephus, *Jewish Antiquities*
Jub.	*Jubilees*
Justin, *Dial.*	Justin, *Dialogue with Trypho*
1–4 Macc.	1–4 Maccabees
Pss. Sol.	*Psalms of Solomon*
1 QS	Serek Hayahad (Rule of the Qumran Community)
Sir.	Sirach/Ecclesiasticus
T. Levi	*Testament of Levi*
Wis.	Wisdom of Solomon

Bible versions

ASV	American Standard Version (1901).
CSB	Christian Standard Bible (2016). The Christian Standard Bible. Copyright © 2017 by Holman Bible Publishers. Used by permission. Christian Standard Bible®, and CSB® are federally registered trademarks of Holman Bible Publishers, all rights reserved.
ESV	The ESV Bible (The Holy Bible, English Standard Version), copyright © 2001 by Crossway, a publishing ministry of Good News Publishers. Used by permission. All rights reserved.
KJV	Extracts from the Authorized Version of the Bible (The King James Bible), the rights in which are vested in the Crown, are reproduced by permission of the Crown's Patentee, Cambridge University Press.
NASB	The NEW AMERICAN STANDARD BIBLE®, Copyright © 1960, 1962, 1963, 1968, 1971, 1972, 1973, 1975, 1977, 1995 by The Lockman Foundation. Used by permission.
NEB	New English Bible (1961). Extracts from the New English Bible, copyright © The Delegates of the Oxford University Press and The Syndics of Cambridge University Press, 1961, 1970. Used by permission.
NIV	The Holy Bible, New International Version (Anglicized edition). Copyright © 1979, 1984, 2011 by Biblica. Used by permission of Hodder & Stoughton Ltd, an Hachette UK company. All rights reserved. 'NIV' is a registered trademark of Biblica. UK trademark number 1448790.
NKJV	The New King James Version. Copyright © 1982 by Thomas Nelson, Inc. Used by permission. All rights reserved.

SELECT BIBLIOGRAPHY

Commentaries on Hebrews

Attridge, Harold W. (1989), *The Epistle to the Hebrews*, Hermeneia (Philadelphia: Fortress).

Bruce, Frederick F. (1964), *The Epistle to the Hebrews* (London: Marshall, Morgan & Scott; Grand Rapids: Eerdmans).

Cockerill, Gareth Lee (2012), *The Epistle to the Hebrews*, NICNT (Grand Rapids: Eerdmans).

deSilva, David A. (2000), *Perseverance in Gratitude: A Socio-Rhetorical Commentary on the Epistle 'to the Hebrews'* (Grand Rapids: Eerdmans).

Ellingworth, Paul (1993), *Commentary on Hebrews*, New International Greek Testament Commentary (Grand Rapids: Eerdmans; Carlisle: Paternoster).

Hughes, Philip E. (1977), *A Commentary on the Epistle to the Hebrews* (Grand Rapids: Eerdmans).

Johnson, Luke T. (2006), *Hebrews: A Commentary*, New Testament Library (Louisville: Westminster/John Knox).

Kleinig, John W. (2017), *Hebrews*, Concordia Commentary (St. Louis: Concordia).

Koester, Craig R. (2001), *Hebrews: A New Translation with Introduction and Commentary*, Anchor Bible 36 (New York: Doubleday).

Lane, William L. (1991), *Hebrews*, 2 vols., Word Biblical Commentary 47 (Dallas: Word).

Michel, Otto (1975), *Der Brief an die Hebräer*, Meyers Kommentar, 13th edn (Göttingen: Vandenhoeck & Ruprecht).

Moffatt, James (1924), *A Critical and Exegetical Commentary on the Epistle to the Hebrews*, International Critical Commentary (Edinburgh: T&T Clark).

Montefiore, Hugh W. (1964), *The Epistle to the Hebrews*, Black's New Testament Commentary (London: Black).

O'Brien, Peter T. (2010), *The Letter to the Hebrews*, PNTC (Grand Rapids: Eerdmans; Nottingham: Apollos).

Schreiner, Thomas R. (2020), *Commentary on Hebrews*, EBTC (Bellingham: Lexham) (orig. 2015, BTCP; Nashville: B&H).

Spicq, Ceslas (1952), *L'Épître aux Hébreux*, 2 vols. (Paris: Gabalda).

Westcott, Brooke F. (1914), *The Epistle to the Hebrews: The Greek Text with Notes and Essays*, 3rd edn (London: Macmillan).

Other relevant publications

Attridge, Harold W. (2009), 'God in Hebrews', in Bauckham, Driver, Hart and MacDonald (eds.), *Hebrews and Christian Theology*, pp. 95–110.

Barrett, Charles K. (1954), 'The Eschatology of the Epistle to the Hebrews', in W. D. Davies and D. Daube (eds.), *The Background of the New Testament and Its Eschatology* (Cambridge: Cambridge University Press), pp. 363–393.

Bateman, Herbert W. (1997), *Early Jewish Hermeneutics and Hebrews 1:5–13: The Impact of Early Jewish Exegesis on the Interpretation of a Significant New Testament Passage* (New York: Lang).

—— (2001), 'Psalm 45:6–7 and Its Christological Contributions to Hebrews', *TrinJ* 22, pp. 3–21.

Bauckham, Richard (2009), 'The Divinity of Jesus Christ in the Epistle to the Hebrews', in Bauckham, Driver, Hart and MacDonald (eds.), *Hebrews and Christian Theology*, pp. 15–36.

Bauckham, Richard, Daniel R. Driver, Trevor A. Hart and Nathan MacDonald (eds.) (2009), *The Epistle to the Hebrews and Christian Theology* (Grand Rapids/Cambridge: Eerdmans).

Caird, George B. (1959), 'The Exegetical Method of the Epistle to the Hebrews', *Canadian Journal of Theology* 5, pp. 44–51.

Campbell, Constantine R. (2008), *Basics of Verbal Aspect in Biblical Greek* (Grand Rapids: Zondervan).

Carson, Donald A. (2000), 'Reflections on Assurance', in Thomas. R. Schreiner and Bruce A. Ware (eds.), *Still Sovereign: Contemporary Perspectives on Election, Foreknowledge, and Grace* (Grand Rapids: Baker), pp. 247–276.

Childs, Brevard S. (1974), *Exodus: A Commentary* (London: SCM).

Church, Philip (2017), *Hebrews and the Temple: Attitudes to the Temple in Second Temple Judaism and in Hebrews*, NovTSup 171 (Leiden/ Boston: Brill).

Croy, N. Clayton (1998), *Endurance in Suffering: Hebrews 12.1–13 in Its Rhetorical, Religious, and Philosophical Context*, SNTSMS 98 (Cambridge: Cambridge University Press).

Ebert, Daniel J. (1992), 'The Chiastic Structure of the Prologue to Hebrews', *TrinJ* 13, pp. 163–179.

Eisenbaum, Pamela M. (1997), *The Jewish Heroes of Christian History: Hebrews 11 in Literary Context*, SBLDS 156 (Atlanta: Scholars Press).

Emmrich, Martin (2003), 'Hebrews 6.4–6 – Again! (A Pneumatological Inquiry)', *WTJ* 65, pp. 83–95.

Filson, Floyd V. (1967), *'Yesterday': A Study of Hebrews in the Light of Chapter 13*, Studies in Biblical Theology (London: SCM).

Gaffin, Richard B., Jr (2012), 'The Priesthood of Christ: A Servant in the Sanctuary', in Griffiths (ed.), *Perfect Saviour*, pp. 49–68.

Goldsworthy, Graeme L. (2000), *Preaching the Whole Bible as Christian Scripture: The Application of Biblical Theology to Expository Preaching* (Leicester: Inter-Varsity Press).

Gooding, David (2012), 'The Tabernacle: No Museum Piece', in Griffiths (ed.), *Perfect Saviour*, pp. 69–88.

Griffiths, Jonathan (2012), 'The Word of God: Perfectly Spoken in the Son', in Griffiths (ed.), *Perfect Saviour*, pp. 35–48.

Griffiths, Jonathan (ed.) (2012), *The Perfect Saviour: Key Themes in Hebrews* (Nottingham: Inter-Varsity Press).

Guthrie, George H. (1994), *The Structure of Hebrews: A Text-Linguistic Analysis*, NovTSup 73 (Leiden: Brill; repub. Grand Rapids: Baker, 1998).

—— (2007), 'Hebrews', in G. K. Beale and D. A. Carson (eds.),
Commentary on the New Testament Use of the Old Testament (Grand
Rapids: Baker; Nottingham: Apollos), pp. 919–995.

Harris, Murray J. (1983), *Raised Immortal: Resurrection and Immortality
in the New Testament* (London: Marshall, Morgan & Scott;
Grand Rapids: Eerdmans).

—— (1992), *Jesus as God: The New Testament Use of Theos
in Reference to Jesus* (Grand Rapids: Baker).

Hay, David M. (1972), *Glory at the Right Hand: Psalm 110 in Early
Christianity*, SBLMS 18 (Nashville: Abingdon).

Holmes, Christopher T. (2018), *The Function of Sublime Rhetoric
in Hebrews: A Study in Hebrews 12:18–29*, WUNT 2/465
(Tübingen: Mohr Siebeck).

Hughes, Graham (1979), *Hebrews and Hermeneutics: The Epistle
to the Hebrews as a New Testament Example of Biblical Interpretation*,
SNTSMS 36 (Cambridge: Cambridge University Press).

Joslin, Barry C. (2007), 'Can Hebrews Be Structured? An
Assessment of Eight Approaches', *CBR* 6, pp. 99–129.

Kurianal, James (2000), *Jesus Our High Priest: Ps. 110,4 as the
Substructure of Heb. 5,1–7,28* (Frankfurt/New York: Lang).

Laansma, Jon (1997), *'I Will Give You Rest': The Rest Motif in the New
Testament with Special Reference to Mt 11 and Heb 3 – 4* (Tübingen:
Mohr Siebeck).

Longenecker, Richard N. (1975), *Biblical Exegesis in the Apostolic
Period* (Grand Rapids: Eerdmans).

McKay, K. L. (1994), *A New Syntax of the Verb in New Testament
Greek: An Aspectual Approach*, Studies in Biblical Greek 5
(New York: Lang).

Marrow, S. B. (1982), '*Parrhēsia* and the New Testament', *CBQ* 44,
pp. 431–446.

Marshall, I. Howard (2009), 'Soteriology in Hebrews', in
Bauckham, Driver, Hart and MacDonald (eds.), *Hebrews and
Christian Theology*, pp. 253–272.

Martin, Michael Wade and Jason A. Whitlark (2018), *Inventing
Hebrews: Design and Purpose in Ancient Rhetoric*, SNTSMS 171
(Cambridge: Cambridge University Press).

Meiers, J. P. (1985), 'Symmetry and Theology in Heb 1, 5–14',
Bib 66, pp. 504–533.

Metzger, Bruce M. (ed.) (1994), *A Textual Commentary on the Greek New Testament*, 2nd edn (Stuttgart: German Bible Society; New York: American Bible Society).

Mosser, Carl (2009), 'Rahab Outside the Camp', in Bauckham, Driver, Hart and MacDonald (eds.), *Hebrews and Christian Theology*, pp. 383–404.

O'Brien, Peter T. (2012), 'The New Covenant and Its Perfect Mediator', in Griffiths (ed.), *Perfect Saviour*, pp. 13–33.

—— (2016), *God Has Spoken in His Son: A Biblical Theology of Hebrews*, NSBT 39 (London: Apollos; Downers Grove: InterVarsity Press).

Peterson, David G. (1982), *Hebrews and Perfection: An Examination of the Concept of Perfection in the Epistle to the Hebrews*, SNTSMS 47 (Cambridge: Cambridge University Press).

—— (1992), *Engaging with God: A Biblical Theology of Worship* (Leicester: Apollos; Downers Grove: InterVarsity Press).

—— (1995), *Possessed by God: A New Testament Theology of Sanctification and Holiness*, NSBT 1 (Leicester: Apollos; Downers Grove: InterVarsity Press).

—— (2009), *The Acts of the Apostles*, PNTC (Grand Rapids: Eerdmans; Nottingham: Apollos).

—— (2012a), *Transformed by God: New Covenant Life and Ministry* (Nottingham: Inter-Varsity Press; Downers Grove: InterVarsity Press).

—— (2012b), 'Perfection: Achieved and Experienced', in Griffiths (ed.), *Perfect Saviour*, pp. 125–145.

—— (2020), *Commentary on Romans*, EBTC (Bellingham: Lexham) (orig. 2017, BTCP; Nashville: B&H).

Rapske, Brian (1994), *The Book of Acts and Paul in Roman Custody* (Grand Rapids: Eerdmans).

Schenck, Ken (2009), 'God Has Spoken: Hebrews' Theology of the Scriptures', in Bauckham, Driver, Hart and MacDonald (eds.), *Hebrews and Christian Theology*, pp. 321–336.

Schnabel, Eckhardt J. (2004), *Jesus and the Twelve*. Early Christian Mission Vol. 1 (Downers Grove: InterVarsity Press; Leicester: Apollos).

Schreiner, Thomas R. (2009), *Run to Win the Prize: Perseverance in the New Testament* (Nottingham: Inter-Varsity Press).

—— (2012), 'Warning and Assurance: Run the Race to the End', in Griffiths (ed.), *Perfect Saviour*, pp. 89–106.

Schreiner, Thomas R. and Ardel B. Caneday (2001), *The Race Set Before Us: A Biblical Theology of Assurance and Perseverance* (Downers Grove: InterVarsity Press; Leicester: Inter-Varsity Press).

Thomas, C. A. (2008), *A Case for Mixed-Audience with Reference to the Warning Passages in the Book of Hebrews* (New York: Lang).

Thompson, J. A. (1980), *Jeremiah*, NICOT (Grand Rapids: Eerdmans).

Vanhoye, Albert (1976), *La Structure littéraire de l'épître aux Hébreux*, 2nd edn (Paris: Desclée De Brouwer, 1976); English edn, *Structure and Message of the Epistle to the Hebrews* (Rome: Pontifical Biblical Institute, 1989).

van Unnik, W. C. (1961–2), 'The Christian's Freedom of Speech in the NT', *BJRL* 44, pp. 466–488 (repub. in *Sparsa Collecta*, Vol. 2 [Leiden: Brill, 1980], pp. 269–289).

Walker, Peter W. (2012), 'Access and Arrival: Metaphors of Movement to Motivate', in Griffiths (ed.), *Perfect Saviour*, pp. 107–124.

Wallace, Daniel B. (1996), *Greek Grammar Beyond the Basics* (Grand Rapids: Zondervan).

Webster, John (2003), *Holiness* (Grand Rapids: Eerdmans).

Wenham, Gordon J. (1979), *The Book of Leviticus*, NICOT (Grand Rapids: Eerdmans).

Williams, Garry J. (2015), *His Love Endures For Ever: Reflections on the Love of God* (Nottingham: Inter-Varsity Press).

Williamson, Paul R. (2007), *Sealed with an Oath: Covenant in God's Unfolding Purpose*, NSBT 23 (Downers Grove: InterVarsity Press; Nottingham: Apollos).

Winter, Bruce W. (2012), 'Suffering with the Saviour: The Reality, the Reasons, and the Reward', in Griffiths (ed.), *Perfect Saviour*, pp. 147–162.

INTRODUCTION

1. Character and style

Although this text is commonly called 'the letter to the Hebrews', its epistolary character has been disputed and its purpose much debated. It certainly ends like a letter, with personal exhortations (13:17–19), a benediction (13:20–21) and final greetings (13:22–25),[1] but its sermonic style suggests a different kind of written communication. How and why was it constructed in this way?

a. An unusual beginning

New Testament letters characteristically begin by introducing the author, identifying the readers and revealing something about

---

1. Some have questioned whether chapter 13 was part of the original document, but this challenge has been met with arguments about common vocabulary, use of the OT and conceptual ties with chapters 1–12. Cf. Lane 2, pp. 495–507; Filson, *'Yesterday'*.

the relationship between them. But Hebrews begins with an impressive statement about the way God has spoken in the prophets and ultimately in his Son (1:1–4).[2] As the author extols the person and work of the Son, the claim is made that his heavenly ascension has made him 'as much superior to the angels as the name he has inherited is superior to theirs'. This introduces a linked set of quotations from the Old Testament (1:5–13), comparing the Son and the angels, and substantiating the affirmations in 1:1–4. An exhortation follows (2:1–4), urging the readers to 'pay the most careful attention' to what they have heard from the Son through his agents, so that they do not 'drift away'. This suggests that the author knew much about the situation of those he was addressing and had a passionate concern for their spiritual welfare.

b. Exposition and exhortation

The two genres used in 1:1 – 2:4 occur throughout Hebrews and are linked in various ways. First, there are passages of *exposition*, which are essentially declaratory and descriptive, focused on God's words and actions in the past (e.g. 1:1–13; 2:5–18; 5:1–10). Second, there are passages of *exhortation*, which address believers in the present and regularly draw out the significance of the expository sections (e.g. 2:1–4; 3:1–6; 10:19–25). More complex units have a mixture of exposition, warning and positive encouragement (e.g. 3:1 – 4:13; 5:11 – 6:12; 10:26–39).

The Old Testament is regularly quoted, with certain passages being foundational to major sections of the document. Psalm 8:4–6 is applied to the Messiah in the passage of exposition in 2:5–18, with other texts added to develop the argument. Psalm 95:7–11 is applied to the readers in the extended exhortation in 3:7 – 4:13 (with a supportive text in 4:4). Psalm 110:4 with its reference to the priesthood of the Messiah in 'the order of Melchizedek' is quoted

---

2. The closest parallel in the NT would be the opening of 1 John, which lacks a specific identification of the author or the readers, but makes a profound series of theological claims (1:1–5), followed by related warnings and exhortations (1:6 – 2:2).

several times in 5:5 – 7:28 and supportive texts are introduced to explain the significance of this prediction. The prophecy of the New Covenant in Jeremiah 31:31–34 is foundational to the exposition in 8:1 – 10:18 (with supportive texts in 8:5; 9:20; 10:5–7). The sequence of exhortations in 10:26 – 13:6 includes several biblical citations that will be noted in the commentary. Biblical allusions occur even more frequently than quotations throughout the book.

The claim that 'in many and various ways God spoke in the past to the fathers in the prophets' (1:1, my translation) introduces a major presupposition of the argument. What Christians call 'the Old Testament' is the authority and basis for the author's work. Since, however, he also insists that 'in these days [God] has spoken to us in his Son' (1:2, my translation), his approach is profoundly Christocentric and gospel driven. Indeed, much of the argument is concerned with showing how the Old Testament points to Jesus and his saving work and relates to those who share in 'the heavenly calling' he made possible (3:1). So the two main themes of the opening paragraph (1:1–4) are drawn together throughout the book: God's revelation to his people in the past is intimately linked to his more recent revelation in the person and work of the Son. More will be said about the author's use of the Old Testament in the 'Theology' section below.

c. Rhetorical techniques

The author of Hebrews regularly uses first-person plural pronouns (we, our, us) and verbs of speaking (1:1, 2; 2:3, 5; 3:5; 4:8; 5:5; 6:9; 7:14; 9:19; 11:4, 18; 12:24, 25; 13:7) and hearing (2:1, 3; 3:7, 15, 16; 4:2, 7; 12:19; cf. 5:11) to alert his audience to the way in which God has addressed them in the past and continues to engage with them in the present. Indeed, until the postscript (13:22–25), he

> studiously avoids any reference to actions like writing or reading that would tend to emphasize the distance that separates him from the group he is addressing. Instead he stresses the actions of speaking and listening, which are appropriate to persons in conversation, and identifies himself with his audience in a direct way.
> (Lane 1, p. lxxiv)

They are treated as *hearers*, rather than as readers of his message. Additionally, the author uses various rhetorical techniques that were employed in the Hellenistic world to guide and persuade people in public assemblies. Like the oratory prized by the ancient world, Hebrews appears to have been constructed 'to influence its hearers by reinforcing their perspective and values and/or urging them to pursue a particular course of action' (Cockerill, p. 12).

Some have argued that the document contains 'epideictic' techniques, which were used on occasions in the Graeco-Roman culture to praise certain individuals and persuade an audience to exhibit their virtues and values. The author is said to employ this form of address in 'celebrating the significance of Christ and inculcating values that his followers ought to share' (Attridge, p. 140). Others, however, have argued that the style of Hebrews is more like the deliberative oratory used in public forums to persuade citizens to take one course of action instead of another (deSilva, p. 47 n. 128). This approach highlights the importance of exhortation in the structure of Hebrews, but the author does not exclusively follow one pattern of rhetoric or the other. Epideictic topics are woven into the argument to motivate the readers to pursue the goal of enduring faithfulness to Jesus and to avoid apostasy.

> Hebrews can thus be analyzed as a deliberative speech that uses epideictic topics extensively to amplify the significance of making the right choice between remaining firm and turning away, between pursuing friendship with God and friendship with one's unbelieving neighbors.[3]

d. A 'word of exhortation'

The author's description of his work as 'my word of exhortation' (13:22) is consistent with this view. His pattern of arguing from Scripture and appealing on that basis to his hearers could suggest the more specific influence of Jewish-Hellenistic synagogue

---

3. DeSilva, p. 56. DeSilva (pp. 72–75) offers an outline of Hebrews that reflects the rhetorical priorities of the author's homily, rather than any pattern of arrangement found in Graeco-Roman rhetorical handbooks.

preaching (Lane 1, pp. lxx–lxxiv; Cockerill, pp. 13–15). A similar term is used in Acts 13:15, when the apostle Paul is invited to address the synagogue in Pisidian Antioch. The summary of Paul's message in Acts 13:16–22 recalls God's involvement with the people of Israel from the time of the patriarchs to the appointment of David as king. Paul then argues that Jesus is the promised Saviour for Jews and Gentiles alike, drawing particular attention to the fulfilment of various scriptures in the resurrection of Jesus (Acts 13:23–37; cf. Ps. 2:7; Isa. 55:3; Ps. 16:10). The climactic appeal of this Christocentric sermon is for the hearers to experience the forgiveness of sins made possible by the death and resurrection of Jesus. They should not turn away with scoffing and perish, but should take seriously the warning of Habakkuk 1:5 (Acts 13:38–41). The term translated 'exhortation' in Acts 13:15 and Hebrews 13:22 (*paraklēsis*) is rendered 'preaching' in 1 Timothy 4:13 (NIV), where the sequence is reading, preaching and teaching, suggesting again the influence of the synagogue on early Christian practice.

Given the foregoing observations about the character and contents of Hebrews, many commentators describe it as a sermon or homily in a written form with a letter-like ending. It was designed to be read to a Christian congregation familiar with the Jewish Scriptures and 'heard as a discourse rather than seen as a text, experienced as a whole in its unfolding' (Johnson, p. 11). This pastor aimed to give the impression that he was present with them in their assembly, delivering the message to them personally. Although the contents could point to the recipients as a distinctly Jewish Christian audience, it should be remembered that many of the earliest converts to Christianity were Gentiles, who were attached to synagogues or had even become proselytes to Judaism (e.g. Acts 13:16, 26, 43; 17:1–4, 10–12). They came to Christ with knowledge of the Scriptures and a sense of already belonging to the people of God. A mixed audience with a Hellenistic synagogue background is proposed under 'Occasion and purpose' below.

2. Structure and argument

'Some of the difficulty in analysing the structure of Hebrews is due not to the lack of structural indices, but to their overabundance'

(Attridge, p. 16). Several different approaches to the issue have been taken, including literary analysis and discourse analysis.[4] We will first consider literary indicators of the structure, such as are found in other ancient documents.

a. Literary indicators

Announcements of theme appear at significant turning points in the argument to indicate in advance the focus of the next section. For example, 1:4 announces that the author is about to compare Christ and the angels; 2:17 indicates that the following chapters will consider Christ as a merciful and faithful high priest; and 5:9–10 shows that the central section of Hebrews will focus on Christ as the perfected Son, who 'became the source of eternal salvation for all who obey him and was designated by God to be high priest in the order of Melchizedek'.

Hook words link new sections of the argument with the preceding announcements of theme. For example, 'angels' in 1:5 links with 'angels' in 1:4; Jesus as 'faithful' in 3:2 links with the claim that he became 'a merciful and faithful high priest' in 2:17, while 'mercy' in 4:16 links with a related term in 2:17; and 'Melchizedek' in 7:1 links with 5:10 and the restatement of this theme in 6:20.

Characteristic words are found in particular sections of the argument, showing that the author is exploring a designated topic there. For example, 'angels' occurs ten times in 1:5 – 2:16, and only incidentally again in 12:22 and 13:2; 'faithful' occurs in the Greek text of 3:2, 5 (NIV has added the word in 3:6), and only twice more in 10:23 and 11:11; and 'Melchizedek' occurs five times in 7:1–17 (NIV has added the name in 7:2), after three mentions of the name in 5:6, 10; and 6:20.

Inclusions (or 'sandwich structures') mark the boundaries of sections by using common words or phrases at the beginning and end. For example, a question concerning 'angels' in 1:5 is coupled with a quotation (Ps. 2:7), while a similar question in 1:14 is coupled

---

4. Cf. Guthrie, *Structure*, pp. 21–41; Joslin, 'Can Hebrews Be Structured?', pp. 99–129.

with another quotation (Ps. 110:1) to enclose the comparison of Christ and the angels; four terms common to 3:1 and 4:14 mark a larger inclusion ('Jesus', 'high priest', 'heavenly/heaven' and 'our confession' [ESV]). Parallels between 5:1–3 and 7:26–28 mark off a whole section devoted to comparing the priesthood of Jesus with the levitical priesthood.[5]

Change in genre occurs when the author moves from exposition to exhortation and then back to exposition. Exhortations are generally introduced by an inferential term such as 'therefore', translating different Greek words (e.g. 2:1 [*dia touto*]; 3:1 [*hothen*]; 4:1 [*oun*]; 6:1 [*dio*]). Exhortations employ different types of imperative (first-person and second-person plural), conditional sentences and rhetorical devices to indicate the seriousness of the challenge being presented.

b. Discourse analysis

Literary indicators are helpful for identifying topics and discrete thought units, but they do not provide 'a sufficient foundation for the overall logic and structure of a speech like Hebrews'.[6] Discourse analysis (also called 'text linguistics') builds on the insights of literary analysis and other approaches, seeking to understand 'the relationships between the various sections of an author's discourse' (Guthrie, *Structure*, p. 37). In the case of Hebrews, this must specifically include 'attention to literary and oratorical conventions of the first century' (Guthrie, p. 45). The paragraphs in a work like Hebrews may be grouped to form 'embedded discourses', which may then be grouped to form 'larger embedded discourses within the main, or "macro-", discourse' (Guthrie, p. 48). Various linguistic and rhetorical features give cohesion to units of the text and indicate shifts from one segment to another.

---

5. Cf. Guthrie, ibid., pp. 76–89; Kurianal, *Jesus Our High Priest*, pp. 242–243.

6. Martin and Whitlark, *Inventing Hebrews*, p. 5. In earlier publications, I was much influenced by the literary observations of Albert Vanhoye (*Structure*) concerning Hebrews, but I am now persuaded of the need for a broader approach.

Inclusions are important markers of both shorter and longer sections of the discourse.[7] Particular terms are used to build cohesion between individual units and in the work as a whole. Most obviously, references to God or God's Son function in this way. Terms related to the concept of 'the word of God', or terms identifying the author, his hearers, or both, also have this function (Guthrie, pp. 90–94).

c. The expository strand

After the introduction, which asserts that God has spoken to us definitively in his Son (1:1–4), the author broadly considers the position of the Son in relation to the angels (1:5 – 2:18). A selection of biblical texts is used in 1:5–14 to proclaim the Son's superiority to the angels. But, in a transitional section (2:5–9), Psalm 8:4–6 is used to introduce the new idea that the Son 'was made lower than the angels for a little while'. The purpose of the Son's incarnation is then unfolded in 2:11–18.

According to Guthrie, the second main section of exposition considers 'the position of the Son, our high priest, in relation to the earthly sacrificial system (4:14 – 10:25)'.[8] A large inclusion is formed by transitional exhortations at the beginning (4:14–16) and end (10:19–25), demonstrating the author's fundamental purpose in arguing this way. The first subsection (5:1 – 7:28) is bracketed by an inclusion at 5:1–3 and 7:26–28, and concerns 'the appointment of the Son as a superior high priest'. This subsection involves an application of Psalm 110:4 to Christ. An 'intermediary transition' in 8:1–2 proclaims that 'we do have such a high priest', who is seated at God's right hand and serves in the heavenly sanctuary. The second subsection (8:3 – 10:18) then expounds 'the superior offering of the appointed high priest' and is marked by an inclusion at 8:3 and 10:18. This subsection develops the

---

7. Eighteen inclusions are noted by Guthrie (pp. 76–89), marking different levels of embedded discourse and turning points in the argument of Hebrews.

8. Guthrie, p. 120 (capital letters have been removed from every citation of his headings).

implications of Jeremiah 31:31–34 for understanding what Jesus has achieved.

The argument in the expository strand of Hebrews develops logically and is consistently built upon the explanation of key Old Testament texts. It also has a spatial interest, as it moves backwards and forwards between the earthly and the heavenly realms and shows how they relate.[9]

d. The exhortatory strand

The exhortations develop somewhat differently, sometimes employing Old Testament texts to make a point (e.g. Ps. 95:7–11 in 3:7 – 4:11; Prov. 3:11–12 in 12:4–11) or focusing on the interplay between the earthly and the heavenly realms (as in 4:14–16; 10:19–25; 12:18–24, 25–29). Mostly, however, they reiterate and expand upon a particular range of pastoral concerns, such as sin, falling away, punishment, faith, endurance, promise, reward and inheritance.

With encouraging words, warnings and examples, 'the author hammers home repeatedly the reward of a right decision on the part of the community and the punishment awaiting those who make a bad decision' (Guthrie, p. 139). The foundational warning in 2:1–4 is about paying careful attention 'to what we have heard, so that we do not drift away', since a 'just punishment' awaits those who 'ignore so great a salvation'. There are striking parallels in later warning passages (4:12–13; 6:4–8; 10:26–31; 12:25–29) with respect to the hearers' continuing response to the word of God and the approaching judgment of God.

In 3:1–6, the faithfulness of Jesus as Son of God becomes an example and empowerment for believers as 'sons and daughters' (2:10) to hold firmly to their God-given confidence and 'the hope in which we glory' (cf. 10:35–39; 12:1–3). Psalm 95:7–11, with its reflection on the rebellion of the Israelites who came out of Egypt, is then used to warn about becoming hardened in unbelief and disobedience (3:7–19). Drifting away from what we have heard

---

9. Cf. Guthrie, pp. 121–126. Guthrie restricts these features to the
   expositional units and fails to observe how they can also be seen
   in some passages of exhortation.

results in forfeiting the 'rest' that God has promised to his people, and so believers should encourage one another not to be 'hardened by sin's deceitfulness'.

A transition piece in 4:1–2 reiterates the warning about falling short of what has been promised, before the author explains in 4:3–11 the significance of the 'rest' mentioned in Psalm 95:7–11. This is articulated in terms of Genesis 2:2, where the Creator is said to have 'rested from all his works' and offered the possibility that human beings might share in his rest. Faith issuing in obedience to God's word is the means of entering that rest. A warning to consider the power of God's word to expose and judge 'the thoughts and attitudes of the heart' (4:12–13) climaxes the sequence of exhortations begun at 3:1. Faithfulness is the fundamental challenge in this hortatory strand.

A transitional exhortation in 4:14–16 has significant verbal links with what has gone before ('a great high priest who has ascended into heaven'; 'Jesus the Son of God'; 'let us hold firmly to the faith we profess'). But it also functions to introduce the second main section of exposition, which considers the Son as high priest in relation to the earthly sacrificial system (4:14 – 10:25) and begins to draw out the practical implications for believers. There are forward links with 5:1–10, where the author explains how Jesus was perfected as our high priest and can 'feel sympathy for our weaknesses' (4:15). On this basis, the positive encouragement is given to 'approach God's throne of grace with confidence, so that we may receive mercy and find grace to help us in our time of need' (4:16).

Before the author launches more fully into an exposition of how Jesus became 'a high priest in the order of Melchizedek' (5:10; 6:20), he pauses to warn his hearers about a condition that could prevent them from being taken forward to maturity and expose them to the possibility of falling away (5:11 – 6:12). That condition is first described by the Greek expression *nōthroi tais akouais* (5:11), which means 'sluggish in hearing' (NIV, 'you no longer try to understand'). The adjective *nōthroi* is used again in an unqualified way in 6:12 (NIV, 'lazy') to mark the end of this hortatory unit. In between these markers, the author more fully exposes the problem that he perceives in the community he addresses (5:11 – 6:3), warning about the fate of those who profess faith and fall away (6:4–8), but then expressing confidence that they will heed the warning and diligently express faith, hope and love 'to the very end' (6:9–12).

The exhortation that concludes the central section of the argument in 10:19–25 begins with a recollection of what believers 'have' in Christ (cf. 4:14). They have 'confidence to enter the Most Holy Place by the blood of Jesus' and 'a great priest over the house of God' to sustain them in the new covenant relationship with God expounded in 8:3 – 10:18. On this basis, the challenges of 4:14, 16 are re-expressed in reverse order and in a modified form ('let us draw near to God' and 'Let us hold unswervingly to the hope we profess').[10] The third challenge to 'consider how we may spur one another on towards love and good deeds' (10:24) recalls 6:10–11, while the warning not to give up meeting together but to encourage one another, 'and all the more as you see the Day approaching' (10:25), recalls 3:6, 12–14.

The exhortation in 10:19–25 also bridges to the next main section of the discourse, where four further units of exhortation highlight the need for faithful endurance. The most intense warning passage in Hebrews comes first (10:26–32), echoing and expanding on earlier ones (2:1–4; 4:12–13; 6:4–8). It describes the judgment awaiting those who turn away from 'the knowledge of the truth', which is graphically represented as trampling the Son of God underfoot, treating 'as an unholy thing the blood of the covenant that sanctified them' and insulting the Spirit of grace. But this warning is accompanied by the author's recollection of the faith, hope and love demonstrated by his hearers in the past, which becomes the basis for encouraging them to persevere with their God-given confidence until they receive what has been promised (10:33–39; cf. 3:6; 6:9–12).

The roll call of Old Testament believers and their faith in 11:1–40 is shaped in a way that 'confronts the listeners with the absurdity of following any other course' (Guthrie, p. 131). This climaxes with the challenge to 'throw off everything that hinders

---

10. NIV obscures the close connection between these verses by translating the same verb 'Let us . . . approach' in 4:16 but 'let us draw near' in 10:22. The exhortation in 4:14 ('let us hold firmly to the faith we profess') is paralleled in 10:23 by 'Let us hold unswervingly to the hope we profess'.

and the sin that so easily entangles', and to 'run with perseverance
the race marked out for us, fixing our eyes on Jesus, the pioneer and
perfecter of faith' (12:1–2). The hortatory sequence that began in
10:26 concludes with a series of challenges in 12:3–17. The first is to
'Endure hardship as discipline', reflecting on the significance of
Proverbs 3:11–12. Believers must also 'Pursue peace with everyone,
and the holiness without which no one will see the Lord' (NRSV).
This is necessary to avoid the sort of apostasy demonstrated by Esau.

The pilgrimage motif that is a major rhetorical structuring and
thematic device in Hebrews comes to the fore again in 12:18–29.
Earlier, this was likened to the journey of the Israelites from Egypt
to Canaan (3:7 – 4:11). The hearers have been warned about drifting
away (2:1), turning away (3:12), falling away (6:6), giving up meeting
together (10:25), shrinking back (10:39) or being hindered in running
the race (12:1; cf. 12:12–13). However, whereas Israel related to God
on the basis of the revelation given to Moses at Sinai, Christians
approach God as beneficiaries of the covenant inaugurated by Jesus
in his sacrificial death and heavenly exaltation (8:3 – 10:18). A
pictorial representation of this contrast is given in 12:18–24. Christians have not come to the terrors of Sinai, but they have already
come by faith 'to Mount Zion, to the city of the living God, the
heavenly Jerusalem'.

In one sense, Christians have already arrived at their destination
by coming to God 'the Judge of all' through Jesus 'the mediator of
a new covenant'. In another sense, they must beware of refusing
the one who continues to warn them from heaven (12:25–27,
reflecting on the significance of Hag. 2:6). As those who are
'looking for the city that is to come' (13:14; cf. 11:9–10, 13–16), they
are still on a journey to the heavenly Jerusalem, or the divine 'rest'
(4:1–11), and must persevere in faith, using all the resources God
has provided for them. This eschatological perspective is clearly
reflected in 12:28–29, where the assurance that 'we are receiving
a kingdom that cannot be shaken' is made the basis for being
thankful and serving God acceptably 'with reverence and awe, for
"our God is a consuming fire"'.

A thematic inclusion with 12:28–29 is formed by the exhortation
to offer to God through Jesus 'a sacrifice of praise' and to do good
and to share with others, 'for with such sacrifices God is pleased'

(13:15–16). The intervening exhortations spell out in detail what such worship might involve in practical terms. An epistolary postscript follows (13:17–25).

e. Drawing the strands together

Guthrie notes the structural connections between these two strands and their independent development, and he proposes a complex outline of the whole discourse in two linked columns. This puts 6:4–8 at the centre of the exhortatory strand and 8:1–2 at the centre of the theological strand. The two genres 'move along different lines but hasten toward the same goal' (Guthrie, p. 146).

However, Guthrie's helpful approach often fails to note the theological significance of key terms and the degree of overlap in the argument. In the exhortatory strand, there is a development of the author's pastoral theology that is linked to developments in the expository strand. This is an important observation for those who want to expound Hebrews in a way that reflects the author's rhetorical strategy. Ultimately, the expository and hortatory sections need to be analysed as a unity, since 'each hortatory section has been crafted to fit a particular place in the discourse' (Cockerill, p. 61; cf. deSilva, pp. 71–75).

Like Guthrie, Cockerill views the exhortations in 4:14–16 and 10:19–25 as dividing the main body of Hebrews into three large sections. Whereas Guthrie makes a separate feature of these transitional exhortations, Cockerill identifies them as the beginning of the second and third major divisions of the argument. The first section (1:1 – 4:13) 'proclaims God's revelation in the Son and warns against disobedience'; the second section (4:14 – 10:18) 'presents Christ's high priesthood as the fulfilment of his sonship and the content of God's self-disclosure in the Son'; and the third section (10:19 – 12:29) 'urges faithful endurance until Christ's return, enabled by the sufficiency of his high priesthood'.[11]

---

11. Cockerill, p. 62. He is sensitive to the formal features of Hebrews, to its use of Scripture and to its rhetorical shape, but he puts considerable emphasis on 'the pastor's imagery and on the concrete way in which he has arranged his material to motivate his hearers'.

f. A pattern of comparison

One of the key features of Hebrews is a developing pattern of contrast between Old Testament institutions and Christ. Understandably, the comparison between Old and New Covenants has been viewed as fundamental to the argument, with Christ and various individuals and institutions in the past being understood as 'representatives of their various covenants'.[12] Extended patterns of comparison (*synkrisis*) were a feature of ancient rhetorical practice and it has been argued that Hebrews follows established guidelines for this. Five comparisons

> collectively span nearly the full length of Hebrews: the angels vs. Jesus (1:5–14), Moses vs. Jesus (3:1–6), the Aaronic high priests vs. Jesus (5:1–10), the Levitical priestly ministry vs. the Melchizedekian priestly ministry (7:1 – 10:18), and Mt. Sinai vs. Mt. Zion (12:18–24).[13]

Six deliberative or hortatory comparisons are directly linked to these expositional arguments (2:2–4; 4:2; 6:13–20; 10:28–29; 12:9; 12:25).[14]

g. Conclusion

The Analysis provided below (pp. 57–60) draws together many of the insights outlined above, with the particular aim of helping those who want to expound and apply Hebrews to contemporary audiences. Like many others, I have sought to show how exposition and exhortation progressively interact to achieve the author's theological and pastoral agenda. Some scholars would structure Hebrews

---

12. Martin and Whitlark, *Inventing Hebrews*, p. 24. Guthrie (*Structure*, pp. 1–20) discusses the way the 'Christ is superior' motif has been explored in the history of interpreting Hebrews.

13. Martin and Whitlark, ibid., p. 51. Internal coherence shows that these comparisons should be read collectively and progressively.

14. Martin and Whitlark (ibid., pp. 60–76) argue that the pairing of these expository and hortatory sections progressively advances the author's ultimate aim 'to encourage perseverance in the faith and, correspondingly, to discourage apostasy'.

in terms of the pattern of argumentation in first-century Graeco-Roman rhetorical texts, but Hebrews 'cannot be forced into the mold of a classical speech' (Lane 1, p. lxxix). Moreover, such an approach does not sufficiently expose the intricacies of the author's argument and its originality.

3. Occasion and purpose

Since 'To the Hebrews' is part of the superscription in most of the earliest manuscripts, it has often been concluded that this 'word of exhortation' was addressed to an ethnically Jewish audience. In support of this, it has been argued that the author's use of the Old Testament and rabbinic methods of interpretation would have appealed only to Jewish converts. The warning passages have been taken to mean that the recipients were in danger of reverting to Judaism, so as to avoid further persecution, either from state authorities or from Jewish leaders and supporters.[15]

However, the title 'To the Hebrews' may only express a conjecture concerning those addressed, based on an estimation of its contents. Such headings appear to have been added to the New Testament documents from the end of the second century, when they were being copied and published together for different audiences (cf. Bruce, pp. xxiii–xxiv). The Acts of the Apostles indicates that many of the earliest Gentile converts were attached to Jewish synagogues before turning to Christ (e.g. Acts 13:16, 26, 43; 17:1–4, 10–12). There, they would have been taught how to interpret the Scriptures and have come to regard them as 'the oracles of God' (Heb. 5:12, ESV). It also appears from some of the Pauline letters that arguments about the fulfilment of biblical promises and institutions in Christ were applicable to mixed audiences (e.g. Gal. 3 – 4; Rom. 3 – 4). Those addressed in Hebrews could have been

---

15. For example, Lane (1, pp. lviii–lx) argues that the addressees participated in a small house fellowship in Rome, whose social and religious roots 'are almost certainly to be traced to the Jewish quarters and to participation in the life of a hellenistic synagogue' (p. liv).

both Jewish and Gentile Christians with a synagogue background
(see section 4 below, 'Destination and date of composition').

Even the focus on the levitical cult in Hebrews does not mean
that the original recipients were exclusively Jewish. Both Jewish
and Gentile Christians were socialized into a community 'that
required both an acceptance of the OT as a record of divine revelation *and* a rejection of the contemporary validity of the covenant
and priesthood therein described (or, better, commanded)' (deSilva,
p. 5). The author contrasts the old way with the new way of drawing
near to God through Jesus Christ to enhance 'the significance of
belonging to, and importance of remaining with, the Christian
community' (deSilva, p. 5).

Adopting this socio-rhetorical approach, David deSilva argues
that 'Hebrews supports group definition and identity through
developing a contrast with an alternative group's ideology, stressing
the superiority of Christian ideology as a means of sustaining
commitment' (p. 5). The process by which the audience was
converted and socialized into the Christian community is indicated
in 2:2–4 and 6:1–3. But this made them members of an illegal sect,
not having a status recognized by Roman society at that time. In
10:32–34, the author recalls how the rejection of their former values
and associations provoked significant reactions from their non-
Christian neighbours and 'the community's confession brought
them into a time of conflict with the larger society' (p. 11).[16]

Although the recipients stood firm and supported one another
in former trials, their pastor addresses a deteriorating situation.
Some are perceived to be in danger of drifting from Christ and the
gospel (2:1) and may be hardening their hearts in unbelief (3:12–13).
Some have given up meeting together (10:25), while those who
remain in the assembly are accused of failing to mature in a way
that might be expected 'by this time' (5:11–14). A general faltering
in confidence and zeal is suggested by key verses (3:6; 4:11; 6:11–12;
12:1–3, 12–13). The recipients needed every encouragement to

---

16. DeSilva goes on to describe how 'Christians adopted a lifestyle that,
   in the eyes of their pagan neighbors, would have been considered
   antisocial and even subversive' (p. 12).

endure further suffering, even martyrdom (12:4), and receive what God had promised them (10:35–39; 11:1–40; 12:5–11). All this suggests that 'the author conceives of the threat to the community in two broad but interrelated categories, external pressure or "persecution" . . . and a waning commitment to the community's confessed faith' (Attridge, p. 13).[17] Furthermore, 'their anxiety at present marginalization, anticipated suffering, and perhaps impending martyrdom may have been exacerbated by disappointment that Christ had not yet returned (1:14; 10:36–39) or by their failure to realize and appropriate his full sufficiency as Savior' (Cockerill, p. 17).

Group definition and the need to sustain commitment to the Christian community in the face of alienation and suffering is part of the reason for this 'word of exhortation' (13:22). Such an explanation of its purpose shows how Hebrews could speak directly to readers in our time, who may also have 'begun to consider the cost of discipleship too great in terms of what they have lost in status, acceptance, and wealth in society' (deSilva, p. 58). However, deSilva's emphasis on responding with loyalty to Christ as Divine Benefactor by adopting appropriate evaluations of honour and shame has less relevance in Western cultures today (pp. 59–68).

More than any other New Testament document, Hebrews shows how the biblical institutions of sanctuary, sacrifice and priesthood are fulfilled in Christ. This line of argument is used to highlight the confident access to God that Christians have in the present and the certainty of their ultimate acceptance into God's presence (4:4–16; 6:19–20; 10:10, 11–18, 19–25; 12:22–24). The fact that Jesus suffered 'outside the city gate to make the people holy through his own blood' (13:12) also becomes the basis for encouraging his followers to 'go to him outside the camp, bearing the disgrace he bore' (13:13).[18] The priestly ministry by which he definitively cleansed,

---

17. DeSilva (pp. 17–18) outlines the difficulty of living as Christians in the shame culture of the Graeco-Roman world.

18. Winter ('Suffering with the Saviour', pp. 147–162) relates this to the possibility of exile to a distant place for Christians in the Roman Empire. But see my comment on 13:13.

sanctified and perfected his people is the means by which he enables them to endure immediate struggles, while 'looking for the city that is to come' (13:14; cf. 7:25; 12:2–3) and offering to God the sort of praise and devotion that pleases him (13:15–16; cf. 9:14; 12:28–29).

Some scholars dispute that a lapse into Judaism was the author's concern in arguing this way. For example, Martin and Whitlark contend that the covenant comparison that spans Hebrews has in view 'a *single* people, running from "our fathers/elders" to the present generation, and a *single* faith shared by this people with a single trajectory – a people who will be perfected together in the heavenly Jerusalem (cf. 11:39–40; 12:22)' (*Inventing Hebrews*, p. 265). A positive characterization of the Old Covenant is essential to the author's goal of 'heightening the audience's appreciation of its own new covenant experience' (p. 266). Hebrews 'pits covenant faithfulness past and present against a common apostasy' (p. 267).

These are important observations about the author's convictions and mode of persuasion. But we must also account for the vigour of his insistence on the insufficiency and inadequacy of the old order (e.g. 7:11–28; 8:1–13; 9:6–15; 10:1–4, 11; 13:10). Is this line of argument merely a rhetorical foil to highlight the greatness of the New Covenant and the advantages of being a Christian? Bruce suggests that

> [the author's] insistence that the old covenant has been antiquated is expressed with a moral earnestness and driven home repeatedly in a manner which would be pointless if his readers were not specially disposed to live under that covenant, but which would be very much to the point if they were still trying to live under it, or imagined that, having passed beyond it, they could revert to it.[19]

In this connection, the warning in 13:9–10 may have special significance. Here the author contrasts himself and his hearers with

---

19. Bruce, p. xxvi. Bruce allows that the audience could include Gentiles coming to Christ from a synagogue background, but identifies the recipients as predominantly Hellenistic Jewish Christians, whose background was more 'nonconformist' than 'the normative Judaism represented by rabbinical tradition' (p. xxix). Cf. O'Brien, pp. 9–12.

'those who minister at the tabernacle'. This expression is 'not a reference to OT people but to contemporaries who lived according to the old order after the coming of Christ' (Cockerill, p. 21). Ministering at the tabernacle in this context is associated with 'eating ceremonial foods, which is of no benefit to those who do so'. So, deSilva rightly concludes that 'while others have the shadow, the addressees have the real thing and should not relinquish this privilege for any lesser good' (p. 500). This implies more than a formal contrast with the attractions of Judaism.

Cockerill concludes that 'the pastor's intention has been to encourage his hearers clearly to distinguish themselves from those who still live by the provisions of that former order. To go "outside the camp" (13:13) is to separate from these people' (p. 21). Put another way, it is reasonable to conclude that part of the author's intention was to motivate the recipients 'to rely on Christ rather than take refuge in the synagogue or maintain vestigial Jewish religious practices' (p. 22). More broadly, however, he was 'concerned about his hearers' standing firm against the pressure of and thus separating from unbelieving societies and values, whatever form that unbelieving society may take' (p. 22).

In short, we may conclude that internal and external aspects of the situation addressed by this pastor moved him to compose this word of exhortation. Internally, there were signs of passivity in the congregation, denoting 'a certain weariness in pursuing the Christian goal or making progress along the road of Christian discipleship' (Ellingworth, p. 78). Some may even have showed signs of active, even permanent rebellion. Fundamentally, there seemed to be an unwillingness to progress in understanding the deeper implications of the gospel in the light of Scripture and to live in the light of this teaching. Externally, there was the constant threat of persecution and the attraction of safer options, either withdrawal into the synagogue or choosing to join the unbelieving world of their opponents.

4. Destination and date of composition

Hebrews is addressed to a group of people who had been Christians for some time (5:12) and experienced extensive persecution

(10:32–34). The gospel was initially preached to them by those who heard it from the lips of Jesus (2:3), but the call to 'remember' the leaders who 'spoke the word of God' to them and 'Consider the outcome of their way of life and imitate their faith' (13:7) may mean that those leaders are now dead.[20] Hebrews is likely to have been written some decades after the beginning of the Christian movement.

Various suggestions have been made about the location of those addressed. Several factors point to Rome as a possible destination.[21] First, we know that by AD 60 there was a substantial Jewish population in the city of between forty and fifty thousand people. They mostly lived together in the area across the Tiber known as Trastevere (Philo, *Embassy to Gaius*, 155–157) and belonged to at least four different synagogues.[22] Second, the first use of Hebrews in early Christian literature is in a document known as *1 Clement*, which was composed by Clement of Rome who was an active leader in the city between AD 90 and 100. Third, the expression 'Those from Italy' (13:24) could mean that the author of Hebrews was writing from somewhere in Italy to Christians in the imperial capital or that he was with a group of Italian Christians in a foreign country, sending a message to those in Rome (or elsewhere).[23]

A comparison with Paul's letter to the Romans is relevant to this discussion. It is widely regarded that Paul wrote Romans during the winter of AD 57–58, which he spent in Corinth (Acts 20:1–3 ['Greece']; cf. 1 Cor. 16:6). The final chapter suggests the existence of several house churches in the city, using different terms to

---

20. Cf. Bruce, pp. 394–395. The leaders mentioned in vv. 17, 24 are clearly still alive.

21. O'Brien (p. 15 n. 55) lists those who share this conclusion. However, he notes that 'few exegetical issues depend on determining the geographical location of the addressees'.

22. We know of eleven or twelve synagogues in Rome, 'at least four of which existed in the first century' (Schnabel, *Jesus and the Twelve*, p. 803).

23. Cockerill (p. 37 n. 160) observes that some of the earliest copyists favoured a Palestinian destination and record that Hebrews was written from Italy through Timothy.

identify them (16:5 ['church'], 10, 11 ['household'], 14, 15 ['with them']). Although Paul addresses the Roman Christians collectively as those who are 'among [the] Gentiles' (Rom. 1:6) and as 'you Gentiles' (11:13; cf. 15:15–16), some have Jewish names or are known to have been Jewish from other sources (e.g. 16:3, 7, 11a; cf. Acts 18:2). It is likely that some of these house churches contained more members with a synagogue background than others. Perhaps by the time Hebrews was written, the size and number of gatherings with a distinctly Jewish Christian character had increased.

Paul deals with a specific division that he knows to exist in the Roman churches (14:1 – 15:7). Hostility and suspicion about observing certain Jewish laws was evident, especially regarding food and the observance of holy days. The style of his address to the 'weak' and the 'strong' suggests that there could have been Jewish and Gentile believers on both sides of the argument.[24] Hebrews confronts a more serious situation, where socio-political developments have caused at least some of those addressed to question the finality of the gospel and the need to mature in understanding and commitment to its claims (see particularly 5:11 – 6:12).

Whether or not Hebrews was written to a house church in Rome or to a group of Christians with a synagogue background somewhere else, there are reasons for dating its composition before AD 70. The destruction of the temple in Jerusalem and the cessation of the sacrificial system took place then, but the author speaks as if that ritual were still continuing (e.g. 8:3–5; 9:7–8; 10:1–3, 11; 13:10–11). Admittedly, he refers to details of the tabernacle rather than the temple, 'because of the association of the desert sanctuary with the establishment of the old covenant at Sinai'.[25] But the ritual of the temple was the ritual of the tabernacle, and the worship of the synagogue was linked to what took place in the temple. Some allusion to the disastrous events of AD 70 would surely have

---

24. Cf. Peterson, *Romans*, pp. 20–24, 478–499.

25. Lane (1, p. lxiii). Lane argues that the present tenses are timeless and 'have no bearing upon a determination of a date for the composition of Hebrews'.

strengthened his argument that the 'first covenant' is now 'obsolete and outdated' (8:13).

If Hebrews was written to a group of Christians in Rome, it is possible that the insults, persecution, imprisonment and confiscation of property mentioned in 10:32–34 were associated with the expulsion of Jews from Rome by Emperor Claudius in AD 49 (cf. Acts 18:1–3). According to the Roman historian Suetonius, Claudius did this 'since the Jews constantly made disturbances at the instigation of Chrestus' (*Lives of the Caesars: Claudius* 25.4). Although it is much debated, the Latin name Chrestus could be a confused rendering of 'Christus' (Christ), and the disturbances could have resulted from Christian claims about the messiahship of Jesus.[26] Jewish Christians are likely to have been included in the expulsion from the city with some traditional Jews.[27] But, when Hebrews was written, tensions seem to have been resolved between the two communities. Indeed, some of those addressed may have been attracted to the security of the synagogue, because of a new kind of opposition that was emerging against Christians from the Gentile world.

The fact that the recipients had not yet resisted to the point of shedding their blood (12:4) is significant. Christians in Rome experienced martyrdom after the outbreak of imperial persecution under Nero in AD 64. Hebrews may be specifically preparing the recipients for such an outcome with a section about the torture, imprisonment and execution of men and women of faith who had gone before them, and an encouragement to focus on what Jesus had endured for them (11:35 – 12:3). This could mean that Hebrews was written just before the Neronian persecution began, or in 'the

---

26. Schnabel (*Jesus and the Twelve*, pp. 800–819) discusses missionary work in Rome and Italy and evaluates the evidence for dating the expulsion of Jews from Rome in AD 49. If Jewish Christians were expelled with their Jewish opponents, the witness to the gospel must have been maintained by Gentile Christians at that time.

27. Although Hebrews says nothing about this expulsion from the city, the fact that the recipients 'joyfully accepted the confiscation of [their] property' (10:34) would be consistent with this.

insecure period between the aftermath of the great fire of Rome (AD 64) and Nero's suicide in June, AD 68' (Lane 1, p. lxvi).[28]

5. Authorship and authority

Hebrews appears between Romans and 1 Corinthians in the earliest extant collection of the Pauline letters (Papyrus 46), which dates from about AD 200. Manuscripts from the fourth and fifth centuries mostly locate it between Paul's letters to churches and his letters to individuals (Ellingworth, pp. 6–7). This tradition reflects the widespread assumption that Hebrews was written by the apostle. Only from the sixth century onwards can Hebrews be found among the General Epistles, as in English versions.

As noted previously, the earliest known use of Hebrews is in *1 Clement*, which was written from Rome at the end of the first century. Hebrews is quoted by several second-century writers, who say nothing about its authorship. One exception is Tertullian (AD 155–220), who attributes it to Barnabas.[29] Writers in the eastern part of the Roman Empire generally treated it as Pauline, though some expressed doubts about this because the style and content of Hebrews differ significantly from the acknowledged Pauline letters. Clement of Alexandria (AD 150–215) and Origen (AD 185–253), for example, 'preserved the tradition of Pauline authorship by supposing that the apostle was somehow responsible for the content, but a follower or assistant for the style' (Attridge, p. 1).

---

28. Cockerill (p. 34) considers that 'the mention of Timothy in Heb. 13:23 is the most concrete internal evidence for the date of Hebrews, suggesting a time within the lifetime of Paul's younger associate'. But if Timothy was in his early twenties when Paul met him in about AD 49 (Acts 16:1–3), he could have been in his forties, fifties or older when Hebrews was written. So the mention of Timothy does not give us an easy time reference.

29. Cf. Lane 1, pp. cli–cliii. Hebrews is not mentioned in the Muratorian Canon, which provides a list of the documents recognized in Rome as NT Scripture in the late second century AD and identifies their authorship.

There was a delay in accepting the authority of Hebrews in the West. This was related to a misunderstanding that it taught that 'those who had sinned after baptism could not be forgiven and readmitted to communion' (Ellingworth, p. 35).[30] The Synods of Hippo (393) and Carthage (397) eventually recognized the canonical authority of Hebrews, which was attributed to Paul. Writing in AD 414, Jerome (*Epistle 129*) pointed to the widespread acceptance of Hebrews as Pauline, 'though many think that it is from Barnabas or Clement. And it makes no difference whose it is, since it is from a churchman, and is celebrated in the daily readings of the Churches' (cited by Ellingworth, p. 36).

Pauline authorship largely remained the accepted view until the sixteenth century, when it was once again questioned. At that time, differences of style and content in Hebrews were once again noted. It was particularly observed that Paul, who emphasizes his calling and status as an apostle and eyewitness of the risen Lord (e.g. Rom. 1:1–5; 1 Cor. 9:1; 15:8; Gal. 1:11–16), could hardly have described himself as having received the Lord's message through 'those who heard him' (Heb. 2:3).

Modern scholars agree that arguments against Pauline authorship are decisive. Hebrews is anonymous and is not ascribed to Paul. It develops a portrait of Jesus as high priest and his work as the fulfilment of Old Testament sacrificial ritual that finds few parallels in Paul's writings. Scripture is cited differently in Hebrews (see section 6b below, 'God and Scripture'). Many typically Pauline themes and arguments are lacking in Hebrews or are expressed in different ways.[31] Although the author is not a current leader of the group being addressed (13:17), he has an intimate knowledge of their situation, wants to be restored to them soon, and writes with pastoral authority and insight (13:18–19, 22). Mention of 'our brother

---

30. This teaching was largely due to the influence of the *Shepherd of Hermas*, which was a Christian document written in Rome between AD 120 and 140. Cf. Kleinig, pp. 32–34.

31. Ellingworth (pp. 4–7) provides a full analysis of the differences between Hebrews and the Pauline letters in language, style and theology.

Timothy' (13:23) could mean that he was in some way part of the Pauline circle of early Christian missionaries.

The suggestion that Barnabas was the author is hard to substantiate in the absence of authentic writings by him. As a Levite from Cyprus, this 'son of encouragement' (Acts 4:36) could have been responsible for the 'word of encouragement' (Heb. 13:22, my translation) that deals so exhaustively with the theme of sacrifice, priesthood and worship. But 'the author's cultic information appears to be derived directly from the OT, rather than from contemporary practice' (Ellingworth, p. 15). As a Jew from the Dispersion, Barnabas quite possibly had intimate contact with the Hellenistic and philosophical teaching of Alexandrian Judaism with which the author of Hebrews seems to have had some acquaintance. But why is there no reference in Hebrews to the Gentile mission, with which Barnabas was so intimately involved (Acts 11:22–26; Gal. 2:9)?

Martin Luther proposed Apollos as the author and this theory has continued to appeal to some (e.g. Johnson, pp. 42–44). As a highly educated Alexandrian Jew, Apollos was eloquent, had 'a thorough knowledge of the Scriptures' and operated in the same missionary sphere as Paul (Acts 18:24–28). Nothing we know about Apollos excludes him from consideration. Ellingworth concludes that 'his name is perhaps the least unlikely of the conjectures that have been put forward' (p. 21). However, in the end it must be said that the evidence in favour of Barnabas or Apollos or any other candidate is not decisive.[32] Indeed, we do not need to know the identity of the author to appreciate his work and accept its authority.

Hebrews itself indicates that the human authorship of biblical books is of secondary importance. So, for example, acknowledging David as the writer of Psalm 95 (Heb. 4:7), Hebrews insists that the Holy Spirit was the primary author (Heb. 3:7). Again, the human authorship of Psalm 8 is not mentioned (Heb. 2:6) and is not regarded as essential for receiving it as divinely

---

32. Other suggestions have included Peter, Jude, Stephen, Philip, Silas and Luke (cf. Ellingworth, pp. 15–20).

inspired Scripture. Similarly, we should be willing to accept that it matters little whom God used to write Hebrews. Put another way, the first recipients knew the identity and authority of the author, but its acceptance by churches more widely took place for other reasons.

Lane argues that 'Hebrews was preserved and transmitted because Christian leaders kept picking it up and positive results followed' (1, p. cliv). Its authority was recognized as it was read in churches all over the Roman Empire and its teaching was applied in different contexts. Hebrews proved to be more than a specific response to the original situation addressed by one of its former leaders. Canonical recognition of the work was 'a confessional acknowledgement that the community of believers was able to make meaning of this text for *spiritual and theological formation in new situations*'.[33] Its authority did not come from the declarations of church councils, but from its innate, God-given ability to speak so effectively into the lives of Christ's people. But there is more to be said about its canonical acceptance than this.

As an exposition of the promised New Covenant and its implications (8:1–13; 10:15–18), Hebrews makes an implicit claim to be New Testament Scripture. The author's use of Old Testament texts and his proclamation of their fulfilment in Christ involve Christological and gospel confessions that parallel other New Testament writings at critical points. These intra-canonical connections explain the widespread recognition of the book's authority, even when Pauline authorship was disputed. Moreover, this pastor's desire to facilitate the maturation and perseverance of those he addresses (5:11 – 6:12) caused him to speak with a prophetic authority above and beyond that of a faithful congregational leader (13:17–25). In effect, Hebrews itself explains why it belongs among the collection of New Testament documents attached to Israel's canon of inspired writings. Guided by God's Spirit, Christians in diverse places recognized Hebrews as having divine authority, because it self-consciously and faithfully transmitted the true, transformative apostolic faith.

---

33. Lane 1, p. clv (my emphasis).

6. Theology

a. God as Trinity

The doctrine of God is central to the argument of Hebrews, with a trinitarian perspective emerging in several contexts. Together with the Gospel of John and certain Pauline passages, Hebrews figured significantly in early Christian debates about the divine and human natures of Christ and the relationship between the persons of the Godhead. The author shows that the progressive revelation of God in history has been for the purpose of redemption and fellowship. God's self-presentation as Trinity is 'the free work of sovereign mercy, in which the holy God wills, establishes and perfects saving fellowship with himself, a fellowship in which humankind comes to know, love, and fear him above all things'.[34]

i. God the Father

God speaks of himself as Father in relation to the Son only in biblical citations relating to the Messiah (1:5; cf. Ps. 2:7; 2 Sam. 7:14), though various references to the Son discussed below explore what it means for Jesus to be uniquely related to God as Father.[35] As 'the Father of spirits' (12:9), God engages with our spirits and treats believers as 'sons' (2:10; 12:5–8 [NIV, 'sons and daughters']). By means of his sacrificial death, the Son of God has consecrated these spiritual children to be in a distinctive relationship with his Father. As the divine sanctifier, Jesus calls them his 'brothers and sisters' (2:11–12, citing Ps. 22:22).

God is the Creator of all that exists (1:1–4; 4:3–4; 11:3), living (3:12; 9:14; 10:31; 12:22), glorious, powerful, majestic and worshipped and served by angels (1:6–7), and eternally ruling the universe with justice and righteousness (1:8–12). His justice exposes both the genuineness and the deceit of human behaviour (6:10). His

---

34. Webster, *Holiness*, pp. 12–13.

35. NIV translates the Greek *en hyiō* in 1:2 'by his Son', though see my comment on this verse. Contextually, this points to the eternal relationship of the Son to the Father.

faithfulness means that 'it is impossible for God to lie' (6:17–18;
cf. 10:23). God is gracious and merciful (4:14–16), but he cannot be
treated with indifference, since he is also 'the Judge of all' (12:23).
No-one is hidden from his sight: all are 'uncovered and laid bare
before the eyes of him to whom we must give account' (4:13). In
drawing attention to these characteristics and activities of God,
Hebrews makes many references to God's progressive interactions
with human beings, as recorded in Scripture. Note particularly the
historical sequence in 11:1 – 12:2. In this connection, the author
continually emphasizes that 'God has spoken and continues to
speak in a vivid and compelling way'.[36]

God's judgment of Israel as a nation under the law (2:2; 3:16–19;
10:28) becomes the basis for affirming the judgment of every
human being after death (6:2, 8; 9:27; 10:27, 30–31; 13:4). Since the
damning effects of sin are experienced by all, only the sacrificial
death of God's Son can bring the necessary deliverance (2:14–15,
17). The seriousness of God's judgment against sin forms the background to the author's special focus on the danger of turning away
from the living God (3:12) and then facing him as judge (2:1–3;
4:12–13; 6:4–8; 10:26–31; 12:25–27). God promises vengeance on
those who prove to be his enemies (10:30, citing Deut. 32:35) and
reveals himself to be 'a consuming fire' (12:29, citing Deut. 4:24).
God's fearsome self-manifestation to Israel at Sinai (12:18–21,
25–26), his judgment of the first generation in the wilderness who
turned away from him in unbelief and disobedience (3:16–19) and
his subsequent warnings to those who opposed his people (10:30)
confirm that the coming judgment is to be avoided at all costs. It
will be an 'eternal judgment' (6:2), likened to a 'raging fire that will
consume the enemies of God' (10:27; cf. Matt. 25:30, 41; 2 Thess.
1:6–10). It will involve 'the removing of what can be shaken – that
is, created things – so that what cannot be shaken may remain'
(12:27), and it will usher in 'the world to come' (2:5), which is the
'promised eternal inheritance' of all true believers (9:15).

---

36. Attridge, 'God in Hebrews', p. 110. Attridge (pp. 99–102) summarizes
    key features in Hebrews' narrative of God's engagements with
    humanity.

Despite this emphasis on divine judgment, the focus of Hebrews is on the eternal salvation God has provided through the suffering, death and heavenly exaltation of his Son, inaugurating the New Covenant by his blood (8:6; 9:15; 13:20), and making it possible for believers to persevere in their calling until they actually enter the 'city' he has prepared for them (12:22–24).

ii. God the Son

Hebrews begins with the claim that God's self-disclosure in the past, 'in the prophets', has been surpassed 'in these last days' in the person of the Son, who radiates the glory of God and is 'the exact representation of his being' (1:1–3; 2:3). The pre-existence and full divinity of the Son is emphasized by saying that he is the one through whom God created the whole universe of time and space (1:2; cf. 1 Cor. 8:6; John 1:1–3), who sustains all things by his powerful word (1:3). His earthly existence is implied by the claim that he made purification for sins, which in the light of verse 3a suggests his incarnation, before he ascended to 'the right hand of the Majesty in heaven'. The incarnation of the Son of God is more explicitly asserted when it is said that he was 'made lower than the angels for a little while' (2:9), that he shared our flesh and blood, and suffered and died to deliver his people from the devil's power and the fear of death (2:14–15; cf. 5:7 [ESV, 'In the days of his flesh']). Put differently, when the Son came into the world, he was given a human body in which to do the will of God, to fulfil the sacrificial rituals given to Israel by God, and to cleanse, sanctify and perfect his people once for all by the offering of himself in death (10:5–10, 14).

When the Son is described as the one whom God 'appointed heir of all things' (1:2, alluding to Ps. 2:8), this introduces the messianic dimension to his role and function.[37] The term 'Christ' or 'Messiah' is used without an article in 3:6; 9:11, 24; 10:10; 13:8, 21. With an article, it more formally reflects the Hebrew expression

---

37. Pss 2 and 110 anticipate or reflect the expectation of prophecies such as Isa. 9:6–7; 11:1–9 about the Son of David who will be anointed with God's Spirit to reign with justice and righteousness over the nations for ever and usher in the perfect peace of a new creation.

'the anointed One' or 'the Messiah' (3:14; 5:5; 6:1; 9:14, 28; 11:26).
The fatherly relationship established by covenant between God
and the Son of David in 2 Samuel 7:14 is identified in Hebrews 1:5
as the basis for the promise in Psalm 2:7–9 about the Messiah who
will ultimately rule the nations.

God initially chose to establish his saving purpose for Israel
through the kings who sat on David's throne. But this was only an
anticipation of his intention to raise his incarnate Son from death
and exalt him to his right hand in heaven, there to reign for ever
as the universal Saviour and Lord (1:13, citing Ps. 110:1). The
beneficiaries of his reign are identified in 2:16 as 'Abraham's
descendants', which must finally mean believers from every nation,
because of promises such as Genesis 12:3; 17:5 (cf. Rom. 4:13–17).
The biblical storyline comes to its climax with the triumph of
Jesus the Son of God and Son of David, who defeats sin, death and
the devil, and fulfils the covenant made with Abraham by bringing
many 'sons' to glory with him (2:9–16; cf. Gal. 3:7–14).

The perfecting of the Son (2:10; 5:9; 7:28) relates to the whole
process by which he was equipped by his earthly suffering, death
and heavenly exaltation to be the promised messianic deliverer of
his people.[38] An Adamic Christology is foundational to this presentation of the person and work of Jesus, recalling the effects of
Adam's disobedience in Genesis 3 and the way these are reversed
by the obedience of the Son (cf. Rom. 5:12–21). Sin, death and the
devil prevent human beings from fulfilling their calling and destiny
as described in Psalm 8:4–6. But Jesus is the heavenly man who
does this for us by being 'crowned with glory and honour because
he suffered death' (2:5–9; cf. 1 Cor. 15:20–28, 45–49). The benefits
are experienced by those whom he sanctifies by his blood, calling
them his brothers and sisters, and bringing them to glory with him
(2:10–13; 10:10, 29; 13:12).

Hebrews blends redemptive and covenantal language to explain
the significance of Jesus' death and heavenly exaltation (2:14–16).
Soon, however, his accomplishment of the messianic salvation as
'a merciful and faithful high priest in service to God' (2:17–18) is

---

38. Cf. Peterson, 'Perfection', pp. 125–136.

added to the picture. This was implied in 1:3 ('After he had provided purification for sins'), but it is extensively developed in 4:14 – 5:10; 7:1 – 10:14; 13:11–13. Jesus fulfilled and replaced the whole method of approach to God provided for Israel through the levitical priesthood. He did this in his suffering, death and heavenly ascension as 'a priest for ever, in the order of Melchizedek' (Ps. 110:4). The priestly and sacrificial benefits of the messianic redemption are discussed more fully below under the heading 'Eschatology and salvation'.

In short, then, the Christology of Hebrews focuses on the incarnation of the eternal Son of God to fulfil the divine plan of salvation predicted of the Son of David in Scripture. He did this as the heavenly man, who is high priest and mediator of a new covenant, opening the way for believers into the presence of God to share in the eternal life of the heavenly Jerusalem (12:22–24). God's promises to Israel are foundational to this presentation of the person and work of Jesus, but the implications for humanity in general are suggested in 2:5–16; 9:27–28. The consequent challenge is to go to him 'outside the camp' or earthly community of God's people, previously maintained by the sacrifices and priestly ministry prescribed by the law, to live in this world as citizens of the heavenly Jerusalem, looking for 'the city that is to come' (13:11–14).[39]

iii. The Holy Spirit

The author comes closest to articulating a doctrine of God as Trinity in relation to the achievement of eternal salvation and the application of its benefits to believers. Empowered by 'the eternal Spirit', the Son offered himself without blemish to God in his sacrificial death (9:14). The implications of this verse are teased out in later passages. As predicted in Isaiah 42:1–4 and ultimately explained in Isaiah 53, the Servant of the LORD would be anointed with God's Spirit to 'bring justice to the nations'.[40] The fulfilment of the Servant's Spirit-directed ministry is specifically indicated in

---

39. Cf. Marshall, 'Soteriology in Hebrews', pp. 253–272.
40. In the Gospels, this anointing with the Spirit is associated with Jesus' baptism (Matt. 3:16–17; Mark 1:9–11; Luke 3:21–22; cf. John 1:32–34).

Hebrews when the obedient Son of God is said to 'do away with sin by the sacrifice of himself', delivering many from final judgment by 'bearing' their sins (9:26–28; cf. 10:5–10).

The same Spirit was given to those who first heard the message of the Lord Jesus. God testified to the authority and truth of that message 'by signs, wonders and various miracles, and by gifts of the Holy Spirit distributed according to his will' (2:4; cf. Acts 2:1–4). Enlightened by the message that those early witnesses preached, many were able to taste 'the heavenly gift' and share in the Holy Spirit (6:4; cf. Acts 2:38–39). When they received 'the Spirit of grace', they were also sanctified by 'the blood of the covenant' (10:29). This echoes the promise of Ezekiel 36:25–27 about God cleansing his people from sin, giving them a 'new heart' and putting his Spirit within them, causing them to follow his decrees and keep his laws. The parallel in Jeremiah 31:33–34 does not mention the Spirit, but promises that under the New Covenant God will put his law 'in their minds and write it on their hearts', because he will 'forgive their wickedness and will remember their sins no more' (cf. Heb. 10:15–18). Reading these two passages together, we may conclude that the Spirit works through the gospel to assure believers of the forgiveness of their sins through the sacrifice of God's Son, and sets them free to serve God with gratitude and obedience (9:14; 12:28).

God's continuing work through his Spirit in believers is alluded to in 13:20–21. The author prays that the God of peace, 'who through the blood of the eternal covenant brought back from the dead our Lord Jesus, that great Shepherd of the sheep', might equip his people with everything good for doing his will, and 'may he work in us what is pleasing to him'. Only by God's enabling work 'in us' may we persevere in faithfulness and obedience to the end. The gift of the Spirit to God's people as a consequence of the Messiah's resurrection and ascension is clearly emphasized in other New Testament contexts such as John 15:26; 16:7; Acts 2:33.

In three passages, the Spirit's inspiration of the biblical writers is affirmed and closely linked with his continuing role as illuminator of Old Testament texts for New Testament believers (cf. 2 Tim. 3:16–17; 2 Pet. 1:20–21). The Holy Spirit continues to speak through Psalm 95 about the danger of hardening one's heart against God's 'voice' and falling away from the living God (Heb. 3:7–19).[41] The Spirit shows from the provisions of the law for worship in the Old Testament that the way into the actual presence of God 'had not yet been disclosed as long as the first tabernacle was still functioning' (9:8). God's Spirit testifies through Jeremiah 31:33–34 that the New Covenant has been established by Christ and that no further sacrifices are required for fellowship with God (10:15–18).

b. God and Scripture

The repeated challenge of Hebrews is to hear the voice of God in Scripture and respond appropriately to the author's teaching that is derived from Scripture. Whereas the apostle Paul regularly introduced biblical citations as 'written', Hebrews uses multiple terms for God 'speaking' through what is written.[42] Some scriptures reveal the Father speaking to the Son or about the Son (1:5–13; 2:5–8; 5:5–6; 7:17, 21). But the Son speaks to the Father in 2:12–13; 10:5–7, while other passages portray God speaking directly to his people (3:7 – 4:13; 8:8–13; 10:15–18, 30–31, 36–39; 12:5–11, 26–29; 13:5). Psalm 118:6–7 provides words of confidence for believers to reflect back to God (13:6).

Biblical texts are used to explain the deepest implications of the gospel and urge those who hear to keep responding to God as he requires.[43] The author strikingly expects his hearers to respond to his own teaching with as much care and diligence as to the Scriptures themselves (compare 5:11 – 6:12 with 3:7 – 4:13). In this way, he speaks with prophetic directness and authority to his audience.

In 4:12–13 the author reflects the language and sentiment of Isaiah 55:10–11, that God's word will not return to him empty, but will accomplish what he desires and achieve the purpose for which he sent it. The word of God in creation is the focus in 1:10–12; 11:3, and the implication in 12:26–27 is that his voice will one day bring

---

41. David is acknowledged as the human author of Ps. 95, but it was God who spoke through him (4:7–8). Cf. Griffiths, 'Word of God', pp. 35–48.

42. Cf. O'Brien, *God Has Spoken*, pp. 21–23; Kleinig, pp. 27–28.

43. Cf. Guthrie, 'Hebrews', pp. 919–995; Kleinig, pp. 29–32.

it to an end. Prophetic words spoken to Israel in passages like Jeremiah 31:31–34 or to the Messiah in passages like Psalm 110:1, 4 have been fulfilled by God. As-yet-unfulfilled promises about the return of Christ, final judgment and the shaking of the created order can therefore be confidently trusted (Heb. 10:30, 37–38; 12:26). Biblical texts are regarded as not merely 'windows on God's speaking in the past', but also as 'witnesses to things his Spirit wishes to speak in the present'.[44] Individual texts 'speak' in this way when they are considered within the overarching story of salvation that the Bible presents.

Hebrews has been described as 'one of the earliest and most successful attempts to define the relations between the Old and New Testaments' (Caird, 'Exegetical Method', p. 45). The author believed that the Old Testament contained 'a genuine foreshadowing of the good things to come, not a Platonic illusion of ultimate reality' (Caird, p. 46). Moreover, the Old Testament is 'not only an incomplete book but an avowedly incomplete book, which taught and teaches men to live by faith in the good things that were to come' (Caird, p. 49). This is particularly illustrated by the use of four key texts in the argument of Hebrews (Pss 8:4–6; 95:7–11; 110:4; Jer. 31:31–34). See also my comment on Hebrews 8:7.

Psalm 8:4–6 is applied to Christ in 2:5–9 and is foundational to the argument in 2:5–18 (with supportive citations from Ps. 22:22 and Isa. 8:17; 8:18 in 2:12–13). Psalm 95:7–11 is applied to the readers in an extended exhortation in 3:7 – 4:13 (with a supportive citation from Gen. 2:2 in 4:4). Psalm 110:4 with its reference to the priesthood of the Messiah 'in the order of Melchizedek' is quoted or alluded to several times in 5:5 – 7:28 and is foundational to the argument in those chapters (with Gen. 22:17 cited in 6:14, and Gen. 14:18–20 alluded to in 7:1–10). The prophecy of a new covenant in Jeremiah 31:31–34 is foundational to the exposition in 8:1 – 10:18 (with Exod. 25:40 a supportive text in 8:5; Exod. 24:8 in 9:20; Ps. 40:6–8 in 10:5–7). Allusions to Psalm 110:1 in 8:1 and 10:12 also frame the argument in this central section. Each of these foundational passages, together with many of the ancillary texts, must

---

44. Schenck, 'God Has Spoken', p. 323.

first be interpreted in its Old Testament context, so that its incompleteness in that context can be understood and its fulfilment in and through the person and work of Christ can be appreciated.

Scholars differ about the number of biblical quotations and allusions in Hebrews. Guthrie identifies 'thirty-seven quotations, forty allusions, nineteen cases where OT material is summarised and thirteen where an OT name or topic is referred to without reference to a specific context'.[45] He discerns nine quotations from the Pentateuch and fifteen allusions; nineteen quotations from the Psalms and fifteen allusions; three quotations from Isaiah and four allusions; and two quotations from Jeremiah and three allusions. 'Habakkuk, Haggai, Proverbs, and 2 Samuel each are quoted once and Joshua is alluded to a single time, as possibly are Proverbs and Job' (Guthrie, 'Hebrews', p. 919).

From the Pentateuch the author drew 'the basic structure of his thought regarding redemptive history' and from the Psalms he derived 'primary support for his Christology'.[46] His handling of Old Testament passages is complex and varied, and is discussed progressively throughout the commentary as different texts appear in the argument. The author mostly works from the LXX Greek translation of the Old Testament, adapting this from time to time to suit his rhetorical purpose.[47] He follows certain rabbinic patterns of interpretation, but 'more than any other technique, and sometimes in conjunction with other techniques, the author of Hebrews uses "reinforcement" . . . either to support a theological point just made or to bolster a word of exhortation'.[48]

---

45. Guthrie, 'Hebrews', p. 919. Contrast Longenecker, *Biblical Exegesis*, pp. 164–170.

46. Longenecker, ibid., p. 167. Non-canonical texts are not cited in Hebrews, but allusions to such material have been detected at certain points in the argument.

47. However, there is debate about the type of LXX text that was used by the author of Hebrews. Cf. Ellingworth, pp. 37–38.

48. Guthrie, 'Hebrews', p. 923. Kleinig (pp. 29–30) lists Hillel's seven logical rules for interpretation, which Bateman (*Early Jewish Hermeneutics*) has shown to be operative in Heb. 1:5–13.

One further preliminary observation can be made. In the theological–Christological sections of Hebrews, where the meaning of the death and heavenly exaltation of Jesus is explored, the viewpoint is that what the Old Testament was pointing forward to has been realized (e.g. 8:1 – 10:18). But in the exhortations, Hebrews assumes that Christians are still on a journey to the ultimate experience of salvation that God has in store for them (e.g. 3:7 – 4:13). Thus,

> in the theologically oriented passages ('realized eschatology') the discontinuity with the old covenant is written large: in the exhortatory passages ('futurist eschatology') the continuity between old and new covenant is such that one might almost think the Christian era had never dawned.[49]

The negative example of the Israelites in the wilderness and the warning of Psalm 95 can be applied directly to Christians, together with the positive examples from Scripture listed in 11:1–38. The bipolarity of Christian existence (the 'now–not yet' tension explained below) is a key to understanding the author's method of interpreting Old Testament Scriptures, 'to let them speak to different elements within the Christian experience'.[50]

c. Eschatology and salvation

Eschatology is concerned with the end of human history on this earth and the eternal future of God's people. The conviction that all human beings must ultimately face God as judge means that eschatology and salvation are intimately linked in Hebrews. God has acted to deliver us from the consequences of our sins and will finally usher us into his eternal presence. However, since 'the end' has already been achieved by the saving work of God's Son (9:11–15; 12:22–24), believers can enjoy in advance the benefits he has won for them (4:14–16; 10:19–25), especially those predicted in the prophecy of a new covenant (8:6–13; 10:15–18; cf. Jer. 31:31–34),

---

49. Hughes, *Hebrews and Hermeneutics*, p. 70.
50. Ibid.

while they wait for the consummation of God's plan in 'the world to come' (2:5). Moreover, the author's 'now, but not yet' perspective enables him to combine assurances about intimate access to God in the present with warnings about the need to persevere in faithful obedience.[51]

i. The end achieved by Christ

The author reveals his eschatological perspective with expressions such as 'in these last days' (1:2) and 'the culmination of the ages' (9:26) for the present era, and 'the world to come' (2:5), 'the coming age' (6:5), God's 'rest' (4:1–11) and 'the city that is to come' (13:14) for what lies ahead. Now is the time when most prophetic expectations have been fulfilled, but final judgment is yet to take place and the promised eternal inheritance is yet to be entered (9:15). Meanwhile, believers are called to endure suffering (10:32–35), to persevere in faith until Christ returns (10:36–39) and to wait expectantly for God's unshakable kingdom to be revealed (12:25–29).[52]

The Son fulfilled God's saving plan by sharing in our humanity, suffering and dying for us, and being exalted to God's right hand through resurrection and heavenly ascension (2:5–15; 13:20). Psalm 110:1 is a key text for our author, because it proclaims that the promised Son of David will sit at God's right hand until his enemies are subdued and he rules the nations without opposition (see also Ps. 2:4–8).[53] The Son's resurrection–ascension as Messiah placed him in that position and inaugurated the final stage of God's dealing with humanity. Enemies of God become his friends when they acknowledge the lordship of Christ and turn to him as their only Saviour. The eternal reign of the Messiah has been established in anticipation of final judgment, and as his servants proclaim his

---

51. Cf. Marshall, 'Soteriology in Hebrews', pp. 253–272.

52. Cf. Barrett, 'Eschatology', pp. 363–393.

53. Ps. 110:1 is the most widely used text in the NT, being quoted or alluded to in Mark 12:36; 14:62 par.; Acts 2:34–35; Rom. 8:34; 1 Cor. 15:25; Eph. 1:20; Col. 3:1; Heb. 1:3 (see my comment), 13; 8:1; 10:12; 12:2; 1 Pet. 3:22.

victory, 'many sons and daughters' are being brought to glory with him (2:10).

When the author explores more fully the way in which the Son accomplished our salvation, he introduces the notion that Jesus acted in a priestly way to provide 'purification for sins' (1:3), making atonement 'for the sins of the people' (2:17). He did this by offering himself in 'reverent submission' to 'the one who could save him from death' (5:7), sacrificing for their sins 'once for all when he offered himself' (7:27). As a sinless and unblemished sacrifice (4:15; 9:14), Jesus fulfilled the role of the Lord's Servant in Isaiah 53:11, which was to 'bear' the sin of others. Bearing sin means bearing its punishment (e.g. Gen. 4:13; Lev. 24:15; Num. 14:34; Lam. 5:7; cf. 1 Pet. 2:24). In Isaiah's prophecy, the Lord 'makes his life an offering for sin' (53:10), so that he can 'justify many' (v. 11).[54]

In Hebrews, the sacrifice of Jesus is viewed as giving him access to God's heavenly sanctuary (9:11–12, 24). This opened the way for believers to approach God directly in his majestic holiness, needing no other mediators or sacrifices (4:14–16; 10:19–22), ultimately to spend eternity in his presence (12:22–24). The layout and ritual of the tabernacle, especially on the Day of Atonement, provided the pattern for this new way of relating to God (9:1–10).[55] As the high priest who 'sat down at the right hand of the throne of the Majesty in heaven', Jesus now 'serves in the sanctuary, the true tabernacle set up by the Lord, not by a mere human being' (8:1–2). Thus, he is the promised eternal priest 'in the order of Melchizedek', who is able to 'save completely those who come to God through him, because he always lives to intercede for them' (7:25). The author is keen to explore the implications of Psalm 110:4, because it describes

---

54. O'Brien (*God Has Spoken*, pp. 210–228) rightly opposes the view that Jesus' resurrection and ascension were part of the process of atonement, although they were necessary for his perfecting as high priest. The shedding of his blood enabled him to enter the heavenly sanctuary and continually apply the benefits of his once-for-all sacrifice to us (9:11–14; 10:19–22).

55. Cf. Gaffin, 'Priesthood of Christ', pp. 49–68; Gooding, 'Tabernacle', pp. 69–88.

the enthroned Messiah as having a continuing priestly role (5:6, 10; 6:20; 7:1–28). This has profound implications for the continuing struggle of believers against temptation, sin and persecution, as outlined below.

ii. Experiencing salvation as a present reality

The terminology of salvation in Hebrews has an explicitly future reference in 1:14 ('inherit salvation'), 7:25 ('to save completely') and 9:28 ('to bring salvation to those who are waiting for him').[56] It clearly relates to the salvation from God's final judgment proclaimed by Jesus (2:2–3), which is a promise to be grasped in the present and not ignored. Jesus is the 'source of eternal salvation' (5:9) and the 'pioneer of their salvation' (2:10), who opens the way for others to follow him into the eternal presence of God (compare 6:19–20; 12:1–3). This salvation, though past with respect to its accomplishment and future with respect to its ultimate outcome, has spiritual and moral implications for the present. The author considers 'better things . . . that have to do with salvation' (6:9), meaning signs of God's enabling grace in the lives of those who believe the gospel, especially faith, hope and love (6:10–12). Assured that those he addresses have understood and experienced the implications of that gospel, he urges them to go on responding to God in ways that please him (10:19–25, 32–39; 12:4–17, 28–29; 13:1–25).

The present implications of Christ's saving work are particularly related to the prophecy of the New Covenant (Jer. 31:31–34), which is foundational to the argument in the central section of Hebrews.[57] It is quoted in full in 8:7–13 and repeated in an abbreviated form in 10:15–18, suggesting that we should look for specific indications in the intervening context of the way this prophecy has been fulfilled. It was originally directed to 'the people of Israel' and 'the people of Judah' (8:8) at the time of the Babylonian exile, but its inauguration by Jesus as mediator (8:6; 9:15; 12:24; cf. Luke 22:20; 1 Cor. 11:25)

---

56. It is also used with reference to the prayers of Jesus (5:7, 'to the one who could save him from death') and Noah (11:7, 'to save his family').

57. Cf. O'Brien, 'New Covenant', pp. 13–33.

means that its benefits are available for all who turn to him in faith. As the Messiah enthroned at God's right hand, he will save and bless people from every nation (Pss 2:8; 22:27–28; Isa. 11:10–11). The covenant that Jesus mediates and guarantees by his eternal priesthood (7:22) is eternal (13:20) and provides access to 'the promised eternal inheritance' (9:15).

Hebrews 8:7–9 observes that God finds fault with his people in Jeremiah 31:31–32 for being unfaithful to him and the covenant he made with them through Moses. But the point is also made that this prophecy exposes the weakness of the previous covenant to deal with the problem of continuing sin and enable God's people to be holy and devoted to his service (8:7). The provisions of the Old Covenant were only a shadowy outline and limited anticipation of the salvation that Christ would accomplish (8:5; 10:1). Hebrews explains the superior achievement of the Messiah in his death and heavenly exaltation as the fulfilment of the cultic rituals prescribed for Israel (9:8–14, 23–24; 10:1–10). The predictions of the New Covenant explain the blessings that Jesus has secured for us by that means.

The unbreakable character of the New Covenant rests on several interconnected promises (8:10–12; cf. Jer. 31:33–34). Foundationally, God promised to provide a definitive forgiveness of sins, requiring no further judgment and bringing a new knowledge of God as gracious and faithful. This knowledge would effect a profound change of heart in his people, leading to covenant faithfulness and obedience. Radical forgiveness is the basis for the promised spiritual and moral transformation of God's people. Definitive forgiveness or cleansing from sin flows from the eternal redemption Christ has obtained 'once for all by his own blood' (9:12; cf. 10:17–18; 12:24). This amazing revelation of God's graciousness and faithfulness is the basis for continually approaching him with confidence through Jesus, 'so that we may receive mercy and find grace to help us in our time of need' (4:16; cf. 10:19–22). Spiritual and moral renewal is made possible by the cleansing of consciences from the burden of guilt, 'so that we may serve the living God' (9:14; cf. 12:28).

iii. The sanctification of believers

Jesus is 'the sanctifier' of those whom God is bringing to glory with him, establishing them as 'the sanctified' people of the New

Covenant by his saving work (2:11; 10:5–10).[58] God consecrated Israel to himself as a holy people under the Old Covenant by rescuing them from captivity in Egypt, dwelling among them and giving them his laws (Exod. 19:4–6; 29:42–46; 31:13; Lev. 20:7–8). But the rituals God provided to keep them in that dedicated relationship could only sanctify them outwardly and not cleanse their consciences from guilt (9:9–10, 13; 10:1–4). A new and definitive way of sanctification has been provided 'through the sacrifice of the body of Jesus Christ' (10:10). His perfectly obedient sacrifice enabled him 'to make the people holy through his own blood' (13:12). This is 'the blood of the covenant that sanctified them' (10:29; cf. 9:19–20).

Sanctification is experienced when the benefits of Christ's atoning sacrifice are applied to the consciences and hearts of those who believe the gospel by the grace of the Holy Spirit (10:19–22, 29; cf. Acts 26:18; 1 Cor. 1:2, 30; 6:11; Eph. 5:26; 2 Thess. 2:13–14).[59] Believers have the status of 'holy brothers and sisters, who share in the heavenly calling' (3:1). This status has profound moral and spiritual implications that need to be worked out in everyday life and relationships (12:7–17; cf. 1 Thess. 4:3–8). Certainty about cleansing from sin induces heart-obedience to God (10:16–18, citing Jer. 31:33–34), which may also be described as a life of grateful service or worship (9:14; 12:28; cf. Rom. 12:1). The exhortations to live holy, loving and obedient lives in 13:1–16 show how the worship of the New Covenant is to be expressed in every sphere of life.

God continues to produce the fruit of sanctification in his children by disciplining us 'for our good, in order that we may share in his holiness' (12:10). To share God's holiness in this context means enjoying life in his presence and reflecting his character, now and in the life to come. God's fatherly discipline is particularly experienced by those who endure suffering without losing heart

---

58. Hebrews is not talking about moral transformation or progressive sanctification when the Greek verb is used in the present tense (2:11; 10:14). It simply describes God's way of bringing people to himself and consecrating them to his service (10:10–18, 29).

59. Cf. Peterson, *Possessed*, pp. 33–40, 71–77.

(12:5–10). This 'produces a harvest of righteousness and peace for those who have been trained by it' (12:11). But peace and holiness must be actively pursued by believers as part of the process of transformation, even as they endure suffering (12:12–17; cf. 10:32–35). Those who have no concern for practical holiness will not 'see the Lord', that is, live in his presence and share in his eternal kingdom.

iv. The perfecting of believers

The perfection that Christ has achieved is first considered in relation to the levitical priesthood (7:11) and the whole means of approaching God under the Old Covenant (7:19, 'for the law made nothing perfect'). This prepares for the positive assertion that in the high-priestly ministry of Jesus a better hope is introduced, 'by which we draw near to God' (7:19). All the institutions of the law – the priesthood, the sacrifices and the tabernacle – failed to bring about the open access to God and security of fellowship with him that Jesus makes possible under the New Covenant (4:16; 7:25; 10:1, 22; 12:22–24).

A link between drawing near to God and perfection is made again in 10:1, where it is argued that the law, having only 'a shadow of the good things that are coming – not the realities themselves', can never, by the same sacrifices that are continually offered every year, 'make perfect those who draw near to worship'. Those who would draw near to God can only be perfected in that desire through Christ and his saving work (10:1, 14). Thus, the verb 'perfect' (*teleioun*) is used consistently throughout Hebrews in a vocational way to mean 'qualify' or 'complete'. Jesus is perfected as the Saviour and messianic high priest (2:10; 5:9; 7:28) and his people are perfected as those who would draw near to God through him. His perfecting makes their perfecting possible.[60]

Christians have already 'drawn near' to the heavenly Jerusalem and are members of the heavenly church, because they have come to God through Jesus, 'the mediator of a new covenant' (12:22–24). At the same time, because of the continuing struggle

---

60. Cf. Peterson, 'Perfection', pp. 125–145.

with temptation and the need to persevere in faith, hope and love, they are urged, literally, to 'keep on drawing near to God' (4:16; 10:22), relying on the continuing high-priestly intercession of Jesus (7:25; 8:1–2). The 'better hope' by which Christians draw near to God is not simply the hope of future resurrection: it is the *present* hope that Jesus gives of approaching God 'with confidence' (4:16; 10:19), to be sustained in that relationship until final glorification.

The perfecting of 'the worshipper' begins with respect to 'conscience' (9:9, 14; 10:1–2, 22). When hearts are cleansed from a guilty conscience, direct access to God through the 'new and living way' provided by Jesus is experienced (10:19–20). When Christ appeared as 'a high priest of the good things that are now already here', what was foreshadowed in the Old Testament became a reality. Jesus definitively fulfilled the role of the high priest on the annual Day of Atonement (9:7, 11–12; cf. Lev. 16:1–19). When he ascended 'through the heavens' (4:14 NIV mg.), he passed through 'the greater and more perfect tabernacle that is not made with human hands, that is to say, is not a part of this creation', opening the way into the sanctuary of 'heaven itself' (9:11, 24; cf. 8:1–2).

Jesus did not enter the heavenly presence of God by means of 'the blood of goats and calves', but by means of 'his own blood' (9:12). Since his sacrifice was perfect, he entered the Most Holy Place 'once for all' and secured 'an eternal redemption'. This is another way of speaking about the complete and lasting forgiveness promised in Jeremiah 31:34 (Heb. 8:12; 10:17–18). Jesus died as a ransom to liberate believers past and present from the consequences of their sin and enable them to receive 'the promised eternal inheritance' (9:15). Hebrews combines eschatological and cultic terms to explain the perfecting work of Jesus.

In contrast with the priests of the Old Covenant, who stand daily at the altar to offer repeatedly the same sacrifices which can never take away sins, Jesus sits at God's right hand, his sacrificial work completed (10:11–14). The result is that by a single offering 'he has made perfect for ever those who are being made holy'. The Greek grammar here stresses that perfection is accomplished by Christ's sacrifice in the past, and that the benefits are permanently enjoyed by those whom he has sanctified. Definitive cleansing from sin makes definitive sanctification possible, which means that we can draw near to God 'with a sincere heart and with the full assurance that faith brings' (10:22). Expressed in terms of access to the heavenly sanctuary, our present experience of drawing near with confidence is the assurance of ultimate transfer to the presence of God in the heavenly city (6:19–20; 9:15; 12:22–24).

The death of Jesus has a retrospective effect for believers 'under the first covenant' (9:15), but the author indicates that they did not experience the benefits of Christ's saving work in their lifetimes. They looked forward to life in the heavenly city (11:10, 13–16), but 'none of them received what had been promised' (11:39). This is explained in terms of God's gracious provision to bring us to glory *together*: 'since God had planned something better for us, so that only together with us would they be made perfect' (11:40). Put another way, this stresses the enormous privilege of living in the era when the messianic perfection was achieved and its benefits were made available through the preaching of the gospel. 'The church of the firstborn who are enrolled in heaven' (12:23, my translation) must include believers before Christ, whose membership of the heavenly assembly was made possible by his death (12:24). In their journey of faith, however, they could not approach God with the confidence that Christians have been given, nor persevere with the certainty that Christ had gone ahead of them as 'the pioneer and perfecter of faith' (12:1–3; cf. 6:19–20). 'The spirits of the righteous made perfect' (12:23) will similarly refer to all the faithful who have now reached the goal of their earthly pilgrimage because of the perfecting work of Jesus.

d. Apostasy and perseverance

Narrowly defined, there are five warnings about apostasy in Hebrews (2:1–4; 3:7 – 4:13; 6:4–8; 10:26–31; 12:25–29). However, scholars differ about the extent of these passages, since some are intimately connected with exhortations to persevere in faith, hope and love (e.g. 5:11 – 6:3; 6:9–20; 10:32–39; 12:22–24).[61] Each of these

---

61. Warnings about missing out on the promised inheritance also occur in 12:14–17. This passage could be read together with 12:18–29 as a mix of warning and encouragement, as in 3:7 – 4:13.

larger units is linked to expositions of the work of Christ designed to give believers assurance about their relationship with God and their eternal destiny. The author demonstrates pastoral insight and wisdom in the way he combines these apparently contradictory aspects of his 'word of exhortation' (13:22). If the warning passages are considered as part of the broader argument of Hebrews, believers should not experience anxiety about the security of their standing with God and ability to persevere in the way he desires.

i. Understanding the warning passages
The dimensions of apostasy and its consequences are progressively revealed throughout Hebrews. Apostasy begins by drifting away from the Lord Jesus and the message he proclaimed (2:1–3). It involves hardening your heart when God's voice is heard and turning away from him in unbelief and disobedience (3:7 – 4:13). Progressive hardening of the heart leads to permanent hardening, because of sin's deceitfulness. Put differently, an unwillingness to be taken forward to maturity and produce the kind of behaviour pleasing to God may lead to a public repudiation of his Son (5:11 – 6:8). Deliberately persisting in sin after receiving 'the knowledge of the truth' expresses open contempt for the Son of God, treating his death as no different from any other, and acting insolently towards God's Spirit by resisting his promptings to turn away from sin and persevere in faithful obedience (10:26–29). Those who have heard the call to come to 'the city of the living God, the heavenly Jerusalem' through Jesus 'the mediator of a new covenant' (12:22–24) should be careful not to turn away from 'him who warns us from heaven', because of the eternal consequences (12:25–27).[62]

These warnings are addressed to the whole church and the pastor includes himself in their scope (2:1–3; 3:14; 4:1–3, 11; 10:26; 12:25, 28; cf. 3:6; 6:1). Like most Christian groups, this congregation probably consisted of people at various stages in their spiritual journey and he does not want any of them to have 'a sinful,

---

62. The Greek verb *apostēnai* (3:12) echoes the description of the Israelites as 'rebels' in Num. 14:9 and highlights the fact that a deliberate turning away from God is meant.

unbelieving heart that turns away from the living God' (3:12). The same concern for each member of their fellowship is reflected again in 3:13; 4:1, 11; 6:11; 12:15–16. When the pastor considers the biblical example of the Israelites in the wilderness, he simply contrasts belief expressed in obedience with unbelief demonstrated in disobedience (3:15 – 4:2). The image of fruitfulness is added to the picture in his parable of two different soils:

> Land that drinks in the rain often falling on it and that produces a crop useful to those for whom it is farmed receives the blessing of God. But land that produces thorns and thistles is worthless and is in danger of being cursed. In the end it will be burned.
> (6:7–8; cf. 10:36–39)

Both lands receive the same rain, but only one produces the crop that pleases God.

The judgment awaiting apostates is portrayed as worse than any punishment prescribed under the law (2:2–3; 10:28–31) or experienced in the history of Israel (3:16–19), because it involves a 'raging fire that will consume the enemies of God' (10:27; cf. 6:8), elsewhere described as 'eternal judgment' (6:2). Those who resist the call of God to persist in faith and grateful service will miss out on the coming kingdom of God (12:26–29) and will not enter his 'rest' (4:1–11). Since apostasy is a deliberate and final rejection of Jesus and the gospel, there can be no forgiveness, because 'no sacrifice for sins is left' (10:26).[63]

Two passages in particular make it clear that the warnings are directed to Christians. The first speaks categorically of the impossibility of restoring to repentance 'those who have once been enlightened, who have tasted the heavenly gift, who have shared in the Holy Spirit, who have tasted the goodness of the word of God

---

63. Given the special nature of apostasy, it should not be confused with other sins, which can be forgiven because of the sufficiency of Christ's atoning sacrifice (2:17; 5:9; 9:12, 28). The present-tense verb 'sinning' (10:26) indicates a pattern of life, rather than one damning transgression.

and the powers of the coming age' (6:4–6). These terms are deliberately chosen to describe people who have had a genuine encounter with Christ and the gospel, though the indirect manner of speech means that the author is not specifically identifying any of his hearers with those who have fallen away. The second passage speaks more personally: 'If we deliberately keep on sinning after we have received the knowledge of the truth, no sacrifice for sins is left, but only a fearful expectation of judgment and of raging fire that will consume the enemies of God' (10:26–27). The author goes on to describe this betrayal as trampling underfoot the Son of God, treating 'as an unholy thing the blood of the covenant that sanctified them' and 'insult[ing] the Spirit of grace' (10:29).[64]

These passages have caused many to question whether genuine Christians can 'lose their salvation', even though this issue is addressed only by implication. This pastor's positive aim is to encourage faithfulness and fruitfulness in the lives of those he addresses. In fact, he speaks confidently about them as a group and encourages them to press on with trust in God and his promises (6:9–20; 10:32–39). His warnings are not hypothetical, however, because he is concerned about signs of spiritual sluggishness in this church (5:11 – 6:3) and notes that some have already abandoned their fellowship (10:25). His warnings are intended to be a means of preserving from apostasy those who may be struggling. The broader evidence of the New Testament is that those whom God has elected will be saved for all eternity (e.g. John 6:37–44; 10:28–29; Rom. 8:28–39; 1 Cor. 1:8–9; Eph. 1:13–14; Phil. 1:6; 1 Thess. 5:23–24; 1 Pet. 1:5; Jude 24–25), but those who are elected will continue to express repentance and faith.[65] Faith is generated and sustained by the message of salvation through Christ and the encouragements and warnings that accompany it.

Within this theological framework, 'Hebrews recognizes a kind of transitory faith or form of conversion which has early signs of

---

64. This warning particularly reflects 'the author's explanation of the new covenant offering of God's appointed high priest (7:1 – 10:18)' (O'Brien, *God Has Spoken*, p. 182).

65. Following Schreiner, pp. 489–490.

life but does not persevere.'[66] Jesus identified this problem with reference to the second and third soils in his parable about the sowing of God's word (Mark 4:1–9, 13–20 par.). The author of Hebrews addresses his 'holy brothers and sisters' as those who 'share in the heavenly calling' (3:1), but he insists that we are God's 'house' or family 'if indeed we hold firmly to our confidence and the hope in which we glory' (3:6). Then he warns that 'We have come to share in Christ, if indeed we hold our original conviction firmly to the very end' (3:14). This is not cause-and-effect language, but an evidence–inference argument, in which 'the observation of a piece of evidence leads the observer to infer a certain logical conclusion'.[67] If they hold firmly to the confidence and hope God has given them in the gospel they will show themselves to be truly members of his family and partakers of Christ. Perseverance is a mark of the genuine believer and warnings are an aid to perseverance.

ii. Encouragements to persevere

Each warning passage is followed either by a significant exposition of the work of Christ (as in 2:5–18) or an encouragement to appropriate the benefits of that work and persevere in the life of faith (as in 4:14–16; 6:9–20; 10:32–39). Jesus himself is the greatest encouragement to persevere because of what he suffered and achieved (2:9, 10, 17–18). Therefore, believers must fix their thoughts on him (3:1; 12:2), approach God confidently through him (4:14–16; 7:25; 10:19–22), consider him (12:3), and 'go to him outside the camp, bearing the disgrace he bore' (13:13).

The exhortation in 4:14–16 focuses first on the need to 'hold firmly to the faith we profess', because we have a high priest who has ascended into heaven. Second, since Jesus can empathize with our weaknesses, having been tempted in every way as we are, yet without sin, we may keep drawing near to God's throne of grace through him, to 'receive mercy and find grace to help us in our

---

66. O'Brien, *God Has Spoken*, p. 165, following Carson, 'Assurance', p. 267.
67. Thomas, *Mixed-Audience*, pp. 184–185, endorsed by O'Brien, ibid., p. 166.

time of need'. The exposition of Christ's high-priestly work in 2:17–18; 5:7–10; 6:19 – 10:18 is the inspiration and motivation for these two vital pursuits. The challenge is to hold on to the 'confession' (ESV), which may refer to a formal confession of faith that the pastor shared with his congregation and that formed the basis of their commitment to Jesus (3:1; 4:14; 10:23). His atoning death and heavenly ascension give believers confidence to approach God in the present (3:6; 4:16; 10:19) and the hope of everlasting life in God's presence (12:22–24).

Faith and hope come into focus again in 6:9–20, where the pastor also urges his community to continue loving one another in practical ways. Hope is realized by imitating those 'who through faith and patience inherit what has been promised'.[68] The three imperatives come together a second time in the pivotal exhortation in 10:19–25. Faith and hope are further encouraged on the basis of the past experience of the recipients and God's trustworthy promises (10:32–39), and by recalling many witnesses to persevering faith in the long history of God's people (11:1–38). Climactically, they are urged to 'throw off everything that hinders and the sin that so easily entangles' and 'run with perseverance the race marked out for us, fixing our eyes on Jesus, the pioneer and perfecter of faith' (12:1–2). Jesus has blazed the trail for us to follow on our journey to the heavenly city and has given faith a perfect basis and certain outcome in his high-priestly work, achieving our salvation by his obedient faith. The challenge to show love to fellow believers in various ways emerges again in 13:1–8, 16, 17–19.

Faith, hope and love are signs of God's enabling grace. When they are exercised, they bring the assurance of a genuine relationship with God and of truly belonging to his family. Guided and empowered by the promises and warnings of Scripture, believers may avoid apostasy and persevere in the way of Christ. Put differently, God equips those who seek his Spirit's help 'with everything good for doing his will', working 'in us what is pleasing to him, through Jesus Christ' (13:21). The relationship between Christ and

---

68. 'Significantly, however, the focus of the paragraph is God's absolute fidelity rather than Abraham's persevering faith' (O'Brien, ibid., p. 197).

his people is living and dynamic, so that assurance of ultimate salvation is linked to the heeding of his voice: 'My sheep listen to my voice; I know them, and they follow me. I give them eternal life, and they shall never perish; no one will snatch them out of my hand' (John 10:27–28). Hebrews portrays this response as grateful service with reverence and awe, and then provides detailed examples of what that might mean in practice (12:28 – 13:16).

e. Maturity and ministry

The pastor's aim is not merely to encourage perseverance or endurance, but also to enable his fellow believers to be 'taken forward to maturity' (6:1). In an exhortation preceding the central doctrinal section, he expresses his concern that they have become (lit.) 'sluggish in hearing' (5:11; NIV, 'you no longer try to understand') and are unprepared to receive the teaching he is about to impart. They are immature, desiring only 'milk', whereas 'the mature' thrive on 'solid food', having their powers of discernment (lit.) 'trained to distinguish good from evil' (5:13–14). His understanding of the nature of Christian maturity and how it is obtained is more fully articulated in later passages such as 6:9–20; 10:32–39; 12:1–15. The style and content of his word of exhortation serves as a model for the mutual ministry he seeks to encourage in the congregation he addresses (3:12–13; 5:12; 10:24–25; 12:15).

i. The path to maturity

The charge that the recipients have become 'sluggish in hearing' (5:11) recalls previous warnings about paying the most careful attention to what has been heard in the gospel (2:1) and heeding God's voice in Scripture (3:7–19; 4:12–13). The issue is not simply an unwillingness to progress to a higher stage of understanding the Christian message, but an unwillingness to work out its deeper implications and respond appropriately. Proof of this is first given in the claim that 'though by this time you ought to be teachers, you need someone to teach you the elementary truths of God's word all over again' (5:12). Being willing to teach others is a mark of maturity, either in the form of mutual exhortation in the church or confessing Christ openly before unbelievers. Needing to be taught 'the elementary truths of God's word all over again' is likened to wanting 'milk' rather than 'solid food', which is a sign of immaturity.

The intellectual, moral and spiritual dimensions of maturity are linked when the pastor says 'everyone who lives on milk is unskilled in the word of righteousness' (5:13 ESV) and identifies the mature as (lit.) 'those who have their powers of discernment trained to distinguish good from evil' (5:14). The challenge is to understand and apply Scripture in the light of its fulfilment by Christ, as illustrated in the argument of Hebrews itself. Although the adjective *teleios* (5:14, 'mature') is clearly a cognate of the verb *teleioun* ('perfect'), it is not used here with reference to the perfecting of believers. Maturity and perfection are two different, but related, strands of thought. Perfection is the gift of God to those who draw near to him through Jesus, on the basis of his once-for-all sacrifice and heavenly exaltation. Maturity results from paying careful attention to the sort of profound teaching the author wishes to give and applying it to everyday life and relationships. This is the intention of his encouragement to 'move beyond the elementary teachings about Christ and be taken forward to maturity' (6:1).

However, teaching about perfection through Christ is central to the solid food that the author seeks to impart. Such teaching is appropriate not only for the mature, but also to draw the immature along the path to maturity. Just as children are encouraged to grow physically by being fed more and more solid food, so the pastor intends to mature his hearers spiritually by teaching them about the high-priestly ministry of Jesus and how it fulfils God's plan of salvation. What he says about the perfecting of Jesus and his perfecting of believers should encourage them to be confident about their relationship with God and to persevere in that confidence, even in the face of hostility and suffering.

In the flow of the argument, the warning passage in 6:4–8 implies that resistance to spiritual growth may lead people to fall away or completely rebel against God, because they are hardening their hearts against him. However, the commendation and exhortation in 6:9–12 shows that the pastor has confidence in his 'dear friends' collectively and does not believe they are sliding into apostasy. Rather, he urges them to continue showing love to each other and to realize their God-given hope through trust in God's character, and to imitate 'those who through faith and patience inherit what has been promised'. Theologically and pastorally, the author prepares the recipients here and in 6:13–20 to respond appropriately to the exposition of Christ's high-priestly work in 7:1 – 10:18 and the extensive section of application in 10:19 – 13:22.

ii. Learning through suffering

Suffering is a prominent theme in Hebrews. The suffering of Jesus is both the means of our salvation (2:9, 10, 18; 5:8; 9:26; 13:12) and in certain respects a pattern for Christians to follow (12:2–3; 13:13; cf. 1 Pet. 2:20–25). The author particularly recalls that, when his hearers came to faith in Christ, they endured 'in a great conflict full of suffering' (10:32). The public nature of this suffering involved insults and persecution, some being imprisoned and others having their property confiscated (10:33–34). These punishments were consistent with Roman law and were designed to make them conform to the religious and social demands of the culture.[69] Paradoxically, it had been a time of spiritual maturation, as they 'stood side by side' with those who were mistreated, 'suffered along with those in prison' and 'joyfully accepted the confiscation of [their] property', knowing that they had 'better and lasting possessions'. In other words, they expressed genuine love for one another (6:10) and gave practical expression to their hope of living for ever in God's eternal city (13:13–14).

The pastor is concerned that they should not throw away their 'confidence', which will be 'richly rewarded' (10:35). This God-given confidence was mentioned previously in 3:6; 4:16; 10:19, the last verse clarifying that it refers to the right of access to God's presence achieved by Jesus' sacrificial death and entrance into heaven. Christians should hold firmly to this confidence, which is another way of speaking about faith and hope (4:14; 10:23), express it in prayer to God (4:16) and confess it openly, even in the face of opposition and insult (10:35; cf. 13:15, 'openly profess his name'). The pastor's concern may be related to the sluggishness he identifies in this congregation (5:11–14) and the possibility that some might

---

69. Cf. Winter, 'Suffering with the Saviour', pp. 147–162.

'shrink back' in the face of further persecution (10:36–39). Examples of enduring faith and hope in the history of God's people are given (11:7–38), climaxing in the challenge to look to these 'witnesses' for encouragement and pre-eminently to Jesus as 'the pioneer and perfecter of faith' (12:1–3).

A further call to endure suffering emerges in 12:4–13, based on Proverbs 3:11–12, where God speaks to Christians 'as a father addresses his son'. Although the author highlighted the need to put away personal sin in 12:1, the struggle in 12:4 is more likely to be against the sin of unbelief expressed in the behaviour of persecutors. The citation from Proverbs is a reminder that God's fatherly love can be experienced in such situations. The application of this text focuses on the educative and training aspect of God's discipline, which all genuine believers experience in some form or another (12:7–8). Experiencing God's discipline through suffering can actually confirm the 'sonship' of God's children (cf. Rom. 8:17–27). Submitting to God's will in times of trial is necessary for the enjoyment of life in its fullest sense: 'God disciplines us for our good, in order that we may share in his holiness' (v. 10). Using terms that particularly refer to the outcome of God's fatherly discipline, the point is made that God 'exercises' or 'trains' those he loves, to produce in them 'the peaceful fruit of righteousness' (ESV). A challenge to pursue practical expressions of peace and holiness in 12:14 arises from this reflection on the purpose of divine discipline. This is a call to understand and co-operate with God's plan to mature and strengthen his people.

iii. Ministering to one another

'Sharing' is an important theme in Hebrews. Christ shares the experience of humanity; the saints have a share in a heavenly calling, in Christ, and in the Spirit; they are partners in the suffering of others; they receive a share in God's holiness; they are reminded to practise sharing in their community.[70]

Challenges to minister to one another as fellow Christians arise from this theological context.

---

70. Croy, *Endurance*, pp. 200–201. Cf. 2:14; 3:1, 14; 6:4; 10:33; 12:10; 13:16.

The pastor calls for members of this church to 'Remember your leaders, who spoke the word of God to you. Consider the outcome of their way of life and imitate their faith' (13:7). They are also to have confidence in their current leaders and submit to their authority, 'because they keep watch over you as those who must give an account' (13:17). Believers in general should care for one another (3:12–14; 12:15–16), but leaders have a special responsibility to watch over the 'souls' in their flock (cf. Acts 20:28–31). They do this knowing that they are accountable to God for their own lives (Heb. 4:12–13) and for the way they conduct their ministry (1 Pet. 5:1–4). Church members care for leaders as they submit to their authority and enable them to do their work with joy.

We cannot be certain of the particular status of the author or the history of his relationship with this congregation. However, when he seeks their prayers, he claims to have a clear conscience and a desire 'to live honourably in every way', desiring to be restored to them soon (13:18–19). He links himself with leaders past and present with respect to his manner of life and his pastoral concern for them. In this context, he urges them to bear with his word of exhortation (13:22), perhaps anticipating that they may have been tempted to resist its complexity and challenges. Although he addresses them in an authoritative way, he does so with spiritual insight, understanding of their situation and compassion, proving a model for the ministry of exhortation he commends to them all.

Exhortation is necessary to prevent sinful, unbelieving hearts from being 'hardened by sin's deceitfulness' and turning away from the living God (3:13–14). What has been learned by believers from Scripture and the author's own work may be shared in individual or group encounters, as long as the promise of entering God's rest remains (4:1). A similar concern for the spiritual welfare of others is encouraged in 12:15–16. They are all to accept responsibility for the care of one another, in case someone forfeits the grace of God and misses out on the eternal inheritance God has secured for those who trust him. A concern for the health and welfare of the church is also mentioned here, using the imagery of Deuteronomy 29:18, 'that no bitter root grows up to cause trouble and defile many'.

Positively speaking, meeting together for mutual exhortation, whether formal or informal, is the way for believers to stir one another towards 'love and good deeds' in everyday life (10:24–25; cf. 13:1–6, 15–16). Such a ministry becomes all the more significant as 'the Day' of Christ's return approaches, when believers will experience the fullness of salvation that he has achieved for them (9:28) and be gathered together in the eternal celebration of the heavenly assembly (12:22–24).

ANALYSIS

1. GOD'S FINAL WORD IN HIS SON (1:1–4)

A. The new revelation compared with the old (1:1–2a)
B. The nature and work of the Son (1:2b–3)
C. The Son and the angels (1:4)

2. THE GREATNESS OF THE SON AND THE NEED TO PAY CAREFUL ATTENTION TO HIS MESSAGE (1:5 – 2:4)

A. The Son's superiority to the angels (1:5–14)
B. A warning about holding fast to the Son and his message (2:1–4)

3. THE SON'S INCARNATION, DEATH AND HEAVENLY EXALTATION IS THE MEANS OF OUR SALVATION AND THE BASIS OF HOPEFUL CONFIDENCE (2:5 – 3:6)

A. The world to come subjected to the glorified Son (2:5–9)
B. Many sons brought to glory by the pioneer of their salvation (2:10–16)
C. The Son as a merciful and faithful high priest (2:17–18)

D. A challenge to be faithful and hold firmly to the confidence and hope the Son has given us (3:1–6)

4. A WARNING NOT TO HARDEN OUR HEARTS IN UNBELIEF, TOGETHER WITH ENCOURAGEMENTS ABOUT THE WAY TO ENTER THE REST THAT THE SON HAS MADE POSSIBLE (3:7 – 4:13)

A. The negative example of the Israelites who failed to enter the Promised Land (3:7–19)
B. A warning about falling short of God's promised rest (4:1–2)
C. Identifying the rest and those who enter it (4:3–11)
D. A warning about the power of God's word to expose and judge (4:12–13)

5. THE SON'S HIGH-PRIESTLY MINISTRY IS THE BASIS FOR PERSEVERING FAITH AND OBEDIENCE (4:14 – 5:10)

A. A challenge to hold firmly to the faith we profess and approach God with confidence for mercy and timely help (4:14–16)
B. The perfecting of the Son as 'the source of eternal salvation for all who obey him' (5:1–10)

6. A CHALLENGE TO AVOID SLUGGISHNESS AND FULLY REALIZE THE HOPE SET BEFORE US (5:11 – 6:12)

A. The pathway to maturity in Christ (5:11 – 6:3)
B. A warning about the fate of those who profess faith and fall away (6:4–8)
C. The need to express faith, hope and love 'to the very end' (6:9–12)

7. THE HOPE CONFIRMED AND SECURED BY THE ENTRANCE OF OUR HIGH PRIEST INTO HEAVEN (6:13 – 7:28)

A. Responding to God's guaranteed promise (6:13–20)
B. The priesthood of Melchizedek (7:1–10)
C. The eternal high priesthood of the Son of God (7:11–28)

8. THE SUPERIOR MINISTRY OF OUR GREAT HIGH PRIEST (8:1 – 10:18)

- A. Enthroned in heaven and serving in the 'true tabernacle' (8:1–6)
- B. Mediator of a new covenant (8:7–13)
- C. Opening the way to the Most Holy Place and cleansing consciences (9:1–14)
- D. Providing the sacrifice that makes eternal salvation possible (9:15–28)
- E. Sanctifying believers once for all and perfecting them for ever (10:1–18)

9. REFLECTING ON THE PRIVILEGES WE HAVE AS CHRISTIANS AND RESPONDING APPROPRIATELY (10:19–39)

- A. Realize the benefits of Jesus' high-priestly ministry (10:19–25)
- B. Don't turn away from the Son of God and his achievements for us (10:26–31)
- C. Persevere and obtain what God has promised (10:32–39)

10. EXAMPLES OF PERSEVERING FAITH, CLIMAXING WITH A CHALLENGE TO REJECT SIN AND FOCUS ON JESUS 'THE PIONEER AND PERFECTER OF FAITH' (11:1 – 12:3)

- A. Faith in the unseen (11:1–7)
- B. The faith of Abraham and his descendants (11:8–22)
- C. The faith of Moses and those associated with him (11:23–31)
- D. Further examples of enduring faith (11:32–40)
- E. Looking to Jesus (12:1–3)

11. CHALLENGES TO ENDURE SUFFERING AND PURSUE PEACE, HOLINESS AND GRATEFUL SERVICE TO GOD (12:4–29)

- A. Submitting to God's discipline (12:4–13)
- B. Pursuing peace and holiness (12:14–17)
- C. Living as citizens of the heavenly Jerusalem (12:18–24)

D. Being attentive to the voice of God (12:25–27)
E. Serving God with reverence and awe (12:28–29)

12. FINAL ENCOURAGEMENTS, BLESSINGS AND GREETINGS (13:1–25)

A. Love that pleases God (13:1–6)
B. Faithfulness that endures (13:7–19)
C. Grace that equips and enables perseverance (13:20–25)

COMMENTARY

1. GOD'S FINAL WORD IN HIS SON (1:1–4)

The author introduces his 'word of exhortation' (13:22) with 'an elaborate display of rhetorical devices to gain his audience's attention' (Guthrie, *Structure*, p. 118), but with no personal greetings or expressions of thanksgiving and prayer for the recipients. One long sentence in Greek is broken into four by NIV. God is the subject of the first part (vv. 1–2), where the focus is on his revelation in the prophets and in his Son. The Son is the subject of the second part (v. 3), where it is claimed that the one who shares in the glory, being and creative power of God made purification for sins in his earthly ministry and then sat down at God's right hand in heaven. The concluding clause (v. 4) leads to an extended contrast between Christ and the angels (vv. 5–14), using a linked series of biblical quotations. This prepares for a warning about the danger of drifting from the message of salvation that was first announced by the Son (2:1–4). Topically, a symmetrical or chiastic pattern may be observed in 1:1–4:[1]

---

1. Cf. Ebert, 'Chiastic Structure', pp. 163–179; O'Brien, pp. 46–47.

1–2a The Son contrasted with the prophets
    2b The Son as messianic heir
        2c The Son's creative work
            3a–b The Son's threefold mediatorial relationship
                  with God
        3c The Son's redemptive work
        3d The Son as messianic king
4   The Son contrasted with the angels

A. The new revelation compared with the old (1:1–2a)

Context

Three comparisons are made with respect to the time of God's speaking, the method by which he spoke and the recipients. The fullness and finality of the revelation in the Son is highlighted, but the author does not imply that the former revelation is outmoded and irrelevant. Rather, by his own use of Scripture he shows how 'God's self-disclosure in his Son is the climax and fulfillment of all previous revelation' (Cockerill, p. 87; cf. Guthrie, 'Hebrews', pp. 919–995).

Comment

1–2a. From the author's standpoint, the former revelation was given *in the past*, when God spoke to the spiritual *ancestors* of Christians (or 'to the fathers'; cf. 6:13–15; 11:4–28; Acts 3:13, 25; Rom. 9:5; 1 Cor. 10:1). This communication came *at many times and in various ways* 'in the prophets' (*en tois prophētais*), referring to the writings of those who 'spoke from God as they were carried along by the Holy Spirit' (2 Pet. 1:19–21), that is, all the Old Testament Scriptures.[2] Hebrews identifies certain prophets by name (e.g. Moses [Heb. 3:5; 7:14; 8:5] and David [4:7]), but mostly cites biblical texts as divine speech (e.g. 1:5–13; 2:12–13; 3:7–11). Passages are cited from the

---

2. Cf. Luke 24:25–27; Justin, *Dial.* 128.4; 129.1 ('the prophetic word'). NIV assumes that the preposition *en* with the dative expresses personal agency (*through the prophets*), but there are no clear examples of this in the NT (Wallace, *Greek Grammar*, p. 373). Cf. Cockerill, p. 90.

Law (e.g. Exod. 25:40 in 8:5), the Prophets (e.g. Jer. 31:31–34 in 8:8–12) and the Writings (e.g. Ps. 40:6–8 in 10:5–7). These span the whole era of Israel's encounter with God and include different forms of communication such as promises (2 Sam. 7:14 in 1:5; Gen. 22:17 in 6:13–15), praises (Pss 45:6–7; 102:25–27 in 1:8–12), predictions (Ps. 110:1 in 1:13), warnings (Ps. 95:7–11 in 3:7–11), commands (Exod. 25:40 in 8:5) and encouragements (Prov. 3:11–12 in 12:5–6).

In these last days, however, the same God who spoke 'in the prophets' has spoken definitively and decisively 'in his Son'. 'The new revelation is a continuation of the old so far as God is the author of both. It is wholly new and separate in character so far as Christ is the Mediator of it' (Westcott, p. 7). The Greek expression without an article (*en hyiō*) highlights the special character and significance of the personal revelation the Son brings.[3] The Son's speaking about eternal salvation is the focus in 2:3, but the Son also reveals the glory and being of God in his character and actions (1:3; 2:5–10; cf. John 1:14, 18). The meaning of the title 'Son' continues to be exposed in the rest of the chapter.

In these last days (lit. 'at the end of these days') reflects the biblical concept of two ages. The present evil age is coming to an end because the predicted era of judgment and salvation has been inaugurated by the coming of God's Son (2:1–4; 5:9–10; 9:15, 26; cf. Mark 1:15).[4] Nevertheless, full enjoyment of the benefits of that new era will come only with the return of Christ and the end of this created order (1:14; 4:9–11; 9:28; 10:36–37; 12:25–29; cf. Mark 8:38; 10:29–30). Those who trust in the Son and continue in his word belong to the coming world (2:5), but they must live in the overlap of the ages, enduring the challenges and testing that brings

---

3. Wallace (ibid., p. 245) observes that this expression should probably be translated 'in a Son'. The force is clearly qualitative: God has spoken to us 'in one who has the characteristics of a son'.

4. The shorter expression 'at the end of the days' can be found in Num. 24:14; Jer. 23:20, where it is rendered by NIV 'in days to come', and in Dan. 10:14, where it is translated 'in the future'. Parallel expressions occur in texts such as Jer. 30:24; 31:31; Hos. 3:5; Mic. 4:1.

(3:1 – 4:16; 10:32–39; 12:1–17; 13:13–16). See Introduction 6c, 'Eschatology and salvation'.

Theology

Fundamental to the argument of Hebrews is the conviction that God has revealed himself over the course of history in word and deed. Foundationally, God revealed his character and will to the prophets of Israel, who wrote over an extensive period the many forms of literature in the Old Testament (narratives, songs of praise, laments, prayers, genealogies, laws, oracles of judgment, predictions). Some of these prophetic writings are applied directly to Christians in Hebrews (3:7 – 4:11; 12:5–8), while others are used to describe the pattern of relating to God that was given to Israel and has now been fulfilled by Jesus (8:1–6; 10:1–18). Supremely, however, God has spoken at the climax of this period of revelation to the inheritors of these Scriptures through his Son. By implication, the Son is God's final word to us, revealing all we need to know to experience the blessings of the promised era of salvation.

B. The nature and work of the Son (1:2b–3)

Context

The fullness and finality of the revelation given in the Son is affirmed in seven statements about his person and work. These reveal the pre-existence of the Son and prepare for the argument that he became fully human to provide eternal salvation for his people (2:10–18).[5] The incarnation and atoning death of the Son is implied when it is said that he 'provided purification for sins'. His heavenly ascension to be enthroned as messianic king is implied by the assertion that he 'sat down at the right hand of the Majesty in heaven'.

---

5. Some have argued that the three clauses in vv. 2b–3a describing the greatness of the Son derive from an early Christian hymn or confession of faith. But the author himself more likely composed these lines, which are integral to his presentation of Christ and the symmetrical structure of vv. 1–4 (see note 1 above).

Comment

2b–c. It might have been expected that the Son's role in creation would be mentioned first, but the author begins by claiming that the Son is the one whom God *appointed heir of all things*. This prepares for the climactic statement about his heavenly enthronement (v. 3), which is supported and explained by Psalm 2:7 in verse 5 and Psalm 110:1 in verse 13. These are messianic texts, promising a universal dominion to God's Son. As the incarnate Son, Jesus entered this dominion when he suffered and was exalted to reign at God's right hand in heaven (cf. 12:2).[6]

The Son destined for universal dominion was the one *through whom also [God] made the universe*. Here and in 11:3 the Greek phrase *tous aiōnas* is translated *the universe*, but in 9:26 it is rendered 'the ages' (6:5, 'the coming age'). Since it can have both temporal and physical applications, it serves to express the totality of God's creation through the Son (John 1:3; 1 Cor. 8:6; Col. 1:16) and explains what is meant by his inheritance of *all things*. The Son who suffers and is raised up for us inherits what he was instrumental in making: the 'whole created universe of time and space' (Bruce, p. 47).

3. Three claims are made about the Son's divine nature and continuing role in creation, and two are made about the achievement of his incarnate life and its consequence. First, a present-tense participle (*ōn*, 'being') points to his continuing existence as *the radiance of God's glory and the exact representation of his being*. These descriptions are complementary, the first indicating that God's glory radiates from the Son as light does from a source like the sun.[7] God's glory is equivalent to 'all his goodness' (Exod. 33:18–23) or his true character. This was revealed to Moses and his people in

---

6. The verb *appointed* (*ethēken*) also echoes LXX Ps. 88:28 (MT 89:28; ET 89:27), where God promises to appoint David 'my firstborn, the most exalted of the kings of the earth'.

7. The active meaning of *apaugasma* is 'radiance' in the sense of 'brightness from a source' and the passive meaning is 'reflection' in the sense of 'brightness shining back' (BDAG). The former seems more likely in this context, since the term *charactēr* conveys 'the truth suggested by "reflection"' (Westcott, p. 11).

varying ways (e.g. Lev. 9:23; Num. 14:21–22), but it was supremely manifested in the person and work of the Lord Jesus (John 1:14; 11:40; 2 Cor. 4:4–6). The second expression indicates that the Son is a distinct identity (*exact representation*), who bears the perfect imprint of God's *being*.[8] In ordinary Greek usage, the word *charactēr* described an impression placed on an object, especially coins, which came to signify a *representation* or mark of ownership (BDAG). Here, the meaning is that the Son is the true embodiment of God as he really is (cf. 2 Cor. 4:4, 'the image of God'; Col. 1:15, 'the image of the invisible God').

Another present-tense participle (*pherōn*, 'bearing') introduces the third claim about the Son *sustaining all things by his powerful word*.[9] The author later affirms that 'the universe was formed at God's command' (11:3). But the role of the Son in the process of creation was asserted in 1:2c, and his continuing involvement with the created order is revealed here (cf. Col. 1:17). The Son maintains and moves the universe of time and space forward to its God-appointed end (cf. John 1:1–4).

A change of tense signals a focus on the earthly ministry of the Son of God and its sequel. 'The "timeless" description of the Son in v. 3ab is brought into relationship with the once-for-all acts of atonement and exaltation in v. 3cd' (Cockerill, p. 96). *After he had provided purification for sins* alludes to his high-priestly work of making atonement for the sins of his people (2:17). The noun *katharismos* (*purification*) occurs only here in Hebrews, but the related verb *katharizein* is employed in 9:13–14, 22–23; 10:2, 22, contrasting the cleansing made possible by the sacrificial rituals of the Old Testament and the cleansing power of Jesus' atoning death.[10] Such

---

8. The noun *hypostasis*, which is translated *being* here, means 'fundamental reality' or 'essence' (Attridge, p. 44). Cf. 3:14; 11:1.

9. NIV has rightly adopted the shorter and better-attested textual variant *autou* ('his'). Cf. Metzger, *Textual Commentary*, p. 592; Ellingworth, p. 101.

10. Cf. 2 Pet. 1:9. The noun *katharismos* refers to Jewish cleansing rites in Mark 1:44; Luke 2:22; 5:14; John 2:6; 3:25. The verb *katharizein* ('make clean, purify') is used in the LXX for the cleansing of altar and people from the defilement of sin (e.g. Exod. 29:37; 30:10; Lev. 16:19).

purification removes the barrier to eternal fellowship with God (9:23–24; 12:22–24).

Although the author mentions the resurrection of Jesus in 13:20, he mostly refers to his ascension (4:14; 6:19–20; 9:11–12, 24) and enthronement at God's right hand (1:13; 2:9; 7:26; 8:1–2; 10:12–13; 12:2). These are three related aspects of his heavenly exaltation, the significance of which is progressively unfolded. The claim that the Son *sat down at the right hand of the Majesty in heaven* is based on Psalm 110:1, which is cited in 1:13 and alluded to in 8:1; 10:12; 12:2. Jesus pointed to the messianic significance of this text (Matt. 22:41–45 par.), and ultimately indicated that he would fulfil it (Matt. 26:64 par.). Hebrews uses Psalm 110:1 in conjunction with other texts to proclaim the completion of the Son's earthly work, the inauguration of his heavenly rule as Messiah and the certainty of his victory over all his enemies. In the symmetrical structure of verses 1–4, this statement matches the assertion that the Son was *appointed heir of all things* (v. 2b).[11]

Theology

The themes of revelation and redemption are linked together in this passage. Everything God revealed to his people in the past about his character and will was for their salvation and preservation in the covenant relationship he established with them (e.g. Gen. 12:1–4; 15:13–16; Exod. 3:15–17; 19:3–8). The ultimate revelation of God has taken place through the person and work of his Son. A careful balance of words, phrases and tenses in this passage shows the Son as eternally existing with the Father, being his agent in creation and 'sustaining all things by his powerful word', radiating his glory, and yet bearing God's image as a separate personality (cf. John 1:1–18). In his incarnation, suffering and heavenly exaltation, the Son continued to reveal the Father in a way that no prophet or angel ever could. At the same time, he provided the cleansing from sin that enables believers to share the glory of his

---

11. 'What the Son has been from all eternity comes to fruition and full expression in his exaltation and session' (Cockerill, p. 96). Cf. Kleinig, p. 45.

eternal kingdom (2:5–18; 9:15). Put differently, he has opened the way to God's heavenly presence for us (12:22–24). See Introduction 6a, 'God as Trinity'.

C. The Son and the angels (1:4)

Context
In the chiastic structure of verses 1–4, this statement matches the contrast between the Son and the prophets in verses 1–2a. The relationship between the Son and the angels that is announced here is an important theme in 1:5 – 2:4 and beyond (2:5–9, 16). There is no evidence that the first recipients of Hebrews were in danger of identifying Jesus as merely one of the angels (cf. Col. 2:18). Rather, the author is about to affirm a Jewish tradition about angels being involved in the giving of the law as a way of highlighting the superiority and finality of the gospel proclaimed by the Son (2:2–3a). Thus, the focus in 1:5 – 2:4 continues to be on the revelation that comes through the Son.

Comment
4. When his earthly work was completed and his heavenly rule as the crucified and glorified Messiah was inaugurated, the Son *became as much superior to the angels as the name he has inherited is superior to theirs*.[12] Jesus did not 'become' the Son of God through his resurrection and heavenly exaltation. Indeed, 1:2 identifies the Son's role in creation and 5:8 speaks about the Son's humble experience in his earthly suffering and death. The incarnation of the Son made him 'lower than the angels for a little while' and his suffering and exaltation enabled him to be 'crowned with glory and honour' in fulfilment of Psalm 8:4–6 (2:9; cf. Phil. 2:6–11). As the victorious Saviour of his people, the incarnate Son became superior in status to the angels again by entering into the full inheritance promised to the Messiah in Scripture (v. 2, 'heir of all things'). The eternal

---

12. It seems clear from what follows (1:5–13) that 'Son' is the name the author has in mind here, rather than 'Yahweh' or 'the Lord'. However, the latter is argued by Bauckham, 'Divinity', pp. 21–22.

Son inherited the honour, dignity and rule appropriate to that name by means of his heavenly exaltation.[13] The name 'Son' is *superior* to the name *angels* ('messengers') because of what it signifies.

Theology

Given the status of angels in biblical thought, it is not surprising that an extended reflection on the relationship of the Son to angels should follow the mention of his heavenly enthronement. 'Undoubtedly to establish the absolute transcendence of Christ, nothing would be more suitable than to prove his superiority with regard to those creatures who occupy the most elevated position and are closest to divinity, that is, angels' (Spicq 1, pp. 50–51 [my translation]). If the Son is greater than the angels, the revelation he brings is of greater significance, and the penalty for neglecting it is more serious (2:1–4).[14] Additionally, the author is preparing for his explanation of Psalm 8:4–6 and the need for the Son to be 'made lower than the angels for a little while' (2:5–9). The role of angels in relation to Christian believers is not considered until 1:14.

---

13. The perfect tense of the verb *keklēronomēken* (*has inherited*) lays stress on the present reality of the status and dignity of the Son.

14. DeSilva (pp. 93–94) provides a helpful survey of the teaching of Scripture and Jewish intertestamental literature on the subject of angels. See also Johnson, pp. 82–84.

2. THE GREATNESS OF THE SON AND THE NEED TO PAY CAREFUL ATTENTION TO HIS MESSAGE (1:5 – 2:4)

The link between 1:5 and the previous passage is clarified by the opening question ('For to which of the angels did God ever say . . . ?').[1] Two biblical quotations about the Son and one about angels (1:5–6) provide the first confirmation that the exalted Son has become 'as much superior to the angels as the name he has inherited is superior to theirs' (1:4). The central section of the passage extends this comparison with another citation about angels and two about the character and destiny of the Son (1:7–12).[2] Then the opening question is repeated ('To which of the angels did God ever say . . . ?'), together with a further text about the Son's

---

1. 'Angels' as a hook word links vv. 4 and 5 and is a characteristic term of the argument from 1:4 to 2:16. See Introduction 2, 'Structure and argument'.

2. Greek *men* and *de* in 1:7, 8 clearly link these verses together in a contrasting fashion, while the next biblical citation in vv. 10–12 is linked to the former with a simple *kai* ('and').

exaltation and a claim about angels serving 'those who will inherit salvation', forming an inclusion between verses 5–6 and 13–14. Before the author makes a specific reference to the message of salvation God has spoken through his Son (2:3), he allows us to overhear what God says to his Son in the pages of Scripture. These passages are not cited to prove the assertions in verses 1–4 but to draw out more of their implications. They form the basis for a warning to 'pay the most careful attention . . . to what we have heard, so that we do not drift away'.[3] This warning is reinforced with a recollection that 'the message spoken through angels was binding, and every violation and disobedience received its just punishment', which provokes the question: 'how shall we escape if we ignore so great a salvation?' The salvation in view is defined as having been 'first announced by the Lord' and 'confirmed to us by those who heard him'. The final verse highlights ways in which God testified to the divine authority of the message delivered to the author and his audience.

A. The Son's superiority to the angels (1:5–14)

Context
The threefold division of this passage may be outlined as follows: the Son's heavenly exaltation as Messiah demands the worship of angels (vv. 5–6); angels are part of the created order, whereas the Son is creator and ruler of all that exists (vv. 7–12); the Son's enthronement means that angels have a particular role in the furtherance of God's saving plan (vv. 13–14). With only brief links between them, seven biblical texts are cited to support and amplify the bold claims made in 1:1–4.[4] These divine utterances are included 'not just for what they say but also for what they

---

3. 2:1–4 is linked to the previous section by the hook word 'salvation' (cf. 1:14; 2:3) and by *dia touto* ('therefore').

4. A general correspondence between themes and movements of thought in 1:1–4 and 1:5–14 is outlined by Meiers, 'Symmetry and Theology', pp. 504–533. But the Son's 'purification for sins' is not further explained until 2:17; 9:11 – 10:18.

accomplish as they are spoken and what they produce in those who faithfully hear them' (Kleinig, p. 90). The author assumes that his hearers will have a sufficient understanding of these texts in their biblical contexts to discern their significance without explanation. See Introduction 6b, 'God and Scripture'.

Comment

5. A question expecting a negative answer (*For to which of the angels did God ever say . . . ?*) invites reflection on two foundational texts. Angels are sometimes collectively called 'the sons of God' in Scripture (e.g. Gen. 6:2, 4; Pss 29:1 [LXX 28:1]; 89:6 [LXX 88:7]; Job 1:6; 2:1; 38:7), but no angel is ever addressed in the way that God as *Father* speaks to his *Son* in Psalm 2:7 and 2 Samuel 7:14. God promised King David that he would establish a 'house' for him, meaning a dynasty to rule God's people (2 Sam. 7:11c–13). The words *I will be his Father, / and he will be my Son* come from this context (2 Sam. 7:14) and reveal a special relationship with David's son. God would not take his love from him, as he did from Saul, but would establish David's throne for ever (7:15–16). When the people of God and their kings were coming under God's judgment from the eighth century BC onwards, later prophets affirmed and restated God's covenant with the house of David (e.g. Isa. 9:6–7; 11:1–12; Jer. 23:5–6; Ezek. 34:23–24). In this way, the hope emerged of an anointed Son of David or Messiah, who would perfectly relate to God as *Father* and bring everlasting salvation to Israel.[5]

Psalm 2, which alludes to the promises made to David in 2 Samuel 7, refers to the coronation of a Davidic king. In response to the conspiracy of nations and rulers against the LORD and his anointed (Ps. 2:1–3), the LORD laughs and scoffs at them:

He rebukes them in his anger
    and terrifies them in his wrath, saying,

---

5. John 7:42 points to the messianic significance of 2 Sam. 7:12 and Acts 13:32–33 proclaims the fulfilment of Ps. 2:7 in the raising of Jesus from death. See also Luke 1:32–33; Acts 4:25–28.

'I have installed my king
    on Zion, my holy mountain.'
(vv. 5–6)

The anointed king then proclaims the LORD's decree: 'You are
my son; today I have become your father' (v. 7). God invites his Son
to ask for the nations as his inheritance (v. 8), and then gives him
the promise of victory over all his enemies (v. 9). Psalm 2 finishes
with a warning to the rulers of the earth to 'Serve the LORD with
fear' and 'Kiss his son' (vv. 10–12).

The promise in Psalm 2:7 is literally 'today I have given birth to
you'. At the enthronement of a Davidic king, this metaphorical
language signified that the king had come into the sort of relationship with God promised to David's offspring in 2 Samuel 7:14.
Ultimately, however, the psalm points to the one whom God
'appointed heir of all things, and through whom also he made the
universe' (Heb. 1:2). By means of his sacrificial death and heavenly
exaltation (1:3), the incarnate Son 'entered his inheritance as Son
and the fruition of a sonship that had always been his' (Cockerill,
p. 104). Psalm 2:7 is applied to Jesus' ascension and heavenly rule as
enthroned Messiah (see also my comments on vv. 6, 13). His inheritance as victorious king includes those whom he has redeemed
(2:10–16).

6. The first text describing the role of angels in relation to the
Son is introduced in an elaborate way. Some have argued that the
expression *when God brings his firstborn into the world* refers to the Son's
incarnation (as in 10:5). However, incarnation made him tempor-
arily 'lower than the angels' (2:9), not someone whom the angels
might *worship*. Others have argued that the expression refers to his
second coming (9:28), but the indefinite construction in Greek
(*hotan eisagagē, when* [*he*] *brings*) need not point to a future event.[6]
Furthermore, the Son's superiority to angels is a present reality
according to 1:4.

---

6. Cockerill, p. 104 n. 23. The word *again* (*palin*) links the scriptural
   citation to the preceding one (as in 1:5; 2:13; 4:5; 10:30), rather than
   modifying the verb to mean 'when he brings him *again* into the world'.

Contextually, the focus is on the exaltation and enthronement of the Son, which is announced in verse 3, implied in verse 5 and confirmed in verse 13. The expression *eis tēn oikoumenēn* (v. 6, *into the world*) most likely points to the Son's entrance into the sphere that is later described as 'the city of the living God, the heavenly Jerusalem' (12:22). There, 'thousands upon thousands of angels in joyful assembly' are 'summoned to acknowledge their Lord'.[7] A related expression in 2:5 ('the world to come', also using *oikoumenē*) refers to the world of eschatological salvation, which has been inaugurated by Christ's saving work, but is still to come for believers. Since the author adds the words 'about which we are speaking' in 2:5, 'the world to come' is likely to have been his focus in the preceding argument. So 1:6 means 'when he brings his Son into the heavenly realm' (9:15, 'the promised eternal inheritance').

God's Son is described as his *firstborn* here, which is another way of alluding to the fulfilment of the promises in verse 5. This title is given to the Davidic king in Psalm 89:26–29: the one who calls God 'my Father' is exalted above all the kings of the earth and is assured of God's commitment to maintain his covenant with him for ever. Applied to the only Son through whom God made the universe, *firstborn* (*prototokos*) highlights his destiny to inherit all things as the enthroned Messiah (v. 2).[8] It does not mean that there was a time when the Father brought the Son into existence. The call for all God's angels to *worship* his firstborn probably comes from Deuteronomy 32:43 (LXX, 'let all the sons of God worship

---

7. Bruce, p. 17. See Lane 1, p. 27, and my comment on 'glory' (2:10). Most often in the NT *oikoumenē* has the sense of the 'inhabited earth' (e.g. Matt. 24:14; Luke 4:5; Acts 11:28; 17:31), but Hebrews uses *kosmos* for the present 'world' into which Christ came to offer himself as a sacrifice for sin (10:5; cf. 4:3; 9:26; 11:7, 38).

8. Elsewhere, the Son is described as 'the firstborn' in relation to creation (Col. 1:15) and the resurrection from the dead (Col. 1:18; Rev. 1:5), and as 'the firstborn of a new humanity, which is to be glorified as its exalted Lord is glorified' (BDAG; Rom. 8:29). Schreiner (p. 67) draws a connection with the application of this term to Israel in Exod. 4:22.

him'). This line is missing from the Old Testament Hebrew version of the text followed by NIV and CSB, but the Qumran manuscript 4QDeut 32 reads 'let all the gods (divine beings) worship him', which is included in the Old Testament translation of Deuteronomy 32:43 by NRSV and ESV.[9] Moses predicted God's ultimate victory over his enemies and a comprehensive salvation of his people, calling upon the nations to rejoice with Israel and the angels to acknowledge his triumph. Hebrews indicates that God has fulfilled these promises through the one who sits enthroned at his right hand (1:3), so that angels should give *him* the honour and praise (cf. Phil. 2:9–11; Rev. 5:11–12; 7:11–12).

7. The second text about angels is introduced in a way that clearly sets up a contrast with what follows concerning the Son (*men* in v. 7 and *de* in v. 8 could be translated 'on the one hand . . . on the other hand'). As a celebration of God's continuing involvement in the processes of the natural world, Psalm 104:4 MT says,

> He makes winds his messengers,
> flames of fire his servants.

All the forces of nature are subject to God's control and serve his purpose. But Hebrews cites the Greek version of that text (Ps. 103:4 LXX), which reverses the objects in both clauses (*He makes his angels spirits, / and his servants flames of fire*) and identifies God's messengers as personal spiritual beings, 'who receive their rank and task from God'.[10] This serves the author's purpose well. Since the Son's role in creation has already been specified (v. 2), *angels* must be *his servants* in the government of the universe.

---

9. Cf. Cockerill, p. 108. It is also possible that Hebrews conflates LXX Deut. 32:43 with LXX Ps. 96:7 ('worship him, all his angels'), which is a rendering of MT Ps. 97:7 ('worship him, all you gods'). Ellingworth (pp. 118–119) surveys several options.

10. O'Brien, p. 71. The Hebrew can be translated 'his messengers' or 'his angels'. LXX opts for the latter and portrays the angels as 'executing the divine commands with the swiftness of wind and the strength of fire' (Bruce, p. 18).

8–9. In contrast to the previous citation, Psalm 45:6–7 (44:7–8 LXX) is presented as a prophetic word that God speaks *about the Son*.[11] Originally a wedding song extolling the virtues of a Davidic king (vv. 1–9) and his bride (vv. 10–12), the psalm contains this extraordinary address to the king: *Your throne, O God, will last for ever and ever.* The psalmist recalls the promise of an everlasting throne for the house of David in 2 Samuel 7:16, but goes beyond the language of father and son in 2 Samuel 7:14 and Psalm 2:7, calling the king *God* (reading *ho theos* as a vocative [*O God*]). In effect, the Davidic king is praised 'for his rule over Israel in a manner that is supposed to resemble God's ruling authority over the universe'.[12] He rules with *a sceptre of justice*, which means that his kingdom is characterized by justice, both in the executive and in the punitive sense.

No Davidic king is actually treated in Scripture as divine, although they were supposed to reflect God's character and rule over his people. Psalm 45:6, however, can be applied literally to the Messiah Jesus, articulating what is implied by Psalm 110:1. As the eternal Son of God, who radiates the glory of God and is 'the exact representation of his being', he came among his people to provide 'purification for sins' (v. 3) and has been exalted to God's right hand, where he now exercises the everlasting rule of justice identified by the psalmist.

The king's enthronement in Psalm 45:7 is related to the fact that he has *loved righteousness and hated wickedness.* The sinlessness of Jesus and his faithfulness in doing the will of his Father is highlighted in 5:7–10; 9:14; 10:5–10 as the mean by which he obtains our salvation and is exalted to God's right hand. *Therefore,* God has set him above

---

11. It would be more accurate to translate *pros ton hyion* 'to the Son' here. As in v. 5, God the Father is viewed as speaking to his Son in Ps. 45:6–7. Bruce (p. 19 n. 84) points to a messianic application of this psalm in some Jewish texts.

12. Bateman, 'Psalm 45:6–7', p. 10. Alternative translations such as 'God is your throne' or 'your divine throne' are unconvincing. Cf. Harris, *Jesus as God*, pp. 209–212. Compare the use of 'Mighty God' as a title for the Messiah in Isa. 9:6–7.

his *companions* by *anointing* him *with the oil of joy* (cf. Isa. 61:3).[13] Kings were traditionally anointed with oil as part of the coronation process (e.g. 1 Sam. 10:1; 16:13), but the image here is of *joy* being the overwhelming experience of this king's induction. Applied to the Son of God, this text points to his exaltation above his *companions* (*metochoi*, 'partners', as in 3:14), who are the many 'sons and daughters' he brings to glory by his saving actions (2:10). They are also identified as 'brothers and sisters' who share in his 'heavenly calling' (3:1; cf. 2:11–18). This interpretation suits the flow of the argument better than an identification of the companions with angels or earthly kings. Following his faithful and obedient earthly service, the Son entered 'the joy that was set before him' (12:2; cf. 2:9; 5:7–10), providing believers with the hope of sharing the joy of his glorious kingdom (cf. 6:19–20; 10:23).

10–12. A citation of Psalm 102:25–27 (101:26–28 LXX) is linked to the previous one with the simple conjunction 'and' (*kai*), rendered by NIV *He also says*. This prayer of a distressed person to the LORD for deliverance is not specifically a messianic psalm. The psalmist expresses great confidence in the LORD's commitment to his people and intention to hear their plea (vv. 12–22, 28). Although he is very much aware of the brevity and pain of human life (vv. 1–11, 23–24), he celebrates the enduring power of God as Creator (vv. 25–27). Since the author of Hebrews has already identified the Son as God's agent in creation and as sustainer of all things (1:2–3), he has no difficulty in assigning what is said here about Israel's *Lord* to the Son (cf. Rom. 10:9–13; 1 Cor. 1:30–31; 2:16; Phil. 2:10–11). Even the heavens and the earth will *perish*, but the Son will *remain*. The first part of this affirmation compares what happens to clothing (*they will all wear out like a garment*). Indeed, the Son *will roll them up like a robe; / like a garment they will be changed* (cf. 12:26–28). But the eternity of the Son is once again asserted by the final words of the citation:

---

13. It is possible to translate *ho theos* in v. 9 as a vocative (*O God*, as in v. 8) and take this as another address to the king/Son in relation to his heavenly Father (*ho theos sou, your God*). But NIV reads *God, your God*, taking both expressions as nominative and referring only to God the Father. Cf. O'Brien, p. 74 n. 182.

you remain the same,
  and your years will never end.
(Cf. 5:6; 7:25; 13:8)

13. A question like the one in verse 5a (*To which of the angels did God ever say . . . ?*) is followed by a citation from Psalm 110:1 (109:1 LXX). This messianic text expresses the significance of the Son's enthronement as the citation from Psalm 2:7 does (v. 5b).[14] So an inclusion is formed between Hebrews 1:5 and 13, with a rhetorical question about angels in verse 14 also matching the claim of verse 6. There is an echo of the first line of Psalm 110:1 in verse 3 ('he sat down at the right hand of the Majesty in heaven'), but the citation in verse 13 focuses on the consequences of his enthronement (*until I make your enemies / a footstool for your feet*). This seventh citation is the climax of the author's demonstration of the Son's glory, authority and power in comparison with the angels. The defeat of his enemies is necessary if he is to inherit all things (v. 2b; cf. Ps. 2:8-9). This points to the 'fearful expectation of judgment' that is outlined in 10:26-31 (cf. 2:2-3).

14. A question expecting a positive answer provides a final perspective on the role of angels: *Are not all angels ministering spirits, sent to serve those who will inherit salvation? Ministering spirits* recalls verse 7, implying that their service is to the Son, but they serve him by being sent 'on earthly missions for the benefit of those to whom God is to give salvation'.[15] Believers are identified as those who will share in the inheritance of the Messiah (v. 2b), because of the *salvation* he has achieved for them (5:9). Salvation involves 'bringing many sons and daughters to glory' (2:10), which is completed at his second coming (9:28). Believers are urged not to neglect the

---

14. Ps. 110:1 is the most widely used text in the NT, being quoted or alluded to in Mark 12:36; 14:62 par.; Acts 2:34-35; Rom. 8:34; 1 Cor. 15:25; Eph. 1:20; Col. 3:1; Heb. 1:3 (see my comment), 13; 8:1; 10:12; 12:2; 1 Pet. 3:22.

15. Ellingworth, p. 133. *Ministering* (*leitourgika*) recalls 'servants' (*leitourgous*) in v. 7, while *spirits* (*pneumata*) is used in both verses. *Diakonia* (v. 14) is a parallel term for 'service' (NIV *to serve*).

salvation proclaimed by the Lord himself (2:3), but to be concerned for the things that 'have to do with salvation' (6:9), and to keep relying on their heavenly high priest to save them completely (7:25). Although salvation is yet to be fully inherited, its blessings can be enjoyed in anticipation (6:4–5). The exalted Son, who was served by angels in his incarnate life (Matt. 4:11; Luke 22:43), uses angels to sustain believers in their relationship with him now and to aid them in their service to him (Pss 34:7; 91:11–12; Acts 5:19; 12:6–11; 27:23–24). See Introduction 6c, 'Eschatology and salvation'.

Theology

Biblical citations in 1:5–13 develop the affirmations in 1:1–4 and say more about the Son's relationship to the angels. However, since these texts mostly proclaim the special relationship between God and the promised Messiah, they focus attention on how the Son obtained his eternal inheritance and saves his people. The author does not engage in metaphysical speculation, but seeks to establish a theological foundation for much of the argument to come. As a result of his heavenly ascension, the Son rules with justice and righteousness, waiting for all his enemies to be subdued, and uses angels to sustain 'those who will inherit salvation' (1:14). Angels worship the Son and serve his eternal purpose by ministering to the needs of his people and, by implication, enabling them to reach their heavenly destination.

B. A warning about holding fast to the Son and his message (2:1–4)

Context

Here, the idea that God has spoken 'to us' in his Son (1:2) is developed. Salvation has come to the author and those he addresses as a word of promise from the Lord Jesus, which was confirmed to them by those who heard him, while God bore witness to the authenticity of the message in supernatural ways (vv. 3–4). Drifting from what God has said to them through his Son can only result in a just punishment surpassing any required by the message spoken to Israel by angels (vv. 1–2).

Comment

1. A logical connection between this exhortation and the preceding argument is indicated by the word *therefore* (*dia touto*, 'because of this'). God has spoken to his people in these last days in his Son (1:2), who is greater than the angels (1:4, amplified in 1:5–14). The author as pastor identifies with those he addresses when he uses the first-person plural in 2:1, 3 and warns about the danger of neglecting the message that has come to them from the Son of God. The positive encouragement *to pay the most careful attention . . . to what we have heard* is accompanied by the warning *so that we do not drift away*. Later passages of exhortation in Hebrews tease out these two themes and regularly link them together (3:7 – 4:13; 5:11 – 6:12; 10:26–39; 12:14–17, 25–29). The encouragement to *pay . . . attention* (*prosechein*) is picked up in 3:6, 14; 10:23, where the challenge is to 'hold fast' (*katechein*) to the confidence and hope that the gospel brings.

In the immediate context, *what we have heard* is specifically the message of salvation proclaimed by the Lord Jesus (v. 3). Careful, continuing attention to this message is necessary, because of the greatness of the one who delivered it and the serious consequences of abandoning it. Hence the argument of Hebrews as a whole! The image of a boat drifting off course is used to warn about the danger of 'a gradual, unthinking movement away from the faith' (O'Brien, p. 84). As the warning passages unfold, different perspectives on apostasy are given. Hardening one's heart in unbelief (3:12–19), being unwilling to be taken forward to maturity (5:11 – 6:3), giving up meeting together (10:25) and abandoning confidence in Christ in the face of suffering and testing (10:26–39) are all signs of drifting. See Introduction 6d, 'Apostasy and perseverance'.

2–3a. A conditional sentence assuming the truth of two claims is linked to the preceding verse by the word *For.* The first assumption reflects a Jewish tradition about angels being involved in the giving of the law to Moses (*the message spoken through angels was binding*).[16]

---

16. LXX and Targum on Deut. 33:2 ('The Lord came from Sinai . . . at his right hand were angels with him') appears to have been the foundation for this tradition found in texts such as *Jub.* 1:27–29; 2:1; Josephus, *Ant.* 15.136; Gal. 3:19; Acts 7:38, 53. Cf. deSilva, pp. 93–94.

The passive participle *lalētheis* (*spoken*) suggests that it was God who spoke *through angels*. Quite apart from this tradition, the law's divine authority was recognized in every stream of Judaism. The second assumption recalls the clear teaching of the law that *every violation and disobedience received its just punishment* (e.g. Exod. 21:1 – 22:20). Based on these assumptions, the pastor urges his audience to acknowledge the truth of his challenging question: *how shall we escape if we ignore so great a salvation?* By implication, the salvation provided by the Son is the only way to escape the coming judgment of God and experience the glory of God in 'the world to come' (2:5–18; cf. 10:26–31). See Introduction 6c, 'Eschatology and salvation'.

3b. Although there is one long sentence in the Greek text of verses 2–4, NIV begins a new sentence here, explaining that this salvation *was first announced by the Lord*. Jesus is not mentioned by name until verse 9, but he is identified by the title *Lord* that is so often applied to God in the Old Testament. The incarnate Lord proclaimed the fulfilment of Old Testament predictions and offered the blessings of the coming kingdom of God to those who responded with repentance and faith (e.g. Mark 1:14–15; Luke 4:16–21). Continuity between the preaching of Jesus and the message that brought the author and his audience to faith is indicated by the unusual expression *archēn labousa laleisthai* ('having first been spoken'). They themselves did not actually hear Jesus preaching, but God's revelation through Jesus was *confirmed* to them *by those who heard him.*[17]

4. As Jesus proclaimed his message of salvation and those who heard him confirmed it to others, *God also testified to it by signs, wonders and various miracles*. Supernatural events bore witness to the divine origin and authority of Christ's gospel and confirmed his promise of eschatological salvation (Matt. 11:2–6; Acts 2:22). *Signs, wonders and various miracles* are regularly associated in Scripture with Israel's rescue from Egypt (e.g. Exod. 7:3; Deut. 6:22; Ps. 135:9; Jer. 32:20, 21).

---

17. The verb *confirmed* here (*ebebaiōthē*) means 'to put something beyond doubt, confirm, establish' (BDAG). The cognate adjective *bebaios* ('binding') is used in v. 2 with reference to the message spoken through angels.

In the present context, they suggest that the preaching and mighty works of Jesus and his apostles signalled a comparable, but even more significant intervention of God in history for the salvation of his people (Acts 2:43; 3:1–16; 5:12–16). Jesus was the ultimate 'prophet like Moses' (Deut. 18:15–18; 34:11), who brought a redemptive message for 'these last days' (1:2; cf. Acts 3:17–26). *Signs, wonders and various miracles* demonstrated the powerful presence of God, bringing tangible proof of his promised new creation (e.g. Isa. 35:5–7; 65:17–25).

God continued to testify to the authenticity of the gospel to the recipients of Hebrews *by gifts of the Holy Spirit distributed according to his will*. Such 'distributions' most likely included the sort of ministry gifts mentioned in Romans 12:6–8; 1 Corinthians 12 and 14; Ephesians 4:11–13; 1 Peter 4:10–11.[18] Although 'healing', 'miraculous powers' and 'miracles' are listed together with speaking gifts in 1 Corinthians 12:9, 10, 28, Acts suggests that such signs and wonders were mostly performed by apostles and key figures like Stephen and Philip in the early stages of the gospel's outreach, not by believers in general.[19] Hebrews does not expand on the notion of spiritual gifts, but the author may have understood that the Spirit would enable believers to exhort and teach one another (3:13; 5:12; 10:25) and openly profess Christ's 'name' in the world (13:15). See Introduction 6a(iii), 'The Holy Spirit'.

Theology
This brief exhortation arises from the preceding exposition and includes both warning and encouragement, establishing a pattern that will be repeated throughout Hebrews. Christians need to be reminded about the authority and significance of the message that brought them to faith in the Lord Jesus and gave them the hope of

---

18. The phrase *pneumatos hagiou merismois* ('distributions of the Holy Spirit') sounds like 1 Cor. 12:11 and is best taken to mean 'various gifts proceeding from the Holy Spirit' (BDAG, *merismos*), rather than a distribution of the Spirit himself.
19. On the use of this terminology in Acts 2:43; 4:30; 5:12; 14:3; 15:12, see Peterson, *Acts*, pp. 83–87. See also Rom. 15:19; 2 Cor. 12:12.

eternal salvation. The primary challenge of this 'word of exhort-ation' (13:22) is to pay the most careful attention to what God has spoken and achieved through his Son, because the gospel itself is the antidote to drifting from the Son and the salvation he made possible. The gospel initiates a relationship that requires a con-tinuing response of faith and obedience. Since God has further testified to the truth of the message by the ministry of his Spirit in the fellowship of his people, 'they are faced with a reality – and a demand – from which they truly cannot "escape"' (Johnson, p. 89).

3. THE SON'S INCARNATION, DEATH AND HEAVENLY EXALTATION IS THE MEANS OF OUR SALVATION AND THE BASIS OF HOPEFUL CONFIDENCE (2:5 – 3:6)

The great salvation mentioned in 2:3 is explained now, laying a foundation for much of the argument to come. A major inclusion is formed between 'not to angels' (2:5) and 'not angels' (2:16). A minor inclusion is formed between 'subjected' (2:5) and 'not subject' (2:8), and between the references to 'death' in 2:9 and 2:15. However, 2:9 also concludes the first paragraph with its focus on the way Psalm 8:4–6 is fulfilled. A new argument begins in 2:10 and extends to 2:16. The psalm is quoted and explained in terms of its fulfilment by the Son in his incarnation, death and heavenly exaltation. The Son brings many sons and daughters to glory, expressing his solidarity with them through suffering and death, and delivering them from the devil's power. The next theme is announced in 2:17–18, stating that the Son achieves this victory as 'a merciful and faithful high priest in service to God ... [making] atonement for the sins of the people' and providing help for them when they are tested. The linked exhortation that follows is to 'fix your thoughts on Jesus, whom we acknowledge as our apostle and high priest [who] was faithful to the one who appointed him, just as Moses was faithful in all God's house' (3:1–6).[1] Christ's faithfulness as the Son who rescues and leads God's people provides the encouragement believers need to hold firmly to the confidence and hope he has given them.

A. The world to come subjected to the glorified Son (2:5–9)

Context
The claim that God has not subjected the world to come to angels (2:5) introduces Psalm 8:4–6 (8:5–7 LXX), which is used to explain how everything will be subjected to the exalted Lord Jesus. This recalls the promise of Psalm 110:1 that God would make the enemies of the Messiah a footstool for his feet (1:13) and the claim that the Son was appointed 'heir of all things' (1:2). God's plan for humanity to share the Son's dominion over creation required him to be 'made lower than the angels for a little while' and then 'crowned with glory and honour because he suffered death'.

Comment
5. The word *gar* (NRSV, ESV, 'Now') links this verse immediately with the preceding exhortation (2:1–4). Three other terms, however, signal that the author is more broadly resuming his exposition of the relationship between the Son and the angels (1:5–14). The hook word *angels*, together with *subjected*, specifically recalls the use of Psalm 110:1 to establish the Son's exalted heavenly status in comparison with the subservient role of angels (1:13–14). *The world to come* echoes 1:6, where a related term describes the sphere into which God has already brought his exalted Son.[2] This verse is not

---

1. The exhortation in 3:1–6 is linked to the exposition in 2:5–18 by subject matter and the strong development marker *hothen* ('Therefore'). This passage forms a bridge to the next main section of the argument in 3:7 – 4:13.

2. This is another way of describing 'the coming age' (6:5) or 'the city . . . to come' (13:14). Many of its benefits can be enjoyed by believers in advance of the consummation of all things with the return of Christ (9:28; cf. 12:22–24). See also my comment on 'glory' (2:10).

opposing any known view about angels ruling the coming world order, but simply reaffirming the Son's eschatological rule (*about which we are speaking*), using Psalm 8:4–6 as an explanation of how he entered that rule. His crowning with glory and honour makes it possible for the human beings he came to save to share in his dominion.

6–8a. The formula introducing the psalm citation (*But there is a place where someone has testified*) implies that we need not know the identity of the author to appreciate its authority and significance. The verb *testified* suggests that the citation is a further testimony to the salvation announced by Christ (vv. 3–4). Psalm 8:4–6 (8:5–7 LXX) is understood prophetically as explaining how the promise of Psalm 110:1 in 1:13 is fulfilled for Jesus (no other citation intervenes between them). These two texts are also used together with reference to Christ in 1 Corinthians 15:25–27; Ephesians 1:20–23; and 1 Peter 3:22, indicating 'a common exegetical tradition upon which Christian writers drew'.[3]

NIV has translated the singular *anthrōpos* as *mankind* and the pronouns *auton* ('him') and *autou* ('his') as plurals (*them* and *their*), using inclusive language to acknowledge that God created us male and female. The psalm celebrates God's purpose and care for human beings, but the singular form of the LXX text enabled Hebrews to apply the citation directly to Jesus.[4] Meditating on what Genesis 1:26–30 says about human beings created in the image of God, the psalmist focuses on God's commissioning of humanity to rule over his creation. However, apparently alluding to what Genesis 3 says about humanity's rebellion against God, Hebrews 2:14–18 implies that we are not free to exercise the sort of

---

3. Lane 1, p. 46. Although some ancient texts include the words 'you have made him ruler over the works of your hands', the shorter reading reflected here is more likely to be the original (cf. Metzger, *Textual Commentary*, pp. 593–594; Ellingworth, pp. 150–152).

4. In the parallelism of Ps. 8:4 (LXX 8:5), 'the son of man' (*hyios anthrōpou* [Heb. *ben adam*]) is simply another way of talking about 'man' (*anthrōpos*). It is not a messianic title here in line with Jesus' use of the term (e.g. Mark 2:10, 28; 8:31, 38). Cf. Cockerill, p. 128 n. 21.

dominion God originally intended for us. Death is now the lot of us all, and the devil holds people in slavery with a fear of death. Sin needs to be atoned for and divine help must be provided for us to share in the rule of Christ in the world to come. So the claim in verses 8–9 is that the incarnate Son who died for us is the Man truly *crowned . . . with glory and honour* (Ps. 8:5), who fulfils the psalmist's ideal and enables others to share in his triumph.

8b–9. The author begins to explain the prophetic significance of the citation by drawing attention to the concluding line (ESV, 'in putting everything in subjection to him'). Two negative expressions are combined to highlight the absoluteness of God's promise to humanity about sharing in his dominion (*nothing that is not subject*). However, a third negative expression is introduced to emphasize that 'At present, we do not yet see everything in subjection to him' (ESV). Applied to the present state of humanity, this points to the problems of sin, death and the devil's power over us (vv. 14–18). Applied to the Son of God, it refers to the fact that we do not yet see all his enemies made a footstool for his feet (1:13, citing Ps. 110:1). Opposition to Christ and his message continues in many forms and sometimes overwhelms his followers (10:26–35). But Christians can view Psalm 8:4–6 in the light of its fulfilment for us by Jesus. In the gospel, we *see Jesus, who was made lower than the angels for a little while, now crowned with glory and honour because he suffered death.*

Although the Hebrew of Psalm 8:5 (*mēelohîm*) could be translated 'than God' or 'than divine beings', the LXX opts for the second possibility (*par' angelous, than the angels*). This clearly helped the author of Hebrews expound the Christological implications of the text.[5] The psalm is only truly fulfilled by the incarnation of the Son of God in the person of *Jesus*, who is mentioned by name for the first time (cf. 3:1; 6:20; 7:22; 10:19; 12:2, 24; 13:20). His being *crowned*

---

5. The LXX expression *brachy ti* can also be understood either qualitatively ('a little lower than'), which is the meaning of the Hebrew original, or temporally ('for a little while'). Hebrews reads the latter sense, changing the word order for emphasis (lit. 'for a little while than the angels made lower'), understanding the original in the light of its fulfilment.

with glory and honour is then taken to refer to his heavenly exaltation and rule at God's right hand, which guarantees that everything will finally be subjected to him (cf. 10:12–13).

Psalm 8 gives no hint of the need for Jesus' suffering, but the author wants to highlight this important feature of the gospel tradition and adds the words *because he suffered death* (ESV, 'because of the suffering of death'). This expression focuses on the suffering associated with death itself (9:26; 13:12), though other verses point to the broader experience of suffering in Jesus' life and ministry (2:10, 18; 5:8; cf. 10:32). As in Philippians 2:8–9, his death on a cross is treated as the grounds for his exaltation. A preliminary indication of the purpose of that suffering is given in the final clause: *so that by the grace of God he might taste death for everyone.* The Semitic expression *taste death* alludes to 'the harsh reality of the violent death on the cross that Jesus endured for the benefit of others' (Lane 1, p. 49): it does not mean that he only partially experienced death. In a sense yet to be defined, his death *for everyone* was a death in their place (cf. Mark 14:24; John 6:51; 2 Cor. 5:14; Gal. 3:13).[6] The following context, with its focus on those who actually benefit from the sacrifice of Jesus, suggests that *everyone* means 'everyone without distinction', rather than 'everyone without exception' (Schreiner, p. 91). God's initiative in this work of salvation is implied by the passive verbs *made lower* and *crowned*, and it is made explicit with the words *by the grace of God.*[7] The word *grace* (*charis*) expresses the favour of God as a generous benefactor (cf. 4:16).

Theology
As the one 'appointed heir of all things', through whom also God made the universe (1:2, 10–12), the Son entered into his inheritance in fulfilment of Psalm 110:1 (1:3–4, 13). He did this by fulfilling Psalm 8:4–6, which reveals God's intention for humanity to rule

---

6. The preposition *hyper* (*for*) is used in a substitutionary way here ('on behalf of'). Cf. Wallace, *Greek Grammar*, pp. 383–389.

7. The poorly attested textual variant *chōris theou* ('apart from God') is discussed by Metzger, *Textual Commentary*, p. 594, and Ellingworth, pp. 155–157.

over the creation, as originally stated in Genesis 1:26–30. Fallen human beings are under the dominion of sin, death and the devil, but they can experience the ideal set forth in the psalm through the Son, who became 'lower than the angels for a little while'. Psalm 8:4–6 is given a Christological application, because it points beyond our fallen human condition to the incarnation and heavenly exaltation of the Saviour. But the author adds the interpretive phrase 'because he suffered death' to clarify that it was by this means that he was crowned with glory and honour, dealt with the problem of death and makes available to us the blessings of 'the world to come'. The significance of Jesus' suffering death is more fully explored in the passage that follows.

B. Many sons brought to glory by the pioneer of their salvation (2:10–16)

Context

A logical development of the claims in verse 9 is provided. First, the author identifies more specifically those who benefit from Jesus' suffering as the 'many sons and daughters' God is bringing to glory (v. 10). They are further identified as 'those who are made holy' (v. 11a). Then, with scriptural support, they are called the 'brothers and sisters' of Christ (vv. 11b–12) and 'the children' God has given him (v. 13). The grace of God was definitively expressed in the incarnation of his Son and his saving death for sinful humanity (vv. 14–15). God acted in this way to save not angels, but 'Abraham's descendants' (v. 16).

Comment

10. An unusual reference to what was *fitting* for God signals that the author intends to develop what he said about the grace of God in verse 9. NIV does not translate the conjunction *gar* ('for'), which makes the logical flow even clearer while signalling the beginning of a new section of the argument. God's provision for us in Jesus was consistent with his gracious, merciful and faithful character, meeting our greatest need as fallen human beings. As the one *for whom and through whom everything exists* (cf. 1:1–2; Rom. 11:36), God as Creator does what is necessary and appropriate to fulfil his purpose

for humanity, here defined as 'bringing many sons to glory' (ESV).[8]
Glory recalls the Son's crowning with glory and honour in verse 9:
his glorification makes it possible for many others to share with
him the glory of 'the world to come' (v. 5; cf. Rom. 5:2; 8:17, 18–21,
30). In Hebrews, this is also identified as the 'rest' promised to
God's people (4:1–11), which is enjoyed in 'the coming age' (6:5);
'the promised eternal inheritance' (9:15); 'a kingdom that cannot be
shaken' (12:28); and 'the city that is to come' (13:14; cf. 11:10, 14–16).
What was particularly *fitting* for God in this process of glorification
was to *make the pioneer of their salvation perfect through what he suffered.*

The noun *archēgos* is rightly translated *pioneer* here and in 12:2
('the pioneer and perfecter of faith'). Although the term could
mean 'author' (as in Acts 3:15), Hebrews uses another word to
convey that idea (5:9 [*aitios*], 'source of eternal salvation'). The
verbal association with *agagonta* (*bringing*) in 2:10 suggests that Jesus
is the one who opens the way for others to follow him ('forerunner'
in 6:20 has a similar meaning). The whole expression (*the pioneer of
their salvation*) means that Jesus is the leader who saves them. The
perfecting of the Son of God is mentioned in two other contexts
(5:9; 7:28), while the perfecting of believers is affirmed in 10:14;
11:40; 12:23 (contrast 7:11, 19; 9:9; 10:1). The verb used here should
not be understood in a strictly moral or cultic sense, but more
broadly in a vocational sense: Jesus was 'qualified' or 'made completely adequate' as *the pioneer of their salvation.*[9] This happened *dia
pathēmatōn* (lit. 'through sufferings'), which NIV renders *through what
he suffered.* The plural noun here embraces more than the singular
expression in verse 9 ('the suffering of death'). It refers to all the
suffering that climaxed in the cross (2:17–18; 5:7–9), which enables
the exalted Son to bring many sons and daughters through testing

---

8. NIV has translated *hyious* ('sons') in an inclusive way (*sons and daughters*),
   but the Son–sons comparison is critical to the argument: 'by fulfilling
   his own sonship through providing redemption the Son brings theirs
   to fruition as well' (Cockerill, p. 137).

9. Cf. Peterson, *Hebrews and Perfection*, pp. 66–73. Against Lane (1, p. 57)
   and Kleinig (pp. 145–150), it is inappropriate on linguistic grounds to
   narrow the meaning of the verb to 'consecrate' or 'ordain' as a priest.

and suffering to the glory of his eternal kingdom (see comments on 4:14–16; 7:25; 12:1–3). The perfecting of Christ involved his proving in temptation and suffering, his sacrificial offering of himself in death, and his heavenly exaltation and enthronement as the triumphant priest-king of Psalm 110:1, 4 (cf. 5:5–10).[10]

11a. The pioneer of salvation is now described as *the one who makes people holy* (*ho hagiazōn*, 'the sanctifier'), while the many sons and daughters he brings to glory are called *those who are made holy* (*hoi hagiazomenoi*, 'the sanctified'). God sanctified or consecrated Israel to himself as a holy people by rescuing them from captivity in Egypt, dwelling among them and giving them his laws (Exod. 19:4–6; 29:42–46; 31:13; Lev. 20:7–8). God has provided a new and decisive way of sanctification 'through the offering of the body of Jesus Christ once for all' (10:10 ESV; cf. 9:13–14). More specifically, Jesus suffered 'to make the people holy through his own blood' (13:12). His blood is 'the blood of the covenant that sanctified them' (10:29; cf. 9:19–20). Sanctification is a definitive work of God achieved through the atoning sacrifice of Christ and applied to those who believe the gospel (cf. Acts 26:18; 1 Cor. 1:2, 30; 6:11; Eph. 5:26; 2 Thess. 2:13–14).[11] Their holy status and calling has profound moral and spiritual implications (Heb. 12:7–17; 1 Thess. 4:3–8), but Hebrews is not talking about moral transformation or progressive sanctification when the verb (*hagiazō*) is used in the present tense here (2:11; cf. 10:14). These relational and covenantal terms speak of God's foundational work in bringing people to himself and consecrating them to his service.

Two parties are identified with this terminology ('the sanctifier' and 'the sanctified'), but they are nevertheless *of the same family* (*ex henos pantes*, 'all of one'). Some take this last expression to refer to the common humanity shared by Jesus and those he came to save, opting for either Adam or Abraham as the 'one' in question. But it is more

---

10. Against deSilva (pp. 197–198), the perfecting of Jesus cannot simply be identified with his exaltation after death. His sufferings are presented in Hebrews as part of the process by which he was equipped to be the empathetic high priest portrayed in 2:18; 4:14–16; 7:25.

11. Cf. Peterson, *Possessed*, pp. 33–40, 71–77.

likely that God is the implied subject: the author envisages a spiritual bond between the Son and 'the sons and daughters' that originates in the will and purpose of God (cf. Eph. 1:3–4). Put another way, 'the Son's solidarity with God's "sons and daughters" is rooted in God's redemptive purpose and thus was prior to and the basis for his becoming a human being' (Cockerill, p. 141). The rightness of this interpretation is confirmed by the argument that follows.

11b–12. The link between verse 11a and the quotation that follows is emphatic (*di' hēn aitian*, 'for which reason'). Given the spiritual bond between the Son and 'the sons and daughters' just mentioned, the sanctifier (NIV, *Jesus*) *is not ashamed to call them brothers and sisters* (lit. 'brothers'). In every experience of persecution, suffering and disgrace, such as those experienced by the recipients of Hebrews (10:32–34), Christians should remember that their crucified and exalted Lord identifies with them fully. The verse that is cited (Ps. 22:22 [21:23 LXX]) comes after the psalmist's lengthy cry for God's help, which recounts the alienation, pain and derision he experienced. Numerous features of this lament anticipate the suffering of Jesus, not least the opening cry, 'My God, my God, why have you forsaken me?' (Matt. 27:46/Mark 15:34). When God's deliverance comes, the psalmist turns to praise:

> *I will declare your name to my brothers and sisters;*
> *in the assembly I will sing your praises.*

Those who fear the LORD will join in praising him for the deliverance of his 'afflicted one' (Ps. 22:23–24). This text anticipates the raising of the Son from death to proclaim God's character and purpose to his disciples (Luke 24:13–49; Acts 1:1–8), and to celebrate the victory of God in the heavenly assembly of the redeemed (Heb. 12:22–24; Rev. 5; 7; 14).[12]

---

12. The word *ekklēsia* in 2:12 (*assembly*) and 12:23 ('church') forms a link between these passages and suggests that the author saw Ps. 22:22 as a prediction of the Son's exaltation to participate in the worship of heaven. Those who come to Christ by faith share with him in that heavenly celebration (12:22–24).

13. The link words *And again* are used twice in this verse, introducing two further citations that reveal more about 'the sanctifier' and his relationship with 'the sanctified' (v. 11). In Isaiah 8:17 (*I will put my trust in him*), the prophet expresses his intention to go on trusting God in a situation where opposition was mounting against him and his disciples. Then, in Isaiah 8:18 (*Here am I, and the children God has given me*), he highlights the significance of his *children* for that context. When many Israelites were turning away from God in fear and unbelief, Isaiah was told to give his sons special names, making them 'signs and symbols in Israel from the LORD Almighty, who dwells on Mount Zion' (Isa. 8:18b; cf. 7:3–9; 8:1–4). Hebrews views the trust of Isaiah as prefiguring the trust of Jesus, when he endured rejection and suffering for the sake of those he came to save (5:7–8; 12:2–3). The prophet's children are viewed as typifying the family of believers, who benefit from their Saviour's trust and obedience.[13] Christians are *children* of Christ in a figurative or spiritual sense (contrast Rom. 8:16–17, where 'God's children' are 'co-heirs with Christ'). As a special group within humanity *given* to the Son by the Father, they signify God's intention to bring many sons and daughters to glory with him. As those who belong to the Son, they require his continuing help in testing and suffering to reach their heavenly destination (2:14–18; 12:1–11). Each of the terms used to describe believers in 2:5–18 ('sons', 'brothers', 'children', 'Abraham's descendants', 'the people') says something different about their relationship with the one who is called 'the pioneer of their salvation', 'the sanctifier' and 'a merciful and faithful high priest'.

14–15. To express historically his relationship with *the children* and bring about their salvation, the Son had to enter upon a physical unity with them by incarnation (John 1:12–14; Gal. 4:4–5; Heb. 10:5–10; 1 John 4:1–3). A logical connection with the previous verse is indicated by the word *oun* ('therefore' [not translated by NIV]) and by the conjunction *epei* (*Since*). The perfect tense of the

---

13. Isaiah's disciples and his children were at the heart of the righteous remnant, 'the faithful Israel within the empirical Israel, the group in whose survival the hope of the future was assured' (Bruce, p. 83).

verb translated *have* (*kekoinōnēken*) means that the children continue to 'share' *flesh and blood* (NIV reverses the order of the Greek nouns 'blood and flesh'). But the aorist tense of the following verb signals a new development: at a particular point in time, the eternal Son of God 'partook of the same things' (*meteschen tōn autōn*).[14]

The purpose of the incarnation is then stated in one long sentence with two main verbs. First, the Son of God became a human being 'so that by death' *he might break the power of him who holds the power of death – that is, the devil*. Second, he came to *free those who all their lives were held in slavery by their fear of death*. The notion that death is the divine penalty for sin (Gen. 2:16–17; 3:22–24; Rom. 5:12) is implicit in this context, because Jesus' death is said to make atonement 'for the sins of the people' (v. 17). But Hebrews also picks up the Jewish tradition about the devil's role in humanity's rebellion against God and its consequences (e.g. Wis. 2:23–24 [NRSV]: 'God created us for incorruption, / and made us in the image of his own eternity, / but through the devil's envy death entered the world, / and those who belong to his company experience it').

The devil wields the power over death that hinders human beings from sharing in 'the world to come' (2:5). This power is experienced as the *fear of death*, which keeps people *in slavery all their lives*. 'The devil did not possess control over death inherently but gained his power when he seduced humankind to rebel against God' (Lane 1, p. 61). This power is broken only when people come to experience the liberation from fear that Jesus makes possible by his death (cf. John 12:31–33).[15] Jesus provides complete forgiveness of sin through his atoning sacrifice (10:12–18). The substitutionary nature of his death was hinted at in 2:9 and the penal aspect of his

---

14. The difference in tenses is important, but the verbs themselves are similar in meaning. The second verb is modified by the adverb *paraplēsiōs* (not translated by NIV), which means 'in just the same way' (BDAG). See my comment on 'fully human in every way' in v. 17.

15. The phrase *dia tou thanatou* ('through death') strictly refers to Jesus' death as the means by which the devil's power was broken. This was followed by his resurrection and heavenly exaltation (4:14; 7:26; 9:11–12; 13:20–21), opening the way to 'glory' for others (2:10).

sacrifice is implied in 2:14–15, 17. As a 'ransom' from sin, his death makes it possible for people to pass through death into 'the promised eternal inheritance' (9:15; cf. 1 Cor. 15:54–57).[16]

Some take the *fear of death* to refer to the particular context of the addressees, who are facing a resurgence of persecution and whose fear of death is making them waver and drift from Christ (e.g. Lane 1, pp. 54, 61). Others draw attention to Graeco-Roman literature considering the fear of physical death as 'an obstacle to commitment to what is right' (deSilva, p. 118). But the parallelism between verses 14–15 and 16–17 suggests that death as the punishment for sin is the focus and that the fear of death in this sense is used by the devil to intimidate people and keep them from serving God. On this reading, the fear of death is related to a guilty conscience (cf. 9:9, 14; 10:2, 22).

16. A strong link with the preceding argument is made using two terms together (*gar dēpou, For surely*). Resuming the contrast between angels and human beings from verses 5–9 and continuing the focus on Jesus' special relationship with those described in verses 10–15, the author concludes that *it is not angels he helps, but Abraham's descendants*. God's concern for humanity in general is shown with the use of Psalm 8 in verses 5–9, but Jesus came as a Jewish man specifically to 'take hold of' (*epilambanetai*, cf. Jer. 31:32 [38:32 LXX]; Heb. 8:9) *Abraham's descendants* to rescue them.[17] This verse highlights the Jewish particularity of Jesus and his work, which is about to be described as a fulfilment of God's provisions through Moses for 'the sins of the people' (v. 17). However, although Hebrews nowhere mentions Gentile believers as such, *Abraham's descendants* ultimately includes all who have the faith of Abraham and therefore benefit from God's commitment to bless

---

16. Hebrews does not imply that a ransom was paid to the devil to liberate those held in slavery by their fear of death. The death of the sinless Son of God (7:27), who 'bore the sins of many' (9:28), was the price he willingly paid to liberate us from the divine penalty for sin.

17. The related verb *antelabomēn* ('I took') is used in Isa. 41:8–10 LXX to remind Israel of God's calling and gathering of them to be his people, based on his choice of them as 'descendants of Abraham my friend'.

the nations through Abraham's offspring (Gen. 12:3; 17:5; cf. Rom. 4:9–12; Gal. 4:4–7).[18]

Theology
Sin, death and the fear of death are ever-present factors in human experience (vv. 14–17), preventing human beings from exercising the dominion intended by God for them in this world and the next (vv. 5–9). The Son of God became fully human and experienced suffering, testing, death and heavenly exaltation to deal with this problem and bring 'many sons and daughters to glory' (v. 10). Although Jesus tasted death 'for everyone' (v. 9), the focus narrows in verses 11–16 to those who in fact benefit from his saving work. They are identified in terms of their relationship with Jesus, which is established by God's gracious initiative. They are the ones he makes holy, whom he calls his brothers and sisters, who are the children God has given him and the true descendants of Abraham. The Man who fulfils Psalm 8 is the pioneer of their salvation, who sanctifies them definitively, breaks the devil's power over death and liberates his people from the fear of death.

C. The Son as a merciful and faithful high priest (2:17–18)

Context
This paragraph restates the significance of the Son's incarnation for his particular role as 'a merciful and faithful high priest in service to God' and draws out some of the implications for believers. These verses prepare for much of the argument to come by clarifying the atoning significance of Jesus' death and explaining how his testing through suffering enables him to help his brothers and sisters in all their struggles with sin.

---

18. Israel's Messiah tasted death 'for everyone' (v. 9), 'outside the camp' of Judaism and its rituals to enable believers from every nation to be sanctified by his blood (13:11–14).

Comment

17. The adverb *hothen* (*For this reason*) introduces a further statement about the incarnation of the Son of God, arising here from
his commitment to rescue those who are 'Abraham's descendants'
(v. 16). In verse 14 the focus was on the Son's adoption of flesh and
blood, but now it is asserted that he had to be 'made like his
brothers in every respect' (ESV). This recalls the claim that it was
fitting for God to perfect the pioneer of their salvation through
sufferings (v. 10). It also relates to the following claim that Jesus can
help those who are tested because of his own experience of suffering and testing (v. 18). Not only Jesus' death, but the totality of
his human experience was designed to make him *a merciful and
faithful high priest in service to God* (the last expression could be
rendered 'in matters relating to God'). A hint of this high-priestly
ministry was given in 1:3 ('After he had provided purification for
sins'), but the implications begin to be drawn out more fully
now.[19] Jesus' faithfulness to God is highlighted again in 3:1–6;
5:7–9; 10:5–10; 12:2, and his ability to provide mercy to those who
approach God through him is explained in 4:14 – 5:10.

A second purpose clause indicates that the foundational role of
Jesus as high priest was that *he might make atonement for the sins of the
people* (cf. 5:1). The expression *eis to hilaskesthai tas hamartias tou laou*
has been variously translated. The rendering 'to make expiation for
the sins of the people' (RSV, REB) recalls the actions of the high
priest on the annual Day of Atonement, purifying the people from
the effects of sin by sprinkling animal blood in the Most Holy Place
(Lev. 16:15–17; cf. Heb. 9:5, 7).[20] Blood was also sprinkled on the

---

19. Jesus is called 'a high priest' (*archiereus*) in 3:1; 4:14, 15; 5:5, 10; 6:20; 7:26;
    8:1; 9:11; 'a great priest' (*hiereus megas*) in 10:21; and 'a priest' in 7:11,
    15–16, 21. Hebrews uses this terminology to show how Jesus fulfilled
    the role of the high priest in Israel, especially regarding the annual
    Day of Atonement ritual in Lev. 16. Cf. Ellingworth, pp. 183–188.
20. The compound verb *exilaskomai* is used several times in Lev. 16 for
    the purification of objects, because of the uncleanness and rebellion
    of the Israelites. The same verb is used with the sense of pleading with
    God to be gracious in LXX Zech. 7:2; 8:22; Mal. 1:9.

altar outside (Lev. 16:18–19), after which the high priest confessed the sins of the people over a live goat and it was sent into the wilderness (Lev. 16:20–22). Expiation expresses the idea of removing sin and its consequences as a barrier to fellowship with God. However, since divine punishment could be avoided by faithful priestly ministry (Lev. 10:1–3), the expression in Hebrews 2:17 has sometimes been translated 'to make propitiation for the sins of the people' (RV, ESV). Propitiation involves appeasing God's anger (3:11; 4:3, citing Ps. 95:11), which is ultimately expressed in the eternal judgment awaiting those who reject his rule in their lives (6:2, 8; 9:27; 10:27, 30–31; 12:29; 13:4). Animal sacrifice in some Old Testament contexts is characterized as providing a ransom payment for sins to escape the penalty of death (Lev. 1:4–5; 17:11),[21] thus anticipating the need for the eternal redemption from sin achieved by the sacrifice of Jesus (9:12, 15).

Purification or cleansing from sin is the effect of Christ's sacrifice mentioned in 1:3; 9:14, 22–23 and implied in 10:2. But 2:14–15 relates his high-priestly work to release from the devil's power over death, suggesting that a ransom from the penalty of death is also in view (as in 9:12, 15). There is no indication that a 'payment' was made to the devil: death is the divine penalty for sin and God views his innocent Son as bearing that penalty for others (see my comments on 9:12, 28). The infinitive *hilaskesthai* is translated by NIV and CSB *make atonement for the sins of the people* (NRSV 'to make a sacrifice of atonement for the sins of the people'). This rendering embraces what is meant by both the expiation of sins and propitiation with reference to God. It anticipates the comprehensive portrayal of Jesus' sacrifice and its implications in the chapters to follow.

As in the Old Testament, *the people* means national Israel (e.g. Deut. 4:20; 7:6–8; 14:2; 21:8). This term has a similar sense in

---

21. Richard E. Averbeck (*NIDOTTE* 2, pp. 689–710) argues that the base meaning of the underlying Hebrew verb *kpr* is 'wipe away', but the derived meaning is 'ransom' when it refers to the overall effect of the action. God is propitiated when the issues that would cause his wrath are wiped away. Cf. Wenham, *Leviticus*, pp. 59–63.

Hebrews 5:3; 7:5, 11; 9:7, 19, but sometimes it more specifically refers to those who benefit from the ministry of Jesus (2:17; 4:9; 7:27; 10:30; 13:12). As with the provisions for atonement in the Mosaic law, God is both the originator and the recipient of the atoning sacrifice offered by Jesus. It is a magnificent expression of his grace (2:9).

18. A causal link with the preceding verse (*en hō gar*, 'for because') clarifies that the Son's atoning work was achieved through his previously mentioned sufferings (v. 10). These are described in an intensive way with the words *he himself suffered*.[22] But the author moves from a focus on the redemptive effect of Jesus' suffering (v. 17; cf. 5:8; 9:26; 13:13) to consider another implication for believers. NIV translates *peirastheis* in a temporal fashion (*when he was tempted*), giving the impression that the suffering of Jesus arose from his experiences of testing. But the meaning could simply be that 'he suffered and was tested' or the participle could function causally in relation to the following verbs ('and because he was tested, he is able to help'). According to 5:7–10, Jesus' final struggle began in the Garden of Gethsemane (Mark 14:32–42 par.) and culminated with his last loud cry from the cross (Mark 15:37 par.). The suffering associated with the cross was his supreme test, qualifying him to help those who are being 'tested' (*tois peirazomenois*). The primary meaning of the verb here is 'test' (as clearly in 11:17), but the secondary meaning 'tempt' should be understood as 'a negative element within it'.[23] Testing can become a temptation to sin. The author primarily has in mind the challenge to faithfulness and perseverance he will address in 3:1 – 4:13, for which the earthly experience and continuing empathy of the exalted Son remains the basis of confidence and continuance (4:14 – 5:10; cf. 7:25; 12:1–4; 13:12–14).[24]

---

22. The perfect tense of the Greek verb with an emphatic pronoun (*peponthen autos*) suggests that Jesus himself 'certainly suffered' (O'Brien, p. 122 n. 206).

23. Ellingworth, p. 191. See also my comment on 4:15.

24. 'Grace to help us in our time of need' is mentioned in 4:16, using the noun *boētheia* ('help'), which is related to the verb *boēthēsai* ('to help') in 2:18.

Theology

Jesus achieves the salvation of his people specifically by becoming 'a merciful and faithful high priest in service to God' in a way that remains to be further unfolded. In this capacity, his fundamental task was to 'make atonement for the sins of the people', thus fulfilling and replacing the sacrificial ministry ordained by God for the purification and preservation of his people from judgment (9:1 – 10:18). But the testing of Jesus through suffering also equipped him as the exalted Messiah to empathize with his struggling people in a personal sense and provide them with the continuing help they need to persevere in faith and hope (cf. 4:14 – 5:10; 7:25).

D. A challenge to be faithful and hold firmly to the confidence and hope the Son has given us (3:1–6)

Context

The author as pastor turns again to address his audience more directly with a mixture of encouragement and warning, as in 2:1–4. The challenge to 'fix your thoughts on Jesus, whom we acknowledge as our apostle and high priest' (v. 1) is clearly based on the preceding argument. This is then supported by a comparison of the faithfulness of Christ as 'the Son over God's house' with the faithfulness of Moses as 'a servant in all God's house' (vv. 2–6a). A conditional clause in verse 6b functions as an implied warning to 'hold firmly' to the confidence and hope given by God's Son, forming a transition to the extensive warning in 3:7 – 4:13. Although 3:1–6 is often viewed as the beginning of the next section of the argument, this bridge passage begins as a challenge arising from the exposition in 2:5–18. Then, the mention of Moses and God's 'house' leads to a comparison between the situation of those addressed in Hebrews with the situation of those led by Moses out of Egypt (3:7 – 4:13).

Comment

1. Several terms in this verse show how the exhortation arises from the teaching in 2:5–18. *Therefore* (*hothen*, 'for which reason') is a marker for action based on what has just been said. The recipients are addressed as *holy brothers and sisters*, because they have been 'made holy' by Christ and named as his 'brothers and sisters' (2:11–12; 10:10; 13:12). Consequently, they are brothers and sisters to one another (reading *adelphoi* ['brothers'] inclusively). They are further described as those *who share in the heavenly calling*, in line with God's plan to bring many sons and daughters to glory (2:10).[25] More broadly, God has called them from heaven through the preaching of the gospel (2:3b; 12:25) to belong to 'the church of the firstborn, whose names are written in heaven' (12:23).[26] Their destiny is to share in 'the world to come' (2:5), which is also called God's 'rest' (4:1–11) and 'the promised eternal inheritance' (9:15). They are on a pilgrimage to that destination, as is made clear in 3:7 – 4:11. To reach their goal they must fix their thoughts ('consider, contemplate') on Jesus as 'the apostle and high priest of our confession' (ESV). The Greek text holds back the name of Jesus for rhetorical effect until the end of the phrase (as in 2:9; 6:20; 7:22; 10:19; 12:2, 24; 13:20).

High priest is clearly a hook word, linking this exhortation to what is said about Jesus in 2:17. Nowhere else in the New Testament is he given this title, though Paul describes him as being at the right hand of God and 'interceding for us' (Rom. 8:34). Jesus is also not called *apostle* (*apostolos*) anywhere else, though his being 'sent' by God is often mentioned (e.g. Matt. 10:40; 15:24; Mark 9:37; Luke 10:16; John 3:17, where the related verb *apostellō* is used). These titles, together with 'Son of God', appear to have been part of the formal 'confession' (*homologia*) of faith that the pastor shared with his audience (cf. 4:14; 10:23).[27] In the developing argument of Hebrews,

---

25. They are *metochoi* ('sharing/participating in') a heavenly calling. The secondary meaning of this term is 'partners' or 'companions' (as in 1:9), but the primary meaning is more suited to the context here and in 3:14; 6:4; 12:8.

26. The noun *klēsis* ('calling') is used only here in Hebrews, but the verb *kalein* ('call') is employed in 2:11; 3:13; 5:4; 9:15; 11:8, 18.

27. Cf. Lane 1, p. 75; Kleinig, pp. 168–170. NIV renders this noun in a verbal fashion (*whom we acknowledge*), but references to 'the confession' in 4:14; 10:23 suggest that there was a form of words that expressed the key beliefs of the community. The word *homologia* can describe the act of confessing something or the content of that confession (BDAG).

apostle most naturally refers to Jesus as the one sent by God to reveal his character and will more fully than the prophets (1:1), the angels (2:2) or Moses (3:2–5), and *high priest* refers to his redemptive and reconciling work.

2. *Faithful* is another hook word, linking this passage with 2:17 and showing that the pastor intends to expound this aspect of Jesus' high-priestly role first. In his earthly ministry, Jesus was loyal and obedient to God, *the one who appointed him*. For this reason, he can be relied upon to help his people in the journey of faith to reach their heavenly destination (12:2). A comparison with the faithfulness of Moses follows, based on the wording of Numbers 12:7. The significance of Moses as prophet and leader of God's people is acknowledged, even as the superiority of Jesus as 'apostle and high priest' is asserted.

Miriam and Aaron challenged whether God had spoken to his people only through Moses (Num. 12:1–2). The Lord responded by saying that he revealed himself to prophets in visions and dreams,

> But this is not true of my servant Moses;
>> he is faithful in all my house.

God spoke to Moses uniquely, 'face to face, clearly and not in riddles', enabling him to see 'the form of the Lord' (12:7–8). Moses was a foundational channel of divine revelation for Israel, because he saw the glory of the Lord and heard his words directly (Exod. 24:1–18; 33:17–23; 34:29–35). This is hinted at in Hebrews 3:5, though the author has a bigger picture in mind when he says *just as Moses was faithful in all God's house*. In 3:16, Moses is identified as the one who led the Israelites out of Egypt, inviting a comparison with Jesus as the leader appointed by God to bring many sons and daughters to glory (2:10). Moses' trustworthiness *in all God's house* included every aspect of his leadership of God's people (11:24–29). The word *house* can mean 'dwelling, temple' or 'household, family' (as in 'the house of Israel'). The Israelite community is meant here, as in Numbers 12:7, where the faithfulness of Moses is affirmed in contrast to the unfaithfulness of the people (Num. 11:1–15; 12:1–2; cf. 1 Chr. 17:14).

3–4. Jesus and Moses were both faithful to God in their different responsibilities, but *Jesus has been found worthy of greater honour than Moses.* God honoured Moses by what he said about him and by the way he used him to rescue and establish his people. But God deems Jesus to be worthy of *greater honour* (*doxa*, 'glory').[28] A specific allusion to his crowning with glory and honour could be intended here (2:9). But the difference in honour due to Moses and Jesus is articulated in more general terms: *just as the builder of a house has greater honour than the house itself.* This is clarified with a simple maxim (*For every house is built by someone*), which is applied with the words *but God is the builder of everything.* Contextually, this means that God as creator of the physical universe is also builder of *the house* (household) that consists of his holy people. The Son of God has already been identified as God's agent in creation (1:2b, 10–12) and should also be acknowledged as God's agent in rescuing his people (household) and bringing them to glory with him (2:10–17). In a way that is yet to be explained, 'both those who lived before the incarnation, including Moses (compare 11:26), and those who live after, reach their goal through him (11:39–40)' (Cockerill, p. 166; cf. 9:15).

5–6. Returning to the language of Numbers 12:7, the pastor identifies the distinctive function of Moses as a faithful *servant in all God's house.* The word *servant* (*therapōn*) is included now because he wishes to make a contrast with Christ as the faithful *Son over God's house.*[29] *Servant* in this context particularly expresses the honour and authority of being a channel of revelation to God's people. Special attention is drawn to the role of Moses in *bearing witness to what would be spoken by God in the future* ('as a witness of what would be spoken'). The revelation given by God to Moses was foundational for the establishment and maintenance of Israel as *God's house.* In the

---

28. The perfect tense of the verb *ēxiōtai* conveys the impression that this judgment is a present reality, while the passive voice implies that God is responsible for this ('considered worthy [by God]').

29. This is the only use of *therapōn* in the NT, though it occurs sixty-four times in the LXX and elsewhere in Greek literature. It describes 'one who renders devoted service, esp. as an attendant in a cultic setting, *attendant, aide, servant*' (BDAG).

providence of God, however, this revelation was also a testimony to the pattern of salvation that would ultimately be revealed and accomplished by God's Son (8:5; 9:8–10; 10:1).[30]

For the first time in Hebrews, Jesus is called *Christos* ('the Anointed One'), though his identity as Messiah was established by various biblical allusions and citations in 1:1–14,[31] where his character and role as Son of God is set forth. Here also, Christ is faithful as *the Son over God's house* (compare 10:21, 'a great priest over the house of God'). At a critical moment in history, Moses was a servant in the household Jesus came to save and preside over for ever as Son (1:13; 7:23–25; 8:1–2; 10:12–14). Indeed, Moses looked forward to the 'reward' made possible by the Christ (11:26). Christian believers are part of the same extended household/family/community (*And we are his house*), though this pastor is about to argue that we have greater resources available for us to persevere and reach our destination than the people in Moses' time (4:14–16; 7:11 – 10:25; 12:1–3, 18–24). Coupled with the assurance that *we are his house*, a note of warning is introduced with the words *if indeed we hold firmly to our confidence and the hope in which we glory.*[32]

A prospective conditional clause acknowledges that the pastor and those he addresses already possess by faith what is required, but they need to *hold firmly* to what they have been given (the same verb is used in 3:14; 10:23). They must hold on to the *confidence* (*parrēsia*) that God has given them in his Son and 'the boast that consists of hope'. In 4:16 the noun *parrēsia* refers to the confidence with which believers can approach God for mercy and find grace

---

30. The related verb (*martyreō*) is used of the witness of Ps. 110:4 to Christ (7:8, 17), and to describe the way God commends the faith of various people in Scripture (11:2, 4, 5, 39).

31. The term is similarly used in 5:5; 6:1; 9:11, 28, and in the combination 'Jesus Christ' ('Jesus Messiah') in 10:10; 13:8, 21. When it is used with an article, it more formally reflects the Hebrew expression 'the Anointed One'/Messiah (3:14; 5:5; 6:1; 9:14, 28; 11:26).

32. Some manuscripts add *mechri telous bebaian* ('firm to the end'), though this is likely to be an interpolation from v. 14. Cf. Metzger, *Textual Commentary*, p. 595.

to help in time of need. Confident access to God has been made possible 'by the blood of Jesus' (10:19). This has a future, as well as a present, dimension, enabling believers to endure opposition and suffering with the certainty of a rich reward (10:35).[33] *Hope* is a related gift that is based on the promises of God and their realization by Christ (6:11, 18–20; 7:19; 10:23). There is an objective basis to the Christian's confidence that needs to be subjectively expressed. Similarly, the *hope* that is given to us in Christ needs to be something *in which we glory* (CSB, 'the hope in which we boast').[34] This hope should be confessed and held unswervingly (10:23), to enable joyful acceptance of whatever affliction or deprivation comes our way (10:34; cf. 12:1–13; Rom. 5:2–4).

Theology

Those who share in God's heavenly calling are exhorted to focus on Jesus as the ultimate revelation of God, looking back to the claims made in 1:1 – 2:4. They should also contemplate Jesus as the high priest who has opened the way into God's presence for them, as expressed in the argument to come. A doctrine of the one people of God is implied by the assertion that Moses was a faithful servant in the household of God over which the Son now rules as heavenly high priest (3:1–6; cf. 8:1–6). Old Testament believers are ultimately ransomed and brought to glory by the saving work of Christ (9:15; 11:39–40). But the finished work of Christ provides Christians with an immediate access to God and an assurance of acceptance that was not possible for believers under the Mosaic covenant. We have an eternal hope that encourages perseverance

---

33. The term *parrēsia* is used in Greek literature for frankness or plainness of speech, which in some contexts means openness or boldness in a public situation or before someone of high rank (BDAG). Cf. Marrow, '*Parrēsia*', pp. 431–446; Kleinig, pp. 171–174 (Excursus 7, 'The Privilege of Free Speech in Hebrews').

34. The noun *kauchēma* literally means 'pride' (NRSV, 'the pride that belong[s] to hope') or 'boast' (ESV, 'and our boasting in our hope'). *To kauchēma tēs elpidos* signifies that the hope given to us in the gospel is what we are to boast about or glory in.

and endurance in the present. We show that we are genuinely part of the household of faith when we hold firmly to what we have been given in Christ. The faithfulness of the Son 'over God's house' assures us that he will sustain and keep those who put their trust in him.

4. A WARNING NOT TO HARDEN OUR HEARTS IN UNBELIEF, TOGETHER WITH ENCOURAGEMENTS ABOUT THE WAY TO ENTER THE REST THAT THE SON HAS MADE POSSIBLE (3:7 – 4:13)

In this lengthy passage of exhortation and exposition, the warning in 3:6 is reinforced and applied more vigorously. Psalm 95:7–11 is cited and related to the situation of the recipients, both as a warning and as an encouragement to persevere in faith and obedience (3:7–15). A series of rhetorical questions highlights the significance of Israel's unbelief and disobedience on their journey to the Promised Land, which is the focus of the citation (3:16–19; cf. Num. 14:1–38). Hardness of heart prevented the generation that came out of Egypt with Moses from entering the 'rest' promised to them by God. The theme of entering God's rest is then applied to those who have received the gospel.

The author includes himself in a transitional warning about falling short of what has been promised (4:1–2). He gives a comprehensive biblical perspective on 'the rest' that remains to be entered and urges his hearers not to follow the example of those who perished in the wilderness (4:3–11). When God as Creator 'rested from all his work' and 'blessed the seventh day and made it holy' (Gen. 2:2–3), he implicitly offered human beings the possibility of sharing in his rest. The land that God promised to Israel was a foretaste of that rest. If Joshua had brought the people into the fullness of God's rest, God would not have spoken later in Psalm 95:7–11 about the danger of missing out on his rest. The rest that remains for the people of God lies beyond this creation, and the means of entering it is continued trust in Christ, issuing in obedience to God's word. A warning to consider the power of God's word to expose and judge 'the thoughts and attitudes of the heart' (4:12–13) climaxes the argument.

A. The negative example of the Israelites who failed to enter the Promised Land (3:7–19)

Context

The pastor quotes Psalm 95:7–11 (94:7–11 LXX) as part of his address to his congregation (vv. 7–11) and applies it in the manner of a sermon. They are warned about having 'a sinful, unbelieving heart that turns away from the living God' (v. 12) and encouraged to exhort one another daily to avoid being hardened by sin's deceitfulness (v. 13). A conditional statement about sharing in Christ 'if indeed we hold our original conviction firmly to the very end' is backed up by repeating the opening three lines of the psalm citation (vv.14–15). A series of rhetorical questions is finally posed, recalling the historical context to which the psalm points, and suggesting the relevance of this tragic story to the audience (vv. 16–19).

Comment

7–8. *The Holy Spirit* continues to speak to believers through Psalm 95:7–11. 'God' is the ultimate source of these words (4:3, 8), though the human author is identified as 'David' (4:7). According to 2 Samuel 23:1–2, 'The Spirit of the LORD' spoke through David when he wrote his songs, giving them a prophetic quality. The LXX identifies David as the author of Psalm 95, though the MT does not.[1]

---

1. The expression 'in David' in 4:7 may suggest that the psalm is part of the collection broadly attributed to David and resulting from his prophetic inspiration. Cf. O'Brien, p. 169 n. 81.

The expression *as the Holy Spirit says* suggests that the Spirit continues to show Christians the contemporary relevance of what was written long ago (cf. 9:8; 10:15). You can hear God speaking to you when you listen to this psalm!

The first clause of the psalm citation is conditional (*Today, if you hear his voice*), and this is followed by a command (*do not harden your hearts*). The recipients of Hebrews heard the message of salvation that was first announced by the Lord Jesus and confirmed to them by those who heard him (2:1–3). The psalmist's challenge is to listen to the voice of God *today*, especially as Scripture conveys his promises and warnings (4:1–13; 12:22–27). Faithful listening involves not hardening your heart in unbelief and disobedience (3:18–19; cf. Num. 14:22). David's warning to his own generation was based on a recollection of Israel's history when they left Egypt and journeyed to the Promised Land. God's people hardened their hearts against him, with terrible consequences (*as you did in the rebellion, / during the time of testing in the wilderness*). The Hebrew version of Psalm 95:8 reads 'as at Meribah, as on the day at Massah in the wilderness', but the LXX replaces these names with terms describing what happened there (Meribah in Hebrew signifies 'quarrelling, finding fault with' and Massah means 'testing'). At the beginning of their journey, they quarrelled with Moses about having no water to drink and put God to the test with their grumbling (Exod. 17:1–7). But the LXX version of the psalm and the rhetorical questions in 3:17–19 focus on the climactic events described in Numbers 14, suggesting that rebellion and testing God characterized their whole journey.

9–10. Speaking directly and personally through the psalmist, God says to subsequent generations of believers that this was

> *where your ancestors tested and tried me,*
> *though for forty years they saw what I did.*[2]

---

2. Hebrews modifies LXX Ps. 95:9 to read 'tested me *with proving*' (*en dokimasia*). This suggests that they were cynically trying to prove the genuineness of God's promises and warnings to them, regardless of the consequences.

When the Israelites reached Kadesh Barnea, they refused to
accept Joshua and Caleb's report about the Promised Land, prefer-
ring to believe the fearful account of the spies who had gone in
with them (Num. 13:26–33). They grumbled against Moses and
Aaron and misrepresented God, suggesting that he had brought
them to that place only to let them fall by the sword (14:1–4). They
treated the LORD with contempt, refusing to believe his promise,
which had been confirmed with an oath to their ancestors (14:16,
23, 30). Despite the many signs of his grace they had witnessed
(14:11), such as the manna (Exod. 16:1–36), water from the rock
(17:1–7) and deliverance from their enemies (17:8–16), they provoked God to destroy them and 'make . . . a nation greater and
stronger than they' through Moses (Num. 14:12).

The author of Hebrews adds the Greek conjunction *dio* ('therefore, for this reason') to the LXX version of Psalm 95:9. This implies
that the behaviour of the Israelites at Kadesh Barnea and during
their forty years of wandering in the wilderness was the reason why
God was *angry with that generation*.[3] They continued to be faithless
and disobedient, and experienced God's judgment again and again
(e.g. Num. 14:39–45; 15:32–36; 16:1–50). Their behaviour led God to
conclude that

Their hearts are always going astray,
   and they have not known my ways.

Although they regularly *saw* what God did, they would not acknowledge his trustworthiness and accept his will for their lives.

11. Psalm 95 concludes by expressing God's anger in the form
of an oath of judgment:

So I declared on oath in my anger,
   'They shall never enter my rest.'

3. Without this conjunction, the words *for forty years* most naturally relate
   to what follows ('I was angry with that generation for forty years').
   But the addition of the conjunction links the forty years more closely
   with the preceding events. Cf. O'Brien, pp. 143–144.

This echoes God's words in Numbers 14:23: 'not one of them will ever see the land I promised on oath to their ancestors' (cf. Num. 14:30; Deut. 1:34–35). God's judgment in that context was confirmed with these words: 'as surely as I live and as surely as the glory of the LORD fills the whole earth' (Num. 14:21; cf. 14:28). LXX follows the MT, providing an incomplete conditional sentence: (lit.) 'if they shall enter my rest . . .' This idiom suggests the need for an impossible conclusion to be supplied, such as 'I would not be God', to reinforce the seriousness of the proposition (Cockerill, p. 181 n. 32). Hebrews alludes to these words of exclusion again in 3:18. Speaking through the psalmist, however, the Holy Spirit challenges later generations not to miss out on the *rest* promised to them, which is identified with the hope set forth in the gospel. Although the term 'rest' is not used in Numbers 14, the inheritance promised to Israel is specifically identified as a place where they will find rest from their enemies (Deut. 3:20; 12:9, 10; 25:19; Josh. 1:13, 15; 21:44; 22:4; 23:1).

12. With a direct address to his audience (*See to it, brothers and sisters*) the pastor begins to apply the specific warning of Psalm 95:7–11.[4] Collectively, they must 'watch out' in case 'any one of them' (*en tini hymōn*) *has a sinful, unbelieving heart that turns away from the living God*. The same concern for individual members of their fellowship is reflected again in 3:13; 4:1, 11; 6:11. Individuals need to be nurtured for their own sake, but also because their unbelief could harm the congregation as a whole (12:15–16; cf. Num. 14:36–38; 32:9; Gal. 5:9). Hearts are mentioned twice in the psalm citation: in the warning not to 'harden your hearts' (v. 8), and in God's declaration that 'Their hearts are always going astray' (v. 10).

The 'heart' in Scripture refers to the centre of a person, where reason, emotions and the will interact. A *sinful . . . heart* is characterized by 'unbelief' ('an evil heart of unbelief') *that turns away from the living God*. The verb *apostēnai* (*turns away*) echoes the description of the Israelites as 'rebels' in Numbers 14:9 LXX (*apostatai*) and

---

4. The present tense of the imperative *blepete* ('see') makes this a warning about habitually watching out for one another as members of Christ's family (cf. 2:11–12; 3:1).

highlights the fact that a deliberate turning away from God is meant.[5] A 'sincere heart', on the other hand, is characterized by 'the full assurance that faith brings' (10:22, my translation), enabling someone to keep drawing near to God. Hebrews has in mind the example of the Israelites, who experienced both the grace and the judgment of God in their wilderness years, yet refused to know his ways (v. 10) and respond with faith and obedience (vv. 16–19; cf. Num. 14:11; Deut. 1:32).[6] The challenge for people in every generation is to be aware of the condition of their hearts and to face each new situation with a genuine desire to trust God and obey him.

God is sometimes characterized in Scripture as *living* in contrast to the dead idols of the nations (Jer. 10:8–10; Acts 14:15). As *the living God*, who gives life, he has continually spoken and acted for his people in history (Josh. 3:9–10; 1 Sam. 17:26). If some of the recipients of Hebrews were in danger of abandoning their commitment to Christ and returning to the security of Judaism (see my Introduction), they too would be turning away from the living God by rejecting Jesus as 'the climax of all God has been doing through his people' (Cockerill, p. 185). Indeed, anyone who professes faith in Christ and turns away from him abandons the living God and his gracious plan of salvation.

13. The antidote for sinful, unbelieving hearts is now given. Although the verb *parakalein* can mean *encourage* (NIV), it is commonly used in contexts where 'appeal to, urge, exhort' is the better translation (BDAG). Using the related noun, the author of Hebrews describes his work as a 'word of exhortation' (13:22, *logos tēs paraklēseōs*). It is a mixture of warning and encouragement, designed to motivate those who receive it to persevere in faith, hope and love (cf. 6:9–20; 10:19–25; 12:5–6). In this way, Hebrews itself provides a model of how Christians should minister to one another. It is

---

5. The Greek infinitive construction *en tō apostēnai* is explanatory here, defining what is meant by 'an evil heart of unbelief' (Ellingworth, p. 222).

6. Lane (1, p. 86) rightly observes that the unbelief envisaged in 3:12 is a culpable 'refusal to believe God' (cf. Num. 14:11; Deut. 1:32).

therefore best to translate the verb in 3:13 and 10:25 'exhort', to embrace the positive and negative dimensions of this ministry.

Exhorting one another *daily* does not necessarily mean gathering as a church each day. What has been learned from Scripture may be shared one-to-one or in small-group encounters at any time. In this broader sense, mutual exhortation is an essential aspect of Christian fellowship. A brief allusion to Psalm 95:7 (*as long as it is called 'Today'*) indicates that the time for individuals and churches to hear God's voice in this way and respond may be limited.[7] Each time God's word is articulated and shared in ministry to one another is a 'day' in which God speaks to his people. When we withdraw from Christian fellowship, we distance ourselves from this possibility. Consequently, every opportunity to minister God's word to one another should be grasped and taken seriously (cf. 4:12–13).

The aim of such mutual ministry is *that none of you may be hardened by sin's deceitfulness*. As noted in 3:12, there should be a concern for each member of the church (ESV, 'any of you'; as also in 4:1, 11; 6:11). The warning not to 'harden your hearts' if you hear God's voice (3:8) is accompanied now by the revelation that progressive hardening of the heart may lead to the condition of being permanently *hardened by sin's deceitfulness*. Sin is personified as a power that leads people to doubt God's word and resist his will (cf. Gen. 3:1–7; 4:7; Rom. 7:7–13, esp. v. 11). Persistence in such behaviour leads to an insensitivity towards God and the possibility of missing out on his 'rest'. Sin's deception (*apatē*) is to make people believe that ignoring the will of God will have no consequences.

14. The reason for the preceding warnings and encouragements is now given, showing why they need to be taken seriously (NIV does not translate the link word *gar* ['for']). In fact, the author repeats the conditional argument of 3:6 in different terms: *We have come to share in Christ* amplifies the previous assertion that 'we are his house', while *if indeed we hold our original conviction firmly to the very end* parallels 'if indeed we hold firmly to our confidence and the

---

7. The limiting event is doubtless the return of Christ, which is alluded to in 3:14; 10:24–25, 37–39; 12:25–27.

hope in which we glory'. In both contexts, an indicative statement points to the present benefits of believing in Christ. Believers are members of God's family or household (3:6; cf. 2:11–13), who *share* (*metochoi*, as in 3:1; 6:4; 12:8) in the promises and expectations of a relationship with Christ now and in the future (NRSV, 'we have become partners of Christ').[8] The perfect tense of the verb *gegonamen* (*We have come*) in this verse highlights the present reality of that relationship, paralleling the use of the present tense in 3:6 (*esmen*, 'we are'). The whole sentence could be rendered 'we have (really) come to share in Christ if we keep our initial attitude firm to the end'.[9]

The conditional clause beginning with 'if' indicates the need to *hold . . . firmly* to what has been received (the same verb is used in 3:6; 10:23). Genuine participation in Christ demands a continuing response to him (*eanper, if indeed* or 'if only' [NRSV]), because that is the nature of a personal relationship. The Greek expression *tēn archēn tēs hypostaseōs* requires a more objective rendering than NIV (*our original conviction*). The noun *hypostasis* is used in 1:3 with reference to God's 'being' and in 11:1, where it is asserted that faith gives to things hoped for 'a substantial reality, which will unfold in God's appointed time' (Lane 2, p. 329). This term commonly refers to 'the essential or basic structure/nature of an entity' (BDAG).[10] Most likely, 3:14 identifies the need to hold on to the substance or 'original foundation' of the faith, which is given in the gospel (2:1–4), and thereby to hold on to Christ. Addition of the words

---

8. NIV rightly takes *metochoi* in an adjectival sense here, meaning that believers are 'sharing' or 'participating' in Christ and the benefits and obligations of that relationship. But this also makes them 'partners' with one another (1:9, 'your companions'). Cf. Ellingworth, pp. 226–227.

9. McKay, *Syntax*, p. 172. O'Brien (p. 152) concludes that perseverance 'will demonstrate that their faith is genuine'. Cf. Carson, 'Assurance', p. 267.

10. The second definition of *hypostasis* in BDAG is 'a plan that one devises for action, *plan, project, undertaking, endeavour*'. Heb. 3:14 may be inviting addressees 'to draw on the semantic component of obligation familiar in commercial usage of the term'.

firmly to the very end accentuates the need to do this until everything promised in the gospel is fully realized (cf. 6:11–12; 10:23, 36–39). Compare the objective dimension to the Christian's 'confidence', which is given by the work of Christ (3:6; 10:19–22). The 'hope in which we glory' (3:6) is similarly God's gift to those who believe the gospel and trust his promises (10:23).

15. *As has just been said* introduces a repeated quotation from Psalm 95:7b–8a. This ties off the warning in 3:12–14 with a reference back to the essential message of the psalm:

> *Today, if you hear his voice,*
> *do not harden your hearts*
> *as you did in the rebellion.*

Each of the terms *Today, if you hear his voice* and *do not harden your hearts* has already been applied to the recipients of Hebrews. When the psalmist alerts his generation to the rebellion of their spiritual ancestors (*as you did in the rebellion*), this serves to warn them about provoking God to judge them in a similar way. With a series of rhetorical questions, Hebrews proceeds to restate the implications of that rebellion for Christians.

16–19. Three rhetorical questions based on the language of Psalm 95 are posed. These are answered with further questions, pointing to key features of the relevant biblical narratives. In this way, the significance of the psalmist's message is driven home. The people who *heard and rebelled* against God in the wilderness were *all those Moses led out of Egypt.* They experienced God's mighty deliverance from Pharaoh's army when they passed through the sea on dry ground (Exod. 14). As they continued on their way, they were regularly assured of his constant care for them (Exod. 16 – 19). They had every reason to believe he could bring them into the land he had promised them with an oath. But God was *angry* with them *for forty years* because they *sinned* in such a way at Kadesh Barnea that their *bodies perished in the wilderness* (Num. 14). They *disobeyed* God when they were called to take possession of their inheritance, and God swore to the majority of them that *they would never enter his rest.* This tragic outcome was the culmination of many rebellious actions arising from their *unbelief.* Those who have come to God in

Christ and experienced the powerful presence of his Spirit in their midst (2:1–4) are warned again about drifting away and missing out on the salvation promised to them as the Israelites in the wilderness did.

Theology
When the conditional argument in verse 6 is repeated in verse 14, it becomes clear that the intervening warnings are designed to encourage a persevering confidence in the hope given to us in Christ. The failure of the first generation of Israelites to enter the 'rest' of Canaan is identified in Psalm 95:7–11 as the result of hardening their hearts in unbelief and disobedience (Heb. 3:16–19). Three verbs are used to describe what the Israelites did (v. 16, they 'rebelled'; v. 17, they 'sinned'; v. 18, they 'disobeyed'), but the root cause of this behaviour was their unbelief (v. 19).[11] The lesson that the Holy Spirit continues to teach from this psalm is that believers should not harden their hearts against God when they hear his voice. God's voice can be heard directly from Scripture or when Christians exhort one another with biblical warnings and encouragements not to be hardened by sin's deceitfulness. The importance of mutual ministry to sustain faith and obedience to God is emphasized again in 4:1–2; 6:10–12; 10:24–25, 32–36; 12:12–17; 13:1–8, 16–19. See also the Introduction 6d, 'Apostasy and perseverance'.

B. A warning about falling short of God's promised rest (4:1–2)

Context
These two transitional verses reiterate and further apply the warning about missing out on what God has promised. After the direct, second-person plural challenges in 3:7–15, which follow the lead of Psalm 95:7–11, the pastor uses a first-person plural form of exhortation, inviting his hearers 'to join him in acting corporately' (Kleinig, p. 199). He resumes this pattern of exhortation in 4:11,

---

11. Cockerill (p. 194) describes their unfaithful behaviour as a 'rejection of the veracity of God's promises and the reality of his power'.

emphasizing that this is a message for professing Christians to heed together. Although Jesus is not explicitly mentioned here as the one who brings believers into God's rest, he has already been identified as the one to whom God has subjected 'the world to come' (2:5) and through whom God brings 'many sons and daughters to glory' (2:10).

Comment

1. The conjunction *Therefore* (*oun*) links this exhortation with the preceding reflection on the incident recorded in Numbers 14. Christians are in a similar position to the Israelites about to enter Canaan, *since the promise of entering his rest still stands*. The Greek indicates that this promise remains open to be believed and acted upon. Given the insistence on 'today' as the time to respond, the sense is more likely to be temporal (ESV, 'while the promise . . . still stands') than causal (NIV, *since*). A parallel term for *still stands* is used in 4:6, 9. If the parallel with 3:12 ('watch out') is noted, the verb *phobēthōmen* may be translated *let us be careful*, though literally it means 'let us be fearful'. Once again, there should be a concern for each individual ('any of you'; cf. 3:12, 13), *that none of you be found to have fallen short* [*of it*]. The language here suggests that some who have begun the journey to God's promised rest may 'appear to be lagging behind', or even 'be found to have come short'.[12]

Promise terminology is used in Hebrews to refer either to God's act of promising or to the content of his promises. God's promises are regularly linked to Old Testament texts and shown to be applicable to Christians. The noun 'promise' (*epangelia*) is found in 4:1; 6:12, 15, 17; 7:6; 8:6; 9:15; 10:36; 11:9 (twice), 13, 17, 33, 39, and the corresponding verb in 6:13; 10:23; 11:11; 12:26. Psalm 95:7–11 extends the promise of entering God's rest, originally made to the ancestors of Israel, to a generation already living in the Promised

---

12. If the verb *dokein* means 'seems' or 'appears' (as in 12:11), the perfect infinitive *hysterēkenai* can be understood to highlight a present reality ('to be falling short'). But the first verb can mean 'found' or 'judged', leading O'Brien (p. 160) to argue that it refers to God's final judgment, and the infinitive is rightly rendered 'to have fallen short'.

Land. The author of Hebrews contends that the psalmist's promise must relate to the foundational 'rest' of God mentioned in Genesis 2:2, and so applies the psalmist's message more broadly. In each extension of the promise, the exact notion of 'rest' is reconfigured and clarified, but the 'alive and active' voice of God (4:12) continues to speak 'today' in a direct and similar way to each successive generation, calling for the same response of obedient faith.

2. The parallel between professing Christians and the Israelites who left Egypt with Moses is expressed in a surprising way: *For we also have had the good news proclaimed to us* (cf. 2:1–4). The verb *euangelizomai* ('to bring good news, announce good news' or 'to evangelize') is widely used in the New Testament (e.g. Matt. 11:5; Luke 4:43; Acts 5:42; 8:4; Rom. 1:15; 15:20) and in some LXX texts (e.g. Pss 40:9; 68:11; 96:2; Isa. 40:9; 52:7; 60:6; 61:1). Only here and in verse 6, however, is the reception of the Christian gospel likened to Israel's reception of God's promises through Moses (*just as they did*).[13] Moses did not preach Christ to the Israelites, but he prepared them to leave Egypt by proclaiming the impending fulfilment of promises made to their forefathers and urging them to trust in the LORD (e.g. Exod. 3:13–20; 4:29–31; 13:11–16).

The Israelites responded initially with faith and also from time to time during their wilderness wanderings. Ultimately, however, *the message they heard was of no value to them.* Most of that first generation failed to enter the promised inheritance *because they did not share the faith of those who obeyed.* The Greek means that they were 'not joined together with those who heard with faith'.[14] Joshua and

---

13. The verb is in the passive to convey the idea of receiving good news (cf. 2 Sam. 18:31 LXX; Matt. 11:5). This perfect passive participle is used with the present tense of the verb *esmen* ('we are') to emphasize the present reality of having been evangelized. Compare 10:10 ('we have been sanctified'), where the same construction is employed.

14. Cockerill (p. 203 n. 30) observes that 'those who heard' in 3:16 refers to the rebels, so it is better to take *tē pistei* ('by faith') with *tois akousasin* ('those who heard') in 4:2 (NIV, CSB), rather than with the preceding verb (NRSV, ESV 'they were not united by faith with those who listened'), to identify the faithful and obedient spies.

Caleb heard the message of Moses with faith and tried to persuade the people as a whole to trust God, but the majority followed the lead of the unbelieving spies (Num. 13:25 – 14:10). NIV margin provides an alternative reading ('because those who heard did not combine it with faith'). This represents a variant in some ancient manuscripts that is less likely to be what the author wrote.[15]

Theology
The author begins to develop a typological argument here, based on his use of Psalm 95:7–11 in the preceding chapter and amplified in 4:6–11. The Israelites who left Egypt with Moses and failed to enter the 'rest' of Canaan provide a negative example to those who have received the gospel and are in danger of drifting from Christ into unbelief and disobedience. But there were some Israelites who continued to believe God's promises and encouraged others to do the same, namely Joshua and Caleb (Num. 13:30–33; 14:5–9). They stand as positive examples to those who believe the gospel and are on a journey to the promised rest of God, which was previously identified as 'the world to come' (2:5; see also 11:4–38).

C. Identifying the rest and those who enter it (4:3–11)

Context
The pastor now proceeds to explain why the Christian hope can be identified with the 'rest' mentioned in Psalm 95:11. He first affirms that 'we who have believed enter that rest', citing again the oath of rejection concerning those who did not believe in the time of Moses (4:3). A quotation from Genesis 2:2 is then introduced to explain the true meaning of God's 'rest' (4:4–5). This foundational text explains why 'it still remains for some to enter that rest', even though many failed to enter the 'rest' of Canaan (4:6). God spoke 'a long time later' through David in Psalm 95:7 about another day in which to hear his voice and believe (4:7). If Joshua had given the people of Israel the ultimate rest, 'God would not

---

15. Cf. Metzger, *Textual Commentary*, p. 595; Cockerill, p. 204 n. 33.

have spoken later about another day' (4:8). Alluding again to Genesis 2, the pastor affirms that the people of God will be able to rest eternally from their works 'just as God did from his' (4:9–10). The concluding challenge is to 'make every effort to enter that rest', and not to 'perish by following their example of disobedience' (4:11).

Comment

3. Since a conclusion is being drawn from verses 1–2, 'for' would be a better rendering of the Greek conjunction (*gar*) than *now* (NIV may be translating the variant *oun*). A general principle is stated (*we who have believed enter that rest*), allowing for the inclusion of believers past, present and future. As in verses 1–2, a first-person plural verb is used to include the pastor with his audience. This present-tense verb is best understood in a timeless way ('we enter') or, in view of verse 11, in a futuristic sense ('we will enter'). Following the lead of Psalm 95:11, *that rest* should be understood as a place yet to be entered, equivalent to 'the promised eternal inheritance' (9:15), the 'heavenly country' (11:13–16), 'the city that is to come' (11:10; 13:14) and 'a kingdom that cannot be shaken' (12:28). With this physical imagery Hebrews expresses the prophetic hope of a new creation or 'new Jerusalem' (Isa. 11:6–10 [the Messiah's glorious 'resting-place']; 65:17–25; Rev. 21:1 – 22:5), rather than simply a spiritual condition that can be enjoyed by faith now.

The promise that those who have believed enter that rest is confirmed by restating what God said (*just as God has said*) in Psalm 95:11 (*So I declared on oath in my anger, / 'They shall never enter my rest'*). The exclusion of some Israelites in Numbers 14 did not mean the exclusion of all. Indeed, the children of that first generation were allowed to enter Canaan with the families of Joshua and Caleb. So what is meant by the psalmist's challenge to believe and enter God's rest? If the Israelites in David's time were already enjoying the rest that Joshua had won for them (cf. 4:8), what rest were they being warned about? An allusion to Genesis 2:2 (*And yet his works have been finished since the creation of the world*) takes this earlier passage as the key to understanding Psalm 95:11. When God 'completed his work of creation, he "rested", so his people, having completed their service on earth, will enter into his rest' (Bruce, p. 109; cf. Rev. 14:13). Genesis 2:2 is understood to point to a rest beyond the present created order. Psalm 95 takes Israel's 'rest' in the Promised Land as pointing to the rest that God now enjoys and believers may enjoy with him in 'the world to come' (2:5).

4–5. Hebrews follows the practice of ancient Jewish interpreters in noting a verbal link between two biblical passages and using the earlier passage to explain the later.[16] The method by which the citation from Genesis 2:2 is introduced (*For somewhere he has spoken about the seventh day in these words*) echoes the vague formula in Hebrews 2:6. But the words cited here clearly form part of the conclusion to the seven-day creation account in Genesis: *On the seventh day God rested from all his works.* God delighted in what he had created, and when he 'blessed the seventh day and made it holy' (Gen. 2:3), he made his rest a potential source of blessing for those created in his image. This ideal is portrayed in the narrative of the Garden of Eden, but human beings were excluded from that perfect environment because of sin (Gen. 2:4 – 3:24). God's plan to bless humanity by bringing them back to himself was set in motion with the call of Abram and the promises made to him (Gen. 11:27 – 12:3).

God is said to have *spoken* in Genesis 2:2, not in direct speech, but in the words of the narrator. In the linked citation from Psalm 95:11, however, God speaks directly to his people through David (*And again in the passage above he says, 'They shall never enter my rest'*). The introductory formula to this second citation follows the pattern already seen in 1:5, 6; 2:13, using the link word *again*. In this context, the implication is that God spoke twice about the same rest (Gen. 2:2 and Ps. 95:11), and that these texts reflect two different types of divine speech.

6–7. The implications of the preceding argument are drawn out (*Therefore*), first by affirming that *it still remains for some to enter that rest* (cf. 4:1). The failure of the wilderness generation is then retold in

---

16. This approach, which is called *gezera shawa*, works here because LXX Gen. 2:2 uses the Greek verb *katepausen* ('rested'), while LXX Ps. 95:11 uses the noun *katapausis* ('rest').

familiar terms: *those who formerly had the good news proclaimed to them did not go in because of their disobedience.* The expression *those who formerly had the good news proclaimed to them* recalls 4:2, while *did not go in because of their disobedience* recalls 3:18–19. But God confirmed the continuing possibility of entering his rest by speaking *a long time later* through David about another *day* in which to hear his voice and believe his promise. God did this in Psalm 95:7, when he *set a certain day, calling it 'Today'.* He established a new opportunity for his people 'to seize his invitation and persevere until they enter his "rest"' (Cockerill, p. 209).

8. *Joshua* is an implied type or forerunner of Christ in bringing God's redeemed people into their inheritance, though the author makes nothing of the fact that the Greek name for Joshua is *Iēsous* (Jesus). Joshua gave the Israelites an earthly rest that involved deliverance from their enemies, a measure of peace and prosperity in the land, and the blessing of God's presence in limited ways (Deut. 3:20; 12:9–10; 25:19; Josh. 1:15; 14:15; 21:44; 22:4; 23:1). The land given to Israel was sometimes described in Eden-like terms (e.g. Exod. 3:8; Num. 13:27; Deut. 8:6–9; 11:8–15), from which the Israelites would be excluded if they failed to honour God and keep his commands (Deut. 8:10–20; 11:16–32). Hebrews understands the overall structure of biblical revelation to mean that Joshua did not bring the people into the eternal rest mentioned in Genesis 2:2. If he had done so, *God would not have spoken later about another day* (Ps. 95:7), or warned a later generation living in the Promised Land about missing out on his rest (Ps. 95:11). Hebrews goes on to identify this as 'the promised eternal inheritance' secured by Jesus for his people (9:15).[17]

9. There is an echo of verse 6 here, with the word *then* (*ara*) introducing an inference from what has gone before. But a new term (*sabbatismos*) is used to identify what *remains . . . for the people of God.* In later Christian sources this term means more than

---

17. The author exposes a macro-typology concerning the 'rest' promised by God and implies that Jesus enables those who are called to experience the ultimate rest. Cf. Lane 1, p. 101; Goldsworthy, *Preaching*, pp. 97–114.

Sabbath-rest, referring rather to what takes place on the day of rest, namely a 'Sabbath celebration'. When God's rest is entered, there will be 'festivity and joy, expressed in the adoration and praise of God'.[18] Of course, thanksgiving, service and praise should be offered to God in this life (12:28; 13:15–16), but the author's focus in this verse is on eternal participation in the 'joyful assembly' of the heavenly Jerusalem (12:22–24; cf. 2:12).

10. The following argument supports what has just been said (*for* [*gar*]). A reference to the Son, who has ascended into heaven and is enthroned as the messianic high priest and ruler of his people, is suggested by a translation such as 'the one who has entered his rest has rested from his own works as God did from his' (cf. KJV, ASV, NASB, CSB). Jesus has gone ahead to open the way for us, and now rests from his works of redemption (4:14–16; 6:19–20; 9:12, 24; 10:19–25). This approach would strengthen the view that Joshua is presented as a type or forerunner of Christ in bringing his people into their inheritance (4:8).[19] However, NIV, NRSV, ESV and other versions more aptly take this verse to refer to believers, understanding the aorist participle *ho eiselthōn* to refer more generally to *anyone who enters* and rendering the aorist verb *katepausen* in a timeless fashion (*rests*). Just as God rested when he finished his work in creating (Gen. 2:2), so believers will cease the work that God has given them to do in this life when they enter his eternal rest (cf. Ellingworth, pp. 255–257). This work would include the sort of service to God and one another mentioned in 6:10; 10:24, 33–34; 13:1–7, 15–16. 'Rest' *from their works* will make it possible for them to participate fully in the 'Sabbath celebration' just mentioned. The author could have in mind the death of believers as the moment of entering God's rest (cf. 9:27; Rev. 14:13), or the return of Christ (10:36–39).

---

18. Lane 1, p. 102. Cf. Laansma, '*I Will Give You Rest*', pp. 295–300. This term is first attested in Hebrews and appears to derive from the verb *sabbatizō* ('observe or celebrate the Sabbath').

19. Cf. Attridge, p. 131. Cockerill (p. 211) explores this possibility, but he concludes that the author does not appear to have given his hearers sufficient clues to make this identification.

11. In a solemn climax to this section of the argument (*therefore*), a first-person plural form of exhortation is used again: *Let us . . . make every effort to enter that rest.* As in 4:1 (*let us be careful*), the pastor includes himself in the challenge, indicating again that this is a warning for every professing Christian. Contextually, the *effort* that is required is persistent faith in the promise of God about entering his rest (4:1–3a). The purpose clause that follows suggests that genuine faith will issue in obedience, not apostasy: *so that no one will perish by following their example of disobedience.*[20] The failure of the Israelites to enter the Promised Land in Numbers 14 was an *example of disobedience*, but its root cause was unbelief (3:16–19). Once again, the author is concerned about the perseverance of each individual in the church he addresses (*so that no one will perish*; cf. 3:12, 13; 4:1).

Theology

At the heart of biblical revelation lies the promise of entering God's rest. When God spoke in Genesis 2:2 about resting from all his works in creation, it was a sign of his gracious intention for humanity. God called Israel to experience something of that rest by living under his rule in the land he promised to them (e.g. Deut. 12:9–10; Josh. 21:44). But the generation he rescued from Egypt failed to enter that rest because of their unbelief and disobedience (3:7–11). They failed to share the faith of those who brought them the good news that they could seize their inheritance (4:1–2). Even when Joshua brought the next generation into the land, the word of God in Psalm 95:7–11 made it plain that the ultimate rest was yet to come (4:6–11). This is the rest promised in the gospel, which is the 'eternal inheritance' or 'enduring city' secured by the saving work of Jesus (9:15; 13:14). Only those who believe God's promises and continue to trust in the deliverer he has appointed for them enter that rest (4:3, 9–11).

---

20. NIV (*perish*) is a fair translation of *pesē* ('fall'). This verb can mean '*fall* in a transcendent or moral sense, *be completely ruined*' (BDAG). O'Brien (p. 173) takes this 'fall' to refer to God's judgment, noting that this accords well with the challenge in 4:12–13.

D. A warning about the power of God's word to expose and judge (4:12–13)

Context

These verses provide a compelling addition to the challenge of 4:1–11. The word of God is presented as the means he uses to expose and judge 'the thoughts and attitudes of the heart'. The focus turns in verse 13 to God himself, from whom 'nothing in all creation is hidden'. Indeed, 'Everything is uncovered and laid bare before the eyes of him to whom we must give account.' This is a confronting picture, but, linked to the previous claim, it is potentially a message of hope. By exposing sin, the word of God can sustain the faith of God's people in the present, until they finally stand before him as 'the Judge of all' (12:23).

Comment

12. The conjunction *For* (*gar*) links this verse to the warning about perishing through disobedience in verse 11. In this context, *the word of God* most obviously refers to Psalm 95. In various ways, the author has claimed that God continues to speak to his people through this text (3:7, 15; 4:3, 5, 7).[21] God is also said to have spoken through Genesis 2:2, which explains the 'rest' mentioned in Psalm 95:11, where the possibility of entering that rest is implicitly offered. The 'word' about inheriting God's rest that the Israelites heard is the same as the gospel that was preached to the recipients of Hebrews (4:1–2). The scriptures quoted by the author anticipated the message of the gospel. Even though *the word of God* is personified here, there is no ground for taking it as a reference to the Son of God in this context (cf. John 1:1–14; Rev. 19:13).

God's spoken word is *alive and active*, accomplishing what he desires and achieving the purpose for which he sends it (cf. Isa. 55:10–11; Jer. 1:12; 23:29). Sometimes, God's purpose in sending his word is to expose and judge the sin of his people. Hebrews conveys this idea by portraying God's word as being *Sharper than*

---

21. Hebrews regularly uses the word *logos* ('word') to refer to a divine communication (2:2; 4:2; 5:13; 6:1; 7:28; 12:19; 13:7).

any double-edged sword (Judg. 3:16; Ps. 149:6; Prov. 5:4; cf. Rev. 1:16; 2:12; 19:15). A sword that is sharpened on both edges will penetrate *even to dividing soul and spirit, joints and marrow.* The terms *soul and spirit* are used somewhat interchangeably by the author to describe the inner person (*psyche* ['soul'] in 6:19; 10:38, 39; 12:3; 13:17; *pneuma* ['spirits'] in 12:9, 23). *Joints and marrow* refer to the physical side of our existence and may be added to indicate that every aspect of our life is open to God and addressed by his word. But the Bible does not sharply distinguish between physical and psychological functions and the author is 'not concerned to provide here a psychological or anatomical analysis of the human condition' (Hughes, p. 165). These terms together simply point to 'the inmost recesses of human existence' (Ellingworth, p. 263). Penetrating like this into our lives, the word of God *judges the thoughts and attitudes of the heart.* As noted in connection with 3:12, *the heart* is another way of referring to the centre of a person, where reason, emotions and will interact. God's word judges our conscious and unconscious motivations and intentions. If we harden our hearts against his word, *he* is not deceived, but *we* miss out on the benefit of seeing ourselves as God sees us.

13. The searching effect of God's word holds us accountable to him personally. God knows everything about us, since literally 'no creature is invisible before him' (Ps. 139:1–12). He uses his word to expose 'all things' (*panta*), making us *uncovered* or 'naked' (*gymna*) and *laid bare* or 'helpless' (*tetrachēlismena*) in his eyes.[22] The reference to God as the one *to whom we must give account* points to his ultimate judgment of humanity (cf. 9:27; 10:26–31).[23] But his word can also bring to light every form of deceit and sin in advance of that terrible day. Such exposure is a blessing if it causes us to approach

---

22. This word can mean 'with neck twisted', as in a wrestling match when an opponent's windpipe is cut off to render him or her helpless (O'Brien, p. 178, esp. n. 142).

23. Although the verb *give* is not used here (cf. Luke 16:2; 1 Pet. 4:5), the judgment context is clear. Less likely is the view of Kleinig (pp. 220–221) that it refers to our response to God's word by our word to him in prayer and about him in confession.

God now through the high-priestly ministry of his Son to receive mercy and find grace (4:14–16).

Theology
The living God continues to address his people through his word, which is 'alive and active' (4:12). By way of example, Psalm 95:7–11 can expose sin in the deepest recesses of our being and warn us of the consequences of continuing unbelief and hardness of heart (3:7, 15; 4:3, 4, 5, 7). The Holy Spirit who inspired the biblical writings continues to speak through them, challenging those who are tempted to go astray. Persevering faith is maintained by willing exposure and response to the words of God in Scripture, pre-eminently the gospel, which promises salvation in the coming judgment of God. See Introduction 6b, 'God and Scripture'.

5. THE SON'S HIGH-PRIESTLY MINISTRY IS THE BASIS FOR PERSEVERING FAITH AND OBEDIENCE (4:14 – 5:10)

In the process of warning his hearers about the danger of hardening their hearts in unbelief and missing out on God's promised rest, the author has already included several encouragements. In this passage he picks up a number of key terms from the preceding chapters and develops the idea that Jesus is a merciful high priest.[1] As the one who offered himself in sinless obedience to the Father in suffering and death, he became 'the source of eternal salvation for all who obey him' (5:9). As the one who has ascended into heaven, he continues to 'empathize with our weaknesses' and enables us to 'approach God's throne of grace with confidence, so that we may receive mercy and find grace to help us in our time of need' (4:16).

---

1. The term 'high priest' appears in 2:17; 3:1; 4:14; 5:1, 5, 10, while the more general term 'priest' is found in 5:6. Both terms are used extensively in subsequent texts. 'Mercy' in 4:16 recalls 'merciful' in 2:17 and 'help' recalls the use of the related verb in 2:18. Other verbal links are noted in the commentary on 4:14–16.

The transitional exhortation in 4:14–16 'raises the readers' expectations and whets their appetite for the pastor's fuller explanation to follow' (Cockerill, p. 221). A typological comparison of Christ's high-priestly ministry with the ministry of Aaron in 5:1–10 indicates in advance that the central section of Hebrews will focus on Jesus as the perfected Son, who 'became the source of eternal salvation for all who obey him and was designated by God to be high priest in the order of Melchizedek'. A large inclusion is formed by the use of similar exhortations in 4:14–16 and 10:19–25, demonstrating the author's aim in speaking so extensively about the high-priestly ministry of Jesus. So this exhortation is a key element in the structure of Hebrews.

A. A challenge to hold firmly to the faith we profess and approach God with confidence for mercy and timely help (4:14–16)

Context
Two statements are made about what we 'have' in Christ (cf. 8:1; 10:21). The first simply affirms that 'we have a great high priest who has ascended into heaven' (v. 14). The second begins with a negative claim that highlights the significance of what is affirmed about Jesus: 'For we do not have a high priest who is unable to feel sympathy for our weaknesses, but we have one who has been tempted in every way, just as we are – yet he did not sin' (v. 15). The first statement is the basis for the exhortation 'let us hold firmly to the faith we profess' (v. 14), while the second supports the exhortation to 'approach God's throne of grace with confidence, so that we may receive mercy and find grace to help us in our time of need' (v. 16).

Comment
14. The conjunction *Therefore* (*oun*) marks the continuation of a developing argument. The term *high priest* was first used in 2:17, where it was announced that the Son of God became fully human in every way in order to become a merciful and faithful high priest in service to God. The faithfulness of Jesus as 'our apostle and high priest' was articulated in 3:1–6 to encourage continuing trust in

him. That emphasis continues in 4:14 with the exhortation *let us hold firmly to the faith we profess*.² Literally, the challenge is to hold on to 'the confession' (*tēs homologias*), which may have been a formal confession of faith that the pastor shared with his audience (3:1; 10:23). But the next two verses also focus on the way Jesus is experienced as merciful.

Our high priest is *great* because of who he is (*Jesus the Son of God*) and because of what he achieved.³ He suffered and died to 'make atonement for the sins of the people' (2:17) and *has ascended into heaven*. NRSV has 'who has passed through the heavens', which is a better rendering of the Greek. This suggests 'a spatial journey that penetrates through the heavenly realms into God's presence' (Johnson, p. 139; cf. 9:24). This claim is important for the author's argument and will be expanded and explained more fully in subsequent passages (6:19–20; 7:23–26; 9:11–12, 24). Jesus has secured an access to God that is not available by any other means.

15. The conjunction *For* signals that what follows confirms the greatness of our high priest and gives further ground for trusting in him. A double negative statement (*we do not have a high priest who is unable to feel sympathy for our weaknesses*) actually means that we *have* such a caring high priest! This assurance is important, because the claim that he has 'passed through the heavens' could be taken to mean that he is now remote from our struggles. Furthermore, the pastor intends to compare Jesus with the high priests who were 'subject to weakness' and supposed to 'deal gently with those who are ignorant and are going astray' (5:2). Put positively, the ascended Christ is able to *feel sympathy for our weaknesses* (KJV, 'be touched with the feeling of our infirmities'),⁴ because he has been *tempted in every*

---

2. The challenge of 3:6, 14 to 'hold firmly' is repeated here with a different verb (*kratōmen*).

3. In LXX Lev. 21:10; Num. 35:25, 28, 32; Hag. 1:1, 12, 14; 2:3; Zech. 3:1, 9; 6:11, 'the great priest' is the high priest (cf. Heb. 10:21). The adjective *great* (*megan*) is not redundant in Heb. 4:14, but expresses the superiority of Christ as high priest.

4. The verb *sympathēsai* is used to convey more than feelings of compassion: 'it always includes the element of active help (cf. 10:34; 4 Macc. 4:25; 13:23)'

way, just as we are – yet he did not sin. Although *weaknesses* could cover a broad range of physical or emotional conditions, the context specifically concerns vulnerability to sin (cf. 5:2; 7:27–28).

The testing of Jesus through suffering was mentioned in 2:18, where we were told that he was equipped by his earthly experience to 'help those who are being tempted [or 'tested']' (cf. 12:3). Testing situations tempt people to sin against God, and so *tempted* is a valid translation of the verb in both verses.[5] *In every way* recalls 2:17, where it is said that the Son of God had to be made like those he came to save, 'fully human in every way'. However, the emphasis now is on his experiencing every form of testing and temptation that his people do, 'because of his likeness to us' (NEB, 'one who, because of his likeness to us, has been tested every way').[6] The pastor is emphasizing the extent of Jesus' identification with our struggle against sin, though it would be reading too much into the text to say that he was faced with every specific temptation that exists. In every aspect of his earthly life, he consistently rejected the pressure to disobey God and be faithless.

Although tested in every way, *yet he did not sin* (he was 'without sin' [NRSV, ESV]), implying that sinlessness was a proven reality throughout his life (cf. Matt. 4:1–11; John 7:18; 8:46; 2 Cor. 5:21; 1 Pet. 1:19; 2:21–23). The Son of God 'offered himself unblemished to God' (9:14) in a perfectly obedient human life that culminated in his sacrificial death (10:5–10). As the true man and ideal high priest (7:26–28), he resisted sin and remained faithful to the end (3:2; 12:2), so that he could rescue fallen humanity from the consequences of sin (2:5–10; 13:12). This teaching does not question the

---

(note 4 *cont.*) (Lane 1, p. 114). 'Empathize with' may convey the meaning better, as in the American version of NIV (2011).

5. Cf. Ellingworth, p. 191. O'Brien (p. 183 n. 171) argues that the perfect passive participle *pepeirasmenon* may express intensity ('he was severely tested'). Alternatively, it may have a stative meaning, indicating that even in his heavenly exaltation he remains a 'tested' high priest.

6. It is more natural to understand *kath' homoiotēta* to mean 'according to his likeness to us' than 'according to the likeness of our temptations'. Cf. Peterson, *Hebrews and Perfection*, p. 78; O'Brien, pp. 183–184.

reality of his humanity, as argued by some. Rather, like Adam in Genesis 2, Jesus is portrayed as having no history of sin before he was tempted. Unlike Adam, however, Jesus remained true to his calling and never sinned. He reversed the effects of Adam's rebellion by his obedience to the point of death (2:14–18; cf. Rom. 5:12–21).[7]

16. The conjunction *then* (*oun*) signifies that the pastor will now explain the implications of the preceding verse. As in 4:1–3, 11, 14, he includes himself in the first-person plural exhortation *Let us . . . approach*. The verb *proserchomai* ('approach, draw near') is highly significant in the argument of Hebrews. It is applied to the Israelites who came before the LORD at Sinai to receive his words through Moses (12:18; cf. Exod. 16:9), and subsequently to offer sacrifices through the mediation of priests (10:1; cf. Lev. 9:5). The people could draw near to stand before the LORD at a distance, and priests without defects could draw near to the altar to make offerings on their behalf (Lev. 9:7, 8; 21:17, 21, 23; 22:3). Fundamentally, the person who draws near to God must seek him in faith (Heb. 11:6; cf. Jas 4:8). But 'a new and living way' to approach God has been opened by the high-priestly ministry of Jesus (10:20–22). A 'better hope' has been introduced by which we 'draw near to God' (7:19, using the synonym *engizein*).

Christians who have 'come' to God trusting in Jesus and his 'sprinkled blood' already belong to the heavenly city that is their ultimate destination (12:22–24; compare 13:14). But the exhortation to 'keep drawing near' to God through Jesus (4:16; 10:19–22) is a challenge to experience the continuing benefits of that initial approach to God and the relationship flowing from it. The perfect tense in 12:22 highlights the fact that Christians have drawn near to God in their conversion, whereas the imperfective aspect of the verb in 4:16 and 10:22 (*proserchōmetha*) 'views the action as open-ended: the "approach" should therefore be ongoing or occur again and again' (O'Brien, p. 185 n. 181). Jesus the crucified and glorified Son always lives to intercede for those who 'come to God through

---

7. Cf. Peterson, *Hebrews and Perfection*, pp. 188–190; Schreiner,
   pp. 153–154.

him' (7:25). Drawing near is the alternative to 'turning away' and the antidote to 'shrinking back' (3:12; 6:6; 10:38–39).

More specifically in 4:16, drawing near to God through the high-priestly mediation of Jesus suggests a specific form of prayer.[8] Coming 'to the throne of grace' means approaching God as 'an unusually generous king who makes himself available daily for an audience with his subjects in the throne room of his palace' (Kleinig, p. 232). In 10:19–20 this is equated with entering by faith 'the Most Holy Place', which means approaching the Holy One in heaven. This is to be done *with confidence* (*parrēsia*, as in 3:6), which is not self-generated, but is given through the gospel and made possible by 'the blood of Jesus' (10:19).[9] God can only be approached as 'the Judge of all' because Jesus as 'the mediator of a new covenant' provided the perfect sacrifice for our sins (12:22–24). 'Christ's high-priestly ministry has achieved for believers what Israel never enjoyed, namely immediate access to God and freedom to draw near to him continually' (O'Brien, p. 186).

The specific reason for continuing to draw near to God is to *receive mercy and find grace to help us in our time of need*. God's *mercy* was supremely expressed in Jesus' death for the forgiveness of our sins (8:12; 10:17–18), and that forgiveness can be appropriated at any time (cf. 1 John 1:9). The term *grace* (*charis*) has a wider meaning here. It was expressed in Jesus' substitutionary death (2:9), but also in the gift of his Spirit (10:29), and it continues to be experienced in the timely help (*eukairos*, 'well timed') he gives to those facing testing and temptation (2:18).[10] When we fail him, we can receive

---

8. The verb *proserchomai* is used in some OT contexts to signify approaching God in prayer (e.g. LXX Jer. 7:16; Ps. 33:6 [ET 34:5]) or approaching someone else with a request (LXX Jer. 49:1–2 [ET 42:1–2]). The synonymous verb *engizō* relates to prayer in Gen. 18:23.

9. The term *parrēsia* was used outside the NT for frankness or plainness of speech, sometimes signifying openness or boldness in a public situation or before someone of high rank (BDAG). Cf. Marrow, '*Parrēsia*', pp. 431–446; Kleinig, pp. 171–174.

10. The word *eleos* ('mercy') in the LXX usually translates words denoting God's faithful covenant love (e.g. Josh. 2:14; 2 Sam. 2:6; 15:20).

mercy from him, and when we struggle to be faithful and persevere, we can find *grace to help us in our time of need*. Given these provisions, no-one should 'fall short of the grace of God' and miss out on the heavenly inheritance (12:15)!

Theology

The high-priestly significance of Jesus' testing and suffering was signalled in 2:17–18 and it is here developed in relation to the continuing needs of his people. The Son who always existed with the Father, and was destined to inherit all things, shared in our humanity to the extent that, because of his likeness to us, he has been tested in every way, yet without sin (4:15). More will be said about his trials in 5:7–9 and much remains to be said about the significance of Jesus' ascension for us (6:19–20; 7:11–28; 8:1–6; 9:11–12, 24–26; 10:12–14). Here, however, the practical implications of his incarnate life and heavenly exaltation are simply stated. With Jesus as our mediator, we can 'hold firmly to the faith we profess' and 'approach God's throne of grace with confidence, so that we may receive mercy and find grace to help us in our time of need' (4:14, 16).

B. The perfecting of the Son as 'the source of eternal salvation for all who obey him' (5:1–10)

Context

Three times in the argument so far Jesus has been described as high priest (2:17; 3:1; 4:14). A formal comparison is now made between high-priestly ministry under the Mosaic law (vv. 1–4) and the high-priestly ministry of Jesus (vv. 5–10). This lays the foundation for much of the argument to come (6:13 – 10:18), especially the idea that his sacrifice inaugurates a new covenant and a new way of relating to God. There is a distinctive echo of 5:1–3 in 7:27–28,

---

Charis ('grace, favour') in the combination 'find favour' can relate to a person's experience of God (e.g. Gen. 6:8; 18:3) or describe 'the gift of a favourable relationship with a socially superior person' (Kleinig, p. 228; e.g. Gen. 39:4; 2 Sam. 14:22).

where the contrast between Jesus and 'the other high priests' comes to a climax. A chiastic structure can be seen in 5:1–10, with the points made in verses 1–4 being considered again in reverse order in verses 5–10 as they apply to Christ:[11]

> *High-priestly ministry under the Mosaic law*
> v. 1   General description of role
>   vv. 2–3 Effectiveness, humanity and sacrifice
>   v. 4 The necessary calling
> *The high-priestly ministry of the Son of God*
>   vv. 5–6 The necessary calling
>   vv. 7–9 Sacrifice, humanity and effectiveness
> v. 10 General description of role

Comment

1. *Every high priest is selected from among the people* refers to the priesthood instituted by God to minister in accordance with the law given to Moses (v. 4). These men were *appointed to represent the people in matters related to God* and were leaders of a large body of appropriately ordained priests (Lev. 8 – 9). The same Greek expression that is here translated *in matters related to God* (*ta pros ton theon*) is rendered 'in service to God' in 2:17. A purpose clause follows, indicating that they were to do this by offering *gifts and sacrifices for sins*. *Gifts and sacrifices* most likely describes 'all the public offerings that were presented each day for God's people (7:27) and each year on the Day of Atonement (10:1–3)'.[12] The phrase *for sins* puts the focus on the atoning work of the high priest (2:17), the preposition *for* (*hyper*) meaning either 'for the sake of' or 'with reference to' in this context. The sacrificial system enabled sinful Israelites to draw

---

11. Cockerill (p. 230) notes that 'the present tense of general description' is used in 5:1–4, whereas the aorist tense in 5:5–10 is used for 'the acts and events through which Christ fulfilled his high priesthood'. I have followed Cockerill (pp. 231–232) in defining the way vv. 2–3 are compared and contrasted in vv. 7–9.

12. Kleinig, pp. 248–249. Kleinig (pp. 256–257) outlines the broad use of *dōra* ('gifts') and *thysia* ('sacrifices') in the LXX. Cf. Heb. 8:3; 9:9.

near to God through priestly mediation at an earthly sanctuary
(10:1–4).

2–3. An unexpected factor is introduced into the argument with
the claim that *He is able to deal gently with those who are ignorant and are
going astray.* The verb *metriopathein* (*deal gently*) means 'to moderate
one's feelings' (BDAG) and is often used in contexts outside the
Bible where the moderation of anger is involved.[13] It is closely
related to *sympathēsai* (4:15), but it is more muted in meaning. The
Old Testament does not mention the need for the high priest to
function in this way, but Hebrews suggests that it was essential for
effectively dealing with *those who are ignorant and are going astray.* This
expression recalls the requirement that sacrifices of atonement be
offered for those who sinned 'unintentionally' (Lev. 4:2; 5:15; Num.
15:22–29; cf. Heb. 9:7).[14] The high priest could have been justifiably
angry with repeat offenders, but needed to remember that he too
was *subject to weakness* or 'clothed' with weakness (ESV, 'beset with
weakness'), just as they were.[15] Indeed, the high priest had to *offer
sacrifices for his own sins, as well as for the sins of the people* (cf. Lev. 4:3–12;
9:7–14; 16:6–17). This provision was a reminder of his own fallen
nature and need for God's mercy. But Jesus needed no such
sacrifice (7:27), since he was a man without sin (4:15).

4–6. According to the law of Moses, no-one could take the
honour of being high priest on himself, *but he receives it when called by
God.* After Aaron was appointed and ordained according to the
ritual given by God (Exod. 28:1–5, 29–30; Num. 3:10), subsequent
generations of priests had to be physically descended from Aaron
to share in this honour. Although the author says *In the same way*
[ESV, 'So also'], *Christ did not take on himself the glory of becoming a high*

---

13. Attridge, p. 143 n. 89; W. Michaelis, 'μετριοπαθέω', *TDNT* 5, p. 938.

14. The combination *tois agnoousin kai planōmenois* (*those who are ignorant
and are going astray*) can be understood to mean 'go astray through
ignorance'. Sins that were deliberate ('with a high hand') could not
be atoned for by the regular sacrificial system (Kleinig, pp. 240–241,
esp. n. 13).

15. The verb *perikeitai* can mean 'clothed' or 'burdened' (Cockerill, p. 234
n. 26).

priest, in 7:11–17 he indicates that something more than physical descent from Aaron and formal ordination was necessary. A new and different order of priesthood required a different form of divine authorization. This was given by God in Psalm 110:4 (*You are a priest for ever, / in the order of Melchizedek*), which is prefaced here by another text in which God addresses his Son directly (Ps. 2:7, *You are my Son*).

Psalm 2:7 was used in 1:5 to confirm that the eternally existent Son of God, who provided purification for sins in his earthly ministry (1:3), has been exalted to the right hand of God to fulfil the destiny of the promised Son of David. But God also speaks directly to his Son *in another place*, when he identifies him as *a priest for ever, in the order of Melchizedek* (Ps. 110:4), the significance of which is to be explained in 7:11–28. These two citations are brought together to show 'the vital connection between Jesus as Son of God and as high priest for the Christology of Hebrews' (O'Brien, p. 197). Jesus used the opening verse of Psalm 110 to challenge the understanding of his contemporaries about the heavenly rule and authority of the Messiah (Mark 12:35–37 par.). The importance of that text for the argument of Hebrews can be seen in 1:3, 13; 8:1; 10:12; 12:2. But the author takes the further step of explaining how the fourth verse of the psalm identifies the Messiah's priestly role and function (5:10; 6:20; 7:11–28; 8:1–2).

7. A graphic description of the earthly experience of this high priest is introduced by the expression *During the days of Jesus' life on earth* (ESV, 'In the days of his flesh').[16] Jesus *offered up prayers and petitions with fervent cries and tears to the one who could save him from death*. There are echoes of the agony of Jesus in the Garden of Gethsemane here (Mark 14:32–42 par.), though the words *with fervent cries*

---

16. Kleinig (pp. 250–251) argues that the Son was only *prepared* for his heavenly priesthood by his earthly life. But this unnaturally separates his sacrificial self-offering from his heavenly application of its benefits. As the one appointed high priest in the order of Melchizedek, Jesus fulfils the pattern of sacrifice required of the Aaronic high priests in his life, death, ascension and heavenly session (7:25–28; 9:11–12; 10:11–14).

and tears find no exact parallel in the narratives of that incident. These words recall some of the psalms in which a righteous sufferer calls out to God for deliverance (e.g. Pss 6:4–5; 13:3–4; 18:4–6; 22:19–21). The author may have had in mind a pattern of prayer throughout the life of Jesus, culminating in Gethsemane and the cross (cf. Mark 15:34 par.; Luke 23:34, 46). Only in Gethsemane, however, did Jesus explicitly pray for the cup of suffering to be taken away from him (Mark 14:36 par.). The description of God as *the one who could save him from death* could point to that cry, when Jesus was 'under the dread of death and seeking escape from it'.[17] Hebrews uses the sacrificial term *offered* in a novel way to include the prayers of Jesus in the process by which he presented himself in life and death to his Father as a sacrifice for the sins of his people (9:14, 25, 28; 10:10, 12, 14, 18).

The claim that *he was heard because of his reverent submission* reflects the second stage of Jesus' prayers in Gethsemane (Mark 14:36, 'Yet not what I will, but what you will'; cf. John 12:28). The word translated *reverent submission* (*eulabeia*) was regularly used in Greek literature with the sense of being 'cautious about giving offense to deities' or 'reverent awe in the presence of God' (BDAG; cf. Heb. 12:28). Given the emphasis on the Son's obedience in the next verse, *reverent submission* or 'godly fear' is a good rendering. Some argue that the term means 'fear of death' here and that Jesus was simply *heard* in the sense of being delivered from anxiety, but this is less likely. *He was heard*, 'not with respect to his immediate object, exemption from death, but with regard to his final and ultimate object . . . agreement with the will of the Father' (Spicq 2, p. 115 [my translation]). Jesus obtained deliverance from death through bodily resurrection (13:20; cf. Acts 2:31–32) because he submitted to the Father's will in dying for the salvation of his people (cf. 2:14–15).[18]

---

17. Peterson, *Hebrews and Perfection*, p. 87. John 12:27–28 offers something of a parallel to the two-stage prayer of Jesus in Gethsemane recorded in the Synoptic Gospels.

18. Cockerill (p. 245 n. 75) similarly concludes that 'the Son did not actually pray for the resurrection, although his prayer was answered in the resurrection/exaltation'.

8. The identity of Jesus as *Son* is recalled (1:2–13; 3:6; 4:14; 5:5), as the author introduces the paradox that *he learned obedience from what he suffered*.[19] There is much in ancient Greek literature about the educative value of suffering (cf. Croy, *Endurance*, pp. 139–144), and this is also reflected in some biblical texts (e.g. Prov. 3:11–12, which is the basis of the argument in Heb. 12:5–11). But there is nothing in the Gospel records to indicate that Jesus had weaknesses that needed to be overcome or patterns of behaviour that needed to be corrected. His suffering was more like that of Moses, Elijah and Jeremiah, who were attacked and defamed because they were God's prophets (cf. 12:2–3). The Servant of the LORD is similarly portrayed in Isaiah 50:4–9 as willingly submitting to suffering in the cause of his prophetic ministry. The Servant's suffering climaxes in his redemptive death, as described in Isaiah 53 (cf. Heb. 7:27; 9:28). The sequence of thought in Hebrews 5:7–9 is similar.

Experiences of suffering prior to the cross, and especially in Gethsemane, were the means by which the incarnate Son learned to express obedience to the will of his Father and become 'the source of eternal salvation for all who obey him' (v. 9; cf. 2:15–17; 10:10–11). He was prepared for the ultimate act of obedience in his sacrificial death by the various forms of testing he endured throughout his earthly life. But he also needed to be equipped for his continuing role as an empathetic high priest, who could effectively apply the benefits of his saving work to his people (4:15; 7:25; cf. 2:18). For this, he needed to experience 'just what obedience to God involved in practice, in the conditions of human life on earth' (Bruce, p. 103).

9. The expression *once made perfect* (*teleiōtheis*) embraces the earthly experience of the Son of God outlined in verses 7–8, recalling the claim that he was perfected as 'the pioneer of their salvation' through what he suffered (2:10). God the Father is the implied agent who 'perfected' him in both contexts (see also 7:28). The Greek verb should not be understood ethically ('attained

---

19. The Greek expression *kaiper ōn hyios* is clearly concessive and could be translated 'Son though he was' to highlight the paradox in the sentence more emphatically.

moral perfection'), or in a narrowly cultic sense ('was consecrated priest'), but more broadly with a vocational meaning: Jesus was qualified through suffering as the Son who was destined to become the source of salvation for others. Some would restrict his perfecting to his resurrection and ascension, viewing this as the outcome of his suffering. As noted previously, however, the three contexts where his perfecting is mentioned (2:10; 5:9; 7:28) together suggest that it involved his proving in temptation and suffering, his sacrificial offering of himself in death, and his heavenly exaltation and enthronement as the triumphant priest-king of Psalm 110:1, 4 (cf. Peterson, *Hebrews and Perfection*, pp. 96–103). Specifically in this context, he was 'qualified' or 'made completely adequate' as the obedient Son and *became the source of eternal salvation for all who obey him.*

The Son's effectiveness as high priest far outstrips that of his Aaronic predecessors (5:1–3), providing 'permanent access to life in fellowship with God' (Cockerill, p. 250). Jesus is the source of *eternal salvation*, because he has secured 'an eternal redemption' from sin and death (9:12), mediated a new covenant that is eternal in its effect (13:20) and opened the way to 'the promised eternal inheritance' (9:15). Eternal salvation is *for all who obey him*, not in the sense that it is earned by obedience, but because genuine faith will express itself in obedience (3:18–19; 4:2–3; 6:9–12; 10:26–29; 11:8). Those who rely on the Son as their only means of salvation will be moved to obey him in every area of their lives. Jesus models the pattern of obedience that is God's will for all his people (10:5–10; 12:1–3). Obedience to God's will from the heart is one of the benefits of the New Covenant promised in 8:10 (cf. Jer. 31:33). See Introduction 6c, 'Eschatology and salvation'.

10. NIV implies that the Son's appointment as high priest followed his perfecting as the source of eternal salvation (*and was designated by God to be high priest in the order of Melchizedek*). But the aorist passive participle here should not be translated in a sequential way (*and was designated*), since it more obviously refers back to the citation of Psalm 110:4 in verse 6 (NRSV, 'having been designated'). Without doubt, the heavenly ascension and enthronement of Jesus was essential for the exercise of his eternal high priesthood *in the order of Melchizedek* (cf. 4:14; 7:11–28), but the author's point is not that Jesus 'became' that high priest through heavenly exaltation.[20] Rather, having been designated high priest in Psalm 110:4, he assumed that role by fulfilling the type or pattern of the Aaronic priesthood, offering himself as the perfect sacrifice for our sins on earth and entering the heavenly sanctuary, there to appear for us in God's presence (9:11–12, 24). Put another way, 5:5–9 implies that he 'became' high priest in the process of 'proving and accrediting himself as the Son'.[21]

Theology

A comparison is drawn here between the ministry of the Aaronic high priests and the superior ministry of Jesus in its earthly and heavenly phases. Jesus lived a life of prayerful dependence on his Father, as he sought to do his will, and learned obedience from what he suffered (vv. 7–8). This obedience culminated in his sacrificial death for sin and exaltation to God's right hand, enabling him to become 'the source of eternal salvation for all who obey him' (v. 9). His perfecting through sufferings as the pioneer of their salvation (2:10) is thus more fully explained. But his designation by God as high priest in the order of Melchizedek is a new idea (vv. 6, 10), which remains to be explored (v. 11; 6:20; 7:1–28). Put simply, the incarnation, death and heavenly exaltation of the Son fulfil Psalm 110:1 *and* 4, qualifying Jesus to reign for ever in God's presence as our eternal mediator. As heavenly high priest, he continues to make it possible for us to draw near to God through him, 'because he always lives to intercede for' us (7:25).

---

20. Cockerill (p. 239) concludes from the association of Ps. 110:4 with Ps. 2:7 and Ps. 110:1 that 'God proclaimed him High Priest at his exaltation', but it would be better to say that what was revealed in those psalm texts came to full expression in Christ's exaltation and enthronement. See note 16 above.

21. G. Schrenk, 'ἀρχιερεύς', *TDNT* 3, p. 279. Cf. Peterson, *Hebrews and Perfection*, pp. 191–195.

6. A CHALLENGE TO AVOID SLUGGISHNESS AND FULLY REALIZE THE HOPE SET BEFORE US (5:11 – 6:12)

The importance of Psalm 110:4 for understanding the nature of Jesus' high-priestly work and its implications was signalled in 5:6, 10. But, before the pastor develops that argument, he pauses to warn his hearers about a condition that could prevent them from maturing as Christians and expose them to the possibility of falling away. He fears that they have become 'sluggish in hearing' (5:11; NIV, 'you no longer try to understand'), which could result in them becoming 'sluggish' in a more general way (6:12, 'become lazy'). In between these two applications of the same Greek term (*nōthroi*), he more fully exposes the problem of spiritual lethargy that he perceives in this community of believers (5:11 – 6:3), developing and applying the warnings previously given (2:1–4; 3:7 – 4:13). He highlights the awful consequences of professing faith and falling away (6:4–8), but then expresses confidence that his hearers will heed his warning and urges them to persevere in faith, hope and love 'to the very end' (6:9–12). This positive note of encouragement continues in 6:13–20, where the prospect of inheriting what God has promised introduces an extended reflection on the ministry of

Jesus as 'high priest for ever, in the order of Melchizedek' (7:1–28). Different styles of rhetoric in 5:11 – 6:12 seek to elicit a series of emotions – shame, trust, fear and optimism – to move the hearers to benefit from the important teaching he is about to give them.

A. The pathway to maturity in Christ (5:11 – 6:3)

Context
The first paragraph in this exhortation rebukes those addressed for their reluctance to listen and learn, and thus progress to spiritual maturity (5:11–14). Their need for 'milk', not 'solid food', hinders them from teaching others and reaching that state whereby their senses are adequately trained to distinguish between good and evil. The second paragraph (6:1–3) is an encouragement to be taken forward to maturity by paying close attention to the argument that follows. They are to make progress by building on the foundational teaching they have already received. In short, 'they stand in need of renewed commitment and obedience to Christ, based upon deeper insight into what they profess' (O'Brien, p. 206).

Comment
   11. Using the literary convention of speaking about himself in the first-person plural, the pastor admits that he has *much to say* about the matters outlined in verses 8–10, but his message (*logos*) is 'hard to explain' (ESV). There is a complexity to the argument he will unfold about Jesus being 'a high priest for ever, in the order of Melchizedek', who fulfils the ministry of the Aaronic high priesthood, inaugurates the New Covenant and opens the way for believers to enter the promised eternal inheritance (6:13 – 10:18). However, the difficulty is not simply with the subject matter, but with the attitude of those addressed (*because you no longer try to under-stand*). The Greek expression *nōthroi tais akouais* means 'sluggish in hearing' (ESV, 'dull of hearing'). This recalls previous warnings about paying the most careful attention to what has been heard in the gospel (2:1) and heeding God's voice in Scripture (3:7–19; 4:12–13). Now the point is made that the recipients need to hear the specific message the pastor himself wishes to give them, implying that this is a further way of listening to God and avoiding

apostasy. The issue is not simply an unwillingness to progress to a higher stage of understanding the Christian message, but an unwillingness to work out its deeper implications and respond appropriately.[1]

12. Evidence that the audience has become reluctant to listen is now given (*kai gar*, 'for indeed' [NIV, *In fact*]). Sufficient time has passed since they became Christians for them to be teaching others (*by this time you ought to be teachers*). Elsewhere in the New Testament, *teachers* are identified as those with particular gifts for instructing the faithful (Rom. 12:7; 1 Cor. 12:28–29; Eph. 4:11). Here, however, the term is most likely used to describe the sort of mutual instruction that might be given by Christians to one another (3:13; 10:24–25; cf. Col. 3:16). It may also include making a confident confession of their faith before unbelieving outsiders (10:35; 13:15; cf. 1 Pet. 3:15–16).[2] Their unwillingness to teach others is linked to a perceived need for someone to teach them *the elementary truths of God's word all over again*. The word *again* also occurs in 6:1, where the pastor advises against 'laying again' the foundation of basic Christian teaching. He may be speaking ironically and reflecting back to them what they have previously expressed to him, but when he says *You need milk, not solid food*, he exposes their passivity and failure to mature as Christians. He does not agree to feed them more milk!

Their resistance to moving on is surprising in view of what is later said about the faith, hope and love they showed in earlier days (10:32–35). Perhaps they anticipated more persecution and suffering and were inclined to shrink back from the sort of wholehearted commitment to Christ previously demonstrated (10:36–39). Their anxiety 'may have been exacerbated by disappointment that Christ had not yet returned (1:14; 10:36–39) or by their failure to realize and appropriate his full sufficiency as Savior' (Cockerill, p. 17). Their failure to advance was actually a form of retreat. *The elementary*

---

1. Cf. Peterson, *Hebrews and Perfection*, pp. 177–178; Holmes, *Sublime Rhetoric*, pp. 182–186.

2. The pastor appears to shame his audience 'for not being sufficiently proactive in their profession of faith and reinforcement of one another's commitment' (deSilva, p. 214).

truths of God's word are more literally 'the basic principles of the oracles of God' (ESV). The word translated *elementary* (*stoicheia*) is generally used for the basic components of something, and hence for 'things that constitute the foundation of learning, fundamental principles' (BDAG; cf. Gal. 4:3, 9; Col. 2:8, 20; 2 Pet. 3:10, 12). 'The oracles of God' (*tōn logiōn tou theou*) is a way of speaking about Scripture (Rom. 3:2; cf. Acts 7:38; 1 Pet. 4:11). These basic biblical principles, which have come to full and final expression in the gospel, are also called 'the elementary teachings about Christ' in 6:1.

13–14. The contrast in the previous verse between *milk* and *solid food* is now developed. To some extent, this exhortation follows the pattern of Hellenistic philosophers, who sought to move people from an elementary to an advanced stage of instruction and understanding. For the author of Hebrews, however, the issues are not simply intellectual or moral. The person *who lives on milk* is 'unskilled in the word of righteousness' (ESV), and for this reason remains a spiritual infant (cf. 1 Cor. 3:1–3; Eph. 4:13–16). Intellectual, moral and spiritual dimensions are linked here.[3] Arrested spiritual growth is a dangerous position in which to remain (6:1–8).

The expression *logou dikaiosynēs* (ESV, 'the word of righteousness') has been variously interpreted (cf. Lane 1, pp. 137–138; deSilva, pp. 212–214). Most likely, it is another way of referring to 'the oracles of God', which expose the true nature of righteousness, hence NIV *the teaching about righteousness*. Elsewhere in Hebrews, 'righteousness' describes behaviour that arises from faith and reflects the character and will of God (1:9; 7:2; 11:7, 33; 12:11). Although the author does not explicitly say so, such righteousness is one of the outcomes of the New Covenant that Christ has inaugurated (8:10–12; 10:15–18; cf. Rom. 6:16–20; 8:1–4).

The moral dimension of the author's challenge continues to emerge when he describes the mature as 'those who because of their mature state have their powers of discernment trained

---

3. The Greek adjective *apeiros* can mean 'unacquainted', signifying 'lack of knowledge', but the context suggests that 'unskilled' might be a better rendering (lacking the capacity to understand and apply). Cf. BDAG.

to distinguish good from evil' (my translation).[4] But this ability to distinguish good and evil from God's perspective arises from properly discerning what Scripture teaches and putting it into practice (cf. Prov. 1 – 9; Matt. 7:24–27). So *solid food is for the mature*, who have experienced 'the word of righteousness' as the means to discern the will of God and desire to be sustained by it in a pattern of life that pleases God. Nevertheless, as the pastor goes on to show, the immature also need solid food if they are to develop as Christians. Babies are weaned from their mothers' milk by gradually being given solids!

6:1–3. Using the first-person plural in a different way from 5:11, the pastor calls upon his hearers to cooperate with his plan to feed them solid food: *Therefore let us move beyond the elementary teachings about Christ and be taken forward to maturity.* NIV rightly brings out the sense of the passive verb *pherōmetha* ('let us be taken forward, borne along'), which suggests God's action in their lives. The pastor hopes this will happen as he teaches and they willingly receive and digest his solid food (cf. v. 3, 'if God permits'). Although the Greek (*aphentes*) means 'leave', NIV has rightly translated *move beyond*, because the image changes to *not laying again the foundation*. This metaphor conjures up the absurd picture of someone laying again the foundation of a building, but never adding to it! Christians should continually build on the spiritual foundation they have been given, not abandon it altogether.[5]

The *foundation* in 6:1 is 'the message of the beginning of Christ' (*ton tēs archēs tou Christou logon*). This could mean 'the message about how to begin with Christ' or 'the message that is foundational for understanding and following Christ'. In Graeco-Roman philosophical schools, the foundation (*themelios*) was a common expression for elementary instruction, 'referring to the basic tenets

---

4. The noun *exis* does not refer to a process (NIV, *by constant use*), but to the result of a process, namely here 'a state of maturity' (BDAG). 'The spiritual senses of the mature have been trained by exercise in the life of faith' (Cockerill, p. 259).

5. Compare Paul's challenge in 1 Cor. 3:10–15 to build appropriately on the foundation laid by his preaching about Christ.

on which the entire edifice of a life lived in accordance with that philosophy can be lived' (deSilva, p. 216). Surprisingly, however, the summary that follows is not Christologically focused. It consists of biblical themes that are basic to the gospel (*resurrection of the dead, eternal judgment*), moral challenges that are essential responses to the gospel (*repentance from acts that lead to death, faith in God*), and ritual issues that were apparently of special concern to the recipients of Hebrews (*instruction about cleansing rites, the laying on of hands*). These six elements suggest that those addressed came from a synagogue background, even if some had been Gentile converts to Judaism or inquirers, and that conversion to Christ necessitated some re-thinking of this teaching in relation to the gospel.[6] The pastor is concerned to deepen and extend their knowledge of Christ and what he accomplished, so that they can persevere as Christians and 'inherit what has been promised' (v. 12).

As indicated in 5:11–14, Christian *maturity* has intellectual, moral and spiritual dimensions. The noun used here (*teleiotēta*) corresponds with the reference to 'the mature' in 5:14 (*teleioi*). Maturity cannot simply be equated with perfection, though the teaching about perfection in Hebrews is central to the author's method of moving his audience along to maturity.[7] The topics listed in 6:1–2 require further biblical and theological reflection, appropriate moral responses, and the development of a gospel-driven spirituality. The author does not leave the foundational issues completely behind, but he develops them in a Christ-centred fashion within the framework of the biblical-theological argument to come. Divine *judgment* is often mentioned (2:2–3; 3:7 – 4:13; 6:8; 9:27;

---

6. Attridge (p. 163) describes these elements as 'a catalogue of Jewish catechesis'. These Jewish beliefs and practices were possibly used as a foundation for expounding Christian claims in the community addressed by Hebrews. See Introduction 3–4.

7. These terms are cognates of the verb 'perfect' (*teleioō*), which is used in relation to Christ (2:10; 5:9; 7:28) and believers (7:11, 19; 9:9; 10:1, 14; 11:40; 12:23). Believers are perfected by the finished work of Christ, but maturity is a goal yet to be achieved (6:1). Cf. Peterson, *Hebrews and Perfection*, pp. 184–187.

10:26–31, 39; 13:4); *faith* is a major topic (especially in 10:38 – 12:3); *repentance* is explicitly mentioned again in 6:6 and 12:17, and is implied in 9:14; and *resurrection* is highlighted in 11:35 (twice) and 13:20. *Cleansing rites (baptismoi)* are dealt with as the author teaches about purification through 'the blood of Christ' (1:3; 9:9–10, 13–14, 22, 23; 10:2) and approaching God with 'hearts sprinkled to cleanse us from a guilty conscience' and 'bodies washed with pure water' (10:22). There is no further mention of *the laying on of hands* in Hebrews.[8] No hard and fast distinction between 'milk' and 'solid food' can be drawn, because the latter involves a deeper understanding and more Christologically focused application of the former. Spiritual milk is an essential ingredient of the solid food that promotes maturity, but it is the food of infant believers.

Recalling the challenge for his hearers to be willing participants in the process of moving forward (6:1), the pastor concludes this section by saying, *And God permitting, we will do so* (cf. 1 Cor. 16:7; Jas 4:15).[9] This underscores his 'utter dependence on the blessing of God, not only to help them understand the important teaching about the person and work of Christ, but also to attain the goal of spiritual maturity' (O'Brien, p. 216).

Theology
Complacency in the Christian life, which some believers opt for, involves becoming unresponsive to the word of God and unwilling to speak and act for Christ in a public way. The pastor pauses to examine more fully what it means to harden one's heart and turn away from the living God in unbelief and disobedience (3:12–19). A reluctance to listen and learn, and thus progress to spiritual maturity, may be the first danger sign (5:11–14). Arrested spiritual growth can prevent people from standing firm for Christ in the

---

8. Schreiner (pp. 176–177) notes the various ways in which this practice is employed in Scripture, arguing that, in combination with cleansing rites, it may refer to Christian initiation rites here.

9. NIV rightly takes the indicative *poiēsomen* ('we will do') as the best attested and more likely reading here, rather than the subjunctive *poiēsōmen* ('let us do').

face of external pressures and internal struggles with sin. The immature can only be moved beyond the elementary teachings about Christ to moral and spiritual maturity by feeding them the solid food of biblical teaching and challenging them to live out its implications. See Introduction 6e, 'Maturity and ministry'.

B. A warning about the fate of those who profess faith and fall away (6:4–8)

Context

This paragraph is linked to the preceding one by the conjunction *gar* ('for'), which is not translated by NIV. The implication is that resistance to spiritual growth may lead people to fall away or completely rebel against God, because they are hardening their hearts against him. Those who fall away are first defined in terms of what they have previously experienced (vv. 4–6a). The central claim of the passage is that it is impossible for such people to be 'brought back to repentance' (v. 6b). The reason for this is explained in two linked clauses: 'To their loss they are crucifying the Son of God all over again and subjecting him to public disgrace' (v. 6c–d). The warning concludes with a parabolic comparison between two types of land, considering what they produce and what their end will be (vv. 7–8).

Comment

4–6. Previous challenges not to drift from the gospel (2:1–4) or to turn away from the living God in unbelief and disobedience (3:7 – 4:11) are developed here. Some of those addressed by the author have shown worrying signs of spiritual regression (5:11–14), and some appear to have abandoned their fellowship (10:25). The severity of his warning can be appreciated when the opening words (*It is impossible*) are combined with the explanatory clause in verse 6 (*to be brought back to repentance*). 'The author strategically moves the audience to see no middle ground between pressing on to their goal and falling away.'[10]

---

10. DeSilva, p. 220. The topic of the 'impossible' was common in all genres of Graeco-Roman rhetoric. Johnson (p. 163) and Schreiner (p. 181 n. 271)

Five Greek participles are linked together to identify those who cannot be brought back to their initial repentance. The first four describe what happens when people genuinely believe the gospel, viewing that life-transforming event 'from different aspects and manifestations' (Lane 1, p. 141). The fifth participle stands in opposition to the others (*and who have fallen away*). First, they are *those who have once been enlightened* (v. 4). The adverb *hapax* (*once*) emphasizes the decisive and unique nature of this event, while the passive verb (*been enlightened*) points to God's initiative in this regard. A similar expression in 10:32 ('after you had received the light') suggests that this is a metaphor for coming to believe in Jesus as 'the light of the world' (John 8:12; cf. 2 Cor. 4:6; Eph. 5:8–9; 2 Tim. 1:10; 1 Pet. 2:9; 1 John 1:5–7). A parallel expression would be 'after we have received the knowledge of the truth' (10:26). The next three clauses draw out the implications of this coming to the light.

Second, these people have *tasted the heavenly gift*, which could mean experiencing Christ himself or the salvation he offers (2:3, 10; 5:9; 7:25) in advance of its full realization at his return (1:14; 9:28; cf. 1 Pet. 1:3–9). This *heavenly gift* comes from heaven and enables those who receive it to share in God's heavenly calling (3:1). 'Tasting' implies experiencing something in a manner that is real and personal, not merely 'sipping' it (compare Ps. 34:8).[11] Typologically, this could be compared with Israel's enjoyment of the manna from heaven, which was God's gift to them on their journey to the Promised Land (Exod. 16:4–8).[12] In Christian terms, this might include being assured of forgiveness and eternal life through the gospel. It could also mean enjoying the blessings

---

review the way this claim was variously understood and applied by early Christian writers.

11. The same verb in 2:9 describes Jesus' experience of the full reality of death, but here and in v. 5 it more narrowly means 'to experience something cognitively or emotionally' (BDAG). A specific reference to the Lord's Supper seems unlikely.

12. Cf. Emmrich, 'Hebrews 6.4–6', pp. 84–85.

of Christian fellowship and a sense of new purpose and direction in life.

Third, these people have *shared in the Holy Spirit* (or 'become partakers of the Holy Spirit'). When the recipients of Hebrews came to faith in Christ, God testified to the truth of the gospel 'by gifts of the Holy Spirit distributed according to his will' (2:4). The pastor does not develop a theology of regeneration by the Spirit or of the Spirit's transforming work in the life of believers (as in John 3:5–8; Gal. 4:1–7; 2 Cor. 3:3–8, 18; Titus 3:5–6). But a comparison of the language in 6:4 with 3:14 ('We have come to share in Christ') suggests that a personal experience of the Holy Spirit is intended by this claim. The author uses 'expressions that designate Christian believers in the fullest sense of the word' (Schreiner, p. 186), while warning about the possibility of falling away. The apostle Paul similarly assures his believers that '[God] set his seal of ownership on us, and put his Spirit in our hearts as a deposit, guaranteeing what is to come' (2 Cor. 1:22; 5:5). Nevertheless, he challenges those who have the Spirit not to 'gratify the desires of the flesh', but to manifest 'the fruit of the Spirit' and 'keep in step with the Spirit' (Gal. 5:16–25). Later in Hebrews, apostates are characterized as insulting 'the Spirit of grace' (10:29), which suggests acting defiantly against the Spirit.

The next clause (*who have tasted the goodness of the word of God and the powers of the coming age*) effectively summarizes and draws together the previous two claims. *The word of God* (which is the gospel in 2:2–3; 4:2) conveys the *goodness* of God and his saving work to us, while the Holy Spirit manifests in advance *the powers of the coming age* (2:4) and enables belief in the gospel. When they experience God's end-time blessings through the ministry of the Spirit, believers are 'catapulted into the future age of God's reign in the midst of the present evil age' (Schreiner, p. 197). God's word and God's Spirit are sufficient to elicit and sustain faith, but faith needs to be exercised with patience and expressed in obedience to keep us from hardness of heart and apostasy (6:9–12).

The fifth verb in this sequence introduces the possibility that those previously identified as genuine believers have *fallen away* (*parapesontas*). The parallel term in 3:12 (*apostēnai*, 'turns away') describes an act of rebellion or renunciation (cf. 3:18–19;

4:11).[13] Such apostasy involves 'a deliberate choice not to participate in the gift once given' (Johnson, p. 161). The nature of that rebellion is described in graphic terms: *To their loss they are crucifying the Son of God all over again and subjecting him to public disgrace.* Such people reject the Son of God as deliberately as his executioners did, and openly put themselves in the position of his enemies who mocked him. This suggests a public repudiation of the Son of God and a continuing denial of any need for the salvation he accomplished on the cross.

The motivation for this is likely to have been 'an unwillingness to endure society's hostility and to continue without society's approval and gifts (10:32–36; 12:1–11)' (deSilva, p. 225). Although apostates may once have stood against the world and its evaluation of Jesus, they change sides and dismiss the claims of the gospel. The present tense of the participles *crucifying* and *subjecting* implies that the people in view continue in that state and do not seek repentance. Their continuing rejection of Jesus makes it impossible to bring them back to repentance. They have hardened their hearts and burnt their bridges with the Christian community. God cannot provide another way of salvation for them apart from the glorious work of his Son and his Spirit, which they have spurned. Each of the warning passages in Hebrews speaks of God's judgment on apostates (2:1–4; 3:7 – 4:13; 10:26–31; 12:16–17). Some draw a parallel with what is said about God in verse 18 ('it is impossible for God to lie') and conclude that in verses 4–6 the reference is to what is impossible for God.[14] However, the briefer

---

13. The verb *parapiptō* can mean 'go astray' or 'fail to follow through on a commitment, fall away, commit apostasy' (BDAG). It is used more definitively with the related noun to describe Israel's unfaithfulness to God and his covenant in passages such as LXX Ezek. 14:13; 15:8; 18:24; 20:27; 2 Chr. 26:18; 28:19; 29:6; 30:7; Rom. 11:11–12.

14. Cf. Cockerill, p. 275; O'Brien, pp. 225–227. God is committed to saving people according to the plan he revealed in Scripture and accomplished through his Son. He cannot deny himself by providing an alternative, but he must act in judgment against those who refuse his way. This last point is certainly implied by v. 8.

expression in verse 4 (*It is impossible*) more likely introduces a general rule that believers need to be warned about: neither God nor his people can restore those who have fallen away in the manner just outlined.

7–8. An illustration from nature completes the warning in verses 4–6. There are some linguistic parallels with Isaiah 5:1–7 here, but Hebrews could also have been influenced by the challenge of Deuteronomy 11:26–28 to be faithful to God and his covenant and enjoy his blessing, rather than his curse.[15] Jesus' parable of the soils could also have been known to the author (Matt. 13:3–9 par.), though he identifies only two types of soil and their fates, whereas Jesus mentions four.

Land that drinks in the rain often falling on it represents those who persist in hearing and being nurtured by the word of God. By God's enabling, they are spiritually fruitful, producing *a crop useful to those for whom it is farmed*. They receive the ultimate *blessing of God* in 'the world to come' (2:5). Meanwhile, God's grace is experienced in Christian relationships and lifestyle challenges (3:13; 6:10; 10:24–25, 32–34; 13:1–8). These present blessings provide the assurance of life to come in 'the promised eternal inheritance' (9:15; cf. 6:9–12).

Land that produces thorns and thistles is worthless and is in danger of being cursed. Rain may also fall on this land, but it fails to produce the expected crop (cf. Isa. 5:2, 5). The persons illustrated here harden their hearts in unbelief and disobedience, despite their experiences of the grace of God. They are *cursed* in the sense that they merit eternal punishment, not merely loss of rewards. *Worthless* in this context means 'rejected'; *in danger of being cursed* is literally 'near to a curse'. These expressions offer no hope of transformation and rescue by God, because the final assertion is that punishment awaits them (*In the end it will be burned* [ESV, 'its end is to be burned']). Fire is an image of divine judgment, as in 10:27 and 12:29 (cf. Deut. 9:3; 29:20; 32:22; Isa. 26:11), not of

---

15. Note the way this theme is picked up again in Deut. 29 and recontextualized by Ps. 95:7–11, which is the basis for the warning in Heb. 3:7 – 4:13.

disciplinary purging here (cf. deSilva, pp. 232–234; Cockerill, p. 278).

Theology
This pastor does not address his hearers as if all were sliding into apostasy. Rather, he warns that, if they remain sluggish and resist being taken forward to maturity, some of their number may indeed turn their backs on the Son of God and the salvation he has achieved. For maximum pastoral impact, his warning is couched in terms pointing to the reality of their experience of Christ and the Holy Spirit. So the passage is designed to speak to anyone who confidently identifies as Christian. Some people show signs of conversion, but they have a transitory faith. They get caught up in the spiritual experience of a Christian group without being truly regenerate, and drift away from Christ after a while (cf. 1 Tim. 1:18–20; 2 Pet. 2:1–22; 1 John 2:19). Continuance is the test of reality for all professing believers. Those who persevere are the true saints, and a passage with a dire warning like this will be used by God's Spirit to sustain them in faith, hope and love.[16] See Introduction 6d, 'Apostasy and perseverance'.

C. The need to express faith, hope and love 'to the very end' (6:9–12)

Context
Just as the warning in 5:11–14 was followed by the encouragement of 6:1–3, so the warning in 6:4–8 is followed by the hopeful message of 6:9–12. But this passage is not meant to negate the impact of the preceding passage. 'Rather, it is added to restore the sense of mutual goodwill and high estimation between speaker and audience while allowing the force of 6:4–8 to spur the hearers on to the behaviour elevated in 6:9–12' (deSilva, p. 245). Indeed, the

---

16. Schreiner (pp. 480–491) concludes that such warnings are 'always effective in the lives of the elect', because God uses them to preserve believers in their faith (p. 482).

behaviour described here will lead them away from the dangers described in 6:4–8 to inherit what has been promised to them.

Comment

9. Acknowledging the shocking nature of the preceding warning (*Even though we speak like this*), the pastor addresses his hearers affectionately as *dear friends* (*agapētoi*, 'beloved' [ESV]), and expresses his confidence in them collectively (*we are convinced of better things in your case*).[17] The comparative expression *better things* puts them in the category of the 'crop' that 'receives the blessing of God' (v. 7). These better things *have to do with salvation* (cf. 10:39).[18] Such confidence is based on an understanding of God's faithfulness, which is about to be explained in terms of God's dealing with Abraham and his eternal provision for those who rely on Jesus and his saving work (vv. 13–20). But the pastor's confidence also relates to the signs of God's enabling grace that he has perceived in the lives of his fellow disciples, whom he identifies as 'the saints' in the next verse.

10. The conjunction *gar* (ESV, 'For') indicates that what follows is an explanation of the confidence expressed in the previous verse. Fundamentally, the pastor affirms the character of the God they serve (ESV, 'God is not unjust so as to overlook'). The justice of God is an important biblical theme (e.g. Gen. 18:25; Neh. 9:33; Ps. 45:6; Zeph. 3:5), which in positive terms involves remembering the needs of others and acting faithfully to put things right for them (cf. Luke 18:7–8). In this context, what God will *not forget* is *your work and the love you have shown him as you have helped his people and continue to help them*. This refers to the behaviour that was so wonderfully displayed in earlier days (10:32–35), and which the pastor perceives to be in some measure still evidenced among them (13:1–3). Their

---

17. The plural of authorship is used again, as in 5:11, and the perfect tense of the verb (*pepeisometha*) expresses intensity: 'I am *firmly* convinced' (Campbell, *Basics of Verbal Aspect*, p. 128).

18. Attridge (p. 174 n. 98) shows how the verb used here (*echomena*, 'having') is employed in Greek literature to mean 'pertain to, involve'.

love has been 'for his name' and they have shown it in 'having served the saints and continuing to serve' (my translation). 'The saints' (*hoi hagioi*, 'the holy ones') are those whom Christ has sanctified by bringing them into a dedicated relationship with himself (2:11; cf. 1 Cor. 1:2; 6:11). Loving service to other believers is made possible when people are enlightened by the gospel, taste 'the heavenly gift', share in the Holy Spirit and experience 'the goodness of the word of God and the powers of the coming age' (6:4–5). By God's enabling, they have shown the fruit of a genuine relationship with him. In effect, the pastor is affirming that 'he who began a good work in you will carry it on to completion until the day of Christ Jesus' (Phil. 1:6).

11. The confidence expressed in verses 9–10 provokes a strong exhortation. One long sentence in verses 11–12 begins with an emotive verb ('we desire, long for' [*epithymoumen*], NIV *We want*). The author's passionate pastoral concern is for the faithful perseverance of each member of this church (*hekaston hymōn, each of you*). A similar concern for every individual in the group is shown by the expression 'any of you' in 3:12, 13; 4:1, 11, and 'any' in 12:15, 16. His confidence that a true work of God has taken place in their midst (6:9; 10:39) does not exclude the possibility that some may be hardening their hearts and drifting away (2:1; 3:12–14; 4:1–3, 11; 10:25). His simple point is that God's gracious initiative demands a continuing response from each and every believer. The *diligence* they showed in loving God and serving his people in the past was inspired and motivated by the *hope* given in the gospel (10:33–34). The same zeal needs to be shown for 'the full assurance of hope until the end' (ESV).[19] If they confidently express the Christian hope in word and deed, they will be sustained by that hope *to the very end*. Consequently, in the next main section of Hebrews (6:13 – 10:18)

---

19. NIV (*so that what you hope for may be fully realized*) takes the noun *plērophoria* to mean 'full realization' (cf. Bruce, p. 151; Attridge, pp. 175–176). But it can also mean 'full assurance, certainty' (BDAG; cf. Col. 2:2; 1 Thess. 1:5), which seems more likely here because a similar expression in 10:22 is rendered 'with the full assurance that faith brings'. Cf. Cockerill, p. 282; Schreiner, p. 195.

the pastor seeks to deepen their understanding of the hope given to them in the high-priestly work of Christ and inspire them to live by that hope.

12. The sentence that began in verse 11 continues with a purpose clause: (ESV) 'so that you may not be sluggish' (NIV, *We do not want you to become lazy*). The same Greek term (*nōthroi*) that was used in 5:11 ('sluggish in hearing') reappears here in an unqualified way to identify a general spiritual lethargy or apathy. This can be avoided if they listen to their pastor's encouragements and warnings (5:11–14), are willingly 'taken forward to maturity' (6:1) and confidently express their God-given hope in word and deed (6:10–11). Anticipating the argument in 11:1 – 12:3 and 13:7, he concludes with the positive challenge *to imitate those who through faith and patience inherit what has been promised*. The two nouns *faith and patience* may form a hendiadys, with one clarifying the meaning of the other, and meaning either 'faithful perseverance' or 'steadfast faith' (O'Brien, p. 233). Abraham's patient waiting for God's promises to be fulfilled is the first example of this that the author provides (6:13–15).

Theology

Speaking the truth in love is an essential aspect of effective Christian ministry (Eph. 4:15). The author of Hebrews establishes a pattern for such ministry in the way he deals with the recipients of his word of exhortation. Without hesitation, he identifies the dangers in the situation he addresses and speaks plainly about the consequences of spiritual lethargy and unresponsiveness to the word of God (vv. 1–8). But his loving commitment to the welfare of his hearers undergirds his solemn warning and comes to open expression in the encouragement of verses 9–12. Acknowledging the faith, hope and love they have shown in their lives, he urges them to keep expressing this 'to the very end'. God's enabling is stressed in verse 10, but his grace must be sought (4:16), and his direction must be followed. Elsewhere in the New Testament, assurances are given about the way God enables his elect to persevere to the end and obtain what has been promised to them (e.g. John 6:37–44; 10:27–30; Rom. 8:28–39; 1 Cor. 1:8–9; Eph. 1:13–14; Phil. 1:6; 1 Thess. 5:23–24; 1 Pet. 1:5; Jude 24–25). 'The fact that the end (election) will certainly be obtained doesn't preclude the use of means (preaching the gospel and believing). Indeed, the means must be present for the end to be obtained' (Schreiner, p. 490).

7. THE HOPE CONFIRMED AND SECURED BY THE ENTRANCE OF OUR HIGH PRIEST INTO HEAVEN (6:13 – 7:28)

The author's challenge 'to imitate those who through faith and patience inherit what has been promised' (6:12) leads him to focus first on the example of Abraham. God's promise and his oath to Abraham enabled him to persevere and receive what was promised (6:13–15). God's faithfulness in this respect provides a strong encouragement for those who have set their hope on Jesus (6:11, 16–18). The importance of understanding Jesus as 'a priest for ever, in the order of Melchizedek' was signalled in 5:6, 10, 11, and the author begins to explain his work in priestly terms in 6:19–20, where the theme of hope emerges again. But in 7:1–10 he pauses to reflect on what is said about the earthly priesthood of Melchizedek in Genesis 14:18–20, before unpacking the significance of Psalm 110:4 for understanding the nature of Jesus' heavenly priesthood and the hope it brings us (7:11–28). There is a shift of focus from Jesus and the Christian community in 6:19–20 to Jesus, Abraham and Melchizedek in 7:1–10, before the focus changes again to Jesus and the priesthood descended from Levi in 7:11–28.

Parallels between 5:1–3 and 7:26–28 point to a major inclusion in the argument and mark off a whole section devoted to comparing the priesthood of Jesus with the levitical priesthood. In 8:1, the author declares that his 'main point' is that 'we . . . have such a high priest, who sat down at the right hand of the throne of the Majesty in heaven', obviously referring back to the preceding argument. But when he adds that Christ 'serves in the sanctuary, the true tabernacle set up by the Lord, not by a mere human being' (8:2), he introduces the next phase of his exposition, which considers the high-priestly ministry of Jesus in terms of the sanctuary he serves and the sacrificial work he has accomplished (8:1 – 10:18).

A. Responding to God's guaranteed promise (6:13–20)

Context

'Promise' is a key word in this section (vv. 13, 15, 17), where the idea of inheriting what God has promised is expounded (v. 12). The significance of God's oath in guaranteeing his promise to Abraham in Genesis 22:16–17 is the focus of attention in verses 16–18. God's faithfulness to Abraham becomes the basis for encouraging Christians to believe that their hope is 'firm and secure'. It is 'an anchor for the soul', because Jesus has already entered the heavenly sanctuary on our behalf and opened the way for us to enter, having become 'a high priest for ever, in the order of Melchizedek' (vv. 19–20). 'The cardinal point of this passage is to impress upon the audience the reliability of the message they have received and of the mediator in whom they have placed their trust' (deSilva, p. 248).

Comment

13–14. A clear link to the previous verse is provided by a reference to what God promised Abraham.[1] In Genesis 12:1–3, God promised a land and offspring who would become a great

---

1. The noun 'promise' is used in v. 12 and the related verb in v. 13. These verses are also linked by the conjunction *gar* ('for'), which is not translated by NIV.

nation, blessed by God and the source of blessing for all peoples on earth. In later narratives, these promises are expanded and reinforced in various ways (e.g. Gen. 13:14–17; 15:1–21; 17:1–21). But in Genesis 22, Abraham is tested with the challenge to sacrifice his only son, 'even though God had said to him, "It is through Isaac that your offspring will be reckoned"' (Heb. 11:18). When Abraham proved faithful, God provided a lamb for the burnt offering and confirmed his original promises with an oath. Hebrews alludes to the fact that God *swore by himself* in Genesis 22:16 ('I swear by myself, declares the LORD') and then gives a version of the words that God swore in Genesis 22:17 ('I will surely bless you and make your descendants as numerous as the stars in the sky and as the sand on the seashore'). The promise of land is included with the words 'Your descendants will take possession of the cities of their enemies', and the promise to make Abraham's offspring a source of blessing to the nations follows (Gen. 22:18). For reasons that will be explained in verse 16, Hebrews emphasizes that, *since there was no one greater for him to swear by, [God] swore by himself.* This language, which is also found in other biblical contexts (e.g. Exod. 32:13; Isa. 45:23; Jer. 22:5), suggests that God is 'bound to his word by his own character' (O'Brien, p. 236).

15. Picking up again some of the terms from verse 12, the author affirms that *after waiting patiently, Abraham received what was promised.*[2] The words *And so* (*kai houtōs*) suggest that both the testing experience of Genesis 22 and God's confirmation of his promises with an oath were the means by which Abraham was enabled to wait patiently. In a manner of speaking, what he *received* was Isaac 'back from death' (Heb. 11:19), and this assured him that God would multiply his descendants and fulfil his other promises. So, 'in the restoration to Abraham of the son upon whose survival the promise depended Abraham did, in a very substantial sense, "obtain the promise"' (Bruce, p. 153). Although Abraham only ever owned a burial place in Canaan for his wife Sarah (Gen. 23:1–20), 'by faith he made his home in the promised land like a stranger in a foreign

---

2. The participle *makrothymēsas* (v. 15, *after waiting patiently*) recalls the use of the related noun in v. 12 (*makrothymia*, 'patience').

country; he lived in tents, as did Isaac and Jacob, who were heirs with him of the same promise' (Heb. 11:9). In this respect, he is a model for Christians waiting to enter their heavenly inheritance (11:10, 13–16). The promise of a homeland for Abraham was ultimately fulfilled in Christ.

16–17. God accommodates himself in Scripture to human patterns of speech to reassure believers of his character and intentions. The underlying issue is God's absolute truthfulness and inability to lie. God's address to Abraham recognizes that *People swear by someone greater than themselves, and the oath confirms what is said and puts an end to all argument.* In the Old Testament, oaths are often taken in God's name (e.g. Gen. 14:22; 21:23–24; 24:3; Deut. 6:13; 10:20) and lying under oath is clearly a misuse of God's name (Exod. 20:7; Zech. 5:3–4). In the Graeco-Roman world, 'oaths are regularly offered as proofs in forensic speeches, alongside the evidence of witnesses, legal contracts, and the like' (deSilva, p. 249). Of course, God does not need to swear an oath, but he *confirmed* his promise to Abraham with an oath,[3] because he *wanted to make the unchanging nature of his purpose very clear to the heirs of what was promised.* God sought to reassure Abraham and his offspring that he would be faithful in carrying out his revealed will or *purpose* for them (*boulē*, as in Luke 7:30; Acts 2:23; 13:36; 20:27; Eph. 1:11).[4] But the expression *heirs of what was promised* recalls verse 12 and includes Christian believers. The next verse clarifies this.

18. God's promise and his oath are described as *two unchangeable things in which it is impossible for God to lie.* There is an echo here of biblical texts affirming that God is not human that he should lie or change his mind (Num. 23:19; 1 Sam. 15:29; cf. Ps. 89:35; Isa. 31:2; Titus 1:2; 1 John 1:10; 5:10). The trustworthiness of God is the basis

---

3. The verb *emesiteusen* (*confirmed*) can be translated 'mediate' (the related noun means 'mediator' in 8:6; 9:15; 12:24) or 'act as a surety'. The latter sense, meaning 'guarantee' or 'settling a matter', is more likely in this context (BDAG; Attridge, p. 181).

4. *Make . . . clear* (*epideixai*) in this context conveys the idea of giving proof (cf. Acts 18:28; Attridge, p. 180 n. 28), and the comparative adverb *perissoteron* ('all the more') reinforces that sense.

for holding unswervingly to the hope we profess, because 'he who promised is faithful' (10:23). God's faithfulness to Abraham and his descendants was recorded in Scripture 'so that . . . we who have fled for refuge might have strong encouragement to hold fast to the hope set before us' (ESV). The noun translated 'encouragement' (*paraklēsis*) appears again in 12:5 with reference to Old Testament Scripture and in 13:22 with reference to the author's own 'word of exhortation', which regularly shows how Scripture is the basis for both encouragement and warning.

In 7:20–28, God's promise and God's oath in Psalm 110:4 are mentioned with reference to the appointment and function of Jesus as 'a priest for ever, in the order of Melchizedek'. It is likely that the author anticipates that argument in 6:16–18, because he immediately focuses on Jesus' entry into heaven as forerunner and high priest on our behalf (6:19–20). In other words, God's promise and God's oath are associated with the establishment of the foundational biblical covenant with Abraham and with the establishment of the New Covenant by the priest-king Jesus, which enables those who are called to receive 'the promised eternal inheritance' (9:15). This hope is not wishful thinking, but a God-given certainty that literally 'lies before us' (*prokeimenēs*, as in 12:1 ['the race marked out for us'] and 12:2 ['the joy that was set before him']). The promise made with an oath to Christ in Psalm 110:4 has been fulfilled for him and that guarantees the fulfilment of God's promises to us. Christians are portrayed as those who have *fled* for refuge, like the Israelites leaving Egypt, who need to 'hold fast' to the hope that God has offered them in Jesus (cf. 4:14, 'hold firmly').[5]

19–20. This hope is described as *an anchor for the soul, firm and secure*. Like a ship anchored in a storm, *the soul* or self of the believer is held by the promises of God, which are *firm and secure*. Nautical

---

5. ESV takes the infinitive *kratēsai* in 6:18 to explain the content of the 'strong encouragement' we are given, whereas NIV takes it to be the objective of the 'flight', which is to 'take hold' of the hope. Both are possible readings, but the first is more consistent with the use of the same verb in 4:14 and a parallel term in 10:23.

imagery is applied to the problem of drifting here, as possibly also in 2:1. The anchor of hope is then personified as entering *the inner sanctuary behind the curtain, where our forerunner, Jesus, has entered on our behalf.* Mixing his metaphors, the author employs the image of the inner portion of the tabernacle for the first time to describe the heavenly realm where the ascended Christ has gone (8:2; 9:8, 12, 24, 25; 10:19–20).[6] The anchor of hope functions as Christ does, 'providing a means of access by its entry into God's presence' (Attridge, p. 184). This is so because Jesus fulfilled the pattern of approach to God set forth in the Mosaic law and opened 'a new and living way' through the curtain (10:20; cf. 9:11–14). Jesus himself is our hope! This theme is developed in 8:1 – 10:25, once the author has explained how Christ functions as *a high priest for ever, in the order of Melchizedek* (v. 20; cf. 7:11–28). It is unwarranted literalism to conclude from 6:20 (*genomenos*, 'having become') that Jesus became high priest in the order of Melchizedek only when he entered God's presence. Christ's death on the cross was part of his high-priestly work, forming the basis for his continuing ministry of intercession for us (7:25).

The title *forerunner* (*prodromos*) is given to Jesus only here in the New Testament but, together with the phrase *on our behalf*, it parallels the description of him as 'the pioneer of their salvation' (2:10). The unique achievement of Jesus in his death, resurrection and ascension *on our behalf* is coupled with the notion that he has gone ahead to open the way to heavenly glory for others to follow him. This hope, which is an anchor for the soul, enables us to 'approach God's throne of grace with confidence' in the present (4:16; cf. 10:19–22), to endure suffering and persecution with the confidence of 'better and lasting possessions' (10:34; cf. 13:14), and to be certain that in coming to Jesus in the heavenly realm 'we are receiving a kingdom that cannot be shaken' (12:28). Immediate access to God through the glorified Lord Jesus is the means of

---

6. NIV has rightly inserted the words *the inner sanctuary*, when the
    Greek expression in v. 19 literally says 'into the inside of the curtain'.
    The second, inner curtain in the tabernacle is regularly called the
    katapetasma in the LXX (e.g. Exod. 26:31–35; Lev. 16:2, 12, 15).

persevering with faith and patience and ultimately experiencing the full reality of life in God's presence.[7]

Theology

God's confirmation of his promise to Abraham with an oath in Genesis 22:17 was an encouragement for him to persevere in faith. Similarly, the oath guaranteeing the eternal priesthood of Christ in Psalm 110:4 provides Christians with two encouragements to persevere (v. 18; cf. 7:20–22). God's promise and his oath are associated with the establishment of the New Covenant by the Lord Jesus. God adopts this pattern of relating to his people to assure them of his faithfulness. However, since Jesus has already entered into heaven on our behalf, specifically as a high priest for ever, the hope set before us of sharing in God's eternal kingdom has been realized by him (vv. 19–20). Promise, oath and fulfilment are brought together to encourage perseverance. Hope is presented in terms of access to God's heavenly sanctuary through the sacrifice and heavenly ministry of Jesus. This hope is 'an anchor for the soul, firm and secure' because of the faithfulness of God in exalting his crucified Son to heaven.

B. The priesthood of Melchizedek (7:1–10)

Context

In 6:20, the author indicated once more the significance of Psalm 110:4 for understanding the high-priestly ministry of Jesus (cf. 5:6, 10, 11). However, before explaining this more fully, he reflects on the passage that inspired the psalmist's prediction. An inclusion is formed between verses 1 and 10 with references to Melchizedek meeting Abraham in Genesis 14:18–20. This passage helps to explain why Psalm 110:4 can speak about the Messiah being a priest 'in the order of Melchizedek'. The focus is first on Abraham, Melchizedek

---

7. Thus, 'the author urges the hearers to find their stability and rootedness in their hope in God's promises rather than in acceptance by their neighbors and by reclaiming their place in the world that is passing away' (deSilva, p. 252).

and the Son of God (vv. 1–3), and then on Abraham, Melchizedek and the priests descended from Levi (vv. 4–10).

Comment

1–3. A strong link with the allusion to Psalm 110:4 in 6:20 is provided by the introductory words (lit. 'for this Melchizedek'), which preface the citation of several key terms from Genesis 14:18–20. Although Melchizedek is mentioned only twice in the Old Testament, there is a remarkable amount of speculation about his significance in Jewish and early Christian literature. 'In various ways Hebrews seems to reflect and stand critically over against a variety of traditions concerning Melchizedek.'[8] In contrast to other contemporaneous interpreters, the author is restrained in his approach to Genesis 14:18–20. His real interest is in what we can learn from Psalm 110:4 about Jesus and his priestly ministry, but he highlights several features of the narrative about Abraham's encounter with Melchizedek that help to explain why the psalmist could claim that the Messiah would be 'a priest for ever, in the order of Melchizedek'.

The key to understanding the argument in verses 1–3 is the expression translated by NIV *resembling the Son of God, he remains a priest for ever* (v. 3). The Greek perfect passive participle (*aphōmoiōmenos*) could be translated 'made like' (BDAG; cf. KJV, ASV), suggesting that in the record of Scripture, Melchizedek is made to resemble the Son of God in certain respects. Either way, this expression does not mean that Melchizedek is an immortal being or that he was the Son of God in some pre-incarnate form.[9] His resemblance to

---

8. Hay, *Glory*, p. 143 (these traditions are summarized on pp. 19–51). 'The marvel about the argument concerning Melchizedek in Hebrews 5–7 is not that the author has made so much out of so little, but that he has made so little out of so much' (Hay, pp. 152–153). Cf. Schreiner, pp. 207–208 (especially n. 327).

9. Cockerill (pp. 300–301) takes the three expressions in v. 3 to describe 'eternal, uncreated Deity', and yet identifies Melchizedek as a human being, likening him to the three visitors from God in Gen. 18:1–15 and the captain of the Lord's army in Josh. 5:13–15. See, however, the

the Son of God lies 'in the biblical representation and not primarily in Melchizedek himself. The comparison is not between Christ and Melchizedek, but between Christ and the isolated portraiture of Melchizedek' (Westcott, p. 175). In verse 15 it is said that 'another priest in the likeness of Melchizedek' has arisen. This implies that Melchizedek and Christ are separate individuals, but that they share something important in common. The full title *Son of God* is used only here and in 4:14; 6:6; 10:29, though the abbreviated title 'Son' is employed in 1:2, 5 (twice), 8; 3:6; 5:5, 8; 7:28 with the same breadth of meaning. These titles embrace his pre-existence, incarnation, revelatory significance, reverent submission in suffering and death, heavenly exaltation and eternal rule. Melchizedek is simply likened to the Son of God in that *he remains a priest for ever.*[10]

The silences of Scripture are taken to be significant in this respect: Melchizedek is presented in Genesis as being *without father or mother, without genealogy, without beginning of days or end of life.* This argument from silence is 'an interpretive device that Hebrews shares with Philo and rabbinic exegetes' (Attridge, p. 190). In a culture where genealogies were important for evaluating the legitimacy of a person's priesthood (vv. 13–17; cf. Neh. 7:64–65), Melchizedek is acknowledged as *priest of God Most High* (v. 1; cf. Gen. 14:18), but no record of his origin is given: he is *without father or mother, without genealogy.* Nevertheless, when he *met Abraham returning from the defeat of the kings,* Melchizedek *blessed him* in the name of 'God Most High, Creator of Heaven and Earth', and *Abraham gave him a tenth of everything* (vv. 1–2; Gen. 14:19–20). In other words, Abraham acknowledged the authenticity of his priesthood. As suddenly as he appears in the narrative, Melchizedek disappears, giving rise to the comment that he is *without beginning of days or end of life.* These words are best understood in the light of the previous ones (*without father or mother, without genealogy*).

---

arguments against this by Schreiner, pp. 209–211.

10. The expression translated *for ever* here is not the one used in Ps. 110:4 (*eis ton aiōna*), but *eis to diēnekes* (cf. 10:1, 12, 14), which perhaps emphasizes 'the enduring continuity of the priestly status' (Attridge, p. 191), and may be rendered 'perpetually'.

The apparently unending nature of Melchizedek's priesthood, which is suggested by the biblical record, foreshadows the never-ending priesthood of the Son of God.

This understanding of Melchizedek as a limited 'type' or anticipation of Christ is reinforced by noting the significance of his *name*, which is taken to mean *king of righteousness*, and his royal function as *king of Salem*, which is taken to mean *king of peace*.[11] These terms recall prophetic expectations that the Messiah would bring righteousness and peace (Isa. 9:6–7; 11:1–9; 32:16–18; Jer. 23:5; 33:15; Zech. 9:9–10), but nothing is made of these notions in the immediate context. As a priest-king of Salem, Melchizedek prefigures the role and function of the Son, to whom God said,

> Sit at my right hand
> > until I make your enemies
> > a footstool for your feet
> (Ps. 110:1; cf. Heb. 1:13)

and

> You are a priest for ever,
> > in the order of Melchizedek.
> (Ps. 110:4)

The Son now reigns in the heavenly Jerusalem as the crucified and glorified Messiah (12:22–24), where he always lives to intercede for his people (7:25).

> Melchizedek remains a priest continually for the duration of his appearance in the biblical narrative; but in the antitype Christ remains a priest continually without qualification. And it is not the type that

---

11. *King of righteousness* means 'righteous king'. The Greek *Salem* translates the Hebrew place name *Šālēm*, which is occasionally associated with Jerusalem (cf. Ps. 76:2; Josephus, *Ant.* 1.180) and sounds like the Hebrew *šālôm* ('peace').

determines the antitype, but the antitype that determines the type; Jesus is not portrayed after the pattern of Melchizedek, but Melchizedek is 'made like unto the Son of God'.

(Bruce, p. 138)

The 'antitype' is the person, object or event foreshadowed by the 'type' presented in the Old Testament.

4. The focus now turns to the greatness of Melchizedek in relation to Abraham and the priesthood that traces its descent from him (*Just think how great he was*). The aim of verses 4–10 is to prepare for the argument that the priesthood of Jesus is superior to and supersedes the priesthood of the tribe of Levi (vv. 11–19). Melchizedek is said to be greater than *even the patriarch Abraham* in that Abraham gave him *a tenth of the plunder*.[12] Genesis 14:20 reads 'a tenth of everything', but Hebrews has substituted a noun that was used in Greek literature for the spoils of war (*akrothinion*), which is appropriate to the context (Gen. 14:17).[13] Abraham's action appears to have been a spontaneous recognition of the dignity of Melchizedek and a way to devote to God *the plunder* from his battle with the kings.

5–6. Although the law about tithing was not given until much later, Hebrews mentions it here to highlight the significance of Abraham's gift to Melchizedek. The descendants of Levi ('those belonging to the sons of Levi') who receive the priestly office have a command in the law *to collect a tenth from the people – that is, from their fellow Israelites* ('from their brothers'). The author uses present-tense verbs, suggesting that this is current practice as he writes (cf. Luke 1:8–10). All of the priests were descended from Levi, but not every Levite became a priest (Num. 18:1–7). The significance of tithing is clarified by saying *even though they also are descended from Abraham*. The levitical priests were set aside to serve the people in matters relating to God, and the Israelites were commanded to support

---

12. NIV translates the emphatic *kai* (*even*), although this is missing from some reliable Greek manuscripts. Cf. Ellingworth, p. 361.

13. This Greek word means 'topmost/best part of the heap' (BDAG) and came to be used for plunder taken in war.

them by tithing what they had (Num. 18:21–24). Priests and people had different roles, but they were children of Abraham together. Melchizedek, who *did not trace his descent from Levi*, is portrayed in Genesis 14:18–20 as collecting a tithe from Abraham – without the authority of the Mosaic law – and blessing *him who had the promises*. Like the word 'patriarch' in verse 4, this last expression highlights the importance of Abraham as the one through whom God established his saving purpose for Israel and the nations (Gen. 12:1–3; cf. Heb. 6:13–17).

7–10. Three final points are made about Abraham, Melchizedek and the levitical priests. First, it is argued that *without doubt the lesser is blessed by the greater*, meaning that, in the narrative of Genesis, Melchizedek is obviously greater than Abraham (v. 7). Although the same verb (*eulogein*) can be used in situations where inferiors praise or congratulate their superiors (2 Sam. 14:22; 1 Kgs 1:47; 8:66; Job 31:20), Israelite priests blessed God's people as his representatives (Num. 6:22–27). Melchizedek's blessing of Abraham is thus taken as a sign of his greatness. Second, it is argued that, *In the one case* [the levitical priests], *the tenth is collected by people who die, but in the other case* [Melchizedek], *by him who is declared to be living* (v. 8). This anticipates the argument in verses 23–24, where the permanent priesthood of Jesus is contrasted with the priesthood of those who were prevented by death from continuing in office. The verb *martyrein* (*declared*) is significant, because it is used several times in Hebrews to refer to the witness of Scripture (7:17; 10:15; 11:2, 4, 5, 39). As in verse 3, it is the biblical representation of Melchizedek as *living* that makes him a type of Christ and superior to the levitical priests *who die*. Third, *One might even say that Levi, who collects the tenth, paid the tenth through Abraham* (v. 9). The author recognizes the strangeness of his argument with the qualification *one might even say*. His explanation that, *when Melchizedek met Abraham, Levi was still in the body of his ancestor* also seems odd, until it is recognized that 'an ancestor is regarded in biblical thought as containing within himself all his descendants' (O'Brien, p. 254; cf. Gen. 25:23; Mal. 1:2–3; Rom. 9:11–13). In short, verses 7–10 argue from Scripture for the superiority of the priesthood of Melchizedek over the levitical priesthood, even before the latter was established by the law of Moses.

Theology

The promise of an eternal priesthood for God's Son in Psalm 110:4 is based on the portrait of Melchizedek in Genesis 14:18–20. Melchizedek is made to resemble the Son of God in that narrative by the presentation of his priesthood 'without genealogy, without beginning of days or end of life' (v. 3). Like all typological arguments in the Bible, this one views Melchizedek as anticipating Christ in certain limited ways. The author goes on to point out the significance of Melchizedek's name, his royal function as 'king of Salem', and his relationship to Abraham and the priesthood descended from him. This last point prepares for the argument about the way the priesthood of Christ fulfils and replaces the levitical priesthood (vv. 11–28). The divine inspiration of Scripture involved the introduction of characters and institutions in the Old Testament that prepared for the ultimate revelation of God's saving plan in the person and work of his Son (cf. 8:3–6; 9:8–10; 10:1–10).

C. The eternal high priesthood of the Son of God (7:11–28)

Context

In the light of his reflection on Genesis 14:18–20, the author now begins to show how the priesthood of Jesus is superior to and supersedes the ministry of the levitical priests. An inclusion is formed between verses 11 and 19 by references to perfection and the law. Here the point is made that believers can be perfected in their relationship with God only by the ministry of a priest 'in the order of Melchizedek'.[14] A second inclusion is formed between verses 20 and 28 by references to God's oath guaranteeing the eternal priesthood of the Messiah in Psalm 110:4. This makes Jesus 'the guarantor of a better covenant', ever able to save those who come to God through him, and a high priest who 'truly meets our need'. Within this broader division (vv. 20–28), where Melchizedek

---

14. A larger inclusion is formed between v. 19, with its implication that perfection for believers could not be obtained through the law, and v. 28, with an affirmation that the Son who has been perfected for ever is able to provide the necessary perfection.

is no longer mentioned, the superiority of Christ's priesthood is argued in terms of its eternity (vv. 23–25), but also in terms of the character, achievement and status of Jesus as Son of God (vv. 26–28).

Comment

11–12. A strong link with the preceding argument is made with the conjunction *oun* ('therefore'), which is not translated by NIV. The topic of *perfection* is introduced in relation to *the Levitical priesthood* (vv. 6–10) and *the law given to the people* in connection with that priesthood (v. 5). Previously, the perfecting of Christ through suffering and heavenly exaltation was considered (2:10; 5:8–9; see also 7:28). Related terminology will now be applied to believers (see also 7:19; 9:9; 10:1, 14; 11:40; 12:23). Put negatively, 'the law made nothing perfect', but through Christ, 'a better hope is introduced by which we draw near to God' (v. 19). In Hebrews, the perfecting of believers involves qualifying them to draw near to God through Christ in a new and decisive way that is soon to be explained.

A rhetorical question in the form of a conditional clause puts the negative case simply: *If perfection could have been attained through the Levitical priesthood . . . why was there still need for another priest to come, one in the order of Melchizedek, not in the order of Aaron?*[15] Based on his strong belief in the divine inspiration and authority of Scripture (e.g. 1:5–13; 3:7–11; 5:5–6; 7:21), the author argues that God would not have made the promise through David in Psalm 110:4 if the priesthood he initiated through Moses was his ultimate intention for his people (Exod. 28:1–5; Lev. 8:1–4). An additional clause highlights the implication of this change of priesthood for the law as a whole: *and indeed the law given to the people established that priesthood.* This clause could be translated 'for the people have been placed under the law on this basis' (CSB, 'on the basis of it the people received the law'). So foundational was the priesthood to the whole system that *when the priesthood is changed, the law must be changed also.*

---

15. The verb *anistasthai* (NIV, *to come*) refers to the 'raising up' in history of another priest like Melchizedek. It parallels the use of a similar verb in v. 14 (see n. 17 below). An implicit reference to Jesus' resurrection is unlikely, either here or in v. 15.

The weakness of the law as a means of relating to God is thus linked to the weakness of the priesthood that supported it. God's intention to change the priesthood was revealed when Psalm 110:4 was written.

Hebrews uses the Greek term *entolē* for specific commands or regulations of the law (7:5, 16, 18; 9:19) and mostly employs *nomos* for the Mosaic law as a totality (7:5, 12, 16, 19, 28; 8:4; 9:19, 22; 10:1, 8, 28).[16] The author is not primarily concerned with the law in its ethical dimension, but as a sacrificial and purificatory system by which the community of Israel could relate to God and be sustained as his holy and distinct people. A certain correspondence between the Old Covenant and the New emerges as categories and concepts are taken over from the former and applied to the person and work of Christ. But the word 'better' is used to describe the hope (7:19), the covenant (7:22; 8:6), the sacrifices (9:23) and the inheritance (10:34; 11:16) he makes possible. The words 'true', 'heavenly' and 'eternal' are also used to describe the perfection he brings. The New Covenant has better and more effective institutions and outcomes than the corresponding institutions and outcomes of the Old Covenant (8:1 – 10:18). This means that the law was 'a temporary dispensation of God, valid only until Christ came to inaugurate the age of perfection' (Bruce, pp. 166–167).

13–14. *He of whom these things are said* is the priest-king addressed in Psalm 110. The author highlights the novelty of this by recalling that Jesus *belonged to a different tribe, and no one from that tribe has ever served at the altar.* Jesus is reverentially described as *our Lord,* and yet his 'rising up' *from Judah* as a man is acknowledged.[17] This puts the focus on his non-levitical origin, since *in regard to that tribe Moses said*

---

16. Exceptions to this would be the use of *nomos* in the plural in 8:10; 10:16 for specific commands of the law. See also my comments on 7:5, 16; 9:22.

17. The verb translated *descended* in v. 14 (*anatetalken*) literally means 'has arisen'. This echoes LXX Num. 24:17 ('a star shall arise from Jacob'), and some think the author is suggesting the fulfilment of this and other messianic prophecies. Cf. O'Brien, p. 261; Cockerill, pp. 319–320. A different verb with a similar meaning is used in vv. 11, 15.

nothing about priests. Nevertheless, the claim is consistent with biblical expectations that the Messiah would be a son of David (e.g. Isa. 9:6–7; Jer. 23:5–6; Mic. 5:2). In other words, for the Messiah to be a priest, he had to belong to an order other than that descended from Levi.

15–17. A new stage of the argument is introduced by the words *And what we have said is even more clear.* The author first recalls what is said in verse 11 about the possibility that another priest like Melchizedek might 'come'. The same Greek verb is used in verse 15, where it is translated *appears.* As in verse 11, this new stage of the argument is introduced hypothetically ('if another priest in the likeness of Melchizedek appears').[18] But from the way he is described, there is no doubt that such a priest has already appeared. Unlike the descendants of Levi, he has not become a priest *on the basis of a regulation as to his ancestry* (or 'not according to the law consisting of a fleshly command'). The word 'fleshly' (*sarkinēs*) here means 'belonging to the physical realm' (BDAG) and implies weakness and transience (cf. 5:2; 7:18; 9:10, 13–14).

The priesthood established by Moses was based on bodily descent from Aaron (Exod. 28:1–5; Num. 3:1–10) and required physical perfection (Lev. 21:16–23; 22:3–8), but Jesus has *become a priest . . . on the basis of the power of an indestructible life,* that is, by God's power exercised in giving him *an indestructible life.* This most likely refers to the resurrection–ascension of Jesus, which climaxed the process by which he was perfected 'for ever' as high priest of the New Covenant (v. 28).[19] What was said previously about Christ having 'become' high priest (5:10; 6:20) applies to the use of the same verb in 7:17 (*gegonen,* 'has become'). Jesus' priesthood came to

---

18. The expression 'in the likeness' (*kata tēn homoiotēta*) recalls the use of a related verb in v. 3 (*aphōmoiōmenos,* 'made like'). Similarity is indicated between Jesus and Melchizedek, not identity.

19. O'Brien (p. 263 n. 115) considers different ways in which *the power of an indestructible life* has been understood and agrees that the genitive expression *zōēs akatalytou* is best understood as indicating that God's power was manifested in the resurrection life of Jesus. Cf. Peterson, *Hebrews and Perfection,* pp. 110–111.

full expression in his heavenly exaltation and enthronement. The
Son of God, who exists eternally, was born a man, suffered and
died for us, and through resurrection and ascension entered the
heavenly sanctuary as the priest foretold in Psalm 110:4 (cited again
in v. 17 to make the point).

Although some have argued that Jesus as Son of God already
had an indestructible life, which was not destroyed by death, this
is not the author's point in making the comparison with the levitical priests.

> The power of life that the resurrection conferred upon Jesus
> demonstrated that his priesthood is not limited by the temporal,
> transient character of the old priesthood based on physical descent.
> It is undergirded by a power that overcame mortality and corruption
> and consequently is beyond the reach of mortality and corruption.
> (Lane 1, p. 184)[20]

As a human being, he was utterly dependent on 'the one who could
save him from death', and his prayers for deliverance were heard,
'because of his reverent submission' (5:7).

18–19. The claim of verse 12 that a change in the priesthood
means a change in the law based upon that priesthood is now
developed. *The former regulation* refers to the commandment about
priesthood mentioned in verse 16a. This regulation is *set aside because
it was weak and useless.*[21] The levitical priesthood could not perfect
the people of God in the sense of bringing them into an eternal
relationship with God. Indeed, the whole system of relating to God
provided through Moses could not achieve that goal, *for the law made
nothing perfect* (it did not facilitate direct and permanent access to
God as the New Covenant does). Since God gave *the law* in the
first place, he was entitled to set it aside as a means of purification and sanctification when it was fulfilled by his Son (10:5–10;

---

20. Contrast Cockerill, pp. 323–324; Kleinig, p. 343.

21. The noun *athetēsis* that is used here to describe the 'setting aside' of this
    regulation has the technical legal meaning of 'annulment' (BDAG). In
    9:26 it is used for the 'removal' of sin.

cf. Acts 10:9–29; 15:7–9). A dramatic change in the way God deals with his people has taken place, because *a better hope is introduced, by which we draw near to God.* The people of the Old Covenant could certainly hope in God to fulfil the promises he gave to them (11:1–2), but because of his entrance into heaven Jesus provides *a better hope* for those who come to God through him (6:18–20). This hope is *better* because the outcome has already been achieved! The author regularly uses the adjective 'better' in relation to Jesus and what he has achieved for his people (1:4; 6:9; 7:7, 22; 8:6; 9:23; 10:34; 11:16, 35, 40; 12:24) to warn against any failure to appreciate and live in the light of these superior blessings.

Elsewhere, the author indicates that the law provided limited access to God through the levitical priesthood (10:1), but Christians can *draw near to God* directly, confidently and permanently, because of the priestly ministry of Jesus.[22] In 12:22–24, drawing near describes the saving relationship with God in heaven that Jesus makes possible by the shedding of his blood. The present hope we have of drawing near to God with confidence (4:16; 10:19–22) carries with it the hope of sharing for ever in God's (lit.) 'unshakable kingdom' (12:28). Thus, the contrast in verses 11–19 is between 'the limited effectiveness of the former priesthood and the absolute effectiveness of the priesthood of Christ' (Peterson, *Hebrews and Perfection*, p. 112).

20–22. The author continues his argument about the superiority of the priesthood of Jesus by claiming that *it was not without an oath* (CSB, 'none of this happened without an oath'). No oath was given concerning the appointment of the levitical priests,[23] but the promise that the Messiah would be *a priest for ever* in Psalm 110:4 was confirmed with an oath (*the Lord has sworn / and will not change his*

---

22. The LXX applies the verb used in 7:19 (*engizein*) to priestly ministry (Exod. 19:21–22; Lev. 10:3; 21:21) and to the approach of all God's people to him in personal prayer or corporate worship (Gen. 18:23; Eccl. 4:17 [ET 5:1]; Isa. 29:13; 58:2). A parallel term (*proserchesthai*) is used in Heb. 4:16; 7:25; 10:1, 22; 11:6; 12:18, 22.

23. The Bible's silence in this regard is taken to be as significant as its silence about the ancestry of Melchizedek (7:3).

mind). This recalls the argument in 6:13–15 about God's oath to Abraham and its encouraging consequence. In both cases, the divine oath confirms the absoluteness of the promise and its continuing validity, giving confidence and hope to his people. But in the present context the further point is made that because of this oath *Jesus has become the guarantor of a better covenant.*

Once more, the author announces in advance a theme that he will soon develop, namely that Jesus is the mediator of a new covenant (8:6–13). This 'second' covenant (8:7) is 'new' (8:8; 9:15; 12:24), or 'better' (7:22; 8:6), because of the better promises on which it is based and because it is 'eternal' (13:20) in its operation and effect. This *better covenant* clearly relates to the 'better hope' in 7:19. In both contexts, Christology and covenant are tied together, though different terms are used to describe what Jesus does. As 'mediator' of this covenant (*mesitēs*, 8:6; 9:15; 12:24), he acted to put into effect what was promised by God to his people (Jer. 31:31–34), but as *guarantor* (*engyos*, 7:22), he provides the assurance with his 'indestructible life' (v. 17) that the covenant will be eternally effective (13:20).[24] God's oath in Psalm 110:4 confirms the eternity of Jesus' priesthood and consequently the eternity of the covenant he initiates. His resurrection–ascension guarantees the continuance of the covenant.

23–25. Further implications of Jesus being a priest for ever are now drawn out. Over the course of time, the levitical priests were many in number, *since death prevented them from continuing in office.* Aaron and his sons were ordained to a priesthood that would 'continue throughout their generations' (Exod. 40:15), but this priesthood depended on a succession of priests to be effective. Plurality is a sign of incompleteness and imperfection for our author (cf. 1:1–2; 10:1–3). However, as the messianic priest 'in the likeness of Melchizedek', Jesus 'remains [*menein*] for ever' (cf. 1:11–12). Consequently, he has *a permanent priesthood*, the emphasis

---

24. The term *guarantor* (*engyos*) occurs only here in the NT, but it is used in Sir. 29:14–17 for a good man becoming a 'surety' for his neighbour's debts and, in effect, giving his life for the other person (cf. Prov. 17:18; 22:26). In 2 Macc. 10:28 it is used for a 'pledge' of success and victory. The term is regularly used in legal and other documents.

here being on the unchangeable quality of his priesthood, not simply its longevity.[25]

An important logical inference follows in verse 25 (*Therefore*), indicating the significance of this teaching for believers (cf. 3:1). As the eternal priest-king at God's right hand, *he is able to save completely those who come to God through him*. Since eternal salvation is still to be inherited (1:14) and experienced in its fullness by those who await Christ's return (9:28), it must not be neglected by drifting from the gospel (2:1–3). So the emphasis now is on the ability of our heavenly high priest to sustain and continually help those who come to God through him (4:14–16; 10:19–22; 12:22–24).[26] Parallel terms echo verse 19 ('we draw near to God') with its emphasis on the 'better hope' that Christ's entrance into heaven gives us (as in 6:19–20). The reason for confidence in verse 25 is *because he always lives to intercede for them*.

There has been considerable disagreement among interpreters about the meaning of Christ's heavenly intercession (see also Rom. 8:34; 1 John 2:1–2; Isa. 53:12). *To intercede* (*entynchanein*) means 'to approach or appeal to someone' (BDAG). When God is approached, the verb can mean 'to pray' (Rom. 8:26–27). Some have taken a literal view, explaining Jesus' intercession as vocal and impassioned prayer to the Father, or the continuing presentation to his Father in heaven of the sacrifice he offered on earth. Others have given more figurative interpretations.[27] On the one hand, it is important to note that Christ is portrayed as seated at the right hand of God (1:3; 8:1; 10:12; 12:2), not kneeling or prostrating himself before the Father or engaged in any ritual actions. On the

---

25. BDAG, *aparabatos*. In legal papyri, the term means 'inviolable'. As in v. 16, the focus is on Jesus' glorified humanity 'instead of his inherent divine properties' (Schreiner, p. 233, against Cockerill, p. 333).

26. Greek *eis to panteles* can be translated 'for ever' (NRSV), but more likely means 'completely, fully, wholly' (BDAG; NIV, CSB) or 'to the uttermost' (ESV) here, the temporal emphasis being in the next clause (*because he always lives to intercede for them*).

27. Cf. Peterson, *Hebrews and Perfection*, pp. 114–116, especially n. 64; O'Brien, pp. 276–278.

other hand, 7:25 reflects the perspective of the two pivotal exhortations in 4:14–16; 10:19–25, concerning the need to receive
continuing mercy and find help to persevere in the Christian life.

The finished nature of Christ's atoning work is the basis for a
confident approach to God through his Son (see especially 10:11–18).
The very presence of the crucified and yet glorified Jesus with God
'on our behalf' (6:20; cf. 9:24) is the reality behind the concept of
his heavenly intercession or mediation for us. This was foreshadowed in the provision of Exodus 28:29 that 'Whenever Aaron
enters the Holy Place, he will bear the names of the sons of Israel
over his heart on the breastpiece of decision as a continuing
memorial before the LORD.' But the language of intercession suggests that Christ as our representative in heaven echoes or brings
to God the prayers we make through him.[28] Fundamentally, the
image of Christ as heavenly intercessor emphasizes the reality of
Jesus' applying the benefits of his sacrificial death and entrance into
God's presence to those who draw near to God through him.

26. The conclusion to this chapter also draws to an end the
whole consideration of Christ's priestly ministry that began in
5:1–3. A close link to the previous verse is provided by the conjunction *gar* ('For', ESV) and the word *Such* (see also 8:1). Jesus has
not been specifically identified as *high priest* since 6:20, although this
is the author's preferred way of describing him (2:17; 3:1; 4:14, 15;
5:1, 5, 10; 8:1; 9:11; 10:21 ['great priest']). The more general terms
'priest' and 'priesthood' are used in the comparison with Melchizedek and the levitical priests in verses 1–25 (see also 8:4). Now the
author claims that 'such a high priest was indeed fitting for us' (my
translation; cf. 2:10, 'it was fitting'). Given our need as sinful human
beings, there was an appropriateness about the way the Son of God
was perfected as our saviour and high priest. First, his proven character (*holy, blameless, pure*) showed that he was not subject to the
weaknesses that characterized the levitical priesthood (5:2). This

---

28. Forgiveness is implied in the approach to God for mercy (4:16), but
    forgiveness is clearly secured by Christ's atoning work on earth (1:3;
    9:26–28; 10:18), not by his pleading the merits of his death to the Father
    in heaven. Cf. Koester, p. 366; Schreiner, p. 234.

made his sacrifice perfect, requiring no repetition (10:5–10). Although he was truly human and tempted in every way as we are, 'yet he did not sin' (4:15). He learned obedience from what he suffered (5:7–8), and ultimately offered himself 'unblemished to God' (9:14).

Second, because of his perfect self-offering and glorious ascension, he is *set apart from sinners, exalted above the heavens*, where he always lives to intercede for us. We have a high priest who is able to bring us directly and permanently into God's presence. Some relate the clause *set apart from sinners* to the preceding description (*holy, blameless, pure*), but it more likely belongs with what follows, especially since the author switches from adjectives to participial clauses.[29]

27. Christ's proven sinlessness ('holy, blameless, pure') means that, *Unlike the other high priests, he does not need to offer sacrifices day after day, first for his own sins, and then for the sins of the people*. The author returns to an argument he began to make in 5:3, 7–10, possibly applying the pattern of double sacrifice mentioned in Leviticus 9:7; 16:6, 15 to the daily sacrifices, assuming that what was required of the high priest on the Day of Atonement applied also to these.[30] But Jesus offered up himself *once for all* (*ephapax*, as in 9:12; 10:10) to deal with the problem of human sin. This theme will be developed at length in 9:11 – 10:18. The related term *hapax* ('once for all') is used in a similar way with reference to the unique and decisive sacrifice of Christ in 9:26, 28. As in the comparison with Melchizedek, the typological relationship of Jesus' priesthood with the levitical priesthood is limited. He did not need to offer daily sacrifices for his people, nor for his own sins. Instead of animal sacrifices, he offered himself once for all in death. Jesus fulfilled the role and function of the levitical priests and the

---

29. Bruce (p. 157 n. 88) suggests that it embraces both moral separation and heavenly exaltation.

30. Kleinig (pp. 366–367) disputes this, arguing that the author had in mind the daily grain offering for the high priest, morning and evening, in association with the burnt offering and sin offerings for the people (Lev. 6:19–23).

sacrificial system given to Israel as the high priest of a different order.

28. The comparisons made between Christ and the levitical priests in this chapter are now drawn together in a summary fashion. The first comparison is between *the law* and *the oath, which came after the law*. *Law* in this context could refer to the specific command appointing the priests or to the whole system of relating to God that was based on that regulation (vv. 17–19). The *oath* establishing the high priesthood of Jesus was made in connection with the later promise of Psalm 110:4. This guaranteed the eternal effectiveness of the Messiah's priesthood and the covenant he mediated (vv. 20–22). The essential contrast with the levitical priesthood relates to the permanence of Jesus' priesthood (vv. 23–25) and the once-for-all nature of his sacrifice (vv. 26–27).

The second major contrast in this verse is between *men in all their weakness* and *the Son, who has been made perfect for ever*. The *weakness* of those appointed to be priests by the law made it possible for them to 'deal gently with those who are ignorant and are going astray', but required them to offer sacrifices repeatedly for their own sins, as well as for the sins of the people (5:2–3). During his life on earth, the Son of God experienced the struggles of human existence and the full force of temptation without sinning. Consequently, even as the exalted Son he is able 'to feel sympathy for our weaknesses' (4:15) and to offer us the help we need (4:16; 7:25). As 2:10 and 5:9 indicate in their contexts, the Son has been *made perfect* by his proving in temptation, his death as a sacrifice for sins and his heavenly exaltation. So he is now qualified (*teteleiōmenon*) to be the high priest we need to bring us to eternal salvation. The additional words *for ever* recall the specific promise of Psalm 110:4, putting the focus on his being made completely adequate as high priest in the order of Melchizedek.

The perfecting of Christ as high priest involved typologically fulfilling the ritual of the annual Day of Atonement in Leviticus 16, because this was the most important ministry of the high priest under the law. This is portrayed in 9:11–14 in terms of his entrance into 'the Most Holy Place' by means of his own blood. The sacrificial blood of Jesus is effective to cleanse consciences in the present and obtain 'eternal redemption' for his people, since 'through the eternal Spirit [he] offered himself unblemished to God'. In this sequence of events, he showed himself to be the promised high priest of the New Covenant. His life of perfect obedience culminated in his death on the cross, and his resurrection–ascension brought him into heaven itself, 'now to appear for us in God's presence' (9:24). Christ began his priestly ministry on earth, but this ministry was with reference to the heavenly sanctuary, not the temple in Jerusalem. His self-sacrificing death on the cross and his entrance into the heavenly sanctuary were two phases of the same priestly action. 'The crucifixion belongs to the high priestly office of Christ as well as his present rule in the sanctuary.'[31]

Theology

The priesthood of Christ is bound up with the heavenly world and the age to come (6:19–20; 7:26; 8:1–2; 9:11–15, 23–28). Although his suffering and death were a significant aspect of his priestly role (2:17–18), in order to function as a priest for ever in the order of Melchizedek the incarnate Son, who offered himself once for all as a sacrifice for the sins of his people (v. 27), had to be given 'an indestructible life' through resurrection and heavenly exaltation (v. 16). His perfecting in this way (v. 28) makes possible the perfecting of those who would draw near to God through him (v. 19). The divinely guaranteed permanence of his priesthood enables him to save his people completely, because he always lives to intercede for us (v. 25). The perfecting of Christ as a priest for ever in the order of Melchizedek brought to an end the whole way of relating to God through the levitical priesthood. Indeed, he is the mediator and guarantor of a better covenant, as will be explained more fully in the following chapters.

---

31. G. Schrenk, 'ἀρχιερεύς', *TDNT* 3, p. 276. Cf. Peterson, *Hebrews and Perfection*, pp. 191–195.

8. THE SUPERIOR MINISTRY OF OUR GREAT HIGH PRIEST (8:1 – 10:18)

In an obvious bridge with the previous chapter, the author proclaims that 'we do have such a high priest, who sat down at the right hand of the throne of the Majesty in heaven' (8:1). Then he emphasizes two themes that will occupy his attention in the following chapters: Jesus serves in 'the true tabernacle set up by the Lord, not by a mere human being' (8:2), and Jesus makes a superior offering to those prescribed by the law of Moses (8:3–5). A third theme is introduced with the claim that he is the mediator of a better covenant, established on better promises (8:6). The prophecy of a new covenant in Jeremiah 31:31–34 is cited with comments in 8:7–13 and again more briefly with comments in 10:15–18. This indicates a large inclusion in which Jeremiah's prophecy is foundational to the argument, though allusions to Psalm 110:1 in 8:1 and 10:12 also frame the section.[1] The same themes of sanctuary,

---

1. Exod. 25:40 is also cited in 8:5; Exod. 24:8 in 9:20; and Ps. 40:6–8 in 10:5–10, as secondary texts in the author's presentation.

sacrifice and covenant are intertwined in 9:1 – 10:18, as the author explains how Jesus opens the way to the heavenly sanctuary by his death and heavenly exaltation (9:1–14), providing a definitive cleansing from sin that makes eternal salvation possible (9:15–28), sanctifying believers once for all, and perfecting them for ever (10:1–18). All this establishes the ground for the climactic exhortations in 10:19–25 and the warnings that follow in 10:26–39.

A. Enthroned in heaven and serving in the 'true tabernacle' (8:1–6)

Context

A significant turning point in the pastor's word of exhortation occurs here. The main point of what he has been saying, and will continue to say, is that 'we do have such a high priest, who sat down at the right hand of the throne of the Majesty in heaven' (v. 1; cf. 10:11–13). A priestly perspective on the death and heavenly exaltation of Jesus was first hinted at in 1:3, then developed in 2:17 – 3:1; 4:14 – 5:10; 6:19 – 7:28. But it will be further explained now in terms of his service 'in the sanctuary, the true tabernacle set up by the Lord, not by a mere human being' (v. 2). Moreover, the nature and achievement of his sacrifice in comparison with the sacrifices of the levitical priests will be further explored with reference to this heavenly sanctuary (vv. 3–5; cf. 9:1–14, 23–26; 10:1–14). Foundationally, the ministry Jesus has received makes him the mediator of a superior covenant, established on better promises (v. 6), which will soon be recalled (vv. 7–13).

Comment

1. The expression *the main point of what we are saying* focuses attention on what has just been said about the priesthood of Jesus 'in the order of Melchizedek' (7:11–28) and introduces an important development in the argument. The claim that *we do have such a high priest* specifically picks up the language of 7:26 ('such a high priest'), where Christ is described as 'set apart from sinners, exalted above the heavens'. This is now explained in terms echoing Psalm 110:1. Jesus' ascension made it possible for him to sit down *at the right hand*

of the throne of the Majesty in heaven.[2] God the Father is identified in a reverent and solemn way as the majestic ruler of all things. The first and fourth verses of the psalm are brought together to affirm that Jesus is the promised priest-king, who reigns in heaven at the Father's right hand. 'The pastor's burden is for his hearers to realize that this is the High Priest "we have" (4:14–16; 10:19–25) and to appropriate his benefits' (Cockerill, p. 351).

2. The priestly dimension to the Son's heavenly rule is further expressed by saying that he *serves in the sanctuary, the true tabernacle set up by the Lord, not by a mere human being* (cf. 9:11, 24, 'not made with human hands'). Jesus was previously described as entering 'the inner sanctuary behind the curtain' on our behalf as 'high priest for ever, in the order of Melchizedek' (6:19–20). Now, he is identified as a 'servant' or 'minister' (*leitourgos*) of that sanctuary.[3] The nature of his continuing service is identified in 7:25 as interceding for those who come to God through him. He is not engaged in further sacrifice, since he sacrificed for the sins of his people 'once for all when he offered himself' (7:27). He is now seated at God's right hand, not standing in a sacrificial mode (10:11–14).

The sanctuary that he serves is more broadly identified as *the true tabernacle set up by the Lord, not by a mere human being.* The term *sanctuary* sometimes refers to 'the Most Holy Place' entered by the high priest on the Day of Atonement (9:3; cf. 9:25; 13:11, *ta hagia*). But this term is also used with reference to the realm that Christ entered (8:2; 9:12, 24; 10:19), which is nothing less than 'heaven itself' (9:24). This heavenly sanctuary can be understood as *the true tabernacle* in the sense that it is the genuine, authentic or real tabernacle (BDAG, *alēthinos*), of which the earthly tabernacle was only 'a copy and shadow' (v. 5). The opposite to *true* here is not 'false', but 'earthly'

---

2. As in 1:3, the wording of Ps. 110:1 ('Sit at my right hand') is adapted to read *sat down at the right hand of the throne of the Majesty in heaven* (lit. 'in the heights' in 1:3 and 'in the heavens' in 8:1). God's transcendent rule is further emphasized by insertion of *the throne* in 8:1 (cf. 4:16, 'the throne of grace'). Cf. 10:12; 12:2.

3. This term is used as a parallel to 'priests' in LXX Isa. 61:6; Sir. 7:29–30, but more generally for 'servants' in passages such as Josh. 1:1; Ezra 7:24.

or 'symbolic'.[4] The LORD required an earthly structure to be built by Moses according to the pattern shown to him (Exod. 25:40), but the LORD himself established the sanctuary in which his Son reigns and serves as high priest. This heavenly realm is distinct from the material heavens God created, which will ultimately pass away (cf. 1:10–12, citing Ps. 102:25–27). Although the heavenly sanctuary is presented in apparently concrete terms in Hebrews, the imagery simply means that Christ has definitively opened the way for sinners to approach God and live in his holy presence for ever (12:22–24).

3–4. At this point, the author resumes the argument that Christ's sacrifice is superior to the offerings made by the levitical priests (7:27–28). However, he does so specifically in relation to the respective sanctuaries they serve. First, he provides a simplified version of the previous claim that *Every high priest is appointed to offer both gifts and sacrifices* (5:1). Second, he makes the obvious conclusion that *it was necessary for this one* [Jesus] *also to have something to offer.* Third, he reasons that, *If he were on earth, he would not be a priest, for there are already priests who offer the gifts prescribed by the law.* Jesus was not qualified to be a priest in the traditional sense (cf. 7:13–14), and others were legally appointed to *offer the gifts prescribed by the law.* Jesus did not function as a priest *on earth* in the levitical system, though he offered himself as an obedient sacrifice in the context of an earthly life (5:7–10). This unique sacrifice enabled him to enter the heavenly sanctuary as high priest in the order of Melchizedek and achieve 'eternal redemption' for his people (9:11–12).

5. The real difference, then, is that the levitical priests *serve at a sanctuary that is a copy and shadow of what is in heaven* (ESV, 'of the heavenly things'), whereas Jesus serves the sanctuary towards which that earthly tabernacle pointed. The word *copy* is followed by the word *shadow* in a construction that could be rendered 'a shadowy copy'. These two nouns are used separately but with much the same meaning in 9:23 ('copies') and 10:1 ('shadow'; cf. Col. 2:17). The

---

4. Cockerill (pp. 354–357) rightly opposes the view that a distinction between the heavenly sanctuary and the true tabernacle is implied in 8:2.

sense is revealed with reference to Exodus 25:40, where Moses was warned by God when he was about to complete the tabernacle: *See to it that you make everything according to the pattern shown you on the mountain.* This quotation appears to be a blend of Exodus 25:9 and 40 LXX, embracing all the instructions given for the building and furnishing of the earthly tabernacle *on the mountain* (see also Exod. 26:30; 27:8; Num. 8:4).

The Greek word *typos* suggests that God gave Moses a design or model to follow in establishing the tabernacle and its ministry.[5] This does not mean that there is an ideal sanctuary in heaven that Moses was to copy in every detail. Rather, in the original context, the tabernacle was to serve as 'a portable sanctuary of the presence of God whose covenant will have been made known at Sinai. What happened at Sinai is continued in the tabernacle' (Childs, *Exodus*, p. 540). Sinai was the definitive encounter with God for Israel, and this would be remembered when they approached him at the tabernacle. Hebrews, however, takes the further step of relating *the pattern* shown to Moses to 'the heavenly things' that would be revealed by God's Son (3:5), specifically what was to come with his sacrifice and entry into heaven (9:11–14, 23–26). Old Testament institutions such as the priesthood, the sacrificial system and the tabernacle are regarded as foreshadowing the work of Christ, who opened 'a new and living way' into the actual presence of God (10:19–22).

Although the earthly sanctuary and its ritual was designed to sustain God's people in the covenant that he established with them, it actually showed the need for the surpassing grace of the New Covenant (8:6–13; 9:8–10; 10:1–10). The author's conclusion that the earthly sanctuary was a shadowy copy of heavenly realities 'consigns the earthly sanctuary to the realm of the changing and transitory, which has only limited validity, because it must ultimately pass away' (Lane 1, p. 206). Some scholars have taken the contrast between shadow and reality in verse 5 to reflect the kind of dualism taught by the Greek philosopher Plato and applied to

---

5. BDAG (*typos* 6) shows how this word can mean 'an archetype serving as a model, *type, pattern*'.

the Jewish Scriptures by Philo of Alexandria. However, Hebrews contrasts the limited ministry of levitical priests at an earthly tabernacle with the historic accomplishment of Jesus in his death and heavenly exaltation, which is 'antithetical to the serene and unhistorical metaphysics of Plato' (Lane 1, p. 207). The distinction between the earthly and the heavenly in Hebrews is Christologically driven, rather than philosophically inspired. The author attempts 'to reinterpret the OT in the light of the priestly office of Jesus Christ, and conversely to understand this new office in the light of the old' (Childs, *Exodus*, p. 550). See Introduction 6c, 'Eschatology and salvation'.

6. As the author reflects on *the ministry* Jesus has received (*leitourgia*), he alludes back to the description of him as a 'minister' or 'servant' (*leitourgos*) of the heavenly sanctuary (v. 2).[6] This ministry is said to be *as superior to theirs* [the ministry of the levitical priests] *as the covenant of which he is mediator is superior* ['better']. The word *diathēkē* occurs seventeen times in Hebrews with reference to the covenant established through Moses and the New Covenant. But six times in the text the noun is also implied in expressions like 'the first' or 'another' (8:7 [twice], 13 [twice]; 9:1, 18), making a total of twenty-three.[7] The legal term *mediator* (*mesitēs*) was widely used of 'any sort of arbiter or intermediary, especially in disputes' (O'Brien, p. 292; BDAG). However, the New Covenant is a divine gift and not a mutual agreement worked out between God and his people. Jesus acts as mediator in a unique way when he sheds his blood to inaugurate this covenant and makes its benefits available (12:24). As well as reflecting on the way the first covenant was put into effect by a blood sacrifice (9:16–22), the author could have been influenced by Jesus' saying at the Last Supper, which formed part

---

6. In this context, *leitourgia* means 'service of a formal or public type' (BDAG).

7. Hebrews restricts the term 'covenant' to the divine disposition made with Israel at Sinai through the mediation of Moses (Exod. 19:5–6; 24:3–8) and the New Covenant. The author speaks of God's promises to Abraham (6:13–15; 7:4–6; 11:8–12, 17–18) as the foundation of his covenant relationship with Israel.

of the tradition passed on by the apostle Paul and no doubt other early Christian missionaries as well (1 Cor. 11:23–25; cf. Luke 22:20).

As noted in 7:22, Jesus is also the 'guarantor' of this covenant, because of his appointment with an oath in Psalm 110:4 to an eternal priesthood. The covenant that he mediates and guarantees is eternal (13:20), and it provides access to 'the promised eternal inheritance' (9:15). It does so because of who he is and what he has accomplished, but also because it is *established on better promises*. The verb used here and in 7:11 (*nenomothetētai*) means 'legally enacted'. The passive form implies that God was the one who enacted both covenants (cf. 8:8–10). The covenant made through Moses was limited in its scope and effect, particularly because of the inadequacies of the levitical priesthood and its ministry, but the covenant Jesus inaugurated is founded on *better promises*, which the author is about to articulate.

Theology

Hebrews uses two complementary expressions to identify the sphere into which Christ entered when he offered himself as a perfect sacrifice for sin. On the one hand, it is the heavenly sanctuary of God's holy presence. On the other hand, it is 'the true tabernacle set up by the Lord, not by a mere human being'. This last expression asserts the primacy of the heavenly sanctuary over the tabernacle established by Moses as the place to meet with God. The earthly tabernacle was designed to be 'a copy and shadow' of the 'heavenly things' that would be revealed and accomplished by Christ in his death and heavenly exaltation. The regulations for worship associated with the earthly sanctuary were limited in their effect, while positively revealing something of the solution God would ultimately provide for the perfecting of his people (9:1–15, 23–28; 10:1–14). The promises of the New Covenant are foundational to this solution.

B. Mediator of a new covenant (8:7–13)

Context

As in previous contexts, the author has indicated in advance his intention to develop a new theme of major significance. Having just described Jesus as the mediator of a new covenant (8:6), he now begins to draw out the implications of that claim. Jeremiah 31:31–34 (38:31–34 LXX) is cited in full, with introductory comments (vv. 7–8a) and a concluding observation (v. 13). The author then returns to the subject of the first covenant in 9:1–10, focusing on its regulations for worship and earthly sanctuary. But New Covenant allusions begin to emerge as he explains how Christ has fulfilled the ritual provisions of the former covenant and replaced them (9:11 – 10:14). When an abbreviated version of Jeremiah 31:33–34 appears with comments in 10:15–18, it is clear that this whole section is designed to show how the New Covenant has come into effect through the work of Christ.

Comment

7. The conjunction *For* links this verse with the previous claim that Jesus is the mediator of a better covenant (v. 6). The necessity for that covenant is first argued in a conditional sentence proposing something that is not true: *if there had been nothing wrong with that first covenant, no place would have been sought for another. Nothing wrong* translates the word *amemptos* (BDAG, 'blameless, faultless'). The clause *no place would have been sought for another* refers to God's initiative in speaking through Jeremiah about the need for a new covenant. The author has used this sort of argument before to highlight the implications of a later biblical text for an earlier one. In 4:8 he proposed that if Joshua had brought the people of Israel into God's ultimate rest, Psalm 95:7–11 would not have been written for them. In 7:11 he observed that if perfection could have been obtained through the levitical priesthood, Psalm 110:4 would not have proclaimed the need for another priest to come in the order of Melchizedek. Now he notes how Jeremiah's prophecy pointed to the need for a better covenant to deal with the limitations of the *first covenant*, providing the longest quotation of an Old Testament text in the New Testament and leaving it 'largely to speak for itself' (Ellingworth, p. 413).

8–9. God's word through Jeremiah also *found fault with the people.*[8] This is particularly illustrated by the accusation in verse 9 that *they*

---

8. The verb *memphomai* ('find fault') echoes the related adjective in v. 7 (*amemptos*, 'without fault'). The accusative *autous* after this verb means

did not remain faithful to my covenant ('continue in my covenant').
Despite God's saving intervention, when he *took them by the hand /
to lead them out of Egypt*, and his remarkable ratification of the covenant with their ancestors at Sinai (Exod. 24:1–18), they were soon
disobedient and rebellious (Exod. 32:1–10). Jeremiah's perspective
on the history of his people is that they were unfaithful throughout
the whole period from the exodus to his own time (e.g. Jer. 11:1–13).[9]
Consequently, God's declaration (*I turned away from them*) must
include the judgment expressed in the destruction of the northern
kingdom by the Assyrians in the eighth century BC and subsequent
conquest and captivity of the southern kingdom by the Babylonians
in the sixth century. The Hebrew text speaks of the love of God in
persisting with them despite their rebellion against him ('though I
was a husband to them'), but Hebrews follows the LXX.

Jeremiah's expression *The days are coming* introduces expectations
of redemption and restoration after this period of judgment (Jer.
31:27, 31, 38; cf. 9:25; 16:14; 23:5, 7). Three occurrences of the phrase
declares the Lord and extensive use of first-person verbs reinforce the
point that 31:31–34 is a new and authoritative revelation from God.
But some have argued that the promise of *a new covenant* simply
implies renewal of the previous covenant. There are certainly
elements of continuity with the past in this oracle, but the greater
emphasis is on discontinuity. The claim that

> *It will not be like the covenant*
> *I made with their ancestors*
> *when I took them by the hand*
> *to lead them out of Egypt*
> (v. 9; Jer. 31:32)

---

with the people, but the dative variant *autois* is strongly attested (Lane 1,
p. 202). The latter could suggest the rendering 'he finds fault (with the
first covenant) and says to them'.

9. MT ('broke my covenant') may refer specifically to the building of the
golden calf, but the LXX suggests a continuing pattern of unfaithfulness
('they did not remain in my covenant'). Cf. Ps. 95:7–11; Heb. 3:7–19;
4:11.

is followed by 'because this is the covenant I will establish with the people of Israel after that time' (v. 10; Jer. 31:33).[10] Fundamentally, there is to be a restoration of the relationship between God and his people (v. 8; Jer. 31:31), expressed in the familiar covenantal promise 'I will be their God, / and they will be my people' (v. 10; Jer. 31:33; cf. Jer. 7:23; 11:4; 30:22). God's law will still be central to the relationship, but it will be applied in a new way to minds and hearts. Knowledge of God will be direct and personal (v. 11; Jer. 31:34) and forgiveness will be decisively given (v. 12). This final promise provides the link to the subjects of priesthood and sacrifice, which will be taken up again in 9:1 – 10:18.

The promise to *make a new covenant / with the people of Israel / and with the people of Judah* suggests an amazing restoration of God's relationship with the dispersed and alienated tribes of the northern and southern kingdoms (cf. Jer. 31:15–22 [Israel] and 31:23–26 [Judah]; cf. 3:18; 23:6; 31:27; 50:4–5). However, it should be noted that the beneficiaries could also include representatives from the nations, who are predicted to gather to the Lord in Jerusalem (Jer. 3:17), learn the ways of God's people (12:16) and confess the worthlessness of their idolatry (16:19–21). The nations are not mentioned specifically in 31:31–34, but a wider reading of Jeremiah suggests that the blessings of the New Covenant could apply to Gentiles who are caught up in God's saving plan. In this way, God's ancient promise to bless the nations by blessing Abraham's descendants would be fulfilled (cf. Gen. 12:3; Isa. 2:2–4).[11]

10. The second half of Jeremiah's oracle expresses the newness of the covenant God will *establish with the people of Israel after that time* (addressing northern and southern kingdoms together now). The causal conjunction at the beginning of this verse ('For', ESV) indicates that the provisions of this covenant are a direct response to Israel's failure in regard to the first covenant. God first undertakes, not to write his words on stone tablets as before (Exod. 31:18; 34:28), but to put his laws *in their minds* and to write them *on their*

---

10. NIV does not translate the conjunction *hoti* ('because'), which expresses causality here.

11. Cf. Peterson, *Transformed*, pp. 29–39.

hearts (Jer. 31:33), indicating a profound spiritual transformation (Jer. 24:7; 32:39). In ancient Hebrew thinking, the 'will' came from the 'heart', so if the law is written on the heart, the implication is that God's people will want to obey it. This is another way of saying that God would fulfil his promise to circumcise the hearts of his people, so that they might love him wholeheartedly and live (Deut. 30:6). Only such radical heart surgery could overcome their stubborn disobedience and rebellion against him (cf. Ezek. 11:19–20; 36:26–27).

The traditional covenant formula follows (*I will be their God, / and they will be my people*; cf. Exod. 6:7; 19:5; Lev. 26:12; Deut. 29:13; Ezek. 36:28), with the order of the parties reversed to highlight the initiative of God. Giving his law to his people in this new way would make it possible for the relationship to be restored and transformed (cf. Ezek. 36:24–28; Isa. 59:20–21). The promise of Jeremiah 31:33 both enables and obliges the recipients 'to conform to the will of God and live indeed as those who are God's people' (Williamson, *Sealed*, p. 154).

11. The second promise of the New Covenant is expressed in an emphatic way:

> *No longer will they teach their neighbours,*
> *or say to one another 'Know the Lord.'*

The reason for this predicted change is the promised gift of a direct and personal knowledge of the Lord for each individual:

> *because they will all know me,*
> *from the least of them to the greatest.*
> (Cf. Jer. 31:34)

The verb *know* in this context 'probably carries its most profound connotation, the intimate personal knowledge which arises between two persons who are committed wholly to one another in a relationship that touches mind, emotion, and will'.[12] Previous promises

---

12. Thompson, *Jeremiah*, p. 581.

in Jeremiah that shepherds would feed the people with knowledge and understanding (3:15; 23:4) are not negated here. The meaning is that neighbours and friends across the whole spectrum of the community would share the same knowledge of God and his will and express that knowledge in godly behaviour. Other New Testament writers see this transformative knowledge mediated by the gift of God's Spirit (e.g. Acts 2:1–4, 38–47; 10:44–48; 15:8–9; Rom. 5:5; 8:9–11, 14–17; 2 Cor. 3:18).

12. The third promise of the New Covenant appears to be foundational to the others, because it begins with a causal conjunction (as in the Greek of v. 10):

> *For I will forgive their wickedness*
> *and will remember their sins no more.*

God's forgiveness was known and experienced by his people prior to this (e.g. Exod. 34:6–7; Lev. 4:20, 26, 31, 35; Pss 51:1–9; 130:3–4), but the people in Jeremiah's time had come under the curse of the covenant, which involved exile and the destruction of everything they held dear (Jer. 11:9–13; 13:15–27; cf. Deut. 28:25–68). Many must have wondered whether divine forgiveness would ever be possible again. Jeremiah proclaimed that God would show mercy in restoring, forgiving and cleansing his people from all the guilt of their sin and rebellion (33:8). So decisively would he deal with the problem that their sin would not be remembered by him or be held against them any longer. When God 'remembers' sin, he punishes it (14:10), so when he promises not to remember sin (31:34), he indicates that he will no longer act in judgment against it. No indication is given here about the means by which God's justice would be satisfied or human guilt atoned for, but Hebrews goes on to relate this promise to the atoning death of Jesus, climaxing in the conclusion of 10:18.

13. The author's final observation about Jeremiah 31:31–34 matches his opening comments. *By calling this covenant 'new', [God] has made the first one obsolete.* God is obviously the implied subject here (as in vv. 7–8a), since he spoke so directly and authoritatively through Jeremiah's oracle. The use of the word *new* in that prediction implies the replacement of the first covenant, because of its inability to keep God's people faithful to him. The Lord himself treats the first one as obsolete by proclaiming and providing a new way (ESV rightly translates the Greek perfect tense 'he makes the first one obsolete'). A general principle from life draws this section of the argument to a close: *and what is obsolete and outdated will soon disappear* (cf. Mark 2:21–22). The author applies this principle to the first covenant because of what God has done to fulfil his promise of a new covenant. The words *soon disappear* could point to the imminent passing away of institutions associated with the first covenant, such as the temple and its rituals, enabling us to date Hebrews before AD 70, when this happened with the destruction of Jerusalem by the Romans.

Theology

Jeremiah 31:31–34 blames the people of Israel for being unfaithful to God and to the covenant he made with them through Moses. At the same time, God's promises through Jeremiah expose the inadequacy of the Mosaic covenant to deal with the problem of continuing sin and to enable God's people collectively to be holy and devoted to his service. The unbreakable character of the New Covenant rests on several interconnected promises. Foundationally, God will provide a definitive forgiveness of sins, requiring no further judgment and bringing a new knowledge of God as gracious and faithful. This knowledge will effect a profound change of heart in his people, leading to covenant faithfulness and obedience. Radical forgiveness is the basis for this spiritual and moral transformation.

> The New Covenant will be both national and international in its effect, it will involve both continuity and discontinuity with previous divine covenants, and it will be both the climactic fulfilment of those covenants and an everlasting covenant of peace (Jer. 32:40; 33:6–9).[13]

When Israel is renewed in this way, the blessings will flow to the nations, as originally promised to Abraham and his offspring

---

13. Peterson, *Transformed*, pp. 42–43. Cf. Williamson, *Sealed*, pp. 179–181.

(Gen. 12:3; 18:18; 22:18; 26:4–5). Hebrews 9 – 10 goes on to reveal
the way in which these promises have been fulfilled through Christ.

C. Opening the way to the Most Holy Place and cleansing consciences (9:1–14)

Context

This section develops the contrast between the old and the new,
but now it is expressed in terms of the earthly and the heavenly.
Two particular provisions of the former covenant are highlighted
in 9:1 and then treated in reverse order: the earthly sanctuary
(9:2–5) and its regulations for worship (9:6–10). The earthly nature
of the Mosaic sanctuary and its ritual limited its effectiveness as a
means of relating to God. Indeed, the whole system only foreshadowed in a limited way what the New Covenant would bring.
Its rituals could not 'clear the conscience of the worshipper', but
involved 'external regulations applying until the time of the new
order' (9:9–10). The new order has come with the advent of Christ
as 'high priest of the good things that are now already here', who
has entered the heavenly sanctuary by means of his own blood and
obtained 'eternal redemption' (9:11–12). This makes possible a new
kind of 'service' to God: Christ can 'cleanse our consciences from
acts that lead to death, so that we may serve the living God' (9:14).

Comment

    1. A link with 8:6–13 is made with the transitional conjunction
oun ('so, now, then') and a reference to *the first covenant*. As in 8:7, 13,
the adjective *first* is used in a temporal fashion and the word *covenant*
is to be understood. However, the intention now is to say more
about the cultic provisions of that earlier covenant, specifically its
regulations for worship and its *earthly sanctuary* (cf. 8:3–5). Israel's holy
place (*hagion*) was *earthly* (*kosmikon*) or 'worldly' in the sense that it
was a material construction, made with human hands, limited in its
effectiveness and 'only a copy of the true one' (9:24). An inclusion
is formed by the use of the word *regulations* (*dikaiōmata*) in verses 1
and 10, indicating that this is the main concern of the paragraph.
The earthly sanctuary was the context for carrying out these regulations. Since the description broadens in verse 10 to include 'food

and drink and various ceremonial washings', the word translated 'worship' in verse 1 should be understood more generally to mean 'service' or 'ministry' (as in v. 6; cf. John 16:2; Rom. 9:4; 12:1).

2. The two divisions of the earthly sanctuary are now described. Even though the word 'tent' (*skēnē*) can refer to the tabernacle as a whole (8:5; 9:21; 13:10), it is used here with reference to each of its two 'rooms'. 'The first tent' (*first room*) is called *the Holy Place* (v. 2, *Hagia*) and 'the second tent' ('second room') is called 'the Most Holy Place' (v. 3, *Hagia Hagiōn*).[14] The terms 'first' and 'second' are used from the perspective of the high priest going first into one and then into the other. The biblical record concerning the tabernacle is the author's focus of attention because it was intimately connected with the establishment of the first covenant (Exod. 25 – 30). The temple, which was built much later, had the same two sacred spaces at its centre (1 Kgs 6 – 8).

Each tent in the tabernacle contained items necessary for the rituals prescribed by God. These represented God's dealings with his people in the past and signified his continuing commitment to them. In *the Holy Place* was *the lampstand* made of beaten gold (Exod. 25:31–40), whose lamps were kept perpetually burning before the LORD. There was also *the table* overlaid with gold and (lit.) 'the display of the loaves' (Exod. 25:23–30; cf. 2 Chr. 13:11 LXX). Exodus 25:30 MT speaks literally of 'the bread of the face', which means 'the bread of the Presence'. This table was placed 'outside the [second] curtain on the north side of the tabernacle' and the lampstand was 'opposite it on the south side' (Exod. 26:35). Twelve loaves of bread were set forth each Sabbath and were eaten by the priests on the next Sabbath, accompanied by an incense offering (Lev. 24:5–9). The lampstand and the loaves represented God's presence in the midst of the twelve tribes and his intention to guide and sustain

---

14. The singular expression in 9:1 (*to hagion*) refers to the whole sanctuary. The neuter plural *Hagia* in 9:2 uniquely refers to the first tent (NIV, *first room*), whereas in 9:25; 13:11 *ta hagia* is used as an abbreviation for the emphatic superlative expression *Hagia Hagiōn* ('the Holy of Holies'), namely the second tent or inner room. Cf. Kleinig, pp. 402–403, 420.

them, as he did in the wilderness with fire and cloud and the provision of manna (Exod. 13 – 18).

3–5. The author now describes what lay *behind the second curtain* (Exod. 26:31–35), identifying it as *the Most Holy Place*. The first item mentioned is *the golden altar of incense*. The term *thymiatērion* can mean 'censer' (KJV, NKJV), and some commentators have argued that this refers to the instrument used by the high priest to burn incense in the Most Holy Place on the Day of Atonement (Lev. 16:12–13). However, there is also evidence for this term being used to describe the altar of incense in the tabernacle or temple (BDAG; Koester, p. 395). If this is what Hebrews means, there is a difficulty locating this *behind the second curtain*. Exodus 30:6 says it was to be placed 'in front of the curtain that shields the ark of the covenant law' (cf. 40:26–27), that is, in the Holy Place.[15] Twice a day, incense was burned on this altar by the priests (Exod. 30:7–9; Luke 1:8–10). However, Exodus 40:5 situates it 'in front of the ark of the covenant law', without any mention of an intervening curtain, and 1 Kings 6:22 speaks of the altar of incense in Solomon's temple 'that belonged to the inner sanctuary'. Hebrews picks up this close association of the altar of incense with the inner sanctuary, particularly in relation to the Day of Atonement ritual (Exod. 30:10; Lev. 16:12–13, 18–19). Indeed, it could be said that 'the altar of incense bore the same relation to the Holy of Holies as the altar of burnt offering to the Holy Place. It furnished in some sense the means of approach to it' (Westcott, p. 249).[16]

In the Most Holy Place was *the gold-covered ark of the covenant* (Exod. 25:10–16). The ark was carried with the people as they journeyed into the Promised Land. Eventually, it was taken to Jerusalem and housed in a tent (2 Sam. 6:1–17), until it was placed in the Most Holy Place in the temple (1 Kgs 8:3–9). The ark is said to have contained *the gold jar of manna*, which represented God's food for his

---

15. Some manuscripts remove *the golden altar of incense* from v. 4 and place it in v. 2 to get over the difficulty, but this variation is not widely attested (cf. Metzger, *Textual Commentary*, p. 598).

16. It may be that the participle 'having' (v. 4, *echousa*) reflects this sense of association, in contrast with the more specific 'in which' (v. 2, *en hē*).

people on their journey from Egypt to Canaan (Exod. 16:1–18), and *Aaron's staff that had budded*, establishing the authority of his priestly office (Num. 17:1–9). Originally, these items were placed in front of the ark (Exod. 16:32–34; Num. 17:10–11), but Hebrews implies that they were later preserved in the ark itself. Most importantly, the ark contained *the stone tablets of the covenant* that were given to Moses when he ascended the mountain the second time (Exod. 34:1–4). These tablets contained the Ten Commandments (Exod. 34:28), expressing the essential demands of God in his relationship with Israel. At the same time, they represented his commitment to bring them into the inheritance he had promised them (Exod. 34:10–11) and to maintain his relationship with them there, despite their rebellion against him (Exod. 34:5–9).

The climax of the author's review of the inner sanctuary is his reference to *the cherubim of the Glory* that were above the ark, *overshadowing the atonement cover*. The lid of the ark, which was made of pure gold, is called 'the place of atonement' or 'mercy seat' (*to hilastērion*; Exod. 25:17–22; 26:34; 37:6–9; 40:20 LXX). The related verb is used in 2:17 to describe the work of Christ as high priest (to 'make atonement for the sins of the people'). This was where the high priest sprinkled sacrificial blood on the Day of Atonement (Lev. 16:14–16a). The two cherubim of hammered gold were made to face each other, with wings spread upwards, but looking towards the atonement cover (Exod. 37:6–9). They represented 'the radiant presence of God dwelling in the midst of his people'.[17] Their overshadowing of the mercy seat signified that God's presence was gracious. When the author says *But we cannot discuss these things in detail now*, he reveals that he is not interested in exploring every facet of the earthly sanctuary and suggesting how these details might have been fulfilled by the ministry of Christ. Rather, as the following verses show, he is more concerned to highlight 'the

---

17. Bruce, p. 190. Bruce describes the cherubim as 'composite creatures' (cf. Ezek. 10:10–14). In Gen. 3:24, they guard the way to the tree of life, and in other texts they support or flank the throne of God in heaven (Pss 80:1; 99:1; Isa. 37:16). Cherubim were also woven into the curtains in the tabernacle (Exod. 26:1, 31).

significance of the separation of the first chamber from the second, and the progressive limitations on access to God that these chambers and their regulations enforce' (deSilva, p. 298).

6–7. The author moves now from describing the design of the tabernacle and its contents (*When everything had been arranged like this*) to outlining what took place there. The regular *ministry* or service (*latreia*, as in 9:1) of the priests in the *outer room* ('first tent') was to tend the seven lamps on the seven branches of the lampstand and to burn incense twice each day (Exod. 30:7–10). The morning and evening daily burnt offerings took place on the altar outside the first tent (29:38–46). Every Sabbath, they would also consume the twelve loaves of bread on the table and present new ones to the LORD (Lev. 24:5–9). The many priests who served on a daily basis in the first tent are contrasted with the high priest who alone would enter the second tent *only once a year* on the Day of Atonement (Lev. 16:17). This symbolic entrance into God's presence was *never without blood, which he offered for himself* [Lev. 16:11] *and for the sins the people had committed in ignorance* [Lev. 16:15–16a]. Leviticus 16 does not restrict atonement to the sins committed by the people *in ignorance*, but Hebrews alludes to the teaching of Numbers 15:22–31 that sins committed 'defiantly' (lit. 'with a high hand') cannot be purged by sacrificial blood. Animal blood was sprinkled once on the atonement cover and seven times on the floor of the Most Holy Place (Lev. 16:14–15), but Hebrews uses the word *offered* to prepare for what is later said about the fulfilment of this ritual in the self-offering of Jesus on the cross (9:25–28). The author says nothing about the 'scapegoat' ritual (Lev. 16:20–22), because his focus is on what happened inside the tabernacle on the Day of Atonement.

8. Although these rituals had meaning and significance for the Israelites to whom they were given, by these provisions *The Holy Spirit was showing . . . that the way into the Most Holy Place had not yet been disclosed as long as the first tabernacle was still functioning.*[18] The Holy Spirit

---

18. NIV (*was showing*) implies that this was the Holy Spirit's intention when the law was given to Israel, but the participle is present tense (*dēlountos* [ESV, 'indicates']), implying that the Holy Spirit is speaking in the present about the meaning of these biblical provisions.

continues to speak to believers through the Scriptures he has inspired (3:7; 10:15; cf. 2 Tim. 3:16–17; 2 Pet. 1:21), giving insight into the meaning and purpose of the law's provisions in the light of their fulfilment in Christ. As long as the outer tent blocked the way for all but the high priest to enter the Most Holy Place, the way for others to enter was not manifested. However, 'the first tent' can also be understood to represent the tabernacle as a whole (*the first tabernacle*), meaning the Holy Place and the Most Holy Place together. Both the 'first tent' of the tabernacle and the tabernacle as a whole were 'emblematic of the first covenant' (Kleinig, p. 42), providing a way to God that was restricted and limited. As long as that earthly structure was still functioning, the way into the heavenly sanctuary or 'true tabernacle' (8:2) was not yet revealed.[19]

9. The God-given earthly tabernacle and its ministry are now described as *an illustration for the present time*. The word *parabolē* (*illustration*) here means something that serves as 'a model or example pointing beyond itself for later realization' (BDAG). Debate has taken place about whether *the present time* refers to the old era of the first covenant which, from the author's perspective, was still passing away (8:13), or to the new age inaugurated by Christ's coming. The latter seems more likely, since the author goes on to explain how Christ has opened the way into the heavenly sanctuary by means of his sacrificial death and glorious ascension (vv. 11–12), so that Christians now stand 'under the cultic regime characterized by Christ's completed and effective sacrifice' (Attridge, p. 241; cf. O'Brien, pp. 314–315). But the author first pauses to highlight a significant weakness of the former system.

The gifts and sacrifices being offered in connection with the tabernacle and later the temple were 'not able to perfect the worshipper with respect to conscience' (my translation). This ritual way of relating to God was unable to solve the problem of human guilt, as

---

19. NIV has translated *tōn hagiōn* in 9:8 *the Most Holy Place*, but it should be rendered more generally, as in 8:2 ('the sanctuary'), meaning the heavenly realm where Christ reigns as high priest. The expression 'the way into the sanctuary' is used in 10:19 in connection with Christ's 'blood'.

experienced in the continuing accusations of conscience (cf. 10:2).[20]
The inability of the levitical priesthood and the law to perfect
believers was signalled in 7:11, 19, and contrasted with 'the better
hope' by which we draw near to God through Christ (cf. 10:19–22).
Now it is indicated that the definitive cleansing of consciences
from the guilt of sin is fundamental to that perfecting (cf. v. 14;
10:1–2).

10. The failure of the priesthood and sacrificial system to perfect
the worshippers is explained more broadly in terms of the external
operation of the law (see also 10:1–4). The regulations associated
with worship at the tabernacle were *only a matter of food* [Lev. 11;
Deut. 14] *and drink* [Num. 6:15, 17; 28:7–8] *and various ceremonial
washings* [Exod. 29:4; Lev. 8:6; 16:4]. These were 'regulations for the
body' ('fleshly regulations'), providing purification at a physical
level to enable God's people to approach him at an earthly
sanctuary. But they were imposed only *until the time of the new order*
(*diorthōsis*, 'improvement, reformation' [BDAG]). Parallel terms
would be 'change' (7:12) and 'set aside' (7:18). *The time of the new order*
overlaps 'the present time' (v. 9), but it is not simply synonymous
with it. The author speaks of the New Covenant being inaugurated
by Jesus (8:6), but also observes that the old order is yet to disappear
(8:13). The earthbound system of the first covenant was a temporary
provision in God's plans for his people, until Christ came to fulfil
and replace it (9:11–14). By implication, this pastor does not want
any of those he addresses to be satisfied with the practices and
limitations of the old order, however that challenge might be facing
them. See Introduction 3, 'Occasion and purpose'.

11–12. The name *Christ*, meaning 'the Messiah', occurs in an
emphatic position at the beginning of this one long sentence in
Greek. A series of contrasts with the previous section (vv. 1–10)
shows how the institutions of sacrifice, priesthood and tabernacle
find their fulfilment in his death and heavenly exaltation.

---

20. The word *syneidēsis* ('conscience') appears in 9:9, 14; 10:2, 22; 13:18.
    A burdened, smiting 'heart' is the OT way of describing the pain
    of conscience (e.g. 1 Sam. 24:5; 25:31; 2 Sam. 24:10). Cf. C. Maurer,
    'σύνοιδα, συνείδησις', *TDNT* 7, pp. 908–911.

First, it is stated that he *came as high priest of the good things that are now already here.* He 'appeared' (*paragenomenos*) in history to fulfil the role of the high priest who now serves in the heavenly sanctuary (8:1–2). His ministry has brought *the good things* promised in 8:6–12, with all the implications to be teased out in 9:12–15. These blessings are now *already here* and available to be enjoyed.[21]

Second, the priestly ministry of Christ is described in terms of an extended comparison with that of the high priest on the annual Day of Atonement (v. 7). Jesus *went through the greater and more perfect tabernacle that is not made with human hands, that is to say, is not a part of this creation,* so as to enter *the Most Holy Place.* Hebrews speaks of the heavens in three different ways: the created and transitory heavens (1:10–12; 12:26), the heavens through which Jesus passed in his ascension (4:14; 7:26; 9:11), and 'heaven itself', which is a way of speaking about the true sanctuary of God's presence (9:24, 25). In contrast with the earthly tabernacle, the heavenly realms where God can be approached are *not made with human hands* and are *not a part of this creation.* In his crucified and resurrected body, our high priest passed through the supernatural spheres separating us from God to enter his actual presence. 'Soteriological significance is not given to the intermediary heavens *per se*, but to Christ's passage through these, that is to his *ascension* (cf. Eph. 4:8–10; 1 Pet. 3:22)' (Peterson, *Hebrews and Perfection*, p. 143). This placed the crucified Saviour on the throne at God's right hand to serve for ever as our heavenly intermediary or intercessor in 'the true tabernacle' (8:1–2; cf. 7:25; Rev. 5:6–10).

Third, *He did not enter by means of the blood of goats and calves, but he entered the Most Holy Place once for all by his own blood.* Animals had to be killed before the high priest could enter the inner sanctuary of the tabernacle and make atonement for himself, his household and the whole community of Israel (Lev. 6:6–19). *Goats* were the sin offering for the people and *calves* or fully grown bulls the sin

---

21. Some manuscripts read 'that are to come' (NIV mg.), but the reading 'that have come' (NIV) is better attested (Metzger, *Textual Commentary*, p. 598). The variant appears to have been influenced by the wording of 10:1.

offering for the priests. Atonement involved sprinkling sacrificial blood on the ark, the walls of the tent and the altar. But this yearly ritual was unable to perfect those who drew near (7:19; 9:9; 10:1–3), since it secured only a limited approach to God through that earthly sanctuary. Moreover, the author goes on to assert that 'It is impossible for the blood of bulls and goats to take away sins' (10:4). The blood of Christ, however, enabled him to enter *the Most Holy Place* of God's heavenly presence and be seated there for ever (8:1–2; 10:12–13).

The adverb *once for all* (*ephapax*), which was used in connection with his sacrifice for sins in 7:27 (see also 10:10), is here applied to his entrance into the heavenly sanctuary on our behalf. The parallel term *hapax* was used with reference to the high priest's once-a-year entrance into the Most Holy Place in 9:7, but mostly it is applied to Christ's single and decisively unique sacrifice for sins (9:26, 27, 28; 10:2). The phrase *by his own blood* suggests that he willingly made himself the eternally effective sacrifice for sins. This was so because his blood was shed as the climax of a perfectly obedient life (9:14; 10:5–10). The term *blood*, which is critical to the argument in verses 12, 13, 14, 18, 19, 20, 21, 22 and 25, is 'clearly being used in a sacrificial sense – it is a life poured out in death as a sacrifice' (O'Brien, p. 321; cf. Lev. 17:11).

Fourth, Jesus' death on the cross and entry into the heavenly sanctuary through resurrection and ascension obtained for his people *eternal redemption*.[22] The term employed here (*lytrōsis*) refers to the experience of being 'liberated from an oppressive situation' (BDAG; cf. Luke 1:68; 2:38). In the LXX, this word group was used in connection with the buying back of land (Lev. 25:24, 26, 29) or slaves (Exod. 21:30; Lev. 25:48). Most importantly, it was used to describe the release of Israel from slavery in Egypt at the time of the exodus (Exod. 6:6; 15:13; Deut. 7:8; 9:26; 15:15). Jesus spoke about giving his life as a 'ransom' (*lytron*) for many (Matt. 20:28; Mark 10:45), and this notion is variously applied in different New

---

22. The aorist participle *heuramenos* following the main verb *eisēlthen* most likely indicates coordinate action (*entered . . . so obtaining*). Cf. Lane 2, p. 230 n. f.

Testament contexts (Rom. 3:24; 1 Cor. 6:20; 7:23; Gal. 3:13; 4:5; Eph. 1:7; Col. 1:14; Titus 2:14; 1 Pet. 1:18).

According to 2:14–18, human beings are universally subject to temptation, sin, death and the devil's power. To this we could add the prospect of facing God's ultimate judgment against sin (10:30–31; 12:25–27, 29; 13:4). Christ's atoning work for the sins of his people is necessary for release from every aspect of this slavery. The redemption he has made possible is eternally effective and eternally available, because the appropriate 'price' has been paid. A related term is used in verse 15 (*apolytrōsis*), where his death is described as a 'ransom' to set them free from sin's consequences and open the way to 'the promised eternal inheritance'.

13–14. The superior outcome of Christ's atoning and redemptive work is further explained by contrasting it with the achievement of animal sacrifices. *The blood of goats and bulls* recalls what is said about the Day of Atonement ritual in verse 12. But the author adds a reference to the occasional sacrifice of a heifer, the ashes of which were to be sprinkled with water on any Israelite who had touched a dead body (Num. 19:9–13). 'The water of purification' was also used to cleanse the Levites when they were installed for service at the tabernacle (Num. 8:6–7). Purification and sanctification are closely linked when it is said that those who were *ceremonially unclean* or defiled were sprinkled to *sanctify them so that they are outwardly clean* (ESV, 'for the purification of the flesh'). This ritual is mentioned to reinforce the external nature of every ceremony associated with the tabernacle and temple (cf. v. 10).[23] Ritual cleansing simply enabled individuals to keep participating in the worshipping community.

The claim that blood and ashes purified and sanctified under the former covenant, even if only at a ceremonial level, provides the basis for the *how much more* argument that follows. *The blood of Christ* refers not primarily to physical blood, but to his self-offering in death, which achieved the eternal redemption just mentioned (v. 12). The following clause clarifies this by claiming that *through*

---

23. 'Calves' are mentioned in v. 12 (cf. Lev. 16:11–19 LXX [*moschos*]), though MT has 'bull' (*par*). The latter is represented in v. 13 (*tauros*), suggesting that our author saw these as interchangeable terms.

the eternal Spirit [he] offered himself unblemished to God. Although it has been argued that *the eternal Spirit* refers to Christ's inner disposition or divine nature, the author consistently uses the term *pneuma* ('spirit') to refer to the Holy Spirit (2:4; 3:7; 6:4; 9:8; 10:15, 29). The voluntary and rational nature of Jesus' sacrifice as the incarnate Son was the culmination of a lifetime of obedience to God the Father, upheld and directed by God's Spirit (cf. Isa. 42:1; Mark 1:9–11 par.). By implication, God as Trinity was involved in the whole process of redemption.[24]

The sacrifice of Christ was *unblemished* because, although 'tempted in every way, just as we are ... he did not sin' (4:15; cf. 5:7–9; 7:26–27). In the LXX, the term *amōmos* ('unblemished') was applied to animals without physical defect (Exod. 29:1; Lev. 1:3; Num. 6:14), but also to people with blameless lives (Pss 18:23 [17:23 LXX]; 37:18 [36:18 LXX]; Prov. 11:5). This Old Testament teaching anticipated the need for the perfectly blameless self-offering of Jesus.

The blood of the Messiah, which means his sacrificial death, achieved a new and decisive way of cleansing people from sin and sanctifying them (cf. Jer. 31:34; Ezek. 36:25, 33). It can *cleanse our consciences from acts that lead to death, so that we may serve the living God.* A clear contrast with 9:9 is made here: animal blood could not 'perfect the worshipper with respect to conscience', but the blood of Christ can liberate the guilty conscience *from acts that lead to death* (ESV, 'from dead works'). These 'works' are not the rituals of the first covenant that must be left behind, but sins that bring the judgment of God and need to be rejected. The opposite of 'dead works' is 'good works' (10:24), as illustrated in 10:32–35; 13:1–19. Repentance is required from dead works (6:1) and cleansing from sin is necessary to experience sanctification (10:10). The cleansing made possible by the sacrifice of Christ (1:3) must be applied to human hearts to cleanse them from a guilty conscience (10:22). No explanation is given for how this happens, but we may infer that,

---

24. Ellingworth (p. 457) says 'a reference to the Holy Spirit need not imply the later developed trinitarian theology', but Hebrews certainly lays the ground for this.

when people believe the message about Christ's atoning work, they are liberated from the fear of sin's penalty (2:15) and the controlling power of 'dead works', so that they may *serve the living God* (cf. 12:28–29).[25] With such language this pastor shows how the promises of the New Covenant (Jer. 31:33–34) are fulfilled by Christ and applied to the lives of believers. Jesus has provided the definitive forgiveness of sins that brings a new knowledge of God as gracious (2:9) and moves people to serve him with transformed minds and hearts. This is how the purifying work of Christ achieves our sanctification or consecration to God's service (2:11; 10:10, 29: 13:12).

Theology
More is made of the heavenly ascension of Jesus in Hebrews than anywhere else in the New Testament. In his crucified and resurrected body, he moved into another dimension or sphere of existence described as 'heaven itself' or 'God's presence' (9:24; cf. Luke 24:51; Acts 1:9–11). By this means, he was exalted to God's 'right hand' to reign for ever as the messianic Son (1:3, 13; cf. Acts 2:33–36; Eph. 4:7–10; 1 Pet. 3:22) and be the eternal intercessor for his people (7:25; cf. Rom. 8:34). The importance of this for us is teased out in 4:14–16; 6:19–20; 10:19–22. As the fully proven and crucified Saviour, he entered the heavenly 'sanctuary' to open 'a new and living way' for his people. A typological comparison with the entrance of the high priest into the Most Holy Place on the annual Day of Atonement shows how Christ's earthly sacrifice and heavenly ascension meet our greatest needs (9:11–15, 24–26). As the high priest who went into God's presence by means of his own sacrificial blood, he achieved an eternal redemption from sin (9:12), which has present and future consequences (9:14, 15). Cleansing consciences from 'acts that lead to death', he frees us to serve God in the present and ultimately receive 'the promised eternal inheritance'.

---

25. Such service to God involves 'a manner of life which is pleasing to God and which is sustained both by gratitude and a serious sense of responsibility' (H. Strathmann, 'λατρεύω', *TDNT* 4, p. 64).

D. Providing the sacrifice that makes eternal salvation possible (9:15–28)

Context

From this point we begin to see more closely how Christ's entrance into the heavenly sanctuary is related to the bringing of his people into their eternal inheritance. The author returns to the theme of Jesus as mediator of a new covenant (v. 15, recalling 8:6) and focuses on his death as the means by which he fulfils its promises. Animal blood had to be shed to inaugurate the first covenant (vv. 16–22), but Christ's blood inaugurates the second covenant and secures permanent access to God for his people, providing the perfect cleansing from sin (vv. 23–24, recalling vv. 11–12, 14). The final emphasis of the passage is on the once-for-all nature of Christ's sacrifice and its eternal consequences (vv. 25–28). When Christ appears again, it will not be to deal with sin but to 'save those who are eagerly waiting for him' (ESV).

Comment

15. The phrase *For this reason* indicates a close link with the previous argument. Christ's sinless self-offering in death provides a cleansing from sin and its consequences that reveals him to be *the mediator of a new covenant* (cf. 8:6, 10–12; Mark 14:24; 1 Cor. 11:25). A definitive forgiveness of sins has been provided (10:17–18), enabling a decisive turning from 'acts that lead to death, so that we may serve the living God' (9:14). Death as the divine penalty for sin remains the underlying assumption in 9:16–28 (cf. Gen. 3:21–24; Rom. 5:12–21; Heb. 2:14–18).

In the Greek text of verse 15, the claim is first made that a death has occurred *as a ransom to set them free from the sins committed under the first covenant.* The author has argued that the sacrifices and cere-monies of the Sinai covenant were 'external regulations applying until the time of the new order' (vv. 10, 13), and will soon claim that they were unable to 'take away sins' (10:4). But the death of Christ applies retrospectively to those who genuinely expressed their need for forgiveness and cleansing through the sacrificial system (e.g. Isa. 1:16–20). In God's plan, these sacrifices were symbols or types, pointing forward to the *ransom (apolytrōsis)* provided by the death of

Jesus (cf. v. 12). The purpose of this ransom was to provide for release from the penalty for sin throughout time. The term used here (*parabaseōn*, 'transgressions') indicates 'the act of deviating from an established boundary or norm' (BDAG; cf. Rom. 4:15; 5:14). But all forms of sin, deliberate or otherwise, are covered by the atoning death of Jesus. Cleansing and ransom are the related effects of his sacrifice (cf. 2:17). By this means, *those who are called may receive the promised eternal inheritance.*

The first generation of Israelites coming out of Egypt failed to enter their earthly inheritance (3:16–19), and so Psalm 95:7–11 took this as a warning to subsequent generations not to miss out on the 'rest' still awaiting God's people. The pastor employed that text to challenge his Christian audience not to fall short of God's rest by failing to persevere in faith (3:12–15; 4:1–11; 6:10–12). Elsewhere, this rest or promised eternal inheritance is identified with 'the world to come' (2:5), 'glory' (2:10), 'the resurrection of the dead' (6:2; 11:35), a 'better and lasting possession' (10:34), a 'city with foundations, whose architect and builder is God' (11:10), 'a better country – a heavenly one' (11:16), 'Mount Zion . . . the city of the living God, the heavenly Jerusalem' (12:22), 'a kingdom that cannot be shaken' (12:28) and 'the city that is to come' (13:14). These images point to the fulfilment of a range of expectations in the prophetic literature about the ultimate future of God's people. Eternal life in God's presence is only possible if the penalty for sin has been paid. Believers under the former covenant will share with New Covenant believers in the perfection of God's new creation because of the death of Jesus (11:39–40; 12:22–24). This eternal inheritance is God's gracious gift to *those who are called*. The author does not explicitly say so, but *those who are called* must ultimately include anyone who has heard the gospel call and come to faith in Christ, not just believing Israelites (cf. 2:10–11; 3:1, 6, 14).

16–17. Mention of 'the first covenant' in verse 15 will soon lead the author to focus on the way it was put into effect by the shedding of blood (v. 18). But before he explains how that happened, he makes a more general observation. NIV translates *diathēkē* in the standard Hellenistic sense of 'last will and testament' in verses 16–17 (so also NRSV, ESV, CSB), but there are difficulties with that rendering here. First, the term is used throughout Hebrews in line with its more usual LXX sense ('covenant'), and that is its meaning in the surrounding verses (vv. 15, 18–20). Second, if the author is talking about 'a will', what he claims does not correspond to 'any known legal practice Hellenistic or otherwise, with respect to the validation or ratification of a will' (Williamson, *Sealed*, p. 203; cf. O'Brien, pp. 328–332). The terms used in verse 17 speak of the initiation of a covenant, rather than the executing of the terms of a will after the death of a testator. Contextually, it is more likely that the author has in mind the ancient covenant-making practice in which the notional death of the covenant-maker had to be 'borne' sacrificially by the 'dead bodies' of animals (*epi nekrois*; cf. Gen. 15:9–10; 22:13; Jer. 34:18–20) or 'brought forward' in a sacrificial sense (Lane 2, p. 231).[26] This was supremely expressed in the ratification of the first covenant at Sinai, which becomes the particular focus in verses 18–21. Animal sacrifices appear to have represented the deaths of the covenant-makers if they did not fulfil the obligations of the covenant. Thus, verse 17 could be rendered 'for a covenant is ratified [*bebaia*, 'valid'] on corpses, since it is not in force as long as the one who made it lives' (Williamson, *Sealed*, p. 206).

18–19. The general principle articulated in verses 16–17 is now explicitly related to the covenant God made with Israel at Sinai. For the reasons just given, *even the first covenant was not put into effect without blood*. The perfect-passive tense of the verb used here gives prominence to the action of inaugurating this covenant with blood, as recorded in Scripture, so that the clause could be translated 'is not inaugurated without blood'. When the obligations of that covenant had been declared (*When Moses had proclaimed every command of the law to all the people*), and these had been written down, Moses 'built an altar at the foot of the mountain and set up twelve stone pillars representing the twelve tribes of Israel' (Exod. 24:3–4). Young men were sent to offer burnt offerings and sacrifice young bulls to the LORD. Then Moses 'took the Book of the Covenant and read it to

---

26. This translation of the verb *pheresthai* is more natural than *prove* (NIV) or 'establish' (ESV, CSB), which are renderings designed to make sense of the sentence if the reference is to someone's last will and testament.

the people. They responded, "We will do everything the LORD has said; we will obey"' (Exod. 24:5–7).

Hebrews abbreviates this account, but also adds words to the critical description of what Moses did next: *he took the blood of calves, together with water, scarlet wool and branches of hyssop, and sprinkled the scroll and all the people* (cf. Exod. 24:8).[27] The sprinkling of *the scroll* and *the people* with animal blood identified God and his people as the two parties in this covenant, though the initiative was entirely God's (see v. 20). Half the blood was splashed on the altar (representing God) and half on the people, but Hebrews takes *the scroll* to represent God and his demands. 'The blood bound the people, on pain of death, to obey the stipulations proclaimed and now written in "the book"' (Cockerill, p. 408). Sacrificial *blood* is the key to this event, though Hebrews adds ritual elements associated with cleansing in other biblical contexts: *water* (Lev. 14:2–7); *scarlet wool* (Lev. 14:48–52); and *branches of hyssop* (Num. 19:6, 17–18). This anticipates the emphasis on cleansing with blood in 9:22.

20. The significance of blood for the inauguration of the first covenant is emphasized with this adaptation of some words from Exodus 24:8: *This is the blood of the covenant, which God has commanded you to keep.* The verb *commanded* (*eneteilato*) highlights the authority of God in declaring the obligations of this covenant. The demonstrative *this* (*touto*) points to animal blood as the means of putting it into effect. Hebrews substitutes 'God' for 'the LORD', perhaps to avoid confusion with the Lord Jesus as subject. It is noteworthy that Jesus made his own adaptation of Moses' words at the Last Supper, when he indicated that the wine represented his own blood as the means of inaugurating the New Covenant (Mark 14:24: 'This is my blood of the covenant, which is poured out for many'; Matt. 26:28 adds 'for the forgiveness of sins'; cf. Luke 22:20; 1 Cor. 11:25).

---

27. Many manuscripts have 'and goats' after 'calves' (v. 19; cf. KJV, NRSV, ESV, NASB), but this addition is likely to be influenced by the wording of v. 12. Cf. Metzger, *Textual Commentary*, p. 500. Commentators mostly prefer the shorter reading.

21–22. *In the same way* refers to manner, rather than timing. The sprinkling with blood now mentioned actually took place when Aaron and his sons were consecrated as priests and Moses *sprinkled with the blood the tabernacle and everything used in its ceremonies* (Exod. 29:10–21). This inauguration of the earthly sanctuary was typical of other purification rites prescribed by God: *In fact, the law requires that nearly everything be cleansed with blood.* Hebrews draws attention to various uses of blood under the law: it provides access to God's presence (vv. 7, 12), outward purification and sanctification of the people (v. 13), covenant inauguration (vv. 18–20) and sanctuary inauguration (vv. 21–22). But its most fundamental application is highlighted by saying *without the shedding of blood there is no forgiveness.*

The noun *aphesis* literally means 'release' (BDAG) and can be applied to freedom from captivity, obligation, guilt or punishment (compare v. 15 'ransom', *apolytrōsis*). The context implies release from the penalty for sin and so forgiveness (as in 10:18). Animals substituted for humans in paying the penalty for sin and thereby atoning for it with their lives (Lev. 17:11). Sacrificial blood was regularly poured out at the base of the altar as a sin offering to God (Exod. 29:12; Lev. 4:7).[28] However, verse 15 indicates that true release from the penalty for sins committed under the first covenant came only with the death of Jesus (cf. 10:17–18). He not only cleansed, but also 'took upon himself the penalty due his people for breach of covenant' (Cockerill, p. 411; cf. v. 26 'to do away with sin'; v. 28 'to bear sin').

23. The inferential conjunction *then* (*oun*), meaning 'therefore' or 'thus', indicates that the author is about to make further typological connections between the rituals of the first covenant and the work of Christ. A verbal link with verse 22 is formed by the verb *purified* and two 'necessities' are highlighted. First, *It was necessary . . . for the copies of the heavenly things to be purified with these sacrifices.* This recalls

---

28. The term translated *the shedding of blood* by NIV (*haimatekchysia*) combines the noun for 'blood' and the verb 'pour out'. It refers to the application of animal blood to the altar, not to its shedding in death (Kleinig, pp. 444–445).

the claim that levitical priests 'serve at a sanctuary that is a copy and shadow of what is in heaven' (8:5). The meaning there is that God gave Moses a design to follow in establishing the tabernacle and its ministry. This does not mean that there is an ideal sanctuary in heaven he was to copy in every detail. Rather, *the heavenly things* (*tōn epouraniōn*) is a way of describing what was to come with the sacrifice of Christ and his entry into heaven. Earthly purification rites were necessary for an earthly way of approaching God in anticipation of Christ's heavenly way of dealing with the problem of sin.

Second, therefore, it was necessary for *the heavenly things themselves* to be purified *with better sacrifices than these*. The plural expression *better sacrifices* is used in a rhetorical contrast with *these sacrifices*, but the author goes on to clarify that the single sacrifice of Christ achieves this purification and the eternal salvation it brings (9:26–28; 10:12). If the author is still thinking in terms of the consecration of the earthly sanctuary (as in vv. 21–22), he is viewing the purificatory death of Jesus as inaugurating or opening up the heavenly sanctuary (with no suggestion of previous impurity; cf. Kleinig, pp. 460–461). However, if a specific comparison is being made with the yearly process of cleansing the earthly sanctuary, because of the sin of the people (Lev. 16:14–19), the author could mean that Christ provided a definitive cleansing from sin that removed every barrier to fellowship with God that exists, not simply in human hearts. Westcott (p. 272) suggests that the consequences of human sin 'extend throughout creation in a way which we are unable to define', and conversely, 'the effect of Christ's work extends throughout creation, with reconciling, harmonising power (Eph. 1:10; Col. 1:20)'. Less likely is the view that *the heavenly things* refers to the people of God who need to be cleansed at the level of their consciences, as in 9:14; 10:22.[29] Something extra is being claimed here.

---

29. O'Brien (pp. 337–338) expounds this view, which involves identifying the people of God as the sanctuary where God would dwell (cf. 3:6, 'we are his house'), who need to be cleansed from sin. But this idea seems remote from the present context.

24. The causal conjunction *For* indicates that this verse provides a further explanation of the previous one. Picking up ideas from 8:2, 5; 9:11–12, it affirms that *Christ did not enter a sanctuary made with human hands that was only a copy of the true one.* The phrase *not . . . made with human hands* (as in 9:11) substitutes for 'set up by the Lord, not by a human being' (8:2), and the adjective *antitypos* is used as a noun-substitute, meaning 'copy, representation' (BDAG). It functions like *typos* ('pattern') in 8:5, indicating that God gave Moses a design or model to follow in establishing the tabernacle and its ministry. The earthly sanctuary was designed to prefigure the way of approaching God's true 'dwelling place' in heaven where Jesus would go. So the author says plainly that Christ entered *heaven itself, now to appear for us in God's presence.* Only here in Hebrews does the unusual singular form *heaven* denote 'the highest heaven in which the true sanctuary as the dwelling place of God exists' (Lane 2, p. 248). Appearing before the LORD in the Old Testament was associated with the coming of God's people to the earthly sanctuary in celebration (Exod. 23:15, 17; 34:23–24; Deut. 16:16; 31:11). However, the qualification *for us* points to Christ's high-priestly role as our representative and intercessor in this regard (6:20; 7:25). Every day, the high priest was to appear 'before the LORD' in the Holy Place on behalf of the Israelites (Exod. 28:9–12, 21, 29; 30:7–8). The high priest's representative role 'before the LORD' on the annual Day of Atonement was the most important expression of this (Lev. 16:7, 10, 12, 13, 18, 30). As the crucified and glorified Saviour, Jesus has been accepted into God's presence once for all, opening the way for us to draw near to God through him and join in the eternal celebration of his victory (4:14–16; 10:19–22; 12:22–24).

25–26. Although the author has made several typological links with the Day of Atonement ritual, he now highlights important differences in the heavenly fulfilment of this liturgy. Christ did not enter heaven *to offer himself again and again, the way the high priest enters the Most Holy Place every year with blood that is not his own.* If this were the case, *he would have had to suffer many times since the creation of the world,* which is obviously absurd. The singularity of Jesus' sacrifice and its eternal significance is then emphasized: *But he has appeared once for all at the culmination of the ages to do away with sin by the sacrifice of himself.* A different verb is used here (*phaneroun*) to refer to the Son of God's appearance on earth (compare v. 24), which was for the purpose of dealing decisively with sin. The emphatic adverb *once for all* (*hapax*) highlights the uniqueness of this event (see also 9:28; 10:2; 1 Pet. 3:18). Indeed, his death marked *the culmination of the ages* (cf. 1:2, 'in these last days') or 'the climax of history' (Lane 2, p. 249). It had 'eschatological' significance, inaugurating the promised era of salvation. Christ's goal was *to do away with sin by the sacrifice of himself*, indicating a final settlement or 'removal' of sin (10:5–18; cf. 1 John 3:5, 'take away our sins').[30]

27–28. The author continues to emphasize the humanity of Jesus by comparing his death with that of human beings generally, who are *destined to die once, and after that to face judgment*. Eternal judgment was one of the elementary teachings mentioned in 6:2, and more will be said about this topic in 10:26–31; 12:23, 25–27, 29; 13:4. But Christ's human experience was different. Having died once, he entered heaven (v. 24), and did not have to face judgment for his sins. In fact, he *was sacrificed once to take away the sins of many*. On the cross, he bore the judgment due to others. For the third time in verses 26–28 the author uses the adverb *once* [*for all*], but this time with specific reference to the atoning death of Jesus.

A clear allusion to Isaiah 53:12 LXX can be seen from the following translation: 'he was offered once for all to bear the sins of many'. The same verb (*anapherein*) is used in both contexts to convey the sense of 'bearing' or 'paying for' their sins (see also Isa. 53:11 LXX, 'he will bear their sins'). Bearing sin means bearing the punishment for sin (e.g. Gen. 4:13; Lev. 24:15; Num. 14:34; Lam. 5:7; cf. 1 Pet. 2:24). The innocent Servant of the LORD in Isaiah's prophecy experiences God's just judgment against sin (vv. 4–6). The Lord 'makes his life an offering for sin' (v. 10), so that he can 'justify many' (v. 11). Although Hebrews speaks about the fulfilment of this prophecy in passive terms here (*Christ was sacrificed*), the active submission of Jesus to God's will in offering himself as a sacrifice for sin is emphasized elsewhere (5:7–10; 7:27; 9:14, 25, 26;

---

30. The same noun (*athetēsis*), which is used in 7:18 to describe the 'setting aside' of the regulation about levitical priesthood, has the technical legal meaning of 'annulment' (BDAG).

10:5–10). Christ bore the punishment for the sins of his people and in this way made a once-for-all atonement for their sins (2:17). Isaiah 53 seems to have been a reason for Hebrews to combine the ideas of Jesus as sacrificial victim and sacrificing priest. Note also that Isaiah 53:12 speaks about the Servant making 'intercession for the transgressors' (cf. Heb. 7:25).

At this point, the author adds his only explicit reference to the second coming of Jesus (though this is alluded to in 10:25, 37): *he will appear a second time, not to bear sin, but to bring salvation to those who are waiting for him* (*apekdechomenois*, 'eagerly waiting' [BDAG; ESV]). In his fulfilment of the Day of Atonement ritual, Christ went into the heavenly sanctuary by means of his own blood and obtained eternal redemption (vv. 11–12). When he appears again, it will not be to deal with the problem of sin any further, as the high priest did when he came out of the earthly tabernacle (Lev. 16:18–22). Rather, it will be 'to bring the full experience of salvation to those who look forward to his return' (my paraphrase). *Salvation* in Hebrews clearly involves deliverance from God's judgment and his wrath against sin, but it also embraces the positive consequences of being forgiven and brought into an eternal relationship with God (1:14; 2:3, 10; 5:9; 6:9; 7:25). In other words, in this context it corresponds to 'the promised eternal inheritance' (v. 15 and parallel terms). *Those who are waiting for him* are also 'those who are called' (v. 15). They prove their call and election by continuing to hope in Christ and wait for the final experience of the salvation he has already achieved for them (6:11–12; 10:32–39).

Theology

The themes of covenant, blood sacrifice and eternal salvation are neatly tied together in this passage. Jesus shed his blood to inaugurate the New Covenant and its blessings. He did this by acting as our high priest in relation to the heavenly sanctuary (vv. 24–26) and by fulfilling the Suffering Servant's calling to 'bear the sins of many' (v. 28; cf. Isa. 53:12). He frees believers from the penalty of sin and makes it possible for them to enter the promised eternal inheritance (v. 15). Put differently, he will bring eternal salvation to those who await his return (v. 28). So the full implications of the second covenant are teased out by further comparison with the provisions of the first. God's presence can be accessed only because of the perfect sacrifice of our heavenly high priest and his entrance into God's heavenly sanctuary. Believers can now draw near to God in heaven, with confidence in the benefits won for them by Christ (4:14–16; 10:19–22), while they eagerly await his return and the joy of sharing God's 'rest' (4:9–11) in 'the city that is to come' (13:14).

E. Sanctifying believers once for all and perfecting them for ever (10:1–18)

Context

This climactic passage draws together many threads from the previous argument and forms a concluding bracket around the argument that began with 8:1–13. An allusion to Psalm 110:1 in 10:12–13 reasserts the claim that we have a high priest who is enthroned at God's right hand in heaven (8:1). A repetition of Jeremiah 31:33–34 in 10:15–18 reaffirms that he is the mediator of a new covenant (8:6–13). A narrower inclusion is formed between 10:1 and 10:14 with the repetition of key terms.[31] In this section, the many sacrifices that were perpetually offered under the law are contrasted with the one sacrifice of Christ. Those many sacrifices were not able to 'make perfect those who draw near to worship', but by his single sacrifice Christ has 'made perfect for ever those who are being made holy'. More specifically, the ineffectiveness of the sacrificial system is highlighted in verses 1–4; God's will to replace that system with 'the sacrifice of the body of Jesus Christ once for all' is argued in verses 5–10 (based on Ps. 40:6–8); the ministry of priests under the former system is contrasted with the eternally effective ministry of Jesus in verses 11–14; and Jesus' high-priestly ministry is affirmed as fulfilling the promises of Jeremiah 31:33–34 in verses 15–18. These paragraphs are arranged in a concentric way,

---

31. The verb 'offered' (v. 1, not translated by NIV) is matched by the noun 'offering' (v. 14; NIV, 'sacrifice'); the verb '[make] perfect' is used in both verses; and the expression rendered 'endlessly' in v. 1 is translated 'for ever' in v. 14.

'with the law and the new covenant treated in the first and last paragraphs, while the superiority of Christ's sacrifice and priesthood to the Levitical institutions occupy the two middle parts' (O'Brien, p. 344).

Comment

1. Returning to the subject of the sacrificial system, the author emphasizes the limited way it enabled the Israelites to draw near to God through priestly mediation at an earthly sanctuary (cf. 5:1–3; 8:3–5; 9:1–10).[32] In particular, he picks up the argument from 8:5, where it was said that the levitical priests served at 'a sanctuary that is a copy and shadow of what is in heaven'. More broadly, the whole law is now described as having *only a shadow of the good things that are coming*. The word *shadow* (*skia*, as in 8:5; Col. 2:17) implies that the cultic provisions of the law were an anticipation of *the good things* which from the standpoint of the law were still *coming*. Those good things are 'now already here' (9:11) and are about to be described again as the benefits of Christ's sacrifice and heavenly ascension (10:5–14; cf. 9:11–15). The law foreshadowed the way God would meet humanity's greatest need by inaugurating the New Covenant through the high-priestly ministry of his Son (10:15–18), but it did not manifest *the realities themselves* (CSB 'it was not the reality itself of those things').

To illustrate his point, the author reflects again on the ritual of the annual Day of Atonement in Leviticus 16 (as in 9:1–14), which required that *the same sacrifices* be offered *endlessly year after year*. Consequently, the law could *never . . . make perfect those who draw near* (NIV adds *to worship*).[33] As in the LXX, the language of drawing near is used to describe the Israelites gathering in solemn assembly to meet

---

32. The conjunction *gar* in v. 1 (ESV, 'For') indicates that 10:1–4 specifically supports and advances the argument in 9:23–28.

33. Some manuscripts have a plural verb here (*dynantai*), signifying that the sacrifices cannot perfect those who draw near. But the law is the main subject of this verse, suggesting that those manuscripts with a singular verb (*dynatai*) are more likely to be original. Cf. Metzger, *Textual Commentary*, p. 600.

with God (e.g. Exod. 16:9; 34:32; Lev. 9:5; Num. 10:3–4), but they could not be perfected in that relationship. The need for continuing sacrifice is evidence that the system as a whole did not perfect the worshippers.

This assertion recalls the earlier claim that 'the law made nothing perfect', but with the high-priestly ministry of Jesus, 'a better hope is introduced, by which we draw near to God' (7:19; cf. 11:39–40). As noted previously, perfection is not a moral concept in Hebrews, but generally describes the qualification of someone to act in a particular capacity. Jesus has made it possible for believers to approach God with confidence to 'receive mercy and find grace to help us in our time of need' (4:16). We are perfected by the one sacrifice of Christ (10:14), which enables us to approach God in this way now (10:19–22), and ultimately to share the joys of his eternal kingdom (12:22–24).

2. The message that the law was unable to perfect those who approached God through its provisions is driven home with two more significant arguments. First, the author asks rhetorically: if the worshippers had been *cleansed once for all*, would not the sacrifices have *stopped being offered?* The form of this argument suggests that 'the sacrificial ritual was still practised in the temple at Jerusalem' (Bruce, p. 227). Second, the author indicates that the real need was for consciences to be cleansed (lit. 'the worshippers no longer having a consciousness of sins').[34] Previously, he argued that the gifts and sacrifices of the law were 'not able to clear the conscience of the worshipper' (or 'to perfect the worshipper with respect to conscience') (9:9). The 'external regulations' of the law applied 'until the time of the new order' (9:10). These regulations were able to sanctify the people only to the extent that they were made 'outwardly clean' (9:13, 'for the purification of the flesh' [ESV]) or to purify ceremonial objects (9:21–22). But Christ is able to 'cleanse our consciences from acts that lead to death, so that we may serve

---

34. The noun *syneidēsis* can mean 'awareness of information about something' or 'consciousness' (BDAG), which is the most natural reading here. Elsewhere in Hebrews, it refers more specifically to 'the inward faculty of distinguishing right and wrong' or 'conscience' (BDAG; cf. 9:9, 14; 10:22; 13:18).

the living God' (9:14; cf. Acts 15:9). This happens experientially when the gospel is applied to hearts and minds. The challenge in 10:22 is to keep approaching God with 'our hearts sprinkled to cleanse us from a guilty conscience'.

3. Instead of removing 'a consciousness of sins', *those sacrifices are an annual reminder of sins.* The *reminder* in view is more than a personal recollection of sin. The Day of Atonement ritual was a public demonstration of the fact that sin is offensive to a holy God, that it is a pervasive problem even among believers, and that it can only be dealt with in God's way. The people were encouraged to fast and present a food offering to the LORD (Lev. 23:26–32), animal sacrifices were offered for priests and people, and the high priest entered the Most Holy Place to make atonement for himself and the whole community by the sprinkling of blood (Lev. 16:3–19). Finally, the high priest would 'lay both hands on the head of the live goat and confess over it all the wickedness and rebellion of the Israelites – all their sins – and put them on the goat's head', before sending it away into the wilderness to signify the removal of their guilt (16:20–22). But the requirement for this event to be *annual* (the same term is rendered 'year after year' in v. 1) highlighted its inadequacy. 'A pardon that has to be bestowed repeatedly – so far at least as its ceremonial expression is concerned – cannot convey the same peace of conscience as a pardon bestowed once for all' (Bruce, p. 228).

4. The author goes a step further and asserts that *It is impossible for the blood of bulls and goats to take away sins* (cf. 10:11). The sacrificial system could not actually remove sin's 'pollution and dominion from human life' (Cockerill, p. 432). Although prophets and psalmists condemned the sacrifices of the faithless in Israel and spoke about the sacrifices God truly desired (e.g. Ps. 50:7–15; Isa. 1:10–15; Amos 5:21–24), none made the sort of categorical claim that we find here. Hebrews does this because 'the realities' to which the rituals pointed have now been revealed in the saving work of the Lord Jesus (10:1, 17–18). Animal sacrifices were God-given precursors to the once-for-all sacrifice God intended to provide through the death of his Son.

5–7. A logical connection with the preceding verses is signalled by the conjunction *Therefore* (*dio*). The author is about to explore the significance of an important biblical passage, revealing God's plan to set aside the sacrificial system and establish his will 'through the sacrifice of the body of Jesus Christ once for all' (10:10). Remarkably, however, this ancient text is put into the mouth of the Son of God 'as he comes into the world' (my translation). This is a way of speaking about the purpose of his incarnation (cf. 2:14–18). The incarnate Son is represented as addressing his Father in the words of Psalm 40:6–8 (39:7–9 LXX) and expressing his intention to do his Father's will.

Psalm 40 is the testimony and prayer of a godly king, leading his people in corporate worship. It is attributed to David in both Hebrew and Greek versions, which must have been a significant factor in the messianic application of the passage to Jesus. Four technical terms are used in the psalm to summarize the range of sacrifices provided by the law of Moses. The general term *sacrifice* (*thysia*) in this sequence describes the 'fellowship offering' mentioned in Leviticus 3, seeking peace with God; *offering* (*prosphora*) refers to the 'grain offering' mentioned in Leviticus 2, which expressed thankfulness to God; a *burnt offering* (*holokautōma*) involved the total burning of an animal on the altar for atonement and to express Israel's consecration to the LORD (Lev. 1; cf. Exod. 29:38–46); and the *sin offering* (*peri hamartias*) was a means of seeking atonement for unintentional sin (cf. Lev. 4:1 – 5:13).

When the psalmist says 'you did not desire' and 'you have not required' these sacrifices, he speaks negatively and absolutely to highlight God's positive intention.[35] Samuel had challenged David's predecessor Saul with the question,

> Does the LORD delight in burnt offerings and sacrifices
>   as much as in obeying the LORD?

Samuel concluded that

> To obey is better than sacrifice,
>   and to heed is better than the fat of rams.
> (1 Sam. 15:22)

---

35. LXX Ps. 39:7 reads 'you did not require', which corresponds with the Hebrew original, but Heb. 10:6 has the more emphatic 'you were not pleased'.

Later prophets similarly expressed God's preference for obedience over sacrifice, making the sort of stark contrast found in Psalm 40 (e.g. Jer. 7:21–23; Hos. 6:6; Mic. 6:6–9). Major manuscripts of Psalm 39:7 LXX read *but a body you prepared for me*. This interprets a strange Hebrew expression ('ears you have dug for me'; NIV 'but my ears you have opened', Ps. 40:6), which suggests that God's great desire was for the king and his people to open their ears to listen to God and obey him. The version of this clause in the LXX particularly suited the argument of Hebrews that the incarnate Son came to do God's will in the context of an obedient, bodily life (cf. 2:14–18; 5:8–9).

The sacrificial system was designed to facilitate the sort of dedication to God expressed in the words,

> Then I said, 'Here I am – it is written about me in the scroll –
> I have come to do your will, my God.'[36]

On the lips of David, this most likely meant that he was committed to obeying the whole book of the law. As instructed by Moses in Deuteronomy 17:14–20, the godly ruler was to hear and obey the law of God. So, when the Son of God came into the world to do what was written of him as Messiah, he embraced everything said about him in all the Scriptures ('the Law of Moses, the Prophets and the Psalms', Luke 24:44). Most obviously, Jesus viewed the prophecy in Isaiah 53 about the Servant's sacrificial death for the redemption of his people as setting forth God's will for his life (e.g. Mark 10:33–34, 45; Luke 22:37).

8. As the opening clauses of Psalm 40:6–8 (39:7–9 LXX) are restated, they are combined in a way that highlights their two negative claims (*Sacrifices and offerings, burnt offerings and sin offerings you did not desire, nor were you pleased with them*). Repeating the different terms for sacrifice in the plural here 'strengthens the all-encompassing nature of this description' (Cockerill, p. 438). The

---

36. *In the scroll* is a simplified translation of 'in the scroll of the book', which means 'the book in scroll-form' (Bruce, p. 234 n. 44).

surprising nature of the two negative claims is then emphasized with the reminder that these *were offered in accordance with the law.* Only God could replace the law's requirements with something better, in the manner that is now described.

9. An important sequence in the citation is noted with the use of a present-tense participle in verse 8 (*legōn*, 'saying') and then a perfect indicative in verse 9 (*eirēken*, 'he says'), pointing to the way in which Christ now speaks through the psalm (LXX 'I said'). A single clause is repeated (*Here I am, I have come to do your will*) to make the point that the Son of God comes into the world to do the will of his Father, and thereby *sets aside the first to establish the second.* *Sets aside* is 'the strongest negative statement the author has made or will make about the OT cultus' (Ellingworth, p. 504). God's positive intention was to *establish* a way of approach that replaces the sacrificial system (10:1–4). Thus, there is a parallel between the prophecy of Jeremiah 31:31–34, as explained in 8:7–13, and Psalm 40:6–8, as explained in 10:5–10. Both passages declare the replacement of what was formerly prescribed by God with a new way of relating to him. However, the psalm text functions to explain more specifically how the promises of the New Covenant are fulfilled by the obedience of Christ.

10. This verse is closely linked with the quotation from Psalm 40 by the use of similar terms: 'will', 'offering' and 'body'. The *will* of God to replace the sacrificial system is fulfilled by the 'offering' (*prosphora*) *of the body of Jesus Christ.* The words 'a body you prepared for me' (v. 5, citing Ps. 39:7 LXX) naturally apply to the whole of his incarnate life, but the redemptive significance of his death is highlighted elsewhere by referring to the shedding of his 'blood' (9:12, 14; 10:19, 29; 12:24; 13:12). Putting these texts together, we may conclude that Jesus' death was an unblemished blood sacrifice, because it was the culmination of a lifetime of complete obedience to the Father (cf. 4:15; 5:7–9; 7:27; 9:14). 'His obedience was from the heart, but it took concrete form in human life and climaxed with his willing self-offering of that life' (Cockerill, p. 444).

A definitive consecration of believers to God is made possible by the unique self-offering of the Messiah in his death: 'we are sanctified once for all through the offering of the body of Jesus

Christ' (my translation).[37] 'Made holy', 'sanctified' and 'consecrated' are all possible translations of the verb used here. The adverbial expression *once for all* further emphasizes the definitive nature of this sanctification. Using the same verb, the author previously declared that the sprinkled blood of animal sacrifices was only able to sanctify 'those who are ceremonially unclean . . . so that they are outwardly clean' (9:13). But Christ's 'blood' cleanses consciences 'from acts that lead to death, so that we may serve the living God' (9:14). This indicates a form of sanctification that is life changing. Definitive cleansing from sin makes definitive sanctification possible. In 10:29, there is a reference to 'the blood of the covenant that sanctified them', and in 13:12 we are told that 'Jesus . . . suffered outside the city gate to make the people holy through his own blood'. Sanctification in these verses refers to a new covenant relationship with God made possible by the sacrifice of his Son. It is a status that is given to those who believe the gospel and approach the Father trusting in the sufficiency of the Son's atoning work (12:22–24). This status is the motivation and empowerment for living a holy life (12:14; cf. 1 Thess. 4:3–8). The obedience of Christ makes possible the obedience of those whom he sanctifies.

11–12. The author resumes the comparison between Jesus' priesthood and that of the levitical priests, which has surfaced at various stages in the argument so far (5:1–10; 7:1–28; 8:1–6; 9:1–14). A new feature here is the claim that *every priest stands and performs his religious duties* (*leitourgōn*, 'ministering'). Standing represents the continuing need for sacrificial ministry under the law (Deut. 18:5). The focus in 10:1 was on the yearly Day of Atonement ritual, but *day after day* in verse 11 refers to the regular pattern of sacrifice at the tabernacle or temple, which was served by numerous priests. *Again and again* (ESV, 'repeatedly') recalls 'endlessly' (v. 1). Further expressions from verses 1 and 4 are adapted and joined together to

---

37. The Greek construction *hēgiasmenoi esmen* highlights the fact that sanctification is a present reality achieved by Christ's sacrifice for us. The first-person plural makes this a confessional statement for the author and those he addresses. Cf. Peterson, *Possessed*, pp. 33–40, 71–77.

highlight the limitations of this ministry (*he offers the same sacrifices, which can never take away sins*).

But . . . this priest [referring back to Jesus Christ in v. 10] . . . *offered for all time one sacrifice for sins*.[38] This sacrifice was so effective that, after he had ascended into heaven, *he sat down at the right hand of God*. His sitting contrasts with the standing of the levitical priests, expressing the completion and enduring effect of his sacrificial work. No levitical priest ever sat in Israel's earthly sanctuary, but Christ is portrayed as having sat down in the heavenly sanctuary, opening the way for believers to draw near with confidence, because of the access he has made available for them (10:19–22). As enthroned high priest, he always lives to apply the benefits of his once-for-all sacrifice to 'those who come to God through him' (7:25; cf. 4:14–16). Sitting also expresses his eternal rule as Messiah (1:3). 'In his preeminent position as High Priest permanently seated at God's right hand the Son possesses all authority necessary to assist the faithful' (Cockerill, p. 447). The wording here is drawn from Psalm 110:1, which is cited in 1:13 and alluded to in 8:1; 12:2. Since Psalm 110:4 promises that the Messiah will be 'a priest for ever, in the order of Melchizedek', Jesus is viewed as fulfilling the predictions of this psalm both as priest and king.

13. A further aspect of Christ's heavenly session is revealed in the promise that the Messiah will sit at God's right hand until his enemies are made a footstool for his feet (Ps. 110:1b; cf. 1 Cor. 15:25). An allusion to this promise is introduced with the expression *since that time*, which refers back to the moment when he sat down at the right hand of God (v. 12).[39] The Son *waits for his enemies to be made his footstool* in the sense that he waits for everyone who opposes

---

38. Although the adverbial expression *for all time* modifies the verb that precedes it in 7:3; 10:1, 14, it possibly relates to the verb that follows it here ('he sat down for all time').

39. The adverbial expression *since that time* is inserted by Hebrews to show that Ps. 110:1b is in the process of being fulfilled ('until I make your enemies / a footstool for your feet'). The passive verb in Heb. 10:13 gives the same sense as the active verb in 1:13: God is the one who will subdue the Messiah's enemies.

his rule to be subdued (cf. Ps. 2:8). However, this is no passive waiting. Psalm 110:2 promises that

> The LORD will extend your mighty sceptre from Zion, saying,
>   'Rule in the midst of your enemies!'
> (Cf. Ps. 2:9)

The LORD works through the Messiah's willing 'troops' (Ps. 110:3) to crush and judge nations and rulers (vv. 5–6). God's subjection of the king's enemies is coextensive with the king's exercise of his sovereign rights. As the people of Christ proclaim his victory over sin and death, enemies become loyal subjects and his rule is extended (cf. Rom. 5:10–11; 2 Cor. 5:17–19). Judgment will fall on those who fail to respond to his gracious offer of forgiveness and new life (cf. 9:27–28; 10:26–31; 12:25–27; 13:4), but final salvation awaits those who wait for his return (9:28, using a similar verb to the one in 10:13).

14. This verse is closely linked to the preceding one by the conjunction *For* (*gar*). However, the repetition of terms used in verses 1, 10 and 12 shows that it effectively concludes the argument in verses 1–13 as a whole. 'The perfection that was not possible through the levitical priesthood (7:11), the law and its sacrifices (7:19; 9:9; 10:1), is here proclaimed as an act of Christ, already accomplished by his single offering for sins.[40] The phrase *mia prosphora* ('one offering') combines elements from verse 12 ('one sacrifice [*mian thysian*] for sins') and verse 10 ('the offering [*prosphora*] of the body of Jesus Christ'). In verses 5–6, 8, these and other terms are used to describe the different sacrifices prescribed by the law, but the author uses them interchangeably here with reference to the death of Jesus to indicate that he provided the sacrifice to end all sacrifices (cf. 9:25–28).

The perfecting of believers by the one sacrifice of Christ is clearly related to their sanctification (v. 10) and cleansing from sin

---

40. Peterson, *Hebrews and Perfection*, p. 149. The perfect tense of the verb *he has made perfect* expresses the continuing or present effect of Christ's sacrifice. This is further stressed by the adverbial term *for ever*.

(9:14; cf. 10:2), though these terms are not simply synonymous. Cleansing from sin is a negative idea, equivalent to the removal of sin and its consequences. This makes possible a positive consecration of believers to God. Cleansing is another way of speaking about the decisive forgiveness of sins that is foundational to the New Covenant (vv. 17–18, citing Jer. 31:34b). This enables the sort of heart-obedience or consecration to God and his will that is implied by Jeremiah 31:33 (cited in v. 16; cf. Jer. 32:39–40). The verb 'to perfect' (NIV 'make perfect') in Hebrews describes the qualification of someone to act in a certain capacity. Jesus was 'perfected' as our saviour and eternal high priest through suffering and heavenly exaltation (2:10; 5:9; 7:28). We are perfected in the sense that we are enabled through Christ to approach God with confidence in the present (4:14–16; 7:19, 25; 10:19–22) and have the certain hope of sharing in God's eternal kingdom (3:1–6; 6:19–20; 9:15, 28; 12:22–29). Although the language of perfection embraces the final realization of God's promises in resurrection to eternal life (11:39–40; 12:23), it is remarkable that 10:14 locates the perfecting of believers 'in the past with respect to its accomplishment and in the present with respect to its enjoyment'.[41]

In 2:11, the exalted Son is designated as 'the one who makes people holy' and believers as 'those who are made holy'. A present passive participle is similarly used in 10:14 to describe believers as *those who are being made holy*. In neither case can this mean progressive moral sanctification, since the author regularly uses the verb 'sanctify' definitively to mean 'consecrate' in a new relationship with God through the sacrifice of Christ (10:10, 29; 13:12). If any sense of progress is implied, it may be that the author envisages individuals successively being consecrated to God as they believe the gospel and experience the benefits of Christ's finished work. Related nouns in 12:10, 14 are used in exhortations to endure discipline and pursue a lifestyle that reflects the character of the one who has made us part

---

41. Peterson, ibid., p. 152 (emphasis removed). Hebrews uses the language of perfection in 10:14 to stress the realized aspect of our salvation (cf. Rom. 8:29–30).

of his holy people (cf. 1 Cor. 1:2; 1 Thess. 4:3–8). Practical holiness arises from living as those consecrated to God in Christ. The concluding exhortations in 13:1–21 detail different aspects of such a life, dedicated to doing the will of God.

15. A modified version of Jeremiah 31:33–34 is introduced to affirm that Christ has fulfilled these promises and inaugurated the New Covenant by his sacrificial death (cf. 8:6; 9:15). Together with the longer version in 8:7–12, this text forms a bracket around the intervening material, showing that the high-priestly work of Jesus should be understood pre-eminently in covenantal terms. God spoke about the need for a new covenant through Jeremiah (8:8), but *The Holy Spirit also testifies to us* with these words (cf. 3:7), emphasizing the immediate and continuing way in which God speaks to his people through this passage (cf. 9:8). The word *also* specifically suggests that the Spirit's testimony in Scripture explains and confirms the significance of the cleansing, sanctification and perfection already experienced by those who have come to believe the message about Christ's saving work (cf. 2:1–4).

NIV clarifies the meaning of an incomplete expression in verse 15 ('for after saying') by translating *First he says* and inserting 'Then he adds' at the beginning of verse 17. This is designed to show that two separate promises from Jeremiah 31:33–34 are in view. However, if the Greek is translated 'the Lord says' in verse 16, a preliminary statement ('This is the covenant I will make with them / after that time') is followed by two key promises together. Either way, the foundational importance of the second promise is indicated by the comment in verse 18.

16. The author's first modification of Jeremiah 31:33 (38:33 LXX) puts *with them* in place of 'with the people of Israel'. By implication, the *time* so vaguely indicated by the prophet has come, and the New Covenant has been established by Jesus' death (9:15). God's first promise in this covenant is

I will put my laws in their hearts
  and I will write them on their minds.

The parallelism here makes it clear that God's people will know in their *minds* the will of God and desire in their *hearts* to obey him (cf. Jer. 32:39–40).⁴² The fundamental challenge in Hebrews is to obey the call of the gospel and persevere in faith, hope and love (e.g. 4:1–2, 11; 5:9; 6:10–12). The theme of doing the will of God and serving him acceptably continues to emerge in the rest of this 'word of exhortation'. The promise of Jeremiah 31:33 is thus fulfilled in the broad demands of Christian discipleship, not simply in the internalization of the laws given through Moses (cf. Rom. 7:4–6; 8:4; Gal. 5:13–26).

17. God's promise that 'I will be their God, / and they will be my people' (Jer. 31:33c) and the promise about his people truly knowing him, 'from the least of them to the greatest' (Jer. 31:34a), are not repeated here. This omission has the effect of focusing attention on the last promise and its significance for the first. The author adapts the original wording ('For I will forgive their wickedness / and will remember their sins no more'), abbreviating the text, changing 'their wickedness' to *their sins* and adding *lawless acts*. 'The addition of this phrase adds emphasis to the totality of God's remission' (Cockerill, p. 458). The form of the verb is also different in the expression *I will remember no more*, probably to stress the certainty of the promise. When God 'remembers' sin, he punishes it (Isa. 64:9; Jer. 14:10). The Day of Atonement ritual provided 'an annual reminder of sins' (Heb. 10:3), together with a divinely ordained method of cleansing from sin, but an unprecedented act of divine grace is signalled in Jeremiah 31:34. 'Pardon for sins past, present, and future would seem to be necessary to keep God's people in the promised relationship and maintain the covenant' (Peterson, *Transformed*, p. 34). When this is experienced through belief in the atoning significance of Jesus' death, we are set free to serve God in the way that Jeremiah 31:33 envisaged (cf. 9:14; 12:28–29).

18. The author's comment on Jeremiah 31:34 draws several threads in the preceding argument together. *Where these have been forgiven* refers to the sins and lawless acts that God will remember

---

42. The author has reversed the order in 10:16 (compare 8:10, citing Jer. 31:33 [LXX 38:10]), giving prominence to the heart as the seat of emotions and will, as in 3:8, 10, 12, 15; 4:7, 12; 10:22 (twice); 13:9.

no more. The word *aphesis* ('forgiveness, release') was previously used in 9:22, where it is said that 'without the pouring out of blood there is no forgiveness' (my translation). Subsequently, the author asserts that 'It is impossible for the blood of bulls and goats to take away sins' (10:4; cf. 10:11), but by one sacrifice Jesus has 'made perfect for ever those who are being made holy' (10:14). The 'release' he makes possible is a freedom from the guilt, punishment and obligation to serve sin (9:14, 15; cf. 2:14–18; Rom. 6:1–14). Consequently, *sacrifice for sin is no longer necessary*: 'we have been made holy through the sacrifice of the body of Jesus Christ once for all' (10:10).[43]

Theology
As the author concludes his explanation of the levitical system and its limitations, he draws out the implications of two significant biblical passages. In the first, the incarnate Son of God is said to have applied Psalm 40:6–8 to himself and fulfilled every aspect of the sacrificial system by his obedient self-sacrifice. In the second, the Holy Spirit speaks about the way the sacrifice of Jesus has secured the benefits promised in Jeremiah 31:33–34. A fundamental weakness of the former system was its inability to provide a definitive cleansing from sin (10:1–4), but this has been accomplished by the single offering of Christ in his saving death (10:5–14). Jesus' sacrifice also achieved a definitive sanctification. Sanctification is fundamentally a relational and positional concept in Hebrews, meaning that believers are set apart from the world to be God's holy people. The moral implications of this relationship are developed in 12:4–17; 12:28 – 13:25. However, it is already clear from 10:5–18 that Christ's self-consecration to do the will of God was designed to enable believers to obey and serve God in a new covenant way.

---

43. The combination *prosphora peri hamartias* (v. 18, 'offering for sin') identifies the supreme accomplishment of his death. However, inasmuch as he fulfils the whole sacrificial system by his one offering, he also provides a definitive consecration to God and secures an eternal peace between God and his people.

Christ also achieved the perfecting of believers by his saving death (10:14). This term could simply relate to glorification through resurrection to God's eternal kingdom (11:39–40; 12:23). But the author has previously linked perfection with the notion of drawing near to God in the context of worship (7:19; 10:1). He also links the perfecting of believers with the fulfilment of God's promises relating to the forgiveness of sins and the doing of his will (10:15–18). Comprehensively, then, the perfecting of believers has a present and a future dimension. It is a way of speaking about the qualification of believers to come into God's presence now and enjoy the benefits of an eternal relationship with him (12:22–24).

9. REFLECTING ON THE PRIVILEGES WE HAVE AS CHRISTIANS AND RESPONDING APPROPRIATELY (10:19–39)

This passage draws out the implications of the pivotal theological argument in 8:1 – 10:18 and highlights the need for a continuing faithful response, which is the focus of the following chapters. The first section briefly summarizes the author's teaching about Christ's high-priestly ministry and its benefits (vv. 19–21) and on this basis gives three exhortations (vv. 22–25). The second section brings the most explicit warning so far about the significance of apostasy and its consequences (vv. 26–31). The third section begins with a challenge to the hearers to remember previous experiences of persecution and suffering and how they were able to endure these, knowing that they had 'better and lasting possessions' (vv. 32–34). An encouragement not to 'throw away your confidence; it will be richly rewarded' (v. 35) is followed by a call to persevere, to do the will of God and 'receive what he has promised' (v. 36). Habakkuk 2:3b–4 (with words from Isa. 26:20) is used to affirm that Christ will not delay returning and to reinforce the challenge to persevere in faith for salvation, rather than shrink back and be destroyed (vv. 37–39).

A. Realize the benefits of Jesus' high-priestly ministry (10:19–25)

Context

Two privileges that Christians 'have' as a result of Christ's death and heavenly exaltation (vv. 19–21) form the basis for three exhortations (vv. 22–25), recalling previous encouragements to faith, hope and love (4:14–16; 6:10–12). In particular, the parallels with 4:14–16 suggest that these two passages are central to the pastor's concern in his 'word of exhortation' (13:22). Both passages function as turning points in the argument, introducing major new sections of the book. In this case, the focus turns to the need for enduring faith and its expression in everyday obedience (10:26 – 13:25).

Comment

19. The conjunction *Therefore* (*oun*) indicates a close link between verses 19–25 and the preceding passage, but the address to *brothers and sisters* here (also in 3:1, 12; 13:22) functions as 'a discourse marker to indicate a turn in the argument' (O'Brien, p. 362). Summarizing what believers in Christ *have* as a result of Christ's high-priestly work (vv. 19–21), the pastor restates and amplifies the implications of this in the exhortations that follow (vv. 22–25). Essentially, we have *confidence to enter the Most Holy Place by the blood of Jesus.* There is clearly a subjective dimension to this *confidence* (3:6; 4:16; 10:35), namely '*boldness* in spite of the frankest recognition of our sins' (Westcott, p. 320), but the phrase *by the blood of Jesus* provides an objective basis for it. Put simply, this confidence is 'the free right to approach God, given in the sacrifice of Christ, which is the essence of the Christian faith'.[1] Freedom of access to God is presented in terms of 'entrance' (*eisodos*) into *the Most Holy Place* (*tōn hagiōn*, 'the holy places'), which is the heavenly sanctuary entered by Jesus on our behalf (6:19–20; 9:11–12). Such confidence has a present and a future dimension. The right of approach to God

---

1. Van Unnik, 'Freedom of Speech', p. 485. H. Schlier ('παρρησία', *TDNT* 5, p. 884) describes this *parrēsia* as 'freedom of access to God, authority to enter the sanctuary'. See also my comments on 3:6; 4:16.

we enjoy now through Jesus anticipates the ultimate experience of entering God's presence in 'the heavenly Jerusalem' (12:22–24; 13:14).

20. Access to God's heavenly sanctuary is *by a new and living way opened for us through the curtain.* As in 6:19–20 and 9:11–12, the author employs the imagery of the tabernacle with reference to Jesus' entrance into heaven. There is a *new* way into God's presence that did not exist before Jesus opened it. This is a *living way,* because Jesus is the high priest who lives for ever (7:16–17, 24–25) and his work will never be outmoded. Jesus *opened* or 'inaugurated' this new way with his own blood.[2] We are invited to follow him into God's presence, trusting in his high-priestly mediation. A complication is introduced into the argument by the phrase *that is, his body (sarx autou,* 'his flesh'). This expression is best understood as a further reflection on the meaning of *through the curtain.* Previously, the curtain separating God's people from his presence was identified as a barrier, though it was also implicitly 'the point of contact between them' (Cockerill, p. 469). Jesus' 'flesh', meaning his crucified body, is here presented as the true means of access to God's presence. It had to be 'rent before the blood could be shed, which enabled him to enter and open God's presence for the people' (Moffatt, p. 143). Thus, verses 19 and 20 both conclude with a reference to Christ's death as the means by which the way into heaven was opened for us: 'blood' and 'flesh' together refer to the sacrifice that opened the new and living way to God.

21. The related blessing that believers have is *a great priest over the house of God.* The author may be abbreviating the description of Jesus as 'a great high priest' in 4:14 or simply following the lead of Old Testament passages where the high priest is designated as 'the great priest' (e.g. Lev. 21:10; Num. 35:25, 28). In 3:6, the Son was described as being 'over God's house', and the same function is ascribed to him now as our high priest. As the reigning Son of

---

2. The same verb *enekainisen* is employed in 9:18 with reference to the inauguration of the Sinai covenant with blood. But the phrase 'entrance into the Most Holy Place' suggests that 'opened' is a possible rendering here.

God, he intercedes for us as high priest, thus sustaining us on our journey to the heavenly city (7:25).

22. The practical implications of belonging to God's family and benefiting from the high-priestly work of Christ are stated in the challenges that follow (vv. 22, 23, 24–25), where the pastor includes himself in the form of exhortation he uses. The first challenge is to keep on drawing near to God. Previously, he indicated that this involved confident prayer for mercy and grace to help in time of need (4:16). A broader meaning is suggested by the use of similar terminology in 7:19, 25; 11:6; 12:18, 22 and the accompanying phrases in 10:22. The call is for continuing expressions of the saving relationship with God through his Son that began when they came to Jesus as 'the mediator of a new covenant' and first experienced the benefits of his 'sprinkled blood' (12:22–24). The opposite would be to 'drift away' (2:1), to 'turn away' (3:12) or to 'shrink back' and be 'destroyed' (vv. 38–39). Drawing near to God in a corporate way could involve reflecting on Scripture together to 'hear his voice' (3:7–15), praise and thanksgiving for the person and work of Christ with confessions of faith (13:6, 15), sharing the Lord's Supper together, and acts of dedication and commitment.[3]

God is to be approached *with a sincere heart and with the full assurance that faith brings*. Such a heart is 'true' or 'authentic' (*alēthinos*, as in 8:2) because it expresses the devotion of the person to God, thus fulfilling the promises of Jeremiah 31:33 and Ezekiel 36:26–27 (contrast 3:12, 'a sinful, unbelieving heart that turns away from the living God'). A heart can function this way because it is characterized by (lit.) 'the full assurance of faith'. This expression recalls 'the full assurance of hope' in 6:11 (NIV, 'so that what you hope for may be fully realized'). 'Both phrases are descriptive of the certainty

---

3. Some scholars argue for a range of allusions to the Lord's Supper in Hebrews (e.g. Kleinig, pp. 301–307), but none of these can be convincingly established. At best, we may say that if a Supper such as was held at Corinth (1 Cor. 10:16–17; 11:17–34) was experienced by those addressed in Hebrews, it would have been an occasion for the sort of communal response described in 10:22. See also my comments on 13:10, 15.

and stability that are created in Christians as a result of the work of Christ and that enable them to remain loyal to him' (Lane 2, p. 286).

Such assurance comes from hearts being *sprinkled to cleanse us from a guilty conscience* and bodies *washed with pure water*. Some have related this combination of terms to the installation of Aaron and his sons to the priesthood, when they were washed with water and sprinkled with blood (Exod. 29:4, 21; Lev. 8:6, 30), suggesting that believers have experienced a 'priestly consecration'.[4] But the priesthood of believers is not explicitly developed in Hebrews (as it is in 1 Pet. 2:6–10; Rev. 1:5–6). Moreover, the author understands the practice of sprinkling with animal blood more broadly (9:13, 19–22). Every cleansing and consecration rite is now fulfilled and replaced by 'the blood of Christ', which is able to cleanse our consciences from acts that lead to death, so that we may 'serve the living God' (9:14; cf. 12:24; 1 Pet. 1:2). Fundamentally, just as the people of Israel were sprinkled with 'the blood of the covenant' at Sinai (9:18–20; cf. Exod. 24:3–8), so 'the cleansing of believers' hearts from a burdened conscience is associated with Jesus's inauguration of the new covenant through his death' (O'Brien, p. 367). The reality of this is experienced when people come to believe the gospel, which proclaims the atoning significance of that death. The pastor does not view Christians in priestly terms because he focuses on the high-priestly ministry of Jesus, which enables them to come together into the presence of God and celebrate his achievement (2:12; 12:22–24).

Bodies washed with pure water most likely refers to Christian baptism as the outward sign of the washing away of sin and its consequences, when a 'confession' of faith in Christ is made (3:1; 4:14; 10:23).[5] Some understand this washing in purely figurative terms, noting that in Ezekiel 36:25 God promises to 'sprinkle clean water' on his people and to 'cleanse' them from all their impurities and their idols. Ezekiel's imagery corresponds with the promise of Jeremiah 31:34 that God will 'forgive their wickedness' and

---

4. Cf. Westcott, pp. 324–325; Kleinig, p. 503–504.

5. Cf. Bruce, pp. 250–251; Attridge, p. 289.

'remember their sins no more'. Ezekiel 36:26 speaks of God giving his people 'a new heart' and putting 'a new spirit' in them, just as Jeremiah 31:33 promises that God will put his law 'in their minds' and write it 'on their hearts'.[6] Hebrews certainly uses such figurative language to imply that the twin benefits of the New Covenant highlighted in 10:15–18 can now be enjoyed by those who draw near to God through the mediation of Jesus Christ. However, the heart–body parallelism in this verse more obviously represents Christian conversion/initiation in terms of its inward and outward aspects: inner spiritual renewal and outward washing with water (cf. Acts 2:38–39; 22:16).

23. The second exhortation begins with the words *Let us hold unswervingly to the hope we profess*. Literally, the challenge is to 'hold fast the confession of our hope without wavering' (ESV). This exhortation echoes 4:14 (ESV, 'let us hold fast our confession') and the earlier description of Jesus as 'the apostle and high priest of our confession' (3:1, ESV). The pastor appears to have shared with those he addresses a formal 'confession' (*homologia*) concerning the person and work of Christ.[7] Jesus is both the object of faith and the one who gives believers a firm and secure hope, because of his death and heavenly exaltation (6:19–20). Hope is explicitly mentioned in 3:6; 6:11, 18; 7:19; 10:23; 11:1, though the subject pervades Hebrews in other ways. This hope is variously described as participating in 'the world to come' (2:5), 'glory' (2:10), 'God's rest' (4:1, 10), 'the promised eternal inheritance' (9:15) and the better 'country' or 'city' that is to come (11:16; 12:22–24; 13:14). The motivation for holding fast to the confession of this biblical hope is that *he who promised is faithful*, recalling 6:12–18, where it is asserted that 'it is impossible for God to lie'. This hope should be articulated and expressed when Christians gather together, so that it can be held *unswervingly* in everyday life situations (10:32–39).

---

6. This approach to 10:22 is preferred by O'Brien (pp. 367–368) and Cockerill (pp. 473–476).

7. Cf. Cockerill, pp. 476–477; Kleinig, pp. 168–170. The word *homologia* can describe either the act of confessing something or the content of that confession (BDAG).

24–25. The third exhortation begins with the words *let us consider how we may spur one another on towards love and good deeds*. The charge is actually to 'consider one another', implying thoughtful reflection on the needs of other believers, 'with a view to stirring up love and good deeds'. A previous challenge was to 'see to it' that no-one in their community had 'a sinful, unbelieving heart that turns away from the living God' (3:12). A similar concern for the spiritual welfare of other believers is encouraged in 12:15–16. The pastor commends this group of Christians for outstanding demonstrations of love and good deeds in the past (10:32–34), but he wants them to be renewed in zeal for such godly behaviour in the present (6:10–12; cf. 13:1–16).

Two related clauses indicate how this ministry to one another might be conducted. Negatively, it means *not giving up meeting together, as some are in the habit of doing*. Professing believers may drift away from Christian fellowship for a variety of reasons (2:1; 3:12–14; 5:11–14), but the following context and the verb used here identify a deliberate 'abandoning, leaving the assembly exposed to peril in the conflict' (Westcott, p. 327; cf. 2 Cor. 4:9; 2 Tim. 4:10, 16). Fear of further persecution and suffering is likely to have been a compelling concern for withdrawal (10:32–39; 12:1–13). Whatever the reason for doing so, abandoning the fellowship of believers may result in abandoning a Christ-centred relationship with God altogether.

Put positively, meeting together with other believers should be an occasion for *encouraging one another – and all the more as you see the Day approaching*. As noted in connection with 3:13, the verb translated *encouraging* (*parakalountes*) would be better rendered 'exhorting' to embrace the elements of warning and encouragement exemplified in the author's own 'word of exhortation' (13:22). This is the same perspective that the apostle Paul had about the edification of the church (e.g. 1 Cor. 14:1–5, 26–33; Eph. 4:11–16; 5:17–20; Col. 3:16). Christians ought to meet together regularly to give and receive in ministry, especially in view of the Lord's imminent return and the prospect of having to give an account to him (10:37–39). See Introduction 6e, 'Maturity and ministry'.

The Day of Christ's return will be the occasion when believers experience the fullness of salvation that he has achieved for them

(9:28) and be gathered together in the eternal celebration of the heavenly assembly (12:22–24; cf. Mark 13:27; 2 Thess. 2:1). But the Day of the Lord in prophetic perspective involves both judgment and salvation (e.g. Isa. 2:12; 4:2–6). In the New Testament, it is called 'the Day' (1 Cor. 3:13; 1 Thess. 5:4), 'the day of God' (2 Pet. 3:12; Rev. 16:14), 'the day of the Lord' (1 Cor. 5:5; 1 Thess. 5:2), 'the day of our Lord Jesus Christ' (1 Cor. 1:8), 'the day of judgment' (2 Pet. 2:9; 1 John 4:17) and 'the day of . . . wrath' (Rom. 2:5). In the following paragraph (10:26–31) the pastor reflects on the nature of that judgment in relation to apostates.

Theology

The exhortations to faith, hope and love in this passage 'encompass the totality of the Christian life' (Cockerill, p. 465). They pick up and develop similar exhortations earlier in Hebrews and prepare for much of the argument to come. Drawing near to God means continually approaching him with confidence in the finished work of his Son. Holding firmly to the hope we profess emphasizes the forward-looking aspect of the Christian life. Considering how we may spur one another on to love and good deeds highlights the outward-looking, other-person-centred shape of a relationship with our trinitarian God. The order of these exhortations is significant, and they are clearly meant to be pursued together. Drawing near to God through Christ is fundamental, because continuing dependence on his saving work is essential for persistence in hope and the pursuit of love and good deeds. The confidence that the Son gives us to approach the Father also makes us willing 'to invest ourselves fully in our eternal hope . . . and in our interaction with fellow believers' (deSilva, p. 374).

B. Don't turn away from the Son of God and his achievements for us (10:26–31)

Context

The warning in verse 25 not to abandon the gathering of Christ's people, especially in the light of his approaching return, is picked up and developed in a simple conditional clause (vv. 26–27). Instead of enjoying the eternal benefits of his sacrifice for sins, those who turn away from Christ and his people are left with 'a fearful expectation of judgment and of raging fire that will consume the enemies of God'. The logic of this is explained in terms of a 'how much more' argument, based on the fact that 'Anyone who rejected the law of Moses died without mercy on the testimony of two or three witnesses' (v. 28). Abandoning a New Covenant relationship with God exposes a person to even more serious punishment, because of what is being rejected (v. 29). God's character as judge of his enemies and vindicator of his people is briefly stated in verses 30–31, echoing Deuteronomy 32:35, 36.

Comment

26. A link with the preceding passage is indicated by the conjunction *gar* ('for', not translated by NIV) and the flow of the argument. This fourth warning passage follows the pattern of the third (6:4–8), heaping up clauses that identify the true nature of apostasy and explaining its consequences. However, the rhetorical style is different: more attention is given to explaining the fearful outcome, now that the magnitude of God's provision for our salvation has been explained (Cockerill, p. 482). The author tactfully includes himself in the warning by using the first-person plural. NIV has rightly translated the present participle of the Greek verb *keep on sinning* to indicate that a pattern of life is being described, rather than one damning transgression. The immediate context points to the particular sin of abandoning Christ and the fellowship of his people (v. 25; cf. 2:3; 3:12; 6:6). However, the underlying cause of such apostasy in some circumstances may be the desire to indulge in particular sins without restraint or restriction (contrast Moses in 11:25).

The adverb *deliberately* emphasizes the stubborn nature of this determination, especially after having received *the knowledge of the truth* (cf. 6:4–5; 1 Tim. 2:4; 4:3; 2 Tim. 2:25; 3:7; Titus 1:1).[8] For such

---

8. The adverb *hekousiōs* (deliberately) may be used with Num. 15:30 in mind, where a person sinning 'with a high hand' (NIV 'defiantly') must be 'cut off from the people of Israel'. But Cockerill (pp. 483–485) argues that a better parallel would be Israel's rejection of salvation as described in 3:7–19.

people *no sacrifice for sins is left* (ESV, 'there no longer remains a sacrifice for sins'). This is because they have rejected the only one who can help them in the face of God's judgment, namely the Son of God who has 'appeared once for all at the culmination of the ages to do away with sin by the sacrifice of himself' (9:26; cf. 7:27; 9:28). The argument about the sacrifices of the law being fulfilled and replaced by the sacrifice of Jesus (10:1–18) would have been particularly challenging if those addressed here were tempted to withdraw into some form of Judaism (see Introduction 3, 'Occasion and purpose'). Now that Christ has come, however, no forgiveness can be found in the rituals that were only a shadow of the good things that have now been realized.

27. Instead of a sacrifice for sins, there remains for those who have turned their backs on Christ *a fearful expectation of judgment and of raging fire that will consume the enemies of God.* The adjective *phoberos* (fearful) is used again in verse 31, where it is translated 'dreadful'. Fear in this context is related to the *expectation of judgment*, which is affirmed and described in various ways throughout Scripture. The image of a *raging fire that will consume the enemies of God* is taken from Isaiah 26:11, but *fire* appears in many other passages about divine judgment (e.g. Isa. 66:15–16, 24; Zeph. 1:18; 3:8; Matt. 25:41; 2 Thess. 1:7–8; Rev. 11:5; 20:14). The word translated *enemies of God* means 'opponents', and the author uses it with the shocking implication that those who once professed faith in Christ might finally share in the judgment due to God's long-standing adversaries.

28. According to Deuteronomy 17:2–7, anyone in Israel who violated the covenant and worshipped other gods was to be put to death *without mercy on the testimony of two or three witnesses.* The pastor describes this sin as a categorical rejection of *the law of Moses,* because the context to which he refers indicates that the person had deliberately and consistently broken the first and second commandments (Deut. 5:7–10). Stubbornly persisting in this behaviour signified apostasy under the Mosaic covenant, since these two laws were so foundational to Israel's unique relationship with God.

29. Addressing his audience directly again, the pastor asks a rhetorical question: *How much more severely do you think someone deserves to be punished* if he or she turns away from Christ and the superior benefits of the New Covenant? As in 6:4–6, a series of clauses describes the nature of such apostasy. First, the person is described as having *trampled the Son of God underfoot*. Trampling underfoot is an expression of contempt (Isa. 26:6; Dan. 8:10; Mic. 7:10; Matt. 5:13; 7:6). The seriousness of showing contempt for *the Son of God* can be measured by remembering everything that has been said about him: he is the ultimate revelation of God, the messianic king who is enthroned at God's right hand, and the Saviour who brings many sons to glory because he suffered for them. Apostasy is a personal affront to the Son of God and 'the Father, who sent him' (John 5:23).

Second, apostates are said to have *treated as an unholy thing the blood of the covenant that sanctified them*. The blood of the covenant in 9:20 refers to the inauguration of the Mosaic covenant with animal blood, but the New Covenant was put into effect with the blood of Jesus (9:15; 10:17–18, 19–20; 12:24; 13:20). By this means he cleansed and *sanctified* his people (9:14; 10:10, 22; cf. 13:12), secured an 'eternal redemption' from sin (9:12; cf. 2:14–15) and made it possible for them to receive 'the promised eternal inheritance' (9:15). Treating Christ's sacrifice as *an unholy thing* (*koinos*) means denying these claims and regarding his death as being no different from any other (being 'of little value because of being common', BDAG). If Christ's blood is no longer regarded as the means by which we are consecrated to God, his blood has been 'desecrated' (Cockerill, p. 489). The expression 'by which he was sanctified' (ESV) could refer both to the objective work of Christ (10:10) and to the personal experience of consecration to God's service through the cleansing of the conscience from sin (9:14; 10:22). If professing Christians are 'hardened by sin's deceitfulness' (3:13) and reach a point where they no longer see the need for cleansing from sin or sense any obligation to live for Christ, their experience of sanctification proves to be superficial. Those who depart from God in this way 'show that they were only God's people phenomenologically, i.e., in appearance only' (Schreiner, p. 328).

Third, apostates are said to have *insulted the Spirit of grace*. The Holy Spirit has been mentioned in each of the warning passages so far: those addressed experienced the Spirit's *grace* when they came to believe in God's Son (2:2–4; 6:4–5) and continue to do so when he speaks to them through Scripture (3:7–15; cf. 9:8–10; 10:15–18).

The Spirit is also mentioned in connection with the obedience of the Son, who 'through the eternal Spirit offered himself unblemished to God' to achieve our salvation (9:14). God as Trinity has moved towards us in grace, meaning that apostasy involves a personal repudiation of God and all his gifts. The apostate acts insolently towards God's Spirit by resisting his promptings to turn away from sin and persevere in faithful obedience (cf. Acts 5:3; 7:51). Such arrogance is the opposite of respectful gratitude (12:28–29).

30. A twofold appeal to Scripture concludes the 'how much more' argument that began in verse 29 (cf. 2:1–4). The punishment due to apostates in the Old Testament was physical death 'without mercy on the testimony of two or three witnesses' (v. 28; cf. Deut. 17:2–7). By implication, the punishment due to those who turn their backs on Christ and the gospel is worse, because they have rejected every provision of God to bring them to eternal life (cf. John 3:16–21, 36). This is affirmed in language drawn from Deuteronomy 32:35, 36, where Moses predicts the apostasy of Israel and God's wrath against his people expressed in the heaping of earthly calamities on them. Our author prefaces these citations with the words *we know him who said*, indicating that his focus is on what they reveal about the character of God. In the original context, *It is mine to avenge; I will repay* refers to God's ultimate vengeance on those he uses to punish his people.[9] A second citation promises vindication for God's people when he acts in judgment on their behalf. English versions mostly take this clause to imply judgment against his people (NIV, *The Lord will judge his people*; cf. Amos 3:2). The Greek verb (*krinei*) can be translated either way, but it means 'vindicate' in Deuteronomy 32:36 LXX, where the parallel expression is 'and relent concerning his servants'. It is more natural to read the verb that way in Hebrews: he will vindicate his people who have remained faithful. The link *and again* does not mean that the second citation is merely repeating the message of the first. Rather, something new

---

9. Hebrews quotes these words in a version that differs from the LXX, but that is attested in Rom. 12:19 and supported by several Jewish Targums on the Hebrew text.

is being said: God will avenge those who prove to be his enemies, and vindicate the faithful.[10]

31. With no further attempt to define the nature of the judgment awaiting apostates, the author concludes with the warning *It is a dreadful thing to fall into the hands of the living God* (cf. Deut. 32:39–42). In some contexts, falling into God's hands implies experiencing his mercy (e.g. 2 Sam. 24:14; 1 Chr. 21:13; cf. Sir. 2:18), but here it means facing God's judgment after having rejected his offer of salvation through Christ. An inclusion is formed with verse 27 ('fearful') by the use of the same Greek word (*phoberos*), here translated *dreadful*. The author is convinced about this from meditating on what Scripture says about God's judgments in history and concluding that his ultimate response to human rebellion must be serious beyond measure. Although much has been said in the preceding chapters about the grace of God revealed in the person and work of the Lord Jesus, an honest reader of Scripture cannot ignore the eternal consequences of rejecting that grace and turning away from the living God (cf. Matt. 8:12; 13:40–43; 24:50–51; 25:30, 41).

Theology
Apostasy involves rejecting God's Son and the need for the salvation he has achieved, scorning the Spirit's promptings to continue believing the gospel and obeying God. It may be caused by a pattern of deliberately indulging sin, leading to a progressive hardening of the heart (3:13), but essentially apostasy is an expression of unbelief (3:12, 19). Since believers have been cleansed and consecrated by the sacrifice of Jesus, 'they should continue to act on that consecration rather than show contempt for it by turning away (10:26–29) and refusing to press on in the journey for which Jesus' death has prepared them' (deSilva, p. 340). Those who turn their backs on Christ and the Spirit of grace may not understand how serious their situation is, but the pastor pulls no punches in identifying how much they offend God by this rejection. The judgment awaiting them must be greater than any earthly punishments against God's

---

10. Compare the way similar expressions in 1:5, 6; 2:13 ('and again', 'again') introduce new citations that represent a development of the argument.

adversaries described in Scripture, because the grace shown to them has been so much greater. They will share in the judgment due to the enemies of God, who never professed faith but throughout their lives denied his grace and rejected his rule over their lives. See Introduction 6d, 'Apostasy and perseverance'.

C. Persevere and obtain what God has promised (10:32–39)

Context

As in 6:9–12, a passage of warm encouragement follows one of warning, emphasizing the way the hearers demonstrated faith, hope and love in the past (10:32–34), and urging them to persevere in this pattern of life, so that they might receive what God has promised (vv. 35–36). In both contexts, an argument from Scripture concludes the section (6:13–20; 10:37–39), focusing here on being ready for Jesus' return. A transition is thus provided to the celebration of enduring faith in chapter 11.

Comment

32. Given the danger signs the pastor has observed in the community being addressed, he encourages them to *Remember those earlier days after you had received the light* (6:4, were 'enlightened'). This expression refers to 'the saving illumination of the heart and mind mediated through the preaching of the gospel' (Lane 2, p. 298). When they came to faith in Christ, they *endured in a great conflict full of suffering.* The word translated *conflict* often designates a 'contest' (*athlēsis*), suggesting the need for discipline, perseverance and co-operation in the face of suffering. The image of the Christian life as an athletic contest with a great reward is developed in 12:1–13 (cf. 1 Cor. 9:24–27; Phil. 1:27; 3:12 – 4:3; 1 Thess. 2:2; 2 Tim. 4:6–8), but the suffering described in 10:32–34 goes beyond that anticipated in a sporting event. Just as Jesus *endured* the cross (12:2) and 'opposition from sinners' (12:3), so believers are to 'endure hardship' (12:7) for the benefits they will receive. The verb used in these verses (*hypomenein*, 'endure') means 'stay in place beyond an expected point in time' and so 'maintain a belief or course of action in the face of opposition, stand one's ground, hold out' (BDAG). The corresponding noun is used in 10:36; 12:1, where it is translated by NIV 'persevere' and 'perseverance'. Since they have done it before, the addressees should have 'the resources and stamina to succeed again' (deSilva, p. 356)!

33–34. The sufferings the recipients of Hebrews endured are now described in four ways. First, they were *publicly exposed to insult and persecution*, meaning that they were verbally abused and physically afflicted in an openly shameful way. The verb translated *publicly exposed* is related to the noun *theatron* ('spectacle, theatre'; cf. 1 Cor. 4:9) and means 'make a spectacle'. The word for 'insult' or 'disgrace' (*oneidismos*) is used again in 11:26 (Moses) and in 13:13, where Christians are called to 'go . . . outside the camp, bearing the disgrace [Jesus] bore'. Second, they *stood side by side with those who were so treated*, literally being 'partners' with them in suffering (*koinōnoi*, cf. Phil. 1:7; 4:14; Rev. 1:9). The author does not simply mean that one group suffered for their faith and the other sympathized with them: at different times they could all have experienced the same things. Some scholars argue that it is impossible to identify these sufferings with any known outbreak of *persecution* in the first century.[11] But if Hebrews was written to a group of Christians in Rome, it is possible that these tribulations were associated with conflicts between Jews and Christians in the reign of Emperor Claudius (cf. Acts 18:1–3; Introduction 3–4).

The third recollection amplifies the second by saying *You suffered along with those in prison*. Prisoners in the first century needed family or friends to supply their everyday needs, including food, water and clothing (13:1–3; cf. Phil. 2:25; 4:14–18). Such practical care was an expression of their love for one another (6:10). But those who identified with prisoners in this way could easily be penalized themselves. The fourth description of this community's public mistreatment is *you . . . joyfully accepted the confiscation of your property*. 'Seizure of property was a common first-century experience for those in disfavour with greedy authorities, and it left its victims isolated and without resources' (Cockerill, p. 501). Christians who were victims of such injustice would have been left more dependent on one another and trusting in God's provision for their needs.

---

11. E.g. deSilva, pp. 13–16, 20–23; Cockerill, pp. 16–23, 500, esp. n. 19.

Nevertheless, they had a remarkable joy in these circumstances (cf. Matt. 5:11–12; Rom. 5:3–4; Phil. 4:4–7; 1 Pet. 4:14–16), which was driven by an abiding conviction that *you yourselves had better and lasting possessions* (ESV, 'a better possession and an abiding one'). The inheritance that Christ has secured for believers is *better* than any earthly possession, because it is *lasting* and involves eternal life with God and his people in the 'better country' (11:16) or 'city that is to come' (13:14). This hope gave them a willingness to accept the loss of material comforts and security.

35. The conjunction *So* (*oun*) indicates that the exhortation *do not throw away your confidence* is the logical response to the preceding recollection of their past experiences and behaviour. *Throw away* implies that they still collectively have this confidence, even though some may be tempted to abandon it. Maintaining this confidence means enduring in faith and hope (vv. 36–39). In 4:16 and 10:19, the same word (*parrēsia*, 'confidence') was used to describe the right of access to God's presence provided by the high-priestly work of Jesus. Here, it describes a confidence before others, especially those who may be opponents and persecutors (cf. 3:6). This is also the emphasis when the same term is used in Acts (2:29; 4:13, 29, 31; 28:31), and in some of Paul's writings (e.g. 2 Cor. 3:12; Phil. 1:20; Eph. 6:19–20). The Christian's *confidence* in Hebrews has two sides: 'the free right to approach God, given in the sacrifice of Christ, which is the essence of the Christian faith, and the open confession of this faith, which is an unshakable hope'.[12] The claim that this confidence *will be richly rewarded* (ESV, 'which has a great reward') refers back to the hope of a 'better possession and an abiding one' (v. 34, ESV) and embraces everything that eternal life in God's presence will entail. This is not a reward for good deeds, but the promised gift of God's grace to those who continue to express trust in his Son (as in v. 36c).

36. NIV begins a new sentence here (*You need to persevere*), but the text actually reads 'for you have need of endurance' (ESV), using the noun corresponding to the verb 'endured' in verse 32. Thus, the

---

12. Van Unnik, 'Freedom of Speech', p. 485. Stressing that the two sides of *parrēsia* are an inseparable unity in Hebrews, he rightly insists that 'in the situation in which Christians live they need it as a gift and a task'.

author returns to the theme of endurance as the positive counterpart to throwing confidence away (v. 35). The result of standing firm in the face of opposition and continuing to support those who stand with you is *that when you have done the will of God, you will receive what he has promised*. This clause parallels the conclusion to the previous verse with its promise of a great reward. *The will of God* is essentially to live by faith in his Son and what he has accomplished (vv. 37–39; cf. v. 22). Clearly, however, genuine faith will be expressed in obedience (3:16–19), even as Jesus fulfilled the will of God in the face of suffering and opposition (5:7–8; 10:5–10; 12:1–2), so that we might become obedient and faithful children of God (5:9; 9:14; 12:3–11; 13:1–19).

37–38. The challenge to endure and obtain what God has promised is backed up with a quote from Habakkuk 2:3b–4, introduced by the conjunction *For* and reinforced by words from Isaiah 26:20 (*a little while*). Both Old Testament passages allude to the shortness of the time before God will act in judgment against those who oppose his people and will vindicate the faithful. Our author first applies this enhanced text to Christ as 'the coming one', who *will come and will not delay*. The subject of these verbs in Habakkuk 2:3 is the revelation that 'awaits an appointed time' and 'speaks of the end'. By adding the article to the participle 'coming' (*ho erchomenos*), Hebrews points to the returning Christ as the fulfilment of that final revelation (cf. 9:28).[13] 'The coming one' appears to be a messianic title in Matthew 3:11; Luke 7:19; John 1:9; 3:31; 6:14.

The order of the clauses in Habakkuk 2:4 is then inverted to make 'my righteous one' the subject of both parts of the verse.[14]

---

13. In the way it renders the Hebrew, Hab. 2:3–4 LXX already suggests the need to wait for an expected deliverer. It could be translated 'if he is late, wait for him; because he will surely come, he will not delay'. Cf. Bruce, pp. 272–275. The LXX differs from the MT/ET in the way it arranges and translates the words.

14. The Hebrew reads 'the righteous will live by his faith [or faithfulness]' and the LXX B text reads 'the righteous will live by my faithfulness'. Hebrews links the personal pronoun 'my' to 'the righteous one'. LXX A and C texts similarly read 'my righteous one shall live by faith'. Paul drops the pronoun altogether in Rom. 1:17; Gal. 3:11.

My righteous one in this context applies to the Christian believer, tempted to wonder if Christ will ever return in accordance with his promise. The implied challenge to *live by faith* means enduring faithfully, as illustrated in verses 32–34 and in the many examples given in Hebrews 11. The basis of such endurance is that God-given 'confidence' (v. 35), which must not be 'thrown away'. Then, using the same subject, a warning is given about God's displeasure with the believer who draws back from a relationship with him:

> *And I take no pleasure*
>   *in the one who shrinks back.*

The next verse makes it clear that God's displeasure is expressed in judgment.

39. As in 6:9–12, encouragement follows warning: *But we do not belong to those who shrink back and are destroyed, but to those who have faith and are saved.* The pastor picks up the language of Habakkuk 2:4 and emphatically distances himself and those he addresses from *those who shrink back and are destroyed.* Rhetorically, 'the affirmation that the hearers are people "exhibiting trust", rather than "shrinking back" seeks to bring into existence the very commitment to trust it affirms' (deSilva, p. 369). The destruction in view (*apōleia*) is the final judgment that awaits unbelievers (e.g. Matt. 7:13; John 17:12; Rom. 9:22; 2 Pet. 2:1, 3; 3:7, 16). But the author affirms that (lit.) 'we are those who have faith for the preservation of the soul', meaning the possession of final salvation (cf. 1 Pet. 1:9).[15] This saving of the 'soul' is experienced in the 'better resurrection' (11:35b) and fullness of life in the 'kingdom that cannot be shaken' (12:28) that is the Christian's hope.

Theology
We can find encouragement to press on in faith by recalling God's help in past struggles and contemplating the future he has

---

15. The noun *peripoiēsis* in this verse means 'preserving' or 'saving' (BDAG). In 1 Thess. 5:9; 2 Thess. 2:14 the context suggests the meaning 'gaining' or 'obtaining' final salvation.

promised us. Past experiences reveal the sustaining grace of God in a range of trying circumstances. The hope of eternal salvation is a further motivation to do the will of God in the present and wait patiently for his promises to be fulfilled. The awful consequences of shrinking back from a relationship with God and abandoning the confidence that is his gift to us in Christ should also be soberly evaluated. Saving faith is essentially a personal trust in the Son of God and what he has achieved for us (3:1, 6, 14; 4:14; 10:19–22). If this is genuine, it will issue in faithfulness or perseverance (6:12; 10:35–39). Faith and faithfulness, 'though they can be distinguished conceptually, are inseparable in the lives of believers' (Schreiner, p. 335).

10. EXAMPLES OF PERSEVERING FAITH, CLIMAXING WITH A CHALLENGE TO REJECT SIN AND FOCUS ON JESUS 'THE PIONEER AND PERFECTER OF FAITH' (11:1 – 12:3)

Two different rhetorical approaches are linked together here. First, there is an extensive exposition of the theme of faith, arising from the challenge to persevere in faith in 10:36–39 and mostly expressed by way of examples from the Old Testament (11:1–39). Despite the author's emphasis on the failure of the wilderness generation to persevere in faith (3:7 – 4:11) and his insistence on the better provisions of the New Covenant for perseverance (8:1–13; 10:11–25), he chooses to focus on Old Testament examples of faith, rather than contemporary models (though see 13:7, 17). Second, just as 'example lists' in ancient literature frequently ended with a brief exhortation, so here the author climaxes his appeal with an exhortation in 12:1–3 that focuses on Jesus.[1] Several of the cameos of faith in Hebrews appear to 'resonate quite pointedly with the

---

1. Cf. deSilva, pp. 377–378. Heb. 11 is more like Jewish lists than comparable Graeco-Roman ones. Cf. Eisenbaum, *Jewish Heroes*, pp. 56–57, 73–84.

audience's past experiences and choices (10:32–34)' (deSilva, p. 380). Despite the particular similarities between this chapter and the celebration of past heroes in Jewish intertestamental literature (e.g. Sir. 44:1 – 50:21; 1 Macc. 2:51–60; 4 Macc. 16:20–25), this pastor has a distinctively 'eschatological' way of presenting the faith of his exemplars.

A large inclusion is formed between 11:1–2 and 11:39–40 by the words 'faith' and 'commended'. The exhortation in 12:1–3 is explicitly to 'run with perseverance the race marked out for us', looking to these Old Testament 'witnesses' for encouragement and supremely to Jesus 'the pioneer and perfecter of faith', who has achieved faith's ultimate goal for us. Hebrews sets these exemplars 'in historical sequence so as to provide an outline of the redemptive purpose of God' (Bruce, p. 280). The verb 'endure' is a key term in 10:32; 12:2, 3, 7, with the noun 'endurance' in 10:36; 12:1. This shows that the exhortation in 12:1–3 is a direct development of the challenge in 10:36–39, enhanced by testimonies to the faith in 11:4–38 and the climactic description of Jesus.

Three reasons may be suggested for the way these testimonies are presented: they clarify the nature of faith, they serve as a motivation for perseverance in the present, and they provide 'an alternate society that counters the baleful influence of the unbelieving world in which the hearers live' (Cockerill, p. 515). The next section (12:7–11) is linked to this one by the use of the verb 'endure' in 12:7, where God's purpose in allowing his people to suffer for their faith is explored.

A. Faith in the unseen (11:1–7)

Context
The introduction in verses 1–2 defines the nature and function of faith in ways that prepare for the argument to come. But verses 3 and 6 continue to lay theological foundations for identifying the faith that pleases God, even as the examples of Abel and Enoch are explored (vv. 4–5). The story of Noah climaxes this first segment, with its reference to 'things not yet seen' (v. 7), forming a minor inclusion with v. 1 (lit. 'things not seen').

Comment

1. *Faith* is the hook word linking this new section of the argument with the preceding one (10:38–39). Two significant characteristics of faith are then highlighted. From a biblical perspective, faith is oriented towards 'the future, hoped-for realization of God's promised reward (vv. 9, 11, 13, 26, 39–40) and the present, but unseen reality of God's existence, providence (v. 6), fidelity (v. 11), and power (v. 19)' (Cockerill, p. 520). The first claim (*faith is confidence in what we hope for*) relates to 'the attainment of hoped-for goals', and the second (*assurance about what we do not see*) relates to 'the perception of imperceptible realities' (Attridge, p. 308).

Debate has focused on whether the word *hypostasis* should be understood subjectively as *confidence* (NIV; ESV, 'assurance'), or whether it should be understood more objectively as 'reality' (CSB, NLT).[2] The same word is used with reference to God's 'being' in 1:3 and the 'substance' or 'foundation' of faith in 3:14. If the author is consistent in using this noun, the meaning here will be that faith gives to things hoped for 'a substantial reality, which will unfold in God's appointed time' (Lane 2, p. 329). Faith gives substance to the hope that God has set before us, enabling us to live in its light. This conclusion fits well with the way faith is portrayed in 11:10, 13–16, 26.

There has also been debate about whether *elenchos* should be translated *assurance* (NIV; ESV, 'conviction') or 'proof' (CSB, NLT ['evidence']). This term is not used elsewhere in Hebrews, but it regularly signifies 'proof' or 'proving' in Greek literature (BDAG). On this basis, it is best to conclude that faith is being described here as the proof of unseen realities. Faith behaves in a way that is consistent with the character of God and the promises he has made, demonstrating the relevance of *what we do not see* ('things not seen') to life in the present. This last expression is matched by

---

2. Cf. BDAG, *hypostasis* 1. Koester (p. 543) argues that the subjective and objective dimensions of faith are linked as the chapter unfolds, but we must still be careful to determine the precise way in which the terms in v. 1 are used. A different word is translated 'confidence' in 10:35 (*parrēsia*).

'things not yet seen' (v. 7), thus indicating that the unseen is a particular focus for faith in this paragraph (see also v. 3b).

2. Such faith is *what the ancients were commended for.* The passive form of the verb *martyrein* ('confirm, testify, affirm') in verses 2, 4, 5, 39 signifies God's testimony to the faith of those who are identified as 'the elders' of Christian believers (*presbyteroi*; cf. 1:1, 'our ancestors'). God's approval was given to these spiritual ancestors in the biblical witness to their faith and its outcome. The same verb is used in 7:8, 17; 10:15 with reference to the testimony of God about other matters in Scripture. This divine testimony has been preserved in the canon of Scripture for the benefit of succeeding generations of believers (1:1; 12:1; Rom. 15:4).

3. Before turning to examine significant examples of faith in action from the Scriptures, the pastor draws his audience into the frame, using the first-person plural: *By faith we understand that the universe was formed at God's command.* Belief in God as creator is foundational to the faith illustrated in this chapter. As in 1:2, the underlying term for *the universe* is 'the ages' (*tous aiōnas*), suggesting that God is the originator of time and history, as well as physical realities.[3] More precisely, Genesis 1 makes it clear that everything was *formed at God's command* ('by the word of God'; cf. Pss 33:6, 9; 148:5; Rev. 4:11). The verb *katērtisthai* (*formed*) means 'to cause to be in a condition to function well, put in order' (BDAG), which embraces everything Genesis 1 says about God's creative activity. Whatever natural science may discover about the process God used, Scripture affirms his sovereign control of every aspect. Hebrews is talking about faith in the biblical revelation that God has given about his word in the process of creation. Scripture also teaches that the 'voice' of God will ultimately shake the created universe in judgment to leave only his 'unshakable kingdom' (12:25–29, citing Hag. 2:6). So those who believe that God created the universe by his word of command can rely on his power to keep his promises about the future.

---

3. 'As the creator of space and time, God is outside and beyond them. He is present to all times and spaces, but is contained by none' (Williams, *His Love*, p. 116).

A conclusion is drawn from the belief that God created everything by his word of command: *so that what is seen was not made out of
what was visible.* The visible was brought into existence 'by what is
not seen' or 'by the invisible things'. This last expression could
parallel 'by the word of God' in the first half of the sentence.
However, the reference to what is 'not seen' in verses 1 and 7
includes God, the heavenly realm, and everything that awaits the
people of God. This suggests that the claim is more broadly that
'the visible realm is secondary to, and less valuable than the invisible realm'.[4] Such a perspective on the ultimate significance of
unseen realities determined the behaviour of many of the exemplars
of faith in the rest of the chapter (vv. 7, 10, 16, 20, 22, 26b, 27b, 35b).
Those addressed by the author had previously endured persecution
and suffering because they shared this perspective (10:32–34). They
are encouraged now to persist with such faith by considering its
practical impact on the lives of their spiritual ancestors.

4. Genesis 4:3–5 is not specific about Abel's faith, but Hebrews
asserts that it was demonstrated in his actions: *By faith Abel brought
God a better offering than Cain did.* Cain's sacrifice was unacceptable
because he was morally compromised (Gen. 4:6–7), suggesting
that Abel's sacrifice was the expression of a pure faith. In fact,
Abel was *commended as righteous, when God spoke well of his offerings.* As
in verse 2, *commended* means commended by God in Scripture. The
words of Genesis 4:4 explain this ('The LORD looked with favour
on Abel and his offering'). The close connection between faith and
righteousness established by the use of Habakkuk 2:4 in 10:38 is
recalled, confirming that Abel was *righteous* in the sense of being in
a right relationship with God *by faith.* Moreover, *by faith Abel still
speaks, even though he is dead.* The author is probably reflecting further
on God's words to Cain (Gen. 4:10, 'Your brother's blood cries out
to me from the ground'), which figuratively called for justice (Heb.
12:24). More broadly, however, Abel still *speaks* through the biblical

---

4. DeSilva, p. 387. This verse echoes the concept of creation *ex nihilo* ('out
of nothing') implied by Gen. 1 (cf. 2 Macc. 7:28), where the absolute
contingency of creation on God is stressed. But Hebrews says more
about the significance of 'what is not seen' in relation to 'what is seen'.

narrative about the righteousness of his *faith* (cf. v. 7; Matt. 23:35; 1 John 3:12).

5. The brief testimony to Enoch in Genesis 5:21–24 is remarkable in two respects. First, Enoch is the only person in this genealogy of Adam's descendants who is said to have 'walked [faithfully] with God' (Gen. 5:22, 24; compare Noah in 6:9). In contrast with Abel's short life, Enoch lived a long life of fellowship with God, expressing faithfulness and devotion to him. This is significant in view of the general spiritual decline portrayed in Genesis 4 – 6. Second, Enoch is the only person in the genealogy whose death is not mentioned (MT, 'then he was not, because God took him'). Hebrews follows the LXX, which interprets 'walked with God' to mean that 'Enoch was well pleasing to God' and the 'he was not' to mean that he 'was not found because God removed him'. The verb *metethēken* simply means 'convey from one place to another' (BDAG), but our author interprets it to mean that Enoch was *taken from this life, so that he did not experience death.* This reflects Jewish speculation that Enoch was taken into heaven without having to die (e.g. *1 En.* 12:3; 15:1; *2 En.* 22:8; 71:14; *Jub.* 4:23; 10:17). The author goes beyond that tradition by asserting explicitly that Enoch was translated into the presence of God *by faith.* The justification for this is that, before he was taken from this life, *he was commended as one who pleased God.* Once again, the verb *commended* draws attention to the words of God in Scripture. Other than this, the author gives no hint about why Enoch was granted this special blessing.

6. The conclusion that *without faith it is impossible to please God* sums up what has been said about Abel and Enoch. In particular, they illustrate the truth that *anyone who comes to him must believe that he exists and that he rewards those who earnestly seek him.* The first part of this claim uses the verb 'draw near, approach, come to' (*proserchomai*), which has appeared at critical points in the argument so far (4:16; 7:25; 10:1, 22; cf. 7:19) and will be used again in 12:18, 22. Here, the term is used without reference to the person and work of Christ, though verse 40 makes it clear that those who believed before Christ are only 'perfected' in their approach to God because of him (cf. 9:15). Faith is more than intellectual assent and involves approaching God with confidence in his character and will, as revealed in Scripture. Foundationally, however, it is necessary to *believe* certain things in order to draw near and please God. First, we must believe *that he exists*, namely 'that he is' the ultimate reality. This reflects what God said to Moses in Exodus 3:14 ('I AM WHO I AM') concerning his uniqueness and eternal existence. Second, we must believe that *he rewards those who earnestly seek him* ('he is a rewarder of those who earnestly seek him'). Seeking implies searching out what he is like and what he requires of those who approach him (cf. Deut. 4:29; Pss 14:2; 34:4, 10; Isa. 55:6–7; Acts 17:27). The motivation for persevering in faith here is knowing that he eternally rewards those who seek him through the mediation of his Son (10:35).

7. The final example of faith in this first segment of the chapter is *Noah*, who is described as being *warned about things not yet seen*, recalling verses 1, 3 ('things not seen'). Noah was *warned* about the impending flood and the need to prepare for it by following God's instructions (Gen. 6:13–21). 'Noah, then, is the first of the attested witnesses whose faith meant taking God at his word, a faith that is clearly forward-looking' (O'Brien, p. 407). Noah's faith expressed *holy fear* or respect for God (*eulabētheis*), leading him to build an ark to *save his family.*[5] By building an ark and escaping God's judgment, *he condemned the world* for its unbelief and *became heir of the righteousness* that is consistent with faith (*kata pistin*, 'according to faith'). Although Genesis does not explicitly mention Noah's faith, it does say that 'Noah found favour in the eyes of the LORD' (6:8) and that he was 'a righteous man, blameless among the people of his time, and he walked faithfully with God' (6:9; cf. 7:1; Ezek. 14:14, 20). The ultimate demonstration of this was his building of the ark. Alluding to the link between faith and righteousness in 10:38, our author concludes that Noah was an *heir of the righteousness that is in keeping with faith*. Noah was next in the biblical sequence of those like Abel and Enoch who, because of their faith, were attested to be righteous and pleasing to God. By implication,

---

5. In 5:7, the related noun *eulabeia* is used with reference to the 'reverent submission' of Jesus to the will of his Father. In 12:28, it describes the 'reverence' with which Christians are to serve God.

those who inherit eternal salvation through faith in Christ (1:14; 6:12, 17; 9:15) are similarly heirs of *the righteousness that is in keeping with faith.*

Theology

The link made between faith and hope in 3:6 and 6:11–12 is developed here. Faith takes seriously the hope given to us by God and acts accordingly. It proves unseen realities by the way it behaves, as suggested in 11:1. The foundation for a God-honouring faith is the belief that the universe was formed by his word of command and is completely dependent on him. With that same authority God will one day bring the material universe to an end and reveal the unseen reality of his (lit.) 'unshakable kingdom' (12:27–28). Those who would please God must approach him with this confidence and the belief that he rewards those who earnestly seek him. God approves the first three exemplars of such faith in Scripture for their devotion, loyalty and obedience. In different ways, they perceived unseen realities and acted appropriately. For this they are commended as righteous.

B. The faith of Abraham and his descendants (11:8–22)

Context

More space is devoted to Abraham and his descendants because of their significance in God's plan to bring humanity back to himself. Abraham's journey to the Promised Land comes first, with a particular focus on the forward-looking nature of his faith (vv. 8–10). Attention then turns to the miraculous birth of Isaac, making possible the fulfilment of God's promise of numerous offspring (vv. 11–12). A pause in recounting the family history takes place as the pastor dwells on the fact that these men and women, like Christians, were really longing for 'a better country – a heavenly one' (vv. 13–16). The testing of Abraham's faith with the challenge to sacrifice Isaac brought him to the point of trusting that 'God could even raise the dead' and, figuratively speaking, 'he did receive Isaac back from death' (vv. 17–19). Then there are references to the faith of Isaac in blessing Jacob and Esau (v. 20), Jacob's faith when he was dying in blessing each of Joseph's sons (v. 21), and Joseph's faith in speaking about the exodus from Egypt and giving instructions concerning the burial of his bones (v. 22).

Comment

8. The first recorded demonstration of Abraham's faith was when he was *called to go to a place he would later receive as his inheritance*. God's promise of the land as an inheritance was implied in his calling (Gen 12:1), but it was made explicit when Abraham arrived in Canaan (12:7; 13:14–17). Nothing is said about the first steps in the journey, which Abram took at the direction of his father Terah and which ended in Harran (Gen. 11:31–32). Genesis 12:1 records the personal calling by God of Abram, who is named Abraham in Genesis 17:5. Like Noah, Abraham's faith was expressed in obedience to the particular revelation that he received: *he obeyed and went, even though he did not know where he was going*. Abraham's motivation was the hope of obtaining a *place* in which to dwell, thus illustrating the claim that 'faith is the reality of what is hoped for' (v. 1, CSB). This verse also recalls the reward perspective of verse 6, with the notion of *inheritance* signifying God's prior gifting or promise, rather than something to be earned by faith.

9. When Abraham arrived in Canaan, *he made his home in the promised land like a stranger in a foreign country*.[6] The only property he ever owned was the burial place he purchased for Sarah (Gen. 23) and he had no citizen's rights. Although he was in *the promised land*, it was still *a foreign country* to him. The transitory nature of his situation was illustrated by the fact that *he lived in tents, as did Isaac and Jacob, who were heirs with him of the same promise* (cf. Gen. 26:1–6; 28:3–4). Isaac and Jacob are linked together with Abraham here, with respect to both the *promise* of an inheritance and the need to wait expectantly for God to fulfil that promise (vv. 13–16).

10. When the author describes Abraham as *looking forward to the city with foundations, whose architect and builder is God*, he pictures him

---

6. The verb translated *made his home* (*parōkēsen*) is used here with the meaning 'inhabit a place as a foreigner, be a stranger' (BDAG), as in LXX Gen. 17:8; 24:37; 26:3; 35:27; 37:1. Abraham's status as a foreigner is confirmed by the expression 'as an outsider' (*hōs allotrian*).

seeking something more than he could experience then and there (cf. vv. 1, 7; 12:22–24; 13:14). In this respect, his faith became 'the proof of what is not seen' (v. 1, CSB). *Foundations* imply permanence and stability, compared with life in a tent. God would provide this ideal environment as both *architect and builder* (cf. 12:28, 'a kingdom that cannot be shaken'). Waiting for God to provide an earthly inheritance, Abraham came to realize that life is a journey towards a future that God alone can provide. There is no suggestion in Genesis that he engaged in a pilgrimage towards heaven. As a man of his own era, however, he was 'continuously waiting for the consummation of redemption'.[7] In this respect, he became a forerunner and model for those who believe the promises of the gospel.

11–12. God's second promise to Abraham was that he would give him numerous descendants and would make him into a great nation (Gen. 12:2; 13:16; 15:5). But Sarah is emphatically the subject of the first sentence here: 'by faith even barren Sarah herself received power to conceive offspring, even though she was past the age, since she considered him faithful who had made the promise' (my translation). Some have argued that Abraham must be the subject of this sentence, because he is clearly identified in verse 12 as the *one man* from whom *came descendants as numerous as the stars in the sky and as countless as the sand on the seashore* (cf. Gen. 22:17; Isa. 51:2).[8] They also note that the expression translated by NIV *enabled to bear children*, which can be translated 'power for the laying down of seed', normally describes the male function in procreation. However, the two verses can meaningfully be read together if Sarah is regarded as having faith to receive Abraham's 'power for the laying down of seed' (Johnson, pp. 291–292; Cockerill, pp. 544–545). Hebrews implies that Sarah's incredulity about the possibility

---

7. Lane 2, p. 353. Lane shows how the idea of a city that is firmly founded by God echoes biblical descriptions of Zion (e.g. Pss 48:8; 87:1–3, 5; Isa. 14:32; 33:20; 54:11–12). Hebrews takes such language to apply to the heavenly city of God, which is the ultimate destination of all true believers (12:22–24).

8. The author draws together here expressions found in Gen. 15:5; 22:17; Exod. 32:13; Deut. 1:10; 10:22; 28:62.

of conception (Gen. 18:10–15) was overcome. Both Abraham and Sarah were called to ignore their age and circumstances and to trust in the power of God to fulfil his promise (cf. Heb. 6:13; 10:23). She was barren and he was *as good as dead*, but together they experienced 'the real but unseen power of God in the present through the birth of Isaac' (Cockerill, p. 536).

13–16. The author pauses in his reflection on specific examples of faith to draw out the implications of verse 10 and apply them to all of Abraham's immediate descendants. *All these people were still living by faith when they died.* Their number was slowly increasing, but *They did not receive the things promised*, specifically the land of Canaan as an earthly inheritance and the blessing of becoming a great nation in that context (Gen. 12:2). In God's providence, generation after generation had to wait for these promises to be fulfilled. They *saw* these realities by faith *and welcomed them from a distance*, when they described themselves as *foreigners and strangers on earth* (Gen. 23:4; 47:4, 9). Hebrews takes this expression to mean that they were *looking for a country of their own* ('a fatherland' or 'homeland') and adds that, *If they had been thinking of the country they had left, they would have had opportunity to return. Instead, they were longing for a better country – a heavenly one.* In effect, their *longing for a better country* meant that they were just like Christians, longing for the inheritance that awaits them in the heavenly realm (12:22–24) and that will one day be manifested as God's new creation (cf. Rev. 21:1–4).

As in verse 10, a close connection is drawn between the faith of Israel's ancestors and the faith of Christians. The situation of 'the ancients' (v. 2) is presented in terms that show the similarity of their situation to ours, and the need for an earnest, forward-looking faith. The faith that perseveres and reaches its God-given destination will not look back longingly to where it has come from. Neither will it be content with the immediate blessings of life in this world. Israel's early ancestors did not have the clear promise of a heavenly homeland that we do, but God delighted in their faith: *Therefore God is not ashamed to be called their God.* Those whose hope was in God and his promises will not be disappointed because, through Jesus Christ, *he has prepared a city for them* (v. 16; cf. 13:14). This is the heavenly Jerusalem (12:22–24), which is another way of speaking about 'the world to come' (2:5), the 'glory' that awaits

God's people (2:10), the promised 'rest' (4:1–11) and 'the promised eternal inheritance' (9:15).

17–19. Abraham's faith was uniquely *tested* when he *offered Isaac as a sacrifice* (Gen. 22:1–18; Jas 2:21–24). The enormity of that test is stressed by picking up the language of Genesis and describing Isaac as *his one and only son* (Gen. 22:2, 'your only son, whom you love'). The challenge for Abraham's faith is also highlighted when he is described as the one *who had embraced the promises* (as in Heb. 7:6). These included the specific promise of Genesis 21:12 (*It is through Isaac that your offspring will be reckoned*), which is then quoted. Since God had identified Isaac as the one through whom this promise would be fulfilled, Abraham was being asked to abandon his God-given hope in response to God's demand for a sacrifice. However, *Abraham reasoned that God could even raise the dead*. Our author may have discerned this from Abraham's confidence that God would provide a solution (Gen. 22:8, 'God himself will provide the lamb for the burnt offering') and the calmness of his actions. Abraham's expectation about returning with his son (Gen. 22:5) may also have been a factor in the author's conclusion about his 'resurrection' faith. But Hebrews goes a step further and concludes 'from which [death], figuratively speaking, he did receive him back' (ESV). The expression *en parabolē* ('figuratively'; NIV, *in a manner of speaking*) points to the typological significance of this event: it prefigured the resurrection of God's one and only Son and the resurrection of those who believe in him.[9]

20. The faith of Abraham's offspring is briefly described in verses 20–22, with an emphasis on how they demonstrated the reality of their hope and relied on the unseen power and faithfulness of God (cf. v. 1). When Abraham died, the LORD appeared to Isaac and confirmed to him the promises made to his father (Gen. 26:1–6). Without mentioning Jacob's deceit and Esau's selling of his inheritance, Hebrews asserts that *By faith Isaac blessed Jacob and Esau in regard to their future* ('concerning things to come'). Genesis 27:27–40 records the form of that blessing, which actually favoured Jacob

---

9. Cf. Attridge, p. 335. Compare the way *parabolē* is used in 9:9, where it is translated 'illustration'.

over his older brother and was a way of saying that the covenant promises would apply only to his descendants. The mention of Esau at this point prepares for the warning in Hebrews 12:16–17 about the way he forfeited the blessing of his inheritance.

21. Jacob went on to have twelve sons and blessed them all with predictions appropriate to each one (Gen. 49:1–28). Hebrews, however, mentions only the incident recorded in Genesis 48:1–22, indicating that *By faith Jacob, when he was dying, blessed each of Joseph's sons*. Joseph took the initiative in seeking the blessing of his sons, who were born when he was in Egypt. He was concerned that they should be reckoned as Jacob's descendants and share in the promised inheritance. Once again, our author mentions only the fact of this blessing and says nothing about Jacob's favouring of Ephraim over Manasseh. However, one further point is made about Jacob's faith at the end of his life: he *worshipped as he leaned on the top of his staff*.[10] The *staff* represented his life as a stranger and sojourner in the land (vv. 9, 13). In humility and reverence, even as he went on the long journey to Egypt (Gen. 46:1–7), he expressed his devotion to God and his continuing belief that God's promises would be fulfilled (cf. Heb. 12:28–29).

22. Joseph is singled out to complete the survey of Abraham's descendants, not only because his story occupies the whole of Genesis 37 – 50, but also because 'his life far surpassed those of all the other sons of Jacob as an example of one who lived by trusting God' (Cockerill, p. 562; cf. Acts 7:9–16). *By faith Joseph, when his end was near, spoke about the exodus of the Israelites from Egypt and gave instructions concerning the burial of his bones*. This is the only place in the New Testament where the word *exodus* is used to describe the departure of Israel from Egypt. *Israelites* (lit. 'the sons of Israel') refers to all the descendants of Jacob/Israel in Genesis 50:25.[11] This incident,

---

10. The Hebrew text of Gen. 47:31 says he 'bowed down at the head of his bed' (cf. NIV mg.), but the LXX renders this 'bowed down as he leaned on the top of his staff'. Cockerill (p. 561 n. 91) shows how the Hebrew text can be read as LXX does.

11. The verb translated *spoke* (*emnēmoneusan*) is better rendered 'remembered' (BDAG): Joseph kept in mind promises such as Gen. 15:13–15.

which is recorded in Genesis 50:24–25, reflects Joseph's absolute confidence that God would come to the aid of his people and take them out of Egypt to 'the land he promised on oath to Abraham, Isaac and Jacob'. Joseph's request that his brothers should carry his bones with them was a practical expression of this hope. 'Joseph's confidence in being taken to the promised land after his death reinforces the hope that the believer's final rest will be in the place that God has promised (Heb. 12:22–24)' (Koester, p. 500).

Theology

The faith of Abraham and his family is a model for Christian faith in three ways: it had a forward-looking dimension with respect to the promised inheritance; it expressed confidence in the faithfulness of God to fulfil what he had promised for the present; and in Abraham's case it demonstrated a trust that God could even raise the dead. By way of comparison, the apostle Paul focuses on the fact that Abraham believed that God had power to fulfil his promise with regard to the birth of Isaac, and likens this to our believing in the one 'who raised Jesus our Lord from the dead' (Rom. 4:18–25). Hebrews goes further than Paul in articulating the typological significance of the faith of these biblical characters, presenting it in terms that are decidedly Christian. Although they did not know Jesus as the Son of God, they are compelling examples of persevering faith for those who do.

C. The faith of Moses and those associated with him (11:23–31)

Context

The focus now is on characters and events associated with the exodus and the conquest of Canaan. The faith of Moses' parents is mentioned first (v. 23), followed by a reflection on the decision Moses made as an adult to be 'ill-treated along with the people of God rather than to enjoy the fleeting pleasures of sin' (vv. 24–26). Moses' faith was then expressed in the way he left Egypt (v. 27) and kept the Passover (v. 28). The faith of the Israelites is identified in relation to their passing through the Red Sea 'as on dry land' (v. 29) and the capture of Jericho (v. 30). The final example of faith in this section is the Gentile prostitute Rahab, who welcomed the spies sent to Jericho and 'was not killed with those who were disobedient' (v. 31).

Comment

23. *By faith Moses' parents hid him for three months after he was born* ('by faith when Moses was born, he was hidden for three months by his parents'). They did this *because they saw he was no ordinary child*. The adjective here and in Exodus 2:2 LXX could mean 'beautiful' (*asteion*) or more broadly 'well-bred' (BDAG). In Acts 7:20, the expression is understood to mean 'beautiful in God's sight' (ESV, CSB), suggesting that Moses had moral and spiritual qualities that were known to God (cf. 1 Sam. 16:7). Put another way, we could say that Moses' parents perceived something of the character he would grow to display (vv. 24–26). They saw the potential threat to Pharaoh of an outstanding leader among the Israelites, but *they were not afraid of the king's edict*, which was to drown 'every Hebrew boy that is born' (Exod. 1:22). The Hebrew midwives similarly did not fear Pharaoh's edict, because they feared God (Exod. 1:17, 21). Moses' parents expressed confidence that God would protect and nurture their baby, even as they placed him in a basket and put it among the reeds along the bank of the Nile (Exod. 2:3–4).

24. *By faith Moses, when he had grown up, refused to be known as the son of Pharaoh's daughter*. Hebrews moves quickly from the time when Moses lived as *the son of Pharaoh's daughter* (Exod. 2:5–10) to the occasion when he 'went out to where his own people were and watched them at their hard labour' (2:11). Seeing an Egyptian beating a Hebrew, 'one of his own people', Moses killed him and effectively renounced his membership of the royal household (2:12).[12] Without specifically commenting on this killing or its morality, our author proceeds to reflect on the rejection of his ties with Egypt.

25. Refusing to be known as the adopted son of Pharaoh's daughter, Moses *chose to be ill-treated along with the people of God*. The

---

12. Koester (p. 508) suggests that this would have involved renouncing 'honour, influence, and the hope of a princely inheritance'.

mistreatment of the Israelites in Egypt is portrayed in Exodus
1:11–22. Moses began to share that mistreatment when Pharaoh
heard about the killing of the Egyptian and tried to kill him,
forcing him to flee to Midian (Exod. 2:15). Later in the narrative,
Moses goes to Pharaoh many times in God's name, asking for his
people to be released, and he continues to suffer with them until
the exodus takes place. The idea of being *ill-treated along with the
people of God* was familiar to the first recipients of Hebrews (10:32–34;
13:3), and the author wants them to be ready to endure such opposition and alienation again (10:35–39; 12:1–13; 13:12–14). He further
clarifies that Moses chose to identify with the people of God *rather
than to enjoy the fleeting pleasures of sin* ('to have the temporary
enjoyment of sin'). This last expression could refer to 'the sinful
opulence that Moses renounced when he joined the Israelites'
(Koester, p. 508), but also the transitory 'advantage that could be
gained by siding with the Egyptians' (Johnson, p. 300). Genuine
faith has a sanctifying effect, separating people from worldly values
and commitments, motivating them to live openly for God and to
please him (12:14 – 13:19). 'Sin occurs where fellowship with the
people of God is refused or discontinued on account of the temptation to seek place or pleasure in the society of unbelievers'
(deSilva, p. 409). Like Abraham, Moses rejected earthly comforts
and security, in order to serve the living and true God and wait
patiently for the fulfilment of his promises (cf. 2 Cor. 4:16–18;
1 Thess. 1:9–10).

26. In essence, Moses is said to have regarded *disgrace for the sake
of Christ as of greater value than the treasures of Egypt*. The word *disgrace*
is significant here, because the same term was used to describe the
'insults' previously experienced by the recipients of Hebrews (10:33),
and it will be used again to challenge them to bear the 'disgrace'
that Jesus bore (13:13).[13] So the experience of Moses and the Israelites in Egypt is linked to the experience of those who boldly

---

13. The noun *oneidismos* is used for 'an act of disparagement that results
     in disgrace' and can be translated 'reproach, reviling, disgrace, insult'
     (BDAG). Cf. Rom. 15:3 (citing Ps. 69:9 [LXX 68:10]); 1 Tim. 3:7.
     A different word for 'shame' is used in Heb. 12:2.

identify with the suffering Christ. Some commentators suggest that the author envisages a 'prophetic consciousness on the part of Moses' concerning the suffering of Jesus (Attridge, p. 341; cf. 3:5). But it is more likely that he describes Moses' experience in this way retrospectively, because of its similarity to the reproach suffered by Jesus and those who follow him. Moses experienced reproach from his own people (Exod. 2:14; 5:21) and from the ruler of Egypt (5:4; 10:10–11, 28). In this way, he suffered 'the reproach of the coming Messiah with whom he was united by faith' (Hughes, p. 497). Like Abraham and his descendants in verses 10, 13–16, Moses is portrayed as having the sort of faith the author of Hebrews identifies as distinctly Christian. Some understand the expression *ton oneidismon tou Christou* in terms of Psalm 89:50–51 (88:50–51 LXX), which refers to the taunts experienced by the psalmist and God's anointed people (lit. 'the reproach of the anointed').[14] However, since *ho christos* ('the anointed') designates Jesus as the Messiah elsewhere in Hebrews, 'the disgrace of the Christ' is more likely to have been the author's primary meaning, rather than 'the disgrace of God's anointed people'. In fact, Moses accepted the insults and disparagement that would ultimately be experienced by both Christ and his people (12:1–13; 13:12–14; 1 Pet. 4:12–19).

Moses was able to have this self-denying attitude *because he was looking ahead to his reward* (lit. 'to the reward'). This recalls 10:35 and suggests that Moses had the same hope that Christians do. Ultimately, of course, Moses shared in the promised eternal inheritance secured by Christ for believers past, present and future (9:15; 11:39–40; 12:22–24). As in 11:10, 13–16, however, Moses' looking ahead to the reward expressed his immediate confidence that God would fulfil the commitments he made to Abraham, Isaac and Jacob (Exod. 3:6–10, 16–17). Moses' *reward* would be to enjoy with his people the blessings of the inheritance they were promised, both earthly and heavenly.

27. Like his parents before him (v. 23), Moses feared God rather than the anger of Pharaoh. The claim that *he left Egypt, not fearing the king's anger* most naturally refers to the occasion when he 'fled

---

14. O'Brien, pp. 432–433; Johnson, p. 301. Contrast Koester, p. 502.

from Pharaoh and went to live in Midian' (Exod. 2:15). Some have disputed this, because the previous verse says that Moses was afraid that his killing of the Egyptian would be discovered (2:14). They argue that verse 27 has in mind Moses' leading of the people from Egypt at the time of the exodus (Exod. 14:13–20).[15] But the exodus is yet to be mentioned (v. 29), and the author has carefully followed the biblical order of events in this chapter so far. Exodus 2:15 simply says, 'When Pharaoh heard of this, he tried to kill Moses.' Moses was not intimidated, but he fled to preserve his life and endured many years as 'a foreigner in a foreign land' (2:22). Hebrews speaks positively about Moses' motivation at this point: he was capable of acting without fear because he persevered 'as if he saw him who is invisible'.[16] Moses focused on the One who is invisible (Col. 1:15; 1 Tim. 1:17) and believed that 'he rewards those who earnestly seek him' (v. 6; cf. 10:35). This argument prepares for the exhortation to Christians that they should endure and enter into their heavenly inheritance by looking to the exalted Lord Jesus, who is perceived and known by faith (12:2; cf. 2:8–9; 3:1–2).

28. As well as governing his own life, Moses' faith was used to bring deliverance and hope to his suffering people. *By faith he kept the Passover and the application of blood.* Moses obeyed God's command to put animal blood on the door frames of the houses where sacrificial lambs were to be eaten, *so that the destroyer of the firstborn would not touch the firstborn of Israel* (Exod. 12:1–13). God is identified as *the destroyer* in Exodus 11:4–5; 12:27, 29, but 12:23 speaks of God's agent in this event. An angel is most likely meant here (as in 2 Sam. 24:16; 1 Chr. 21:12, 15; Isa. 37:36; 1 Cor. 10:10). This final plague would bring God's judgment on the Egyptians and their gods, but the Israelites would be passed over (Exod. 12:27, 29–30). The

---

15. O'Brien (p. 433) takes this verse to refer to the exodus as the culmination of a series of events in which Moses did not fear the king. Cf. Koester, pp. 503–504.

16. O'Brien, p. 434. The causal translation of *hōs horōn* (*because he saw*) is not as accurate as the qualitative rendering of ESV ('as seeing'). The point is that Moses did not actually see God, even at the burning bush (Exod. 3:1–6) or later (33:12–23).

Passover meal was to be a sign to that generation of their impending deliverance from Egypt and from death in the sea, encouraging them to move out in faith. It was also meant to be a perpetual memorial of God's saving grace to later generations (12:14–28). Like Noah, who constructed an ark before he could see the flood approaching, Moses obeyed God and kept the Passover before there was any indication of the approaching judgment.

29. Attention now turns to the faith of the people when they *passed through the Red Sea as on dry land* (Exod. 13:17 – 14:22).[17] Although they were terrified when Pharaoh and his army caught up with them (14:10–12), Moses urged them to stand firm and see the deliverance God would bring (14:13). 'The Hebrews placed their lives completely in the hands of God who held back the waters' (14:21–22) and 'the reward for their dependence was the destruction of the Egyptians by those same waters' (deSilva, p. 414). Judgment fell on their pursuers, who *were drowned* (14:23–31). Nothing is said about the subsequent behaviour of the Israelites in the wilderness, because it was earlier used as an example of unbelief and disobedience (Heb. 3:7 – 4:11).

30. The conquest of Canaan is introduced with a brief reference to the first major battle fought under Joshua: *By faith the walls of Jericho fell, after the army had marched round them for seven days* (Josh. 5:13 – 6:27). The implied subject of this sentence is the next generation of Israelites. They exercised faith in response to God's extraordinary instructions about the defeat of Jericho, just as their parents had done concerning their escape from Egypt.

31. *The prostitute Rahab* is the last person to be considered in this historical sequence. She appears instead of Joshua as the climactic example of faith, because of the particular challenge she offered to the recipients of Hebrews. *She welcomed the spies* who were sent to Jericho by Joshua and protected them (Josh. 2:1–9). She knew what God had done for the Israelites and sought deliverance for herself and her family from the destruction that was coming upon her city (2:10–13). *By faith*, therefore, she *was not killed with those who were*

---

17. Hebrews follows the LXX in calling it 'the Red Sea' (*hē Erythra Thalassa*), whereas the Hebrew expression is 'the Sea of Reeds' (*yam sûp*).

disobedient (cf. Josh. 6:23–25). 'Rahab is an example of someone who hears "good news", unites herself with the faith of those who obey, and receives salvation.'[18] Her implied status as a Gentile and her reputation as a prostitute were no barrier to this. In each of the events mentioned in verses 28–31, the outcome for those who had faith and were obedient was life, while the outcome for those who were disobedient was death (cf. 10:39).

Theology

The period of the exodus and conquest in Israel's history was characterized by conflict between the people of God and unbelievers. The primary challenge for the Israelites was to overcome fear and the loss of hope, so that God's purpose for them could be fulfilled. The author of Hebrews sees the responses of Moses in this context as particularly relevant to those he addresses. Fearing oppressive rulers who oppose God's people is a natural human reaction, but fear can be contained by focusing on the One who is invisible and trusting in his power to grant what he has promised (vv. 23, 27). The related challenge is not to abandon God and his people to avoid mistreatment and experience temporary gratification or relief (vv. 25, 26; cf. 10:25). Like Moses, this means being convinced about the surpassing wealth of the 'reward' that God promises to those who persevere in faith (10:35). Like Rahab, it involves being certain about God's power to save and choosing life instead of death, whatever the cost (vv. 23, 28–31).

D. Further examples of enduring faith (11:32–40)

Context

The pastor's rhetorical method changes here as multiple examples of faith and its consequences are recorded without much detail. The earlier expression 'by faith' (*pistei*) is missing, though 'through faith' (*dia pisteōs*) appears at two critical points (vv. 33, 39). There are three segments to the argument. In verses 32–34 the focus is on the

---

18. Mosser, 'Rahab Outside the Camp', p. 393. Mosser notes particular links with Heb. 4:1–2; 10:36–39; 13:13–14.

marvellous things achieved by men and women of faith in the past. In verses 35–38 the emphasis is on the suffering, alienation and death of the faithful, of whom 'the world was not worthy'. In verses 39–40 there is a restatement of verse 2 ('These were all commended for their faith'), but with the qualification that none of them obtained the promise. This surprising conclusion is explained in terms of God's plan for them to be perfected 'together with us' through the saving work of Jesus.

Comment

32–34. An attention-grabbing question (*And what more shall I say?*) alerts us to the fact that there is more to be said about faith, but it will be conveyed in a different way. 'The author calls to mind a host of examples even as he protests that he has not the time to do so' (*I do not have time to tell*)![19] First, he mentions four judges by name (*Gideon, Barak, Samson and Jephthah*), one king (*David*), and then *Samuel and the prophets*, identifying key characters in the books Judges to 2 Samuel. The book of Judges identifies the flaws in those mentioned here, and yet it shows how their faith was used by God at particular moments to advance his plan for his people (O'Brien, pp. 439–440). Perhaps David is placed before Samuel to highlight his succession to the judges as ruler of God's people. Second, he describes what these people accomplished in the political and military spheres *through faith*. In general terms, they *conquered kingdoms, administered justice, and gained what was promised*. This last claim could include David, who was promised the kingship in 1 Samuel 16:1–13 and assured of a perpetual dynasty in 2 Samuel 7:1–16. Then there is a particular allusion to Daniel (*who shut the mouths of lions*; cf. Dan. 6:22–23), the three who were cast into the fiery furnace (*quenched the fury of the flames*; cf. Dan. 3:25–28) and those who *escaped the edge of the sword*. These could include David (1 Sam. 17:45–47; 19:10–18), Elijah (1 Kgs 19:1–3), Elisha (2 Kgs 6:26–32) and Jeremiah (Jer. 26:7–24), and the Jews saved by Esther. The

---

19. DeSilva, p. 416. Attridge (p. 347) notes examples of this sort of disclaimer as a segue from one rhetorical style to another in Greek literature.

pastor returns to the theme of what was positively accomplished through faith when he mentions those *whose weakness was turned to strength* [e.g. Gideon, Judg. 7; and Samson, Judg. 16:19–30] *and who became powerful in battle and routed foreign armies* [*parembolas*, can also be rendered 'fortified camps', BDAG].

35. Although the author has just mentioned some who escaped death, he views the supreme goal of faith as victory over death in resurrection (cf. v. 19). *Women received back their dead, raised to life again* in this world (e.g. 1 Kgs 17:17–24 [the widow of Zarephath]; 2 Kgs 4:17–37 [the Shunammite woman]). In addition to these resurrections, *There were others who were tortured, refusing to be released so that they might gain an even better resurrection.* Vivid expressions of this hope occur in the Apocrypha, written after the period of history covered in the Old Testament (e.g. 2 Macc. 6:18 – 7:42; 4 Macc. 5 – 18).[20] But Hebrews makes it clear that a share in the resurrection to eternal life is possible only because of the better sacrifice of Christ (9:22–23), which inaugurates the better covenant (7:22).

36–38. Images of alienation, persecution, imprisonment and death pile up to show the recipients of Hebrews the extent to which their experience so far has been similar to that of believers in former generations (cf. 10:32–34; 13:3), although none has yet been forced to shed his or her blood (12:4). *Some faced jeers and flogging, and even chains and imprisonment. They were put to death by stoning; they were sawn in two; they were killed by the sword.* Jeremiah was taunted (Jer. 20:7–8), beaten (37:15) and imprisoned (20:1–3; 37:15–18), and according to the *Lives of the Prophets* 2:1, he was stoned.[21] Jewish tradition also records that Isaiah was sawn in two (*Lives of the Prophets* 1:1; *Martyrdom of Isaiah* 5:1–14). The prophet Uriah was slain with the sword (Jer. 26:20–23), as were others (1 Kgs 19:10, 14; Jer. 2:30). *They went about in sheepskins and goatskins, destitute, persecuted and*

---

20. DeSilva (p. 419) notes the persistent focus on resurrection in 2 Macc. 7:9, 11, 14, 23, 29 as the expectation of each martyr. They die to leave examples of faithfulness to God and his law for others to follow (2 Macc. 6:28, 31; 4 Macc. 1:7–8; 9:23; 12:16).

21. Matt. 23:37 and Luke 13:34 record the tradition that prophets were stoned. Cf. Stephen in Acts 7:58–59; Paul in Acts 14:19; 2 Cor. 11:25.

ill-treated. Despite the world's evaluation and dismissal of such people, *the world was not worthy of them! They wandered in deserts and mountains, living in caves and in holes in the ground.* Some of these descriptions recall the stories of David (1 Sam. 23:14), Elijah and Elisha (1 Kgs 17 – 19; 21; 2 Kgs 1 – 8), and faithful Jews who lived on the fringes of civilization at the time of the Maccabean revolt (e.g. 1 Macc. 2:28, 31; 2 Macc. 5:27; 10:6). Each of these images 'contributes to the overall picture of a group that is marginalized in the extreme, having no place in society and exposed to every form of disgrace at society's hands' (deSilva, p. 421). By this means, the pastor encourages those he addresses to persevere with similar confidence in God and his promises (10:35–39; 12:1–13) and cope with different degrees of exclusion from the world in which they live and even punishment for their faith.

39–40. Despite the fact that believers in both Testaments share similar circumstances and are called to make similar responses, the pastor concludes by emphasizing a significant difference. Old Testament characters were *commended for their faith,* in the sense that God testified to it in the pages of Scripture, *yet none of them received what had been promised* (v. 39; cf. v. 13). Although they saw the fulfilment of certain promises in this life (e.g. 6:15; 11:11, 33), none of them experienced the comprehensive blessings of the messianic era. The singular noun in verse 39 ('the promise') refers to eschatological salvation as a whole, viewed from the standpoint of Old Testament prophecy (cf. 10:36). The failure of these men and women of faith to experience the promised eternal inheritance was through no fault of their own. In his gracious providence, *God had planned something better for us,* in the sense that *their* enjoyment of perfection through Jesus Christ would only be *together with us.*[22] The author uses the language of perfection previously employed to highlight the total benefits of Christ's saving work for those who believe (cf. 12:2). With reference to Old Testament believers, the focus is on their 'ultimate transfer to the actual presence of God in

---

22. NIV rightly translates *problepsamenou* ('foresaw') as *planned.* The concept is similar to God's foreknowledge in Rom. 8:29, meaning a divine resolution to provide in advance for his elect.

the heavenly sanctuary'.[23] But the situation of those living in the New Covenant age is *better*, because we experience in advance of that eternal inheritance the blessing of being already perfected by the sacrifice of Jesus (10:14).

Perfection could not be attained through the levitical priesthood (7:11), and 'the law made nothing perfect' (7:19; cf. 9:9; 10:1–4). But a better hope has been introduced by the sacrifice of Christ, making it possible for Christians to approach God with confidence in the present (cf. 4:14–16; 10:19–22) and ultimately to share in the promised eternal inheritance (12:22–29; 13:14). That inheritance was offered to the people of God typologically in the gift of the Promised Land and the provision of the sacrificial system, but the reality towards which these institutions pointed has only now become attainable because of the death and heavenly exaltation of Jesus. Those who were called to trust God in the Old Testament era receive the promised eternal inheritance when they are resurrected, because the mediator of the New Covenant has 'died as a ransom to set them free from the sins committed under the first covenant' (9:15). Those who approach God now on the basis of his Son's perfect work become citizens by faith of the heavenly Jerusalem, with their names already 'written in heaven' (12:23).

Theology
Christians must persevere with confidence in God and his promises to obtain the rich reward of eternal life. In this respect, the faithful who are commended in Scripture offer both encouragement and challenge. Alienation from the surrounding culture, ill-treatment, disgrace, persecution and even death may be the consequence, but Christians are in an even better position than their Old Testament counterparts to persevere in faith. 'The unseen truth which God will one day enact is no longer entirely unseen; it has been manifested in Jesus ... the "end" in which all believe and towards which all move, has been anticipated and proleptically disclosed.'[24]

---

23. Lane 2, p. 393. Cf. Peterson, *Hebrews and Perfection*, pp. 156–159.
24. Barrett, 'Eschatology', pp. 382–383. But Hebrews does not teach that
    what was manifested in Jesus was 'entirely unseen' in the OT.

Returning to the pastor's earlier imagery, we can say that the way
into the heavenly sanctuary of God's eternal presence has been
opened by Jesus in his death and heavenly exaltation, so that Christians can draw near with confidence and hold fast to the hope he
has given us (4:14–16; 6:18–20; 10:19–22; 12:22–24).

E. Looking to Jesus (12:1–3)

Context
This brief conclusion to the author's celebration of faith begins
with a reminder that Christians are 'surrounded by . . . a great
cloud of witnesses' to whom we can look for encouragement.[25] The
essential challenge is 'to run with perseverance the race marked
out for us', which is enhanced by two related encouragements. We
are to run this race by throwing off 'everything that hinders
and the sin that so easily tangles' (v. 1) and 'fixing our eyes on
Jesus, the pioneer and perfecter of faith' (v. 2). This last clause
is expanded with several others, outlining the pattern of his
endurance and its outcome ('For the joy that was set before him
he endured the cross, scorning its shame, and sat down at the right
hand of the throne of God'). The challenge to 'Consider him who
endured such opposition from sinners' (v. 3) restates the previous
one in a more focused way, before a purpose clause resumes the
theme of running the race ('so that you will not grow weary and
lose heart'). This passage picks up the theme of endurance from
10:32, 36 and prepares for the call to 'Endure hardship as discipline' (v. 7), which is central to the next segment of exhortation
(vv. 4–13).

Comment
   1. A strong conjunction (*toigaroun*, *Therefore*) clearly links this
exhortation with the previous exposition. *Such a great cloud of witnesses*
refers to those in Scripture commended by God for their faith. The

---

25. Just as 'example lists' in ancient literature frequently ended with a brief
   exhortation, so here the author climaxes his appeal with an exhortation
   that finally focuses on Jesus (so deSilva, pp. 377–378).

noun *martys* ('witness') is related to the verb *martyrein* ('confirm, attest, witness'; 11:2, 4, 5, 39). Those whose faith is 'witnessed' by God become *witnesses* of God-honouring faith to others. The author stresses that (lit.) 'we ourselves [*kai hēmeis*] have such a great cloud of witnesses surrounding us' (*cloud* is a metaphor for 'crowd'), implying that they are a constant source of encouragement for Christian believers to look to. Some have argued that these are heavenly spectators who observe our struggles in *the race marked out for us*, but the author's call to fix our eyes on Jesus (v. 2) suggests that we are to pay attention to them as well. The emphasis is on 'what Christians see in the host of witnesses, rather than on what they see in Christians'.[26]

The main challenge of this verse is the exhortation *let us run with perseverance the race marked out for us*. The noun translated *race* (*agōn*) can have the more general sense of 'competition, contest' or even 'struggle against opposition' (BDAG; compare *athlēsis* ['conflict'] in 10:32), but the verb *run* clarifies that a metaphorical foot race is envisaged. The present tense of this verb and the words *with perseverance* ('endurance', as in 10:36) indicate that the race of faith is a long-distance one, requiring dedication, focus and exertion. However, this is not a competitive event, but one in which all are encouraged to finish well. We can persevere in the race *marked out for us* (ESV, 'set before us') by looking to the example of those who have successfully reached the finishing line. Like them, we must *throw off everything that hinders* (ESV, 'every weight' [*ongkon panta*]).[27] This could include things that may not be sinful in themselves, but which slow down or prevent continuance in the Christian life, such as habits, friendships, ambitions and attachments. We are also to put aside *the sin that so easily entangles*, which is another general expression that could apply to a range of attitudes and behaviours

---

26. O'Brien, p. 451. DeSilva (pp. 427–429) argues for 'spectators' and Cockerill (pp. 602–603) contends that both senses may be intended.

27. The verb *apothemenoi* (*throw off*) is used elsewhere in the NT for putting off qualities as though they were clothes (Rom. 13:12; Eph. 4:22, 25; Col. 3:8; Jas 1:21; 1 Pet. 2:1).

(ESV, 'sin which clings so closely').[28] *The sin* the author has in mind is not specifically apostasy, but anything that constricts or prevents the believer from finishing the race. Some argue that *the sin* is either a closer definition or literal equivalent of *everything that hinders*, but *sin* implies deliberate rebellion against the will of God (3:12–13; 10:26). Hindrances only become sinful when they are retained at the expense of spiritual progress.

2. The primary encouragement for running with perseverance the race marked out for us comes from *fixing our eyes on Jesus* (compare 3:1–2; 12:3), who is the ultimate witness to the faith that triumphs through suffering. Jesus *endured the cross* with all its physical horror, apparent abandonment by his heavenly Father and mockery from his opponents. Crucifixion was a vile and degrading form of execution, but the author focuses on the disgrace of the cross (*scorning its shame*), rather than its physical pain, because he wants this to be the model for his hearers. Jesus was able to do this because his focus was on *the joy that was set before him*.[29] This joy was rather like the prize or the goal that is the focus of the athlete and it embraced everything his ascension and enthronement signified. Jesus shares this joy with his 'brothers and sisters' (2:11–12; 12:22–24; cf. John 17:24). The implied challenge is for them to have the same perspective in their struggle with opposition, persecution, suffering and public disgrace (10:32–36; 13:13). In this respect, Jesus is 'the perfect example – perfect in realisation and effect – of that faith we are to imitate, trusting him' (Westcott, p. 397).

The encouragement to fix our eyes on Jesus must take into account the triumphant conclusion to his suffering: he *sat down at the right hand of the throne of God* (thus fulfilling Ps. 110:1). The

---

28. The best reading is *euperistaton*, which means 'easily ensnaring, obstructing, constricting' (BDAG). The variant *euperispaston* ('easily distracting') is poorly attested and is most likely secondary (Ellingworth, pp. 638–639).

29. The preposition *anti* in v. 2 could give the meaning 'instead of (the joy)', but its use in v. 16 suggests that its most natural sense in both contexts is 'for the sake of' (Croy, *Endurance*, pp. 37–40, 74 ['to obtain the joy'], 177–185).

ascension and heavenly session of the Son of God is central to the
argument of Hebrews (1:3, 13; 2:5–9; 4:14; 8:1; 9:11–12; 10:12–13).
Heavenly enthronement was Jesus' destiny as Messiah, enabling
him to rule in the midst of his enemies (Ps. 110:2) and function as
the heavenly high priest of his people (Ps. 110:4). His heavenly
session concluded the earthly struggle he endured, making it possible for believers to share with him all the blessings of 'the
promised eternal inheritance' (9:15). He has entered God's 'rest'
(4:1–11), and believers are summoned to 'guide their pilgrimage
by looking to Jesus, considering both his earthly career and his
celestial glory. Their conduct should be modelled on his earthly
perseverance; but they are also to meditate on his session, the
reward of the perseverance.'[30] Believers will reign with Christ
in 'the world to come', because of his victory over sin and death
(2:5–10; cf. Rom. 5:17; Rev. 5:10; 20:4, 6; 22:5).

When Jesus is identified as *the pioneer and perfecter of faith*, he is
presented as both the ultimate example of persevering faith and the
enabler of such faith for others. As 'the pioneer of their salvation'
(2:10), Jesus is the leader who delivers his people by being perfected
'through sufferings' and becoming the one through whom they are
brought to glory.[31] As the *pioneer and perfecter of faith*, Jesus goes
ahead of his followers in suffering, dying and being raised to glory,
giving faith 'a perfect basis by his high-priestly work'.[32] Jesus' faith
is articulated in 2:13, using the words of Isaiah 8:17 ('I will put my
trust in him'), his faithfulness to his heavenly Father is indicated in
2:17; 3:1–2, and this is further explained in terms of his 'reverent
submission' (5:7) and obedience (10:5–10). The rare word *perfecter*
(*teleiōtēs*) describes 'one who brings something to a successful conclusion' (BDAG) and recalls the author's teaching about the way

---

30. Hay, *Glory*, p. 95 (emphasis removed). Compare the focus on looking
    to the reward in 11:10, 14–16, 26; 13:13–14.

31. The same noun (*archēgos*) that is used with reference to Jesus in 2:10;
    12:2 is also found in Acts 5:31, where the context gives the meaning
    'prince' or 'leader', but in Acts 3:15 'author' is the more appropriate
    rendering.

32. G. Delling, 'τέλος κτλ.', *TDNT* 8, p. 86.

Christ's perfecting makes the perfecting of believers possible. As *the pioneer and perfecter of faith*, he inaugurated a 'new and living way' for us to approach God (10:20) and has gone ahead of us into the heavenly sanctuary as 'forerunner' on our behalf (6:20). Jesus is both the specific source of Christian faith and 'the first person to have obtained faith's ultimate goal, the inheritance of the divine promise which the ancients only saw from afar' (Attridge, p. 356). The article before *faith* (*tēs pisteōs*) embraces the faith of Jesus and the faith of believers before and since, so that 'our faith' (ESV, CSB) is an inadequate rendering. Jesus perfects the faith of Old Testament believers by bringing them 'to the fulfilment of the thing they were trusting to receive' (deSilva, p. 432). He perfects our faith by giving us the perfect example of persevering faith and the assurance through his finished work that those who trust him will reach their heavenly destination.

3. The challenge to *consider* Jesus heightens the emphasis on looking to him as the pioneer and perfecter of faith, expressing the need to 'reason with careful deliberation' about him (BDAG; a parallel term is used in 3:1). In particular, the author wants his audience to meditate on the fact that Jesus *endured such opposition from sinners*, which included verbal and physical abuse.[33] His opponents were *sinners* in the sense that they acted lawlessly in arresting him and putting him to death (Matt. 26:45; Acts 2:23), but more broadly in the sense that they set themselves against God and his will. The reason for considering Jesus in this way is given in the purpose clause *so that you will not grow weary and lose heart*. The first verb is regularly used for physical weariness (BDAG), but the additional words 'in your souls' (not translated by NIV) suggest a spiritual weariness. This meaning is confirmed by the second verb, which appears again in verse 5, where it clearly means 'lose heart'. Spiritual fatigue prevents endurance in running 'the race marked out for us' (v. 1). Indeed, physical, emotional and spiritual endurance is required in any experience of suffering (10:32–34), and those

---

33. NIV does not include the words 'against himself' (NRSV, ESV) because they are poorly attested in the manuscript evidence. Cf. Metzger, *Textual Commentary*, pp. 604–605.

addressed by the author have been challenged about the need to continue with such perseverance (10:35–39). By implication, '"the One who has endured" is able to sustain them, not primarily by removing the trials but by supplying the inner strength and fortitude they need' (Cockerill, p. 613).

Theology

In the face of impending suffering and a potential unwillingness to endure further trials, believers can be encouraged by the example of many witnesses to persevering faith in Scripture. But the greatest incentive to continue in the race marked out for us is to contemplate what it meant for Jesus to be the pioneer and perfecter of faith and to seek his help. The pastor explains this in terms of Jesus' example, but also his unique achievement. The use of athletic imagery in this passage, together with its climactic focus on the way Jesus endured and reached his goal, has great rhetorical significance. Enduring faith will not be diverted from reaching its goal by physical or emotional pain, the shaming of opponents, hindrances of any kind, or entanglement with sin. Those who feel that they lack the resilience to persevere in the Christian life should consider what Jesus endured and approach God through him to find grace to help them in their time of need (4:16).

11. CHALLENGES TO ENDURE SUFFERING AND PURSUE PEACE, HOLINESS AND GRATEFUL SERVICE TO GOD (12:4–29)

The pastor's focus shifts more specifically now to the struggle his friends are having with unbelieving outsiders (vv. 4–11), though continuity with the preceding section is indicated by the use of endurance language (vv. 1, 2, 3, 7) and related terms.[1] Proverbs 3:11–12 is the basis of the first challenge, in which God is said to speak to Christians 'as a father addresses his son' (vv. 4–13). The emphasis here is on God's discipline or training of his children and how they should respond. God desires that believers share in his holiness and produce 'a harvest of righteousness and peace'.

The challenge to pursue peace and holiness in verse 14 arises from the preceding reflection on the purpose of divine discipline. Then, in verses 15–17, the believing community is warned to look out for anyone who 'falls short of the grace of God', becomes a source of trouble and defilement in their midst, or is 'immoral, or

---

1. Fatigue is mentioned in vv. 3, 5, 12; the struggle against sinners/sin in vv. 3, 4; joy as the outcome of suffering in vv. 2, 11.

is godless like Esau, who for a single meal sold his inheritance rights as the oldest son' (alluding to Gen. 25:29–34). The example of Esau reinforces previous warnings about failing to obtain the inheritance promised by God (2:1–3; 3:7 – 4:11; 6:4–6; 10:26–31).

The warning in verses 15–17 is followed by the encouragement that those who have come to God through Jesus have been given a secure inheritance in the heavenly Jerusalem and belong to the ultimate assembly of God's people (vv. 18–24). To avoid any slide into unbelief and disobedience, they are further warned not to 'refuse him who speaks' or to turn away from 'him who warns us from heaven' (vv. 25–27). Put positively, they are to be thankful for receiving a share in God's unshakable kingdom and serve him acceptably 'with reverence and awe' (vv. 28–29). The nature of God-honouring service is then revealed in the exhortations that follow (13:1–19).

A. Submitting to God's discipline (12:4–13)

Context

The struggle addressed by the pastor here is the sort of 'opposition from sinners' experienced by Jesus and, to some extent, by this fellowship of believers in the past (v. 4; cf. 10:32–34). Proverbs 3:11–12 is quoted as a text they may have forgotten, in which God speaks directly to their situation (vv. 5–6). Here the focus is on the way he disciplines his children and calls upon them not to 'make light' of the situation or to 'lose heart'. The pastor's challenge is to endure hardship as an expression of God's fatherly care, submitting to his discipline as a loving process of training and transformation (vv. 7–9). The specific purpose of God's discipline is 'that we may share in his holiness' (vv. 10–11), which requires cooperation from believers and includes strengthening one another to persevere in the face of suffering (vv. 12–13).

Comment

4. This transitional verse has no formal connection with the preceding one and so NIV rightly indicates that a new paragraph begins here. But a reference to the recipients' *struggle against sin* echoes the mention of Jesus' experience of opposition from 'sinners' (v. 3). The struggle here is against the sin of unbelief expressed in the behaviour of their persecutors (10:32–34), rather than the struggle with personal sin reflected in verse 1. Although the pastor says *you have not yet resisted to the point of shedding your blood*, the implication is that, like the martyrs in 11:35–38 and Jesus in 12:2, death could be the outcome for at least some of them, thus echoing the challenge of Jesus for disciples to 'take up their cross' and follow him, even to the point of death (Mark 8:34–38 par.).[2]

5–6. Those who suffer insult, rejection and persecution because of their identification with Jesus may question God's love and lose heart (*eklyein* as in v. 3). Anticipating this, the pastor reminds them of a significant biblical text with this introduction: 'And you have forgotten the exhortation that addresses you as sons' (CSB).[3] Hebrews itself is called a 'word of exhortation' (13:22), because it blends warning and encouragement to motivate the recipients to persevere in faith, hope and love. Although 'encouragement' is a possible translation of the same noun in 6:18 (*paraklēsis*), 'exhortation' better describes the way the biblical quotation is understood and used in this context. As elsewhere in Hebrews, 'the written word is to be understood as a spoken address' (Attridge, p. 360).

Proverbs 3:11–12 LXX is cited in full, with the pronoun *my* added to *son* (as in the Hebrew text). The sonship of Jesus is highlighted many times in Hebrews (1:2, 5, 8; 3:6; 4:14; 5:5, 8; 6:6; 7:3, 28; 10:29), but the sonship of believers was only previously mentioned in 2:10, where it is coupled with the idea that we are his 'brothers' (2:11–12; cf. Rom. 8:14–17; Gal. 4:1–7).[4] Most of the proverbs addressed to

---

2. In my Introduction section 4 I reflect on the implications of this verse for understanding the situation of the first recipients of Hebrews and the dating of this work.

3. Commentators and translators are divided about whether to read this as a rhetorical question (NIV, ESV) or a statement (CSB). The Greek can be rendered either way.

4. NIV translates 'sons and daughters' in 2:10 and 'brothers and sisters' in 2:11–12 to make it clear that the words 'sons' and 'brothers' should be understood inclusively. In 12:5, a similar inclusivity is to be understood in the paraphrase *as a father addresses his son*.

'my son' (e.g. Prov. 1:8; 2:1; 3:1, 11) are in the form of parental teaching and instruction to children in an Israelite family. However, this particular proverb speaks about the way *the Lord* disciplines his people. It begins with two parallel prohibitions or warnings:

> *do not make light of the Lord's discipline,*
> *and do not lose heart when he rebukes you.*

The reason for not making light of such an experience and losing heart is then given in the form of two parallel statements:

> *because the Lord disciplines the one he loves,*
> *and he chastens everyone he accepts as his son.*

God's discipline expresses his fatherly love for his children.

Discipline (*paideia*) can refer to 'corrective punishment, training, or the end result of training, i.e., education or culture' (Croy, *Endurance*, p. 77; BDAG). A punitive dimension to the Lord's discipline is indicated by the use of the verbs *rebukes* and *chastens* in Proverbs (5:12; 6:23; 9:7; 12:1; 13:18; 15:10, 32), though the application of the text in verses 7–11 suggests that the author is focusing more positively on the educative and training aspect of God's discipline. As they endure opposition from unbelievers because of their commitment to Christ (v. 4), God is working to 'fortify his "sons and daughters" in the way of obedience' (Cockerill, p. 616).[5]

7–8. Picking up the language of Proverbs 3:11–12 LXX, the author's fundamental challenge is to *Endure hardship as discipline* ('for the sake of discipline endure'). This exhortation is then explained in terms of their relationship with God as Father: 'God is treating

---

5. A punitive view of divine discipline is common in many Jewish sources, but 'passages from the Wisdom of Solomon (3.1–12; 11.1–14; 12.19–22), Sirach (2.1–6; 4.17), and Deuteronomy (8.2–5) are evidence that a formative view of suffering is occasionally to be found among Jewish writers' (Croy, *Endurance*, p. 95). Croy points to the influence of Graeco-Roman thinking on the author's formative view of discipline, but Cockerill (pp. 616–618) qualifies this.

you as sons' (ESV [NIV, *children*]). A rhetorical question links this to parental discipline in human experience more generally: 'For what son is there whom his father does not discipline?' (ESV). However, the focus shifts more specifically to believers with the next expression (*If you are not disciplined*). NIV obscures this by translating the following clause *and everyone undergoes discipline*. ESV ('in which all have participated') highlights the significance of the term 'partakers' (*metochoi*) here, which is central to the author's definitions of genuine Christian experience in 3:1, 14; 6:4. At this point he is suggesting that 'all of God's true children have become partakers of and continue to experience his discipline' (Cockerill, p. 623). Indeed, without such discipline *you are not legitimate, not true sons and daughters*. Put positively, experiencing God's discipline through suffering can actually confirm the 'sonship' of God's children (Rom. 8:17–27).

9. Another dimension to God's training and correcting of his people is now explained with a human analogy (*Moreover, we have all had human fathers who disciplined us and we respected them*).[6] Although children may find it difficult to respect their parents when they are being guided and corrected by them, respect can certainly be the outcome over the course of time. Indeed, a godly pattern of instruction will enable children to honour their parents (Exod. 20:12; Eph. 6:1–4). More profoundly and extensively, believers need to *submit to the Father of spirits and live*. This challenge comes in the form of a question expecting a positive answer: 'Shall we not much more be subject to the Father of spirits and live?' (ESV). Given the reference to *human fathers* in the preceding clause, the one to whom we should submit is our spiritual father.[7] Submitting to the will of

---

6. The noun *paideutēs*, which was commonly used for 'an instructor who provided guidance and correction' (Koester, p. 529; cf. Rom. 2:20), describes the role of fathers here. The related verb is used in vv. 6, 7, 10 (*paideuein*) and the noun *paideia* ('discipline') in vv. 5, 7, 8, 11. Cf. 1 Cor. 11:32; 2 Tim. 2:25; 3:16; Titus 2:12.

7. Num. 16:22 and 27:16 LXX refer to God as the giver of all life with the expression 'God of the spirits and all flesh'. A shorter expression appears in 2 Macc. 3:24–25; 1 QS 3:25; *1 En.* 37–71 ('God of the spirits'). *Father of spirits* picks up the more intimate language of the preceding

our heavenly Father in times of trial is necessary for the enjoyment of life in its fullest sense, both now and for ever (vv. 1–2, 14, 22, 28; cf. 10:38).

10. Human parenting may lack wisdom and be limited in its scope (*They disciplined us for a little while as they thought best*). God's parenting, however, is guided by his perfect knowledge of us and concern for the eternal welfare of his children (*but God disciplines us for our good, in order that we may share in his holiness*). The positive intention of God's discipline is stressed by the expression *for our good*, which is then explained in the clause that follows. A rare Greek word for *holiness* (*hagiotēs*) denotes the sanctity of God's character and life (related terms are used in Exod. 15:11; Isa. 6:1–3; Amos 4:2 LXX).[8] To share God's holiness is to enjoy the transforming effect of life in his presence, which ultimately means being brought 'to glory' through Christ (2:10). However, in advance of that, God wishes to produce in us practical expressions of the sanctified relationship we already have with him through the saving work of his Son (10:10, 24; 13:12). Examples of this are given in 12:11; 13:1–6. Elsewhere in the New Testament, transformation into the likeness of Christ is an aspect of the glorification that begins with conversion and is completed when believers meet him face to face (Rom. 8:28–30; 2 Cor. 3:18; 2 Thess. 2:13–14; 1 John 3:2–3).

11. Continuing the analogy with parental discipline, the author admits that *No discipline seems pleasant at the time, but painful*, suggesting that divine discipline can be similarly distressing. *Later on, however, it produces a harvest of righteousness and peace for those who have been trained by it.* Using terms that particularly refer to the outcome of God's fatherly discipline, the point is made that God 'exercises' or 'trains' those he loves in order to produce in them 'the peaceful

---

(note 7 *cont*.) verses and suggests God's initiative in bringing life to the spirits of those who believe in him.

8. The noun *hagiotēs* came into use only late in Hellenistic Judaism (e.g. 2 Macc. 15:2; *T. Levi* 3:4). In the NT it is found only here and as a variant in some manuscripts of 2 Cor. 1:12. Cf. BDAG; Lane 2, p. 425.

fruit of righteousness' (ESV, CSB). This rendering suggests that righteousness is the source of the 'peaceful fruit' God desires to see in us.⁹ 'Peaceful fruit' would be the attitudes and behaviour flowing from a right relationship with God (peace with God). This might include perseverance, a Christlike character, hopefulness, and love for God and for other people (cf. Rom. 5:1–5; 8:29; 12:3–21). The verb *trained* (*gegymnasmenois*) recalls the athletic imagery in verses 1–2, but it is used educatively here (as in 5:14) to reinforce the positive purpose of God's discipline. The Holy Spirit produces the fruit of such a relationship with God in believers (Gal. 5:22–26; cf. Jas 3:13–18), while suffering provides 'fertile soil for the cultivation of a righteous life, responsive to the will of God' (Bruce, p. 361).

12–13. An inference is drawn from the preceding verses (*Therefore*) that effort is required to reach the goals God has set for his people. Continuing the metaphor of training (v. 11) and running the race (vv. 1–3), physical imagery is used to encourage active perseverance, this time adapting words from Isaiah 35:3–4. The prophet was told to

> Strengthen the feeble hands,
>   steady the knees that give way;
> say to those with fearful hearts,
>   'Be strong, do not fear;
> your God will come,
>   he will come with vengeance;
> with divine retribution
>   he will come to save you.'

Those who fear the future are similarly encouraged in Hebrews 10:35–39 not to throw away their confidence, because of the promise that

---

9. Cockerill (pp. 627–628) argues from 10:38; 11:4, 7 that *righteousness* in 12:11 refers to a right relationship with God that is based on faith and that he 'perfects this righteousness and brings its "peaceful fruit" to maturity'. Contrast Lane 2, p. 425; Ellingworth, p. 656.

In just a little while,
he who is coming will come
and will not delay.

Now they are told to strengthen one another for the struggle that lies ahead (*strengthen your feeble arms and weak knees*). Additional words from Proverbs 4:26 are adapted and put into the plural to reinforce this message (*Make level paths for your feet*).[10] Their aim should be 'so that what is lame may not be put out of joint, but rather be healed' (NRSV, ESV). If some of their number are showing signs of weakness, tempting them to 'turn away' or be 'dislocated' (BDAG), they need to be helped back on track by fellow believers (compare v. 3, 'so that you will not grow weary and lose heart'). Even those who are spiritually weak may be 'healed' and kept moving forward in the 'race' of faith (v. 1), through the support and encouragement of other believers. This focus on the need for appropriate ministry to one another continues in verses 14–17.

Theology
Although the focus of this passage is on enduring the sort of opposition and persecution Jesus experienced, the principles outlined by the pastor could be applied to a range of situations in which Christians suffer, such as sickness, deprivation, loneliness and the loss of loved ones. As God's children learn to submit to his will in suffering, his holiness is reflected in their attitudes and behaviour. They learn to trust him as the Holy One, who is sovereign over every circumstance, perfectly loving, wise and righteous. They experience him moulding and shaping them into the kind of people he wants them to be. They become more concerned about helping one another in the journey of faith. They acknowledge that trials are necessary for the formation of godly character (cf. Rom. 5:3–5; Jas 1:2–4; 1 Pet. 1:6–9) and to keep them firm and faithful to the end, when by God's grace they will fully share in his holiness.

---

10. O'Brien (p. 471) observes that Prov. 4:26 refers to 'godly conduct under the direction of divine wisdom', which is relevant to the moral thrust of Heb. 12:1, 4, 14–15.

B. Pursuing peace and holiness (12:14–17)

Context

The notion of cooperating with God as he trains his people to share in his holiness is developed in verse 14. This involves pursuing peace with everyone and expressing what it means to be one of God's holy people in character and lifestyle. In verses 15–17, the community is warned to 'look out' for one another in three related ways: literally, 'lest anyone falls short of the grace of God'; 'lest any root of bitterness grows up to cause trouble and defile many' (alluding to Deut. 29:18); and 'lest anyone is immoral or godless like Esau, who for a single meal sold his inheritance rights as the eldest son' (alluding to Gen. 25:29–34).

Comment

14. There is no grammatical connection between this verse and the preceding one, though it picks up the themes of holiness and peace from verses 10, 11 and the challenge of verses 12–13 to move together in the direction set by God. *Make every effort to live in peace with everyone* could be rendered 'keep pursuing peace with everyone'.[11] In the flow of the argument, this means demonstrate in all your relationships the peaceful fruit of righteousness that God is producing in your lives (cf. 13:1–3, 7, 20–21). This concern for peaceful relationships with *everyone* echoes the more extensive treatment of the subject in Romans 12:9–21. *Peace* in the form of non-retaliation against opponents should be especially pursued in the context of persecution and suffering (cf. 12:3–4).

Although a different word for *holiness* is used,[12] the message is similar to verse 10. First and foremost, holiness denotes the sanctity of God's character and life. Holiness in the sense of a consecrated

---

11. Less likely is the view of Cockerill (pp. 633–634) that the text should be translated 'together with all pursue peace and holiness' and that the challenge is simply to pursue peace in the church.

12. This noun *hagiasmos* is sometimes translated 'sanctification' and occurs also in Rom. 6:19, 22; 1 Cor. 1:30; 1 Thess. 4:3, 4, 7; 2 Thess. 2:13; 1 Tim. 2:15; 1 Pet. 1:2. Cf. Peterson, *Possessed*, pp. 139–142.

relationship with God is imparted to believers through the work of Christ (10:10, 29; 13:12 cf. 2:11). Only those who have been cleansed and sanctified by Christ's blood can approach God with confidence in his heavenly sanctuary (10:19–22). But just as the gift of peace must be expressed in everyday relationships, so holiness is to be pursued in character and lifestyle (cf. 2 Cor. 7:1; 1 Thess. 4:1–8; 2 Tim. 1:9–10; Titus 2:11–14). Indeed, without such a proof of genuine sanctification, *no one will see the Lord*, meaning live in his presence and share in his eternal kingdom (12:22–28; cf. Ps. 15). This does not mean that salvation is achieved by reaching a certain level of moral perfection. Holiness in every area of life should be the constant goal and desire of those who have been set apart to belong to Christ, but salvation is unquestionably by the grace of God (vv. 15–17). As noted in connection with verse 10, transformation into the likeness of Christ is complete only when we *see the Lord* (see especially 1 John 3:2).

15. Continuing the challenge of the preceding verse, the author encourages his hearers to pursue peace and holiness 'by diligently guarding what they have received through Christ from threat of loss' (Cockerill, p. 635).[13] *See to it* renders a present participle (*episkopountes*, 'accepting responsibility for the care of' [BDAG]), highlighting the need for a particular type of continuing care for one another (compare 3:12–14; 5:12; 10:24–25). In this warning passage (vv. 15–17), the possibility of forfeiting the grace of God and missing out on the blessing of seeing the Lord is powerfully articulated. First, there is to be a concern for individuals (*that no one falls short of the grace of God*). God's *grace* was supremely demonstrated in the death of Jesus (2:9) and in the gift of his Spirit (10:29), and it is always available to help those who seek it (4:16). Falling short of God's grace implies not grasping hold of it and missing out on the eternal inheritance God has secured for those who trust him (4:1–2; 9:15). Second, there is to be a concern for the church (*that no bitter root grows up to cause trouble and defile many*). This alludes to Deuteronomy 29:18 (29:17 LXX), which warns about the possibility that

---

13. 'Abandonment of the "holiness" provided by Christ shatters the "peace" of the believing community as well' (Cockerill, p. 638).

someone in the covenant community might turn away from the Lord to go and worship other gods. Such a person, clan or tribe might become a 'root . . . that produces . . . bitter poison', defiling the whole nation of Israel. In Christian communities, apostasy of any kind can similarly *cause trouble and defile many.*

16. The third concern that Christians should have in their oversight of one another is that *no one is sexually immoral, or is godless like Esau.* In effect, Esau spurned God's holiness and became a pattern of the arrogant unbelief that leads to rebellion (Gen. 25:29–34). The Genesis narrative does not describe Esau as being *sexually immoral* (*pornos*), though later Jewish writings make much of his sexual immorality (e.g. *Jub.* 25:1, 7–8; Philo, *Questions and Answers on Genesis* 4.201, 153), especially in marrying two Hittite women (cf. Gen. 26:34–35; 27:46; 28:8–9). Sexual indulgence and apostasy are often connected in human experience, though NIV separates the two ideas with a comma, allowing for the possibility that Esau simply turned away from the LORD and became *godless* (*bebēlos*, 'worldly, common').[14] He devalued his relationship with God and the long-term blessings awaiting him to pursue instant self-gratification (*who for a single meal sold his inheritance rights as the oldest son*). No mention is made of Jacob's self-serving role in this sorry story. 'Esau was drawn into apostasy by his love for the world' (Cockerill, p. 633; contrast Moses [11:24–26] and Jesus [12:1–3]), and he perversely despised his *inheritance rights as the oldest son* (Gen. 25:33–34). As the firstborn, he was destined to be the head of the family and to receive a double share of his father's inheritance (Deut. 21:15–17). If Isaac had blessed him as he did Jacob (Gen. 27:28–29), all the covenant blessings promised to Abraham and Isaac would have been his. But Esau excluded himself from the grace of God.

17. The author assumes that his audience will be familiar with the two biblical accounts he now links together (*as you know*): Esau's rejection of his inheritance rights (Gen. 25:29–34) and *afterwards* his attempt to seek his father's blessing (Gen. 27:34–38). Even though

---

14. This adjective functions as the opposite of 'holy' in LXX Lev. 10:10; Ezek. 22:26; 44:23 ('the holy and the common'), effectively meaning 'unholy' (ESV).

Esau *wanted to inherit this blessing, he was rejected.*[15] NIV has weakened the force of the next two clauses (*Even though he sought the blessing with tears, he could not change what he had done*). A preferable translation is 'for he found no chance to repent, though he sought it with tears' (ESV). Genesis 27:34, 38 stresses that Esau sought the blessing with tears, but repentance is actually the new topic in Hebrews 12:17 and is more likely to be what the author meant by 'it'.[16] The expression 'chance to repent' suggests 'an objective possibility for repentance granted by God' (O'Brien, p. 476), rather than an inability to change his father's mind. The author employs this language to reinforce his earlier warning about the impossibility of bringing back to repentance those who have renounced Christ and the gospel (6:4–6). Esau is viewed as an example of someone who put himself in a position where a second chance was no longer possible. See Introduction 6d, 'Apostasy and perseverance'.

Theology
'Within the community of faith, there is to be no separation of peace and holiness. If "peace" binds the community together as the achievement of Christ, "holiness" is that quality which identifies the community as the possession of Christ' (Lane 2, p. 450). Appropriate ministry to one another within the body of Christ is necessary to maintain these identity markers and avoid the corrupting effect of apostasy (see Introduction 6e, 'Maturity and ministry'). In particular, the pastor is concerned to highlight the danger of forfeiting the grace of God. This may happen through neglect or unbelief, causing an individual to miss out on enjoying eternal life in God's presence. Moreover, anyone whose heart turns away from the Lord may become a disturbing influence on others

---

15. The verb used here means that he was regarded as 'unworthy/unfit and therefore to be rejected' (BDAG). The passive form could mean that he was rejected by God or his father or both.
16. The feminine pronoun *autēn* ('it') can refer either to 'blessing' or to 'repentance'. O'Brien (p. 476 n. 161) argues for the former, because the noun *topos* ('place', 'opportunity', 'chance') is masculine. However, the emphasis could fall on the second noun ('repentance') in this pair.

in the church. Esau is the classic example of a person who devalued his relationship with God and the inheritance that was rightly his to satisfy his immediate needs. Esau functions as a final warning about the impossibility of bringing back to repentance those who have hardened their hearts against Christ and the gospel (cf. 3:12–14; 6:4–6; 10:26–31).

C. Living as citizens of the heavenly Jerusalem (12:18–24)

Context

As an encouragement to persevere in the ways he has just outlined (vv. 7–17), the pastor compares and contrasts the approach of the Israelites to meeting with God at Mount Sinai (vv. 18–21) and the approach to God that is now possible at Mount Zion, 'the city of the living God, the heavenly Jerusalem', through Jesus 'the mediator of a new covenant' (vv. 22–24). Sinai was the place where God gave the law and entered into a covenant with Israel as a nation (Exod. 19 – 24). In that context, the tabernacle, the priesthood and the sacrificial system were established to sustain and bless Israel as God's holy people (Exod. 25 – 30).

> Step by step the writer advances from the physical terrors by which [the revelation] was accompanied (verses 18–20), to the confession of the Lawgiver himself (verse 21), who alone among the prophets was allowed to speak to God face to face.
> (Westcott, p. 412)

The heavenly Jerusalem is the ultimate destination of those who are called under both covenants, but access to this city is possible only because of the New Covenant and the 'sprinkled blood' of Jesus (9:15; 11:13–16, 39–40; 13:12–14). 'Whereas Sinai is characterized by limited access to God, Zion is characterized by the full and final access depicted earlier in the sermon as an eschatological hope (e.g. 6:19–20).'[17]

---

17. Martin and Whitlark, *Inventing Hebrews*, p. 48 (authors' emphasis removed).

Comment

18. This new section is closely linked to the preceding one by the conjunction 'for' (ESV). As in previous contexts, a serious warning is followed by a statement of the hope that is given to those who put their trust in Jesus. The same verb is used in verse 18 (*You have not come*) and verse 22 ('you have come') to highlight the difference between Israel's encounter with God at Sinai (Deut. 4:11–12) and the approach to God in his heavenly city that the New Covenant makes possible.[18] The author uses the perfect tense (*proselēlythate*, 'you have come') to give prominence to the action that determines the situation of believers under these successive covenants. Although it is true that 'the terrifying atmosphere that characterized the theophany at Sinai (vv. 18–21) throws into bold relief the festive joy of Zion' (Lane 2, p. 459), it should be noted that God is still portrayed in the centre of the heavenly city as 'the Judge of all' (v. 23) and as 'a consuming fire' (v. 29). So the contrast between the two scenes should not be drawn too sharply.

Mount Sinai is not actually mentioned, though the author clearly draws on different biblical descriptions of Israel's meeting with God there (Exod. 19:16–22; 20:18–21; Deut. 4:11–12; 5:22–27). Vivid images of dangerous phenomena are employed to invite the hearers 'to re-experience not only the powerful imagery but also a powerful sense of awe suggested by such' (Holmes, *Sublime Rhetoric*, pp. 128–129). Seven terms describe the mountain and the occasion. First, Sinai was 'what may be touched', which emphasizes that it belonged to the earthly realm and was 'perceptible to the senses'.[19] Second, it was 'burned with fire' (Deut. 5:23, 'ablaze with fire'). When God spoke from the fire it was a manifestation of his glory and majesty, which threatened to consume those who witnessed it (Deut. 5:23–26). The next three terms (*darkness, gloom and storm*) continue to portray Sinai as a scene of terror and potential death (cf. Deut. 4:11 LXX).

---

18. Elsewhere in Hebrews this verb is translated 'approach' (4:16), 'come to' (7:25), 'draw near' (10:1, 22), 'comes to' (11:6).

19. Lane 2, p. 461. The term used here reflects the warning in Exod. 19:12–13 about touching the mountain, though a different verb is used in the LXX (cf. Heb. 12:20).

19. More space is devoted to the sixth and seventh features of the Sinai encounter, pointing to its climax. The focus here is on what was *heard*. A *trumpet blast*, which grew louder and louder, caused everyone to tremble with fear (Exod. 19:16, 19; 20:18). Finally, there was *a voice speaking words* ('a voice of words'; cf. Deut. 4:12). This was such an overwhelming experience *that those who heard it begged that no further word be spoken to them*. 'Like God's living, active, and piercing word in Heb. 4:12, God's speech in Heb. 12:18–21 is also threatening and dangerous' (Holmes, *Sublime Rhetoric*, p. 133). Positively, the people said, 'Today we have seen that a person can live even if God speaks with them' (Deut. 5:24). Negatively, they were afraid of being consumed by the great fire and asked Moses to 'Go near and listen to all that the LORD our God tells you' (Deut. 5:25–27; cf. Exod. 20:18–19). They acknowledged the grace of God in speaking to them, but they were aware of their vulnerability in that encounter and their need for a God-appointed mediator.

20. Particular attention is drawn to a command that the Israelites *could not bear*: *If even an animal touches the mountain, it must be stoned to death*. This followed a warning that 'Whoever touches the mountain is to be put to death' (Exod. 19:12–13). Hebrews focuses on 'the most stringent aspect of the command . . . in order to emphasize the gravity of the injunction and the peril of coming before the annihilating holiness of the divine appearing' (Lane 2, p. 463). God's words were meant to facilitate a relationship with him, but the encounter at Sinai showed the danger of being in his presence and the need for him to provide a safe method of approach.

21. *The sight was so terrifying that Moses said, 'I am trembling with fear.'* These words are not found in any narrative about Sinai, but they may have been based on Deuteronomy 9:19 ('I feared the anger and wrath of the LORD, for he was angry enough with you to destroy you').[20] This was Moses' reaction to the later rebellion of the

---

20. There was a Jewish tradition that Moses was fearful at Sinai (*b. Sabb.* 88b), which may have influenced our author. Cf. Bruce, pp. 371–372; Lane 2, p. 464.

Israelites (Deut. 9:7–18), illustrating his fear that God would judge his people (cf. Heb. 10:30–31, citing Deut. 32:35, 36). Another possibility is to see here an allusion to Moses' words when he first encountered God at the burning bush ('Moses hid his face, because he was afraid to look at God', Exod. 3:6; cf. Acts 7:32). Either way, even Moses, appointed by God to be the mediator of the covenant, was fearful of God's holiness, majesty and wrath against disobedience, as a result of his different encounters with God.

22. *But you have come to Mount Zion* begins the positive contrast between Israel's situation under the law and the situation of those who have come to God through Jesus. In a sense, Christians in their conversion have already reached their heavenly destination! Yet this vision is designed to keep them approaching God in the way that he has provided (4:14–16; 7:25; 10:19–25), not falling short of his grace (12:15), so as to enjoy the full experience of salvation that awaits them (6:18–19; 9:27–28; 10:36–39; 13:14). The overall challenge of Hebrews is to realize in daily experience the benefits of being already rescued from final judgment and made members of the ultimate assembly of God's people through faith in Christ.

In the last stages of conquering the land of Canaan, David took the city of Jerusalem from the Jebusites, which was on *Mount Zion* (2 Sam. 5:6–12). It became known as *the city of the living God*, because God promised to be present with his people there and his plans for their future were tied up with that city (e.g. Pss 48; 87; Isa. 14:32; 28:16; 54:11–14). The notion of a new or *heavenly Jerusalem* developed in Jewish and Christian apocalyptic literature as a way of explaining how prophetic hopes such as Isaiah 2:1–4; 35:10; 65:17–25 would ultimately be fulfilled (cf. Bruce, pp. 373–375). Hebrews adopts such terminology to describe the heavenly homeland of God's people, which was earlier identified as 'a better country' and a city prepared for them (11:10, 14–16; cf. 13:14, 'the city that is to come'). Other related terms are 'the world to come' (2:5), God's 'rest' (4:1–11), 'the promised eternal inheritance' (9:15), 'an even better resurrection' (11:35) and 'a kingdom that cannot be shaken' (12:28). Taken together, these terms portray the future for God's people in concrete terms, but as a transcendent reality that already exists and will one day have an earthly manifestation (cf. Rev. 21:1–5).

Developing the vision of this heavenly gathering, the author first points to *thousands upon thousands of angels in joyful assembly*.[21] In contrast with the solemnity of Sinai (vv. 18–21), where angels were associated with the giving of the law (2:2; cf. Deut. 33:2 LXX), this is a scene of celebration (BDAG, *panēgyris*, 'festal gathering'; cf. Ezek. 46:11; Hos. 9:5; Amos 5:21 LXX). Angels celebrate the victory of Jesus (cf. Rev. 5:11–14; 7:11–12) and share the joy that he has entered into. By implication, God's people on earth may join them in this praise, anticipating the joy of the heavenly city.[22]

23. The body to which all true believers belong is called *the church of the firstborn, whose names are written in heaven*. The gathering of Israel to meet with God at Sinai was called 'the day of the assembly' (Deut. 4:10; 9:10; 18:16 LXX; cf. Acts 7:38, 'the assembly in the wilderness'). In Matthew 16:18, Jesus uses the same term (*ekklēsia*) to talk about building his own eternal 'assembly' or 'church', against which 'the gates of Hades' will not prevail.[23] In Hebrews 2:12 (citing Ps. 22:22 [21:2 LXX]), the glorified Jesus proclaims God's name in this 'assembly' of his brothers and sisters. The 'assembly' in these references is the heavenly or eschatological gathering of all who have been saved through him for eternal life. We anticipate the day of ultimate assembly in God's presence when we gather together in earthly congregations to celebrate our redemption and minister to one another (10:24–25).

God called Israel his *firstborn* when he brought them out of captivity in Egypt (Exod. 4:22–23 ['firstborn son']; cf. Jer. 31:9). But

---

21. Greek *myriades* could mean 'ten thousand upon ten thousand' or 'a very large number, not precisely defined' (BDAG).

22. Compare my comment on 4:9 ('Sabbath celebration') and the visions in Revelation 4 – 5; 7; 11:15–18; 12:10–12; 14:1–5; 16:5–6; 19:1–8. Cf. Peterson, *Engaging*, pp. 261–282.

23. In secular Greek, this term could refer to any sort of informal gathering (as in Acts 19:32, 41) or to a legally constituted assembly (as in Acts 19:39). In Christian circles, it became a technical term for gatherings of believers in particular places (e.g. Acts 8:1; 11:26; 14:23; 1 Cor. 1:2) or for the whole company of those belonging to Jesus (e.g. Eph. 3:10; 5:25–27).

when they built the golden calf, Moses was told that those who
sinned in this way would be blotted out of 'the book' God had
written (Exod. 32:32–33), meaning that they would be judged
by him and miss out on the inheritance he had promised them.
Using the same image positively, Jesus encouraged his disciples to
rejoice that their names were 'written in heaven' (Luke 10:20),
meaning that those who put their trust in him in this life could be
certain of a heavenly inheritance. Hebrews similarly speaks of (lit.)
'the firstborn who are enrolled in heaven'.[24] Retrospectively, this
must include believers before Christ, whose membership of the
heavenly assembly was made possible by his death 'as a ransom to
set them free from the sins committed under the first covenant'
(9:15; cf. 11:39–40). The designation *firstborn* (*prōtotokoi* is a plural
term here) now belongs to all who are genuinely children of God
'through their union with him who is the Firstborn *par excellence*'
(Bruce, p. 377).[25]

The reference to God as *the Judge of all* recalls earlier warnings
about final scrutiny and accountability (cf. 2:2–3; 4:13; 6:8; 9:27;
10:26–31; 13:4), but those who have come to Jesus and put their
trust in his saving death have clearly been accepted into God's holy
presence. Nothing is said here about the fate of the faithless and
disobedient, because the focus in this vision is on the positive
outcome for the assembled multitude.

Those specifically identified as *the spirits of the righteous made perfect*
will be the faithful who have finally reached the goal of their
earthly pilgrimage. Although resurrection from the dead is part of
the author's expectation (6:2; 11:35), and the resurrection of Jesus is
ground for confidence about this (13:20–21), he does not explain
how bodily resurrection relates to the present state of these people.

---

24. The verb used in Luke 10:20 is a technical term for recording
    information and the one in Heb. 12:23 (*apogegrammenōn*) is a synonym
    (BDAG, 'registered'). Cf. Rev. 21:27 ('written').

25. Jesus is God's 'firstborn' (1:6), whose destiny is to inherit all things
    as the enthroned Messiah (cf. Col. 1:15, 18; Rev. 1:5). As 'the firstborn
    among many brothers and sisters' (Rom. 8:29), he makes it possible
    for believers to share in his inheritance.

They are called *spirits* to stress 'the spiritual and immaterial nature of the new order of existence' (Montefiore, p. 232).[26] They are called *the righteous* because they have lived by faith and their deeds reflected this (11:4, 7), even in the face of opposition and suffering (10:38–39). The emphatic expression *made perfect* is a deliberate echo of 10:14, indicating that the recipients stand before God forgiven and guiltless because of Christ's high-priestly offering.[27] Those who lived before the time of Christ did not enjoy the confidence of direct approach to God that is the Christian's present privilege (4:14–16; 10:19–22; cf. 11:39–40). Ultimately, however, all God's elect children will share the joys of his eternal kingdom because of his Son's saving work.

24. Believers on earth are already enrolled as citizens of heaven (v. 23; compare Phil. 3:20) and, even now, belong to the ultimate assembly of God's people, because they have come to *Jesus the mediator of a new covenant*. As in 2:9; 3:1; 6:20; 7:22; 10:19; 12:2; 13:20, the personal name *Jesus* is held back for rhetorical effect ('to the mediator of the new covenant – Jesus'), emphasizing here the humanness of the mediator. The additional phrase *and to the sprinkled blood* could simply refer to the redemptive death by which Jesus inaugurated that covenant and its benefits (8:6; 9:15). However, since the sacrifice establishing 'the first covenant' was applied to the Israelites at Sinai when they were sprinkled with animal blood (9:19–20; cf. Exod. 24:8), the focus here might be on the metaphorical application of Jesus' *blood* to the 'hearts' of those who believe the gospel, who are 'sprinkled' to cleanse them from a guilty conscience through Christian initiation (10:22; cf. 9:14).

The next clause in Greek reads 'speaking better than Abel'. If this is an allusion to Genesis 4:10 ('Your brother's blood cries out to me from the ground'), the contrast is between Abel's blood,

---

26. Harris (*Raised Immortal*, pp. 119–142) discusses the nature of the resurrection body and whether the NT envisages a disembodied 'intermediate state'. Cf. 1 Cor. 15:35–57; 2 Cor. 5:1–10.

27. Perfect passive forms of the same verb are used in 10:14 and 12:23 (*made perfect*), expressing the continuing effect of Christ's sacrifice for them.

which metaphorically cried for punishment, and the blood of Jesus, which speaks of forgiveness and acceptance. NIV assumes this reading with a paraphrase (*that speaks a better word than the blood of Abel*). However, in 11:4 it is Abel's faith that is 'speaking' through his 'better sacrifice [or 'offering']' (alluding to Gen. 4:4), not his death. Abel's faith put him in the category of the righteous who suffered and died for their faith (11:36–38), who are now perfected by the blood of Christ (12:23). Abel's faith enabled him to experience something better than he could have hoped for, because the blood of Christ was a better sacrifice than Abel's.[28]

Theology

This description of the heavenly Zion is a portrayal of God's perfected people, who have passed beyond judgment and are rejoicing with the angels in the presence of their crucified and glorified Saviour. As those who have already 'come' to God in this heavenly context through faith, believers on earth are assured that they belong to the ultimate, complete company of the people of God, here called 'the church of the firstborn, whose names are written in heaven'. When the pastor affirms that this access to God's presence is through Jesus 'the mediator of a new covenant' and his 'sprinkled blood', he restates the argument of 8:1–6; 9:11–15, 23–28. When he contrasts Israel's approach to God at Sinai and the approach of Christians to God in his heavenly sanctuary through Jesus, he restates in visionary form the argument of 9:16–22; 10:1–22. Sinai represents the whole system of approaching God under the law through priestly mediators offering sacrifices at an earthly sanctuary. No such continuing ministry is necessary now because of the finished work of Christ. The vision is presented here to inspire endurance and faithfulness in the face of every form of testing and struggle.

---

28. Cf. O'Brien, pp. 489–491. The word *better* is regularly used in relation to the New Covenant and the blessing of eternal salvation (6:9; 7:19, 22; 8:6; 9:23; 10:34; 11:16, 35, 40). No difference of meaning can be read into the use of the Greek adjectives *neos* (*new*) in 12:24 and *kainos* in 8:8; 9:15.

D. Being attentive to the voice of God (12:25–27)

Context
The pastor turns again to exhortation, in this case clearly arising from the preceding visionary material (vv. 18–24). An immediate connection is made between 'the blood [of Christ] that speaks' (v. 24) and the challenge not to 'refuse him who speaks' (v. 25). But the voice that calls from heaven warns, as well as encourages (3:7 – 4:13; 10:26–38). Just as there was no escape for the Israelites at Sinai 'when they refused him who warned them on earth', so there will be no escape for those who approach God through Jesus but 'turn away from him who warns . . . from heaven'. The shaking of the earth at Sinai is contrasted with the promise of Haggai 2:6 about the shaking of earth and heaven 'once more' (v. 26). This is related to the ultimate removal of 'what can be shaken', so as to leave behind 'what cannot be shaken' (v. 27). This last expression prepares for the challenge that begins in verse 28 ('since we are receiving a kingdom that cannot be shaken').

Comment
25. The abrupt warning *See to it* recalls the challenge in 3:12 not to follow the example of the Israelites who failed to enter their earthly inheritance. As in that context, the essential issue is not to *refuse him who speaks*.[29] Israel's refusal to listen to God's voice and obey him began at Mount Sinai (Exod. 32) and continued to the border of the Promised Land (Num. 13 – 14) and beyond. The same God who *warned them on earth* now *warns us from heaven*. God warned the Israelites through Moses concerning the demands of his covenant relationship with them in their earthly inheritance (12:18–21; cf. Deut. 27 – 29). Christians have received a 'heavenly calling' through the glorified Lord Jesus (3:1), inviting them to share in the inheritance of the heavenly Jerusalem (12:22–24). Nevertheless, similar warnings are suggested by the rhetorical

---

29. The verb *paraiteomai* is used here in its negative application 'reject, refuse' (BDAG). The deliberate and decisive nature of this refusal is emphasized by the introduction of another term (*turn away*).

question *If they did not escape when they refused him who warned them on earth, how much less will we, if we turn away from him who warns us from heaven?* The word *escape* recalls 2:3 ('how shall we escape if we ignore so great a salvation?'). The greatness of the salvation achieved and proclaimed by the Lord Jesus brings with it 'an even greater responsibility and danger than Israel faced' (O'Brien, p. 493; cf. 10:26–31).

26–27. The terror of Israel's experience at Sinai is recalled with the words *At that time his voice shook the earth.* Two elements of the biblical account seem to be combined here: the trembling of the mountain (Exod. 19:18) and the trembling of the people when God spoke (Exod. 20:18–21).[30] This dramatic event is compared with what God has *now* promised about another shaking. 'In both cases, the reference to shaking emphasizes the sheer power of God's speech, which fundamentally alters the created order' (Holmes, *Sublime Rhetoric*, p. 148). Haggai 2:6 is abbreviated to read *Once more I will shake not only the earth but also the heavens.* This message was delivered when the second temple was built in Jerusalem after the Babylonian exile. The prophet spoke about the approaching judgment of the nations in terms of the shaking of the heavens and the earth, which would have a positive outcome for God's people in a glorified temple (Hag. 2:7).

Hebrews takes the words *once more* to indicate a connection with the shaking of the earth that occurred at Sinai. However, in tune with the message of Haggai, the shaking that is to come is said to involve *the removing of what can be shaken – that is, created things – so that what cannot be shaken may remain.* All created things, including people who reject the gospel and resist Christ's rule, will be removed (10:13; cf. Hag. 2:21–22), though no details are given here about the judgment this entails (cf. 10:26–31). *What cannot be shaken* refers to the heavenly Jerusalem and its inhabitants, who have been rescued from judgment by the saving work of Jesus (12:22–24). They will

---

30. Exod. 19:18 MT speaks of the trembling of 'the whole mountain', but the LXX records the trembling of the people. The trembling of the mountain was remembered in Judg. 5:4–5; Pss 68:7–8; 77:18. Cf. *4 Ez.* 3:18.

remain with God and his Son (1:10–12) in what was previously described as 'the world to come' (2:5), God's 'rest' (4:1–11), 'the promised eternal inheritance' (9:15), 'a better country – a heavenly one' (11:16) and the city 'he has prepared . . . for them' (11:16), which from an earthly perspective is still 'the city that is to come' (13:14; cf. Rev. 21:1–8). In other New Testament contexts, the destruction of the material universe is variously linked with the return of Christ, final judgment and the resurrection of the dead in the context of 'a new heavens and a new earth' (e.g. Phil. 3:20–21; 1 Thess. 4:13 – 5:11; 2 Thess. 1:5–10; 2 Pet. 3:7, 10–13). Hebrews does not explicitly make all those connections.

Theology

> By 'moving' the hearers into the place where God speaks and calling attention to the hearers' receptivity to that speech, Hebrews 12:18–29 provides the basis for the exhortations to endurance and solidarity with the assembly in the verses surrounding it.
>
> (Holmes, *Sublime Rhetoric*, p. 123)

God continues to speak to his people from heaven through Scripture (3:7–11; 9:8; 10:15–17; 12:5–6) and congregational leaders who apply God's word to them (13:7, 17, 22). Mutual exhortation on the basis of Scripture is clearly another way in which God's voice can be heard (3:12–15; 10:24–25). Access to heaven is provided and sustained when the word of God is heard and received with faith in earthly settings and obedience is excited. This passage provides a vivid re-presentation of the challenge in 4:1–13 to go on heeding the word of God, especially as it comes to us in the gospel of Christ. The word of God enables perseverance in faith, hope and love, but it also warns about the consequences of turning away from the Son and all that he has done for us.

E. Serving God with reverence and awe (12:28–29)

Context

These two verses form a bridge between the general challenge to keep listening to the voice of God (12:25–27) and the particular exhortations in 13:1–19. The heavenly Jerusalem is represented as 'a kingdom that cannot be shaken', picking up a term from the warning in verses 26–27. As in the Old Testament, God is to be served by his redeemed people, but what determines the character of that service now is the heavenly setting, in which Jesus is 'the mediator of a new covenant' (v. 24; 8:1–6). The motivation and empowerment for acceptable service is gratitude for God's gracious gift of eternal salvation through Christ (cf. Rom. 12:1). This service is to be offered 'with reverence and awe, for our "God is a consuming fire"'.

Comment

28–29. The conjunction *Therefore* (*dio*) shows that a conclusion to the preceding passage has been reached. This is also indicated by the causal clause *since we are receiving a kingdom that cannot be shaken*, which relates the hope given in the heavenly vision (vv. 22–24) to the warning that follows (vv. 25–27). The present participle *receiving* suggests that a share in God's kingdom may be enjoyed by faith, in anticipation of the full experience to come. Unlike the kingdoms of the world that rise and fall, God's unshakable kingdom endures: 'it is rooted in God's unalterable character and God's unchanging promises. It signals an established and steady reality that contrasts with the audience's tumultuous existence mentioned earlier' (Holmes, *Sublime Rhetoric*, pp. 149–150; cf. 10:32–39; 12:3–13). This kingdom will be finally and fully manifested in the judgment to come, which his redeemed people will survive to enjoy his new creation. This new environment is portrayed in verses 22–24 as a sanctuary where his victory over sin and death is eternally celebrated.

The certainty that the gospel offers about God's unshakable kingdom is a reason to express our thanks to him (*let us be thankful*).[31] Normally, the noun *charis* is translated 'grace' (as in 2:9; 4:16 [twice];

---

31. Some manuscripts have the indicative *echomen charin* ('we are grateful'), but the subjunctive *echōmen charin* ('let us be thankful') suits the context better and is more likely to be the original. The indicative form occurs in 1 Tim. 1:12; 2 Tim. 1:3.

10:29; 12:15; 13:9, 25), but here it describes the appropriate response to God's grace (BDAG). Thanksgiving and praise are important ways of acknowledging the grace given to us (13:15, 25), but the author indicates that thanksgiving is not an end in itself. Literally, the Greek reads 'through which let us serve God acceptably', meaning that thanksgiving is the basis and means by which we serve God acceptably. Such service is not offered to gain acceptance or open the way into God's presence, but as a grateful recognition that Jesus has achieved what we need through his high-priestly ministry (10:19–22).

NIV translates the verb *latreuein* 'serve' in 9:14, but 'worship' in 12:28, which is unfortunate, because the link between these verses is important. In current English usage, 'worship' is often understood quite narrowly to mean praise or more broadly a corporate engagement with God in a congregational setting. But in 9:14 the verb describes the service to God that is made possible in everyday life by the cleansing of our consciences from 'dead works', because of the sacrifice of Jesus. 'Serve' is also the better rendering in 12:28, because chapter 13 goes on to outline various practical ways in which God is to be obeyed. Words and actions that flow from gratitude to God for Jesus and the promises of the gospel are the way to serve God *acceptably* (13:15–16).[32]

However, the author also insists that God should be served *with reverence and awe*. The word *eulabeia* was used in 5:7 with reference to the 'reverent submission' or 'godly fear' of Jesus as he prayed in the face of death. The same term was used in 11:7 to describe the attitude of Noah as he obeyed the word of God and constructed an ark for the saving of his household from the judgment of the flood. The noun *deos* (*awe*) is used only here in the New Testament, but in Greek literature more generally it describes 'an emotion of profound respect and reverence for deity' (BDAG). The second term (*awe*) reinforces and intensifies the first (*reverence*), especially in view

---

32. The adverb *euarestōs* ('acceptably') should be linked with the related verb in 13:16 ('pleased') and the adjective in 13:21 ('pleasing'). Acceptable service involves doing God's will in every sphere of life, enabled by his grace and power. Cf. Peterson, *Engaging*, pp. 241–254.

of the claim that *our 'God is a consuming fire'*. This is a modified quotation from Deuteronomy 4:24, where Moses refers to the awesome holiness of God experienced at Sinai and subsequently (see also Deut. 5:25; 9:3; Isa. 33:14). The image of fire appeared earlier in Hebrews in two warnings against apostasy (6:8; 10:27). Christians may not have had a tangible experience of God's dangerous and powerful presence as Israel did in the wilderness (12:18–21), but God's nature has not changed. 'Everything is uncovered and laid bare before the eyes of him to whom we must give account' (4:13). Godly fear reflects both a confidence in the saving grace of God and a solemn respect for God as judge.

Theology
Acceptable service is offered to God as we receive with faith and gratitude the promise of 'a kingdom that cannot be shaken' and express that grateful faith in daily obedience. In the Old Testament, the sacrificial service of priests at the earthly sanctuary enabled the people to be ceremonially cleansed from sin and consecrated to his service (9:6–10; 10:1–4), but Jesus' once-for-all sacrifice has provided a definitive cleansing and sanctification for the people of the New Covenant (9:14; 10:10). So the service that Jesus makes possible requires no further priestly mediation or sacrificial rituals. He has given us the right of direct access to God's heavenly presence (10:19–22) in whatever context we find ourselves. This approach to God through Jesus will culminate in the joy and celebration of the heavenly city. Meanwhile, we are called to offer to him the kind of practical, everyday service detailed in the next chapter.

12. FINAL ENCOURAGEMENTS, BLESSINGS AND GREETINGS (13:1–25)

At first glance, this collection of encouragements, blessings and greetings seems to have little connection with the preceding chapters. Some have even argued that chapter 13 was a later addition to the author's work, though this has been satisfactorily opposed.[1] In fact, verses 1–6 give examples of the way the service to God mentioned in 12:28 can be expressed in everyday life and relationships. The next section is framed by passages calling for leaders past (vv. 7–8) and present (vv. 17–19, including the author) to be honoured with respect for their teaching and example. At the centre of this section (vv. 9–16) there is an exhortation to avoid strange teachings and for hearts to be strengthened by grace. This is followed by a comparison between the sacrificial ritual of the high priest on the Day of Atonement and the sanctifying death of Jesus (cf. 9:6–14), which in turn becomes the basis for a challenge to 'go to him outside the camp, bearing the disgrace he bore',

---

1. Cf. Lane 2, pp. 495–507; Cockerill, pp. 673–676.

offering to God a sacrifice of praise and pleasing him with a sacrificial care for one another. In various ways, therefore, the theme of acceptable worship continues from 12:28–29 through to 13:15–16. The author's prayer and praise in verses 20–21 is then a bridge to the final section of the chapter, in which he adds other features more like a letter-ending to his word of exhortation (vv. 22–25).[2]

A. Love that pleases God (13:1–6)

Context

These verses provide a series of exhortations with motivations, essentially on the theme of love. Love for Christian brothers and sisters must continue, and hospitality must not be neglected, especially in view of certain biblical precedents (vv. 1–2). Love for those who are in prison and for those who are ill-treated can be stirred by identifying closely with their situation (v. 3). Marital love and faithfulness can be protected by remembering what Scripture teaches about God's judgment of adulterers and 'all the sexually immoral' (v. 4). Love of money can be avoided by being content with what you have and trusting God to provide what you need (vv. 5–6).

Comment

1. There is no grammatical link between this verse and the preceding ones, but the following exhortations clearly illustrate practical ways in which to offer to God acceptable service 'with reverence and awe' (12:28). Christian worship should have a horizontal as well as a vertical expression (cf. 13:15–16). The charge to *Keep on loving one another as brothers and sisters* (lit. 'let brotherly love continue') assumes that such love has been demonstrated in the past and should be a continuing characteristic of Christ's people (6:10–11; cf. 1 Thess. 4:9; 1 Pet. 1:22; 2 Pet. 1:7). The term *philadelphia*

---

2. Cockerill (pp. 710–711) argues that vv. 18–25 display 'the normal elements of a letter's end', meaning that he divides the chapter differently (vv. 1–6, 7–17, 18–25).

('brotherly love') normally expressed familial love, but it was occasionally applied to those in religious or political associations (e.g. 1 Macc. 12:10, 17; 2 Macc. 15:14). Jesus called his disciples 'brothers' (Mark 3:33–35; Matt. 25:40; 28:10; John 20:17) and encouraged them to treat each other as such (Matt. 23:8; Luke 22:32; John 15:12). The author has previously affirmed the kinship of believers in the 'household of God' (Heb. 2:10–13; 3:6; 10:19–20) and urged them to care for one another in ways that reflect that relationship (3:12–14; 6:9–12; 10:24–25; 12:15–17).

2. The exhortation *Do not forget to show hospitality to strangers* could apply to those outside the Christian fellowship or to believers in need of food and accommodation (e.g. Acts 10:23; 21:16; 28:7; deSilva, pp. 487–488). The word translated *hospitality* (*philoxenia*) was widely used to mean 'receive a stranger as a guest' (Louw and Nida). 'Among Jews and Gentiles alike, hospitality to strangers was highly regarded, and even considered to be a religious obligation' (O'Brien, p. 506). All Christians are urged to engage in this ministry (Rom. 12:13; 1 Pet. 4:9), but especially church leaders (1 Tim. 3:2; Titus 1:8). The author supports his appeal with a biblical allusion: *for by so doing some people have shown hospitality to angels without knowing it.* Most likely, this refers to the way Abraham entertained three men in Genesis 18:1–10, who brought the promise that Sarah would have a son in her old age. These divine representatives are identified as angels in Genesis 19:1–2, 15, when Lot again offered them hospitality. Those to whom we show hospitality may prove to be messengers of God, 'bringing a greater blessing than they receive' (Bruce, p. 371).

3. The exhortation *Continue to remember those in prison* acknowledges that this particular ministry has taken place in the past (10:34) and urges that it should not lapse. *Remember* means act according to their needs, not simply recall their situation. It is likely that members of this church had to supply food, clothing and emotional support to brothers and sisters who had been imprisoned for their faith.[3] Over time, this could have become a significant burden and exposed those who visited the prison regularly to

---

3. Koester (pp. 564–565) describes the terrible conditions of first-century prisons. See more fully Rapske, *Paul in Roman Custody*, pp. 195–225.

possible arrest themselves. The motivation to continue such loving care is to identify with the prisoners *as if you were together with them* (cf. Lev. 19:18; Matt. 7:12). The scope of the challenge is then widened to include *those who are ill-treated* and the motivation is to identify with them *as if you yourselves were suffering*. This last clause could be rendered 'as those who are also in a body', meaning that we have all experienced pain and should be able to empathize with others who are neglected or physically abused for their faith.

4. The style of exhortation changes in verses 4–5, allowing the author to speak 'with striking forcefulness' (Cockerill, p. 683). Two challenges are first presented regarding marriage: *Marriage should be honoured by all, and the marriage bed kept pure*. The term *honoured* (*timios*) means 'of exceptional value' (BDAG) and indicates that the institution of marriage should be highly prized and individual marriages should be valued and protected at all costs (cf. Matt. 19:3–9, citing Gen. 2:24). This is a word to the married, but also to those associated with them in family, church or society (*by all*). It 'recognizes the importance of social support for marriage, since fidelity in marriage is more difficult if marriage is not valued by the community' (Koester, p. 565). The second challenge (*and the marriage bed kept pure*) focuses on the sexual exclusivity that God requires between a man and a woman in marriage (Exod. 20:14; Lev. 18:1–23). *The marriage bed* (*koitē*) is a euphemism for marital intercourse (Wis. 3:13, 16). The adjective *pure* (*amiantos* ['undefiled'], as in 7:26; Jas 1:27; 1 Pet. 1:4) is the equivalent of holy, implying that God has a distinct and special purpose for sex. 'Illicit sexual intercourse defiles the marriage bed (Gen. 49:4) and profanes what God has made holy' (O'Brien, p. 510).

The motivation in this case is that *God will judge the adulterer and all the sexually immoral*. NIV has reversed the order of the words: the more general term *sexually immoral* (*pornoi*, as in 12:16; 1 Cor. 5:9–11; 6:9; Eph. 5:5; 1 Tim. 1:10; Rev. 21:8; 22:15) comes first in the Greek text. This covers all forms of sexual expression outside of the marriage of a man and a woman. It is followed by the more specific term 'adulterers' (*moichoi*, as in Luke 18:11; 1 Cor. 6:9), referring to married people who have sexual relationships outside of their marriage. The future tense (*will judge*) points to the final judgment mentioned in 6:2; 9:27; 10:27, 29–31, 39; 12:23, 27, 29; 13:17. Those who have not repented of adultery or sexual immorality and sought the forgiveness of God will experience his condemnation and exclusion from his presence.

5–6. The implied exhortation to *Keep your lives free from the love of money* ('your manner of life without the love of money') is balanced by the encouragement to *be content with what you have* ('being content with present circumstances'). This reflects the teaching of Jesus about the impossibility of serving both God and money (Matt. 6:24), which is followed by a challenge to trust God for the provision of daily needs, while seeking first his kingdom and his righteousness (6:25–34). Those addressed in Hebrews had suffered for their faith and joyfully accepted the confiscation of their property, knowing that they had 'better and lasting possessions' (10:34). The pastor wants them to maintain that vision and *be content* with what they have. Fearing further persecution and loss, some may have sought to protect themselves by accumulating wealth. This could have impeded their spiritual commitment, hindered their relationships with others in the church, and prevented them from sharing their possessions with those in need (13:16).

The love of money is described in 1 Timothy 6:10 as 'a root of all kinds of evil', even causing some to wander from the faith and pierce themselves with many griefs. In that context, 'godliness with contentment' is set forth as the antidote to greed (6:6–9). Hebrews cites two biblical texts to give a similar perspective. The motivation for keeping lives free from the love of money and being content with what you have is that

> *God has said,*
> *'Never will I leave you,*
>   *never will I forsake you.'*[4]

This restates the promise made to the Israelites as they faced the prospect of taking possession of the land of Canaan (Deut. 31:6).

---

4. O'Brien (p. 510 n. 61) argues that the intensive expression *autos gar eirēken* should be translated 'he himself speaks': God addresses Christians directly through this scripture.

Similar words were spoken to Joshua as their leader (Deut. 31:8; Josh. 1:5), echoing the foundational covenant promise that God would be with his people to sustain them and fulfil his purpose for them (e.g. Exod. 3:12; Judg. 6:16; 1 Kgs 11:38; Isa. 43:2).

Consequently, God's presence with and provision for his people should be acknowledged with certainty (*So we say with confidence*), adopting the confession of the psalmist,

> *The Lord is my helper; I will not be afraid.*
>   *What can mere mortals do to me?*
> (Cf. Ps. 118:6 [117:6 LXX])

Although a different word for *confidence* is used in the introduction to this citation, it recalls the repetition of a similar term in previous passages (3:6; 4:16; 10:19, 35). Continuing his unfolding of the nature of acceptable worship (12:28), the author shows that a godly lifestyle is nurtured by reflecting back to God in a personal way a certainty about the reliability of his promises.

Theology

The challenge to keep loving one another as brothers and sisters is a key to this passage, with some of its implications being unfolded in the exhortations that follow. Hospitality can be a particular expression of love for fellow believers and support for their ministries, as well as a means of building bridges with those outside the church. Caring for prisoners and those ill-treated for their faith is a particularly demanding and sometimes dangerous call for self-sacrificing love. Marriages need to be valued, supported and protected by all, so that marital love can flourish in the exclusive commitment of a man and a woman to each other. God's call to holiness is denied when biblical teaching about appropriate sexual behaviour is rejected (cf. 1 Thess. 4:1–8). Love of money and discontent with what one has can also damage relationships and cause believers to lose sight of God's purpose for their lives. Especially for a persecution context, but also in a materialistic, God-denying secular context, these exhortations provide vital clues about persevering in love together as the people of God.

B. Faithfulness that endures (13:7–19)

Context

Once more, the pastor seeks to encourage faithfulness in God's service and help his hearers reach their heavenly destination. He first calls on them to remember the leaders who brought the gospel to them, to consider the outcome of their way of life and imitate their faith (v. 7). This establishes a pattern for what follows, where there is a focus on matters of faith (vv. 8, 10, 11–12, 14) and exhortations concerning lifestyle (vv. 9, 13, 15–16). In particular, the recipients are to avoid being carried away by strange teachings, reflecting again on the significance of Jesus' suffering for them, and be willing to identify with him 'outside the camp' as those who are 'looking for the city that is to come'. A charge to have confidence in their present leaders and submit to their authority (v. 17) then leads to a personal request for prayer by the author (vv. 18–19).

Comment

7. *Remember your leaders, who spoke the word of God to you* means 'have a special regard for those who first brought the gospel to you' (2:3; 4:2; 6:1).[5] The same verbal term (*hoi hēgoumenoi*, 'those leading') is used later in the chapter for those who are currently their *leaders* (vv. 17, 24; cf. Luke 22:26; Acts 15:22). As in verse 3, *remember* involves taking action, not simply recollecting. This is clear from the following charge: *Consider the outcome of their way of life and imitate their faith.* The word *outcome* most likely refers to 'the whole course of their lives from start to finish' (Bruce, p. 374), suggesting that these leaders could now be dead.[6] The pastor wants his hearers to pursue

---

5. Speaking or preaching 'the word' refers to evangelism in Acts 4:29; 8:25; 11:19; 13:46; 14:25; 16:6; Phil. 1:14 (cf. Mark 2:2; 4:33), though it can also refer to a ministry of the gospel among believers (Acts 4:31; 20:32; 1 Pet. 4:11).

6. This observation does not invalidate the argument that Hebrews might have been written some time between AD 64 and 68 (see Introduction 4). Apart from natural factors leading to the deaths of early witnesses, many died as martyrs in this period.

the same lifestyle, recognizing that it was motivated and directed by *their faith*. In effect, he adds these leaders to the list of those his hearers can *imitate* in running the race of faith (12:1–3; cf. 6:12).

8. The confession *Jesus Christ is the same yesterday and today and for ever* is not linked grammatically to the preceding verse, but it forms a thematic bridge between verses 7 and 9. The Jesus Christ who was preached to them by their leaders *yesterday* has not changed: he remains *the same . . . today and for ever* (1:12; 3:1–6; 4:14–16; 7:25; 8:1–2; 10:19–22; 12:1–3). This Christological claim is foundational for dealing with strange teachings (v. 9) that differ from the gospel message originally announced by the Lord and confirmed by those who heard him (2:3). God-honouring faith holds on to Jesus Christ as proclaimed by the earliest witnesses and expounded by those who first received their testimony (6:1–3; cf. Col. 2:6–8).

9. The warning not to be *carried away by all kinds of strange teachings* ('diverse and strange teachings') recalls the image of drifting from the message that brought these believers to Christ in the first place (2:1; cf. Eph. 4:14–16). Although the pastor speaks quite broadly about *strange teachings*, he goes on to identify a particular error: *It is good for our hearts to be strengthened by grace, not by eating ceremonial foods, which is of no benefit to those who do so*. God's grace was supremely expressed in the sacrificial death of his Son (2:9) and the giving of his Spirit (10:29). Believers should keep approaching God's gracious throne with confidence to find grace to help in time of need (4:16). They should also see to it that no-one in their fellowship 'falls short of the grace of God' (12:15). Guilty human hearts need to be cleansed from sin and renewed by God's grace to serve him effectively (9:14; 10:22; cf. 8:10–12; 10:16–17). They need to be 'confirmed' or 'established' (*bebaiousthai*, as in 2:3) by the gospel of grace, not by eating or refraining from eating certain foods.

Debate has taken place about the specific reference to *foods* 'by which those who walk in them are not benefited' (my translation). The idea of 'walking' in them suggests a 'whole manner of life in which foods played a central role' (O'Brien, p. 519; cf. Attridge, pp. 394–396). The following verse could point to meals associated with Jewish sacrifices. More broadly, however, food and drink and various ceremonial washings were earlier described as 'external regulations' under the Mosaic covenant 'applying until the time of

the new order' (9:10). *Foods* could refer to the dietary laws set forth
in Leviticus 11 and Deuteronomy 14.[7] Some of those addressed in
Hebrews could have been attracted to these Jewish practices and
the suggestion that holiness would be 'maintained and confirmed
by what they ate' (Kleinig, p. 701).[8] But such practices could not
bring the grace promised to the beneficiaries of the New Covenant
(9:11–15; cf. Rom. 14:17–18; 1 Cor. 8:8; Col. 2:16, 20–23).

10. With an abrupt declaration of what *we have* as believers
(compare 4:14–15; 6:19; 8:1; 10:19–21), the author returns to the
imagery of the sacrificial system: *We have an altar from which those who
minister at the tabernacle have no right to eat.* Although some commentators have sought to identify this with the Lord's Supper, Holy
Communion or Christian Eucharist, this is unlikely (contrast
Cockerill, p. 696, with Kleinig, pp. 301–307, 702–704). As in earlier
contexts, an Old Testament cultic term (*altar*) is used to describe
the death of Jesus and its implications for believers. At one level we
may say that the cross was the Christian's altar, and yet the author
implies that it is possible to *eat* from this altar. In effect, this means
continually benefiting from the sacrifice of Christ, who has 'entered
heaven itself, now to appear for us in God's presence' (9:24; cf.
John 6:51–58). Sacrifice, priesthood, sanctuary and altar are all
fulfilled for us in the person and work of our glorified Saviour, and
we continue to appropriate the benefits by drawing near to God
through him (4:14–16; 7:25; 10:19–22). The Lord's Supper may be a
sacramental way of feeding on Christ 'in your hearts by faith with
thanksgiving' (the Book of Common Prayer), but that is entirely
different from identifying this meal or the table from which it is
taken as our *altar* (cf. 1 Cor. 10:14–22; 11:17–34).

---

7. Paul addressed similar issues in Rom. 14:1 – 15:7 in an earlier
   communication with Christians in Rome. It is entirely possible
   that the matter remained unresolved for some.

8. Cockerill (pp. 694–695) argues that the author's delay in dealing
   with the problem until this point was first to allow for a thorough
   presentation of the way Christ fulfils Old Covenant rituals and
   practices, thus showing them to be obsolete. Second, he had more
   pressing concerns about his hearers that needed to be dealt with first.

The verb translated *minister* (*latreuontes*) could refer to 'the worshippers' who approach God at the tabernacle through the priesthood and sacrificial system (as in 9:9; 10:2). However, in view of the argument that follows (v. 11), the reference is more likely to be to priests who *minister at the tabernacle* ('serve', as in 8:5) and 'share in what is offered on the altar' (1 Cor. 9:13; cf. Lev. 6:14–18, 24–29 [MT 6:7–11, 17–22]; 7:1–7). The priests who enjoyed this privilege at the altar outside the tabernacle and the temple could not benefit from the sacrifice of Christ if they remained wedded to this old way of relating to God. Neither can anyone else who continues to pursue the 'shadow' instead of the 'reality' (Heb. 8:5; 10:1).

11–12. The author returns to the detail of the Day of Atonement ritual in order to make a new application to the person and work of Jesus. First, he recalls that *The high priest carries the blood of animals into the Most Holy Place* [*eis ta hagia*, 'into the holy places'] *as a sin offering* (Lev. 16:11–15). The fulfilment of this in the sacrificial death of Jesus and his entrance into heaven was argued in 9:11–12, 24–28. Second, he recalls that the flesh of these animals could not be eaten on the Day of Atonement, but *the bodies are burned outside the camp* (Lev. 16:27–28). In various ways, the ritually clean *camp* of Israel is distinguished in the Pentateuch from the unclean region *outside the camp*, which is a place of death (e.g. Exod. 29:14; Lev. 4:12; 8:17; 9:11; 10:4–5; 24:10–16; Num. 15:35–36). Applied to the sacrifice of Christ, however, this presents a strange anomaly, because he died *outside the city gate*.

A radically new approach to the sanctification of God's people is signified by saying *And so Jesus also suffered outside the city gate to make the people holy through his own blood*. Jesus suffered and shed his blood outside the temple precincts and beyond the gate of the holy city (John 19:17–20). The expression *outside the city gate* is parallel to *outside the camp* (vv. 11, 13), but narrows the application to the historic situation of Jesus' crucifixion outside the walls of Jerusalem. At a human level, this happened because he was 'despised and rejected' by his own people (Isa. 53:3). In God's plan, however, it took place so that he could make his life 'an offering for sin' (Isa. 53:10), providing a new way of cleansing and sanctification for those who come to him as the crucified Messiah (Heb. 10:1–10). As the mediator of a new covenant (12:24), he enables those from a Jewish background to experience the fulfilment of the law's provisions, and Gentiles to come from the unclean space outside the sanctuary of Israel into his holy presence.

13. The practical implication of the teaching in verse 12 is now stated: *Let us, then, go to him outside the camp, bearing the disgrace he bore.* As in 12:2–3, Jesus is portrayed as suffering uniquely and redemptively for his people, but also leaving them an example to follow (cf. 1 Pet. 2:21–25). Jesus endured the 'shame' of the cross and in suffering *outside the camp* he experienced *disgrace* (cf. 11:26). The same term was rendered 'insult' in 10:33, describing the past experience of the addressees. They are challenged to identify with the suffering Jesus once more in *bearing the disgrace he bore.* The expression *outside the camp* could be understood quite broadly to refer to the unbelieving world that has rejected Jesus,[9] but the context points more specifically to 'the worship of the community that lives by the Old Covenant as if Christ had not come' (Cockerill, pp. 702–703).[10] Separation from the temple in Jerusalem and synagogues throughout the Roman Empire exposed the earliest Christians to abuse and attack from Jews and Gentiles alike (e.g. Acts 13:49 – 14:7; 17:1–9; 18:1–17). This was the place of insult and disgrace for them.

14. The challenge to go to Jesus 'outside the camp' seems to detract from the pastor's regular portrayal of him as the exalted Lord (1:3–4, 13; 3:1–6; 8:1–2; 10:11–14; 12:1–2) and his encouragements to approach God through Jesus in the heavenly realm (4:14–16; 7:25; 10:19–22). However, this verse provides a reason for the previous one: *For here we do not have an enduring city, but we are looking for the city that is to come.* The present situation of believers in this world is temporary, but we have the sure and certain hope of

---

9. Winter ('Suffering with the Saviour', pp. 147–162) relates this quite specifically to the possibility of exile to a distant place for Christians in the Roman Empire.

10. The mention of ceremonial foods (v. 9) and an 'altar' at which 'those who minister at the tabernacle have no right to eat' (v. 10), and the explicit reference to the 'camp' of the Israelites (v. 11), alluding to Lev. 16:27, point to 'the established fellowship and ordinances of Judaism, grounded in the tabernacle rituals of the old covenant' (O'Brien, p. 525).

sharing with Christ in his eternal kingdom, which is a 'better and lasting possession' (10:34). By faith, we have already come to Jesus in the heavenly Jerusalem (12:22–24), but as pilgrims on a journey we still welcome this reality from a distance and long for our arrival at *the city that is to come* (cf. 11:13–16). Rather than simply belonging to this world and adopting its fleeting values, Christians are to make hard choices about possessions, security and community, going to Jesus 'outside the camp, bearing the disgrace he bore'. Paradoxically, we can meet the exalted Saviour and identify with him in places of suffering, disgrace and shame, for that is the context in which he died to consecrate us to himself as a holy people.

15. The author has returned to the theme of acceptable worship, arguing once more that Jesus has fulfilled and replaced the cultic provisions of the Old Covenant. The practical consequence of this is that the spiritual life of believers should be nourished by grace, and not by food laws and other such regulations. Moreover, the place of Christian service is not simply in the gathering of believers (10:24–25), but in the world, where there is suffering and disgrace, unbelief and persecution. Another dimension to that service is now teased out in terms of continually offering to God *a sacrifice of praise*. This recalls the challenge to be thankful for receiving a kingdom that cannot be shaken and to serve God on that basis (12:28).[11] Here the point is made that a *sacrifice of praise* is to be offered to God *through Jesus*, meaning as a response to his high-priestly work and because of the access to God he has achieved for us (4:14–16; 7:25; 10:19–22; 12:22–24). In the LXX, the expression *sacrifice of praise* refers both to an animal that was sacrificed (e.g. Lev. 7:12, 13, 15) and to the song of thanksgiving that accompanied it (e.g. Pss 107:22 [106:22 LXX]; 116:17 [115:8 LXX]; 2 Chr. 29:27–28). Psalm 50:14–15, 23 indicates that the essence of the sacrificial system was to be found in thanksgiving, the fulfilment of vows, dependence on God and daily obedience. Since animal sacrifices have been replaced by the

---

11. Some early and important manuscripts do not include the link word *oun* (*therefore*), which seems necessary at the beginning of v. 15. It could have been what was originally written, but accidentally omitted in these manuscripts. Cf. Metzger, *Textual Commentary*, p. 605.

sacrifice of Jesus (Heb. 10:5–10), these ideals are now achievable for all who rely on his perfect work for acceptance by God.

In language borrowed from Hosea 14:2 LXX, this sacrifice of praise is described as *the fruit of lips that openly profess his name* (see also *Pss. Sol.* 15:3; 1 QS 10:8, 22–23). Such praise for the person and work of Jesus could be offered in the church, where he is confessed as the Son of God and high priest who has given his people an eternal hope (3:1; 4:14; 10:23 [*homologia*]).[12] His *name* could also be confessed or acknowledged in the world 'outside the camp' (v. 13), meaning that the verb used here (*homologountōn*) could refer to public testimony about Jesus (cf. Matt. 10:32 par.; John 9:22; 12:42). Clearly, the praise offered to God in the fellowship of believers can be a stimulus for praising him before unbelievers.

16. A related aspect of acceptable worship is revealed in the exhortation *And do not forget to do good and to share with others, for with such sacrifices God is pleased.* The general term *do good* ('well-doing') could apply to the range of behaviours encouraged in verses 1–7. This is followed by the more specific term 'sharing' (*koinōnia*). The latter could refer to material gifts or contributions to fellow Christians as an expression of common participation in Christ (as in Acts 2:42, 44–45; 4:32; cf. Rom. 12:13; Phil. 4:15), though generosity to anyone in need could also be intended (cf. Gal. 6:9–10). *Such sacrifices* cannot be regarded as cultivating God's favour, since service to God is to be motivated by gratitude for what he has already done for us (12:28; 13:15). Transformed cultic language is used to identify actions that express genuine faith, which is pleasing to God (cf. 11:5, 6). Related terms are used in 12:28 ('acceptably') and 13:21 ('pleasing'; cf. Rom. 12:1, 2; 14:18; 2 Cor. 5:9; Eph. 5:10; Phil. 4:18; Col. 3:20).

17. *Leaders* come into focus again, as the author employs the same general term as before (v. 7), but this time applied to those who are currently serving. Members are urged to *have confidence* in their leaders and to *submit to their authority.* NIV translates the first verb (*peithesthe*) in a way that is consistent with 2:13 ('trust') and 6:9 ('convinced').

---

12. Cf. Kleinig, pp. 168–170. However, Kleinig (pp. 707–708) unnecessarily restricts the offering of a Christian 'sacrifice of praise' to the Lord's Supper or Eucharist. See also note 3 on p. 240.

ESV and CSB translate 'obey', which is less likely (BDAG), since this creates a tautology ('obey and submit').[13] Even if the second alternative is adopted, the context is not simply calling for indiscriminate obedience. Congregational members should hold their leaders 'in the highest regard in love because of their work' (1 Thess. 5:13) and submit to those who invite trust and respect by their example and teaching (1 Cor. 16:15–18). If there is no basis for confidence in leaders, submission to their authority becomes an awkward and unreal formality. The specific reason for confidence and submission here is *because they keep watch over you as those who must give an account*. They are 'on the alert' for any threatening peril (BDAG; cf. Mark 13:33; Luke 21:36; Eph. 6:18). Believers in general should care for one another (Heb. 3:12–14; 12:15–16), but leaders have a special responsibility to watch over the 'souls' in their flock (Acts 20:28–31). They do this knowing that they are accountable to God for their own lives (Heb. 4:12–13) and for the way they conduct their ministry (1 Pet. 5:1–4). With this in mind, believers should have confidence in those who have this commitment and submit to their authority, *so that their work will be a joy, not a burden*. Prayerful and supportive congregational members enable leaders to pursue their work with joy, rather than with complaint or groaning (BDAG, *stenazō*). A circle of care is envisaged here, because joyless leaders do not help congregations flourish and grow (*that would be of no benefit to you*).

18. The theme of mutual ministry is continued as the pastor brings himself into the picture and asks for prayer. Plural forms (*Pray for us. We are sure . . . we have*) could include those mentioned in verse 24, but the shift to the singular in verse 19 more likely indicates that the author has used a literary plural to refer to himself alone (as in 5:11; 6:9, 11–12). The reason for this request is (lit.) 'for we are convinced that we have a good conscience, desiring to act well in all things'.[14] Perhaps he has been accused in some way and

---

13. The second verb (*hypeikete*) is found only here in the NT and means 'yield to someone's authority' (BDAG).

14. The verb 'to act' (*anastrephesthai*) here recalls the use of the related noun in v. 7 (*anastrophēs*, 'way of life'), suggesting that the author was following the model of those previous leaders.

is defending himself. More positively, he could simply be per-
suading his hearers of the integrity and sincerity of his life and
ministry. Those whose consciences have been cleansed from guilt
through faith in Christ have been set free from 'dead works' to
'serve the living God' (9:14; 10:22). A good conscience means more
than feeling content with one's own behaviour. Assured of God's
forgiveness for sin, a good conscience testifies to a pattern of life
that is pleasing to God (Rom. 9:1; 2 Cor. 1:12; 1 Tim. 1:5, 19; 3:9;
2 Tim. 1:3; 1 Pet. 3:16). NIV (*a clear conscience*) does not capture the
fullness of this teaching about a transformed conscience. Leaders
with godly convictions and a confirming lifestyle should be supported by the prayers of those to whom they minister.

19. In an intensely personal way (*I particularly urge you to pray*), the
pastor expresses his desire to be with them again (*so that I may be
restored to you soon*). The verb *restored* in this context means 'to return
someone to a former place or relationship' (BDAG, *apokathistēmi*),
implying that he was once part of their congregational life and
presumably one of their leaders. The passive form of the verb
suggests that God must achieve this restoration (cf. Phlm. 22). Little
is revealed about the context from which the author addresses them
(vv. 23–24),[15] but his knowledge of their past struggles and present
needs has moved him to address them with great pastoral concern
and biblical insight. A return visit would enable him to reinforce
the message he is sending them. Such leaders play a vital role in
sustaining and maturing Christ's people in every generation.

Theology
The call to consider the lifestyle of the earliest gospel preachers and
imitate their faith once more links behaviour with right belief (v. 7).
Although there are pressures from unbelieving societies and other
religious traditions to change our beliefs and modify our behaviour, the fundamental challenge of this passage is to remember that

---

15. Koester (p. 573) suggests that the author's insistence on a good
    conscience and acting rightly could mean that he has faced opposition
    and imprisonment: 'being restored would mean being released and
    allowed to return to the community'.

'Jesus Christ is the same yesterday and today and for ever' (v. 8).
What he accomplished once and for all continues to benefit his
people in the present (vv. 9–10) and provide them with the hope of
an enduring city (v. 14). Meanwhile, they are encouraged to live
differently, being willing to suffer and bear disgrace because of
their identification with Jesus (vv. 12–13), but also to live expectantly
(v. 14), thankfully (v. 15), sacrificially (v. 16), submissively (v. 17) and
prayerfully (vv. 18–19).

C. Grace that equips and enables perseverance (13:20–25)

Context
The author has already moved to a letter-like ending with his
request for prayer in verses 18–19. A comparison with the letters
of Paul and 1 Peter shows further similarities: there is a prayer of
blessing (vv. 20–21; cf. 1 Thess. 5:23; 2 Thess. 3:16; 1 Pet. 5:10–11),
a summary exhortation (v. 22; cf. 2 Cor. 13:11; 1 Tim. 6:20; Titus
3:14; 1 Pet. 5:12), a message about future association (v. 23; cf. Eph.
6:21–22; Col. 4:7–9; Titus 3:12–13), final greetings (v. 24; cf. Phil.
4:21–22; Col. 4:10–15, 18; 1 Pet. 5:13) and a concluding blessing
(v. 25; cf. 2 Cor. 13:14; Gal. 6:18; Eph. 6:23–24; Col. 4:18; 1 Tim. 6:21;
2 Tim. 4:22; Titus 3:15; 1 Pet. 5:14). With this ending the pastor
gives himself the opportunity to 'address several personal issues
that would only have distracted from the body of his sermon'
(Cockerill, p. 711).

Comment
20. Having requested prayer for himself (vv. 18–19), the pastor
prays for his hearers in the form of an extended blessing or
benediction. God is first invoked as *the God of peace*, and his work in
bringing Jesus back from the dead as *that great Shepherd of the sheep* is
highlighted. This invocation is followed by a prayer in verse 21 for
God to equip his people 'with everything good for doing his will'
by working in them what is pleasing to him. A doxology or
ascription of praise to God concludes the sequence.

As *the God of peace*, he has established peace between himself and
sinful human beings through the sacrificial death of his Son, inaugurating the New Covenant, which is eternally effective (9:11–12, 15;

10:14–18; 12:24).[16] Although resurrection from the dead was implied in previous statements about the heavenly exaltation and continuing ministry of the Lord Jesus (e.g. 7:16, 25; 8:1–2), this is the first time his resurrection is declared to be an essential part of the process of salvation. It was 'by the blood of the eternal covenant' that Jesus was *brought back from the dead*.[17] His perfect sacrifice made it possible for him to be resurrected and 'appear for us in God's presence' (9:24), thus opening the way for us to follow (2:10; 6:20; 12:2, 22–24). In this way, he is for us *that great Shepherd of the sheep*, who surpasses Moses (Isa. 63:11) and David (2 Sam. 5:2) in rescuing and preserving the flock of God (Matt. 26:31; John 10:11; 1 Pet. 2:25; 5:4; Rev. 7:17). Indeed, as the Son of God he fulfils the pattern of ultimate care attributed to God himself in Psalm 23 and Ezekiel 34, even laying down his life for his people so that he might give them eternal life. Jesus continues to exercise the role of Shepherd in his high-priestly ministry in heaven (7:25).

21. The author's prayer request has two parts. First, he asks the God of peace to *equip you with everything good for doing his will*. The verb translated *equip* is rendered 'prepared' in 10:5 ('a body you prepared for me') and 'formed' in 11:3 ('the universe was formed'). In this context, the mood of the verb expresses a wish or prayer ('may he equip'). *Everything good* here refers not to material blessings, but to spiritual resources *for doing his will*. God has already provided cleansing from sin (9:14), sanctification (10:10) and the perfection of a new covenant relationship with him (10:14–18). The way is always open for believers to 'receive mercy and find grace to help us in our time of need' (4:16). Eternal life in God's presence has already been secured for us (12:22–24). These benefits need to be constantly appropriated and enjoyed, so that minds and hearts

---

16. The designation 'God of peace' can also be found in Rom. 15:33; 16:20; 2 Cor. 13:11; Phil. 4:9; 1 Thess. 5:23.

17. The unusual verb *anagein* ('bring up') is also employed in Rom. 10:7 with reference to the bodily resurrection of Jesus. It recalls OT descriptions of God bringing up Israel from Egypt (e.g. Lev. 11:45; 1 Sam. 12:6; Ps. 81:10; Jer. 2:6) and bringing up people from the realm of the dead (Pss 30:3 [LXX 29:4]; 71:20 [LXX 70:20]; 86:13 [85:13]).

might be motivated and directed in God's way. God may also equip us to do his will through the support and challenge of fellow believers (3:12–14; 10:24–25; 12:15–16), by taking us forward to maturity (5:11 – 6:3) and by enabling us to benefit from his fatherly discipline (12:1–13). *Doing his will* involves persevering in faith, hope and love, and obeying the commands of God, as articulated in various passages throughout Hebrews.

Second, the author includes himself in a request that God may *work in us what is pleasing to him.* The last clause is parallel to *doing his will*: God is pleased with those who live by faith (11:5–6) and express their trust by grateful service (12:28) and daily obedience (13:1–19). But the new emphasis here is on God's enabling *in us*: we must do his will, but we can do that only if God works in us what is pleasing to him (compare Phil. 2:11–12). Although Hebrews says little about the operation of God's Spirit in the lives of his people, we know from elsewhere in the New Testament that the Spirit is given to enable such faithfulness and fruitfulness (e.g. Rom. 8:5–17; Gal. 5:16–26).

These requests are made to God *through Jesus Christ*, meaning on the basis of his saving work and through his mediation as our eternal high priest (4:14–16; 7:25; 10:19–22). The ascription (*to whom be glory for ever and ever*) could apply to the God of peace, to whom the prayer in verses 20–21 is addressed, or to Jesus Christ, who has just been mentioned. This ambiguity reflects the close association between the Father and the Son first proclaimed in 1:1–4 and indicated in various other passages throughout Hebrews. God as Trinity is worthy of eternal praise for every provision he has made for the salvation and perseverance of his people. See Introduction 6a, 'God as Trinity'.

22. The pastor's final appeal is strengthened by identifying the recipients once more as *brothers and sisters* (as in 3:1, 12; 10:19). They share a special relationship with each other because Jesus has called them his brothers and sisters (2:11–12). Literally, he says, 'I exhort you to bear with my word of exhortation.' This suggests that he views his work as a sermon or homily in written form, prepared for oral delivery (cf. Acts 13:15; 1 Tim. 4:13; Cockerill, pp. 11–16). He has skilfully proclaimed the person and work of Christ in the light of Old Testament Scripture, seeking to warn about the consequences of drifting from these blessings and to encourage persistent faith, hope and love. The challenge to *bear with* his word of exhortation perhaps acknowledges that they could resist the complexity of its message (5:11) or its severity (6:4–6; 10:26–31; 12:15–17). This challenge is backed up by the explanation *for in fact I have written to you quite briefly*. Parallels in Jewish and early Christian documents suggest that this was a polite way of encouraging receptivity to the message (Lane 2, pp. 568–569).

23. The announcement that *our brother Timothy has been released* implies that he is well known to the church and that he has been recently released from prison. This was presumably the Timothy who accompanied Paul on his missionary journeys (Acts 16:1–3; 17:14–15; 18:5; 19:22; 20:4), who was associated with Paul in the writing of six of his letters (2 Cor. 1:1; Phil. 1:1; Col. 1:1; Phlm. 1; 1 Thess. 1:1; 2 Thess. 1:1) and who received the two letters from Paul that are in the New Testament. The author of Hebrews may have belonged to the same Pauline circle, though the content and style of his composition are different from Paul's letters. He is eager to visit his Christian friends (v. 19) and, if Timothy arrives *soon*, he promises to *come with him* to see them. This expresses his affectionate concern for them, but it also hints at the fact that he will be able to see how well they have responded to his word of exhortation.

24. The encouragement to *Greet all your leaders and all the Lord's people* may be an indication that the author was addressing a smaller group within the larger company of Christians in a particular city. This would be applicable if, for example, Hebrews was directed to one or more house churches in Rome. Paul used a series of second-person plural exhortations like this to ask individuals and groups in that city to express bonds of fellowship with one another (Rom. 16:3–15).[18] Whatever the author's precise meaning, he echoes his previous challenges to honour their leaders (13:17) and pursue peace with everyone (12:14). *All the Lord's people* means 'all the saints' (*hagioi*, 'holy ones'), which is a common designation for believers in

---

18. Cf. Peterson, *Romans*, pp. 536–544. It is also possible that Paul intended by this means to convey his own greetings to these individuals and groups ('Greet on my behalf').

the New Testament (e.g. Rom. 1:7; 16:15; 1 Cor. 1:2; 6:1–2; 14:33; 16:15; Heb. 6:10). Those who have been sanctified by Christ (Heb. 2:11; 10:10, 14, 29; 13:12) are the holy people of the New Covenant. They are challenged to pursue holiness (12:14) as a practical outworking of the holy status that has been given to them by God. *Those from Italy send you their greetings* could mean that the author is writing from somewhere outside Italy, where there are other believers *from Italy*, or it could mean that he is writing from Italy to somewhere else, including the city of Rome.[19]

25. *Grace be with you all* is a wish-prayer found in various forms at the end of many of Paul's letters (e.g. Rom. 16:20; 1 Cor. 16:23; Gal. 6:18). This is a blessing full of theological significance, because *grace* is a critical term for understanding the gospel and its implications. Although the word itself is used only eight times in Hebrews (2:9; 4:16 [twice]; 10:29; 12:15, 28 ['thankful']; 13:9, 25), the concept is conveyed by every statement about the work of Christ and God's unmerited provision for the eternal salvation of his people.

Theology

The combination of prayers, exhortations and greetings in these concluding verses is revealing. The pastor highlights the need for believers to depend on the grace of God, heed the warnings and encouragements of Scripture conveyed by leaders and his own word of exhortation, and treat one another appropriately as brothers and sisters in Christ. God's grace is expressed unusually in terms of bringing back Jesus from the dead as 'that great Shepherd of the sheep' and doing this 'through the blood of the eternal covenant'. The resurrection of Jesus is normally 'subsumed under the image of his exaltation to God's right hand' (O'Brien, p. 534), but it is explicitly made the basis for confidence here that God can equip his people 'with everything good for doing his will' and, by implication, bring them to share in his own resurrection from the dead.

---

19. Early manuscripts of Hebrews mostly interpret this to mean that the author was writing from Italy. Cf. Cockerill, p. 722 n. 67.